Making Gullah

The

JOHN HOPE FRANKLIN SERIES

in African American History and Culture

Waldo E. Martin Jr. and Patricia Sullivan,

editors

Making Gullah

A History of Sapelo Islanders, Race, and the
American Imagination

MELISSA L. COOPER

THE UNIVERSITY OF NORTH CAROLINA PRESS   Chapel Hill

The University of North Carolina Press has been a
member of the Green Press Initiative since 2003.

Cover illustration: "Christmas at the Big House [Howard Coffin's home on Sapelo
Island]—1913." Courtesy of the University of Georgia Marine Institute.

Library of Congress Cataloging-in-Publication Data
Names: Cooper, Melissa L., author.
Title: Making Gullah : a history of Sapelo Islanders, race, and the
American imagination / Melissa L. Cooper.
Other titles: John Hope Franklin series in African American history and culture.
Description: Chapel Hill : The University of North Carolina Press, 2017. |
Series: The John Hope Franklin series in African American history and
culture | Includes bibliographical references and index.
Identifiers: LCCN 2016042809| ISBN 9781469632674 (cloth : alk. paper) |
ISBN 9781469632681 (pbk : alk. paper) | ISBN 9781469632698 (ebook)
Subjects: LCSH: Gullahs—Georgia—Sapelo Island. | African Americans—
Georgia—Sapelo Island—History. | Gullah Geechee Cultural Heritage Corridor.
Classification: LCC F292.M15 C66 2017 | DDC 975.8/73700496073—dc23
LC record available at https://lccn.loc.gov/2016042809

For the ancestors, and for Menelik and Sundiata

CONTENTS

ILLUSTRATIONS

Making Gullah

PROLOGUE The Misremembered Past

For the past twenty years, on the third Saturday in October, scores of visitors have flocked to the ferry headed for Sapelo Island, Georgia, to partake in the annual Cultural Day festivities. The fund-raising festival hosted by the Sapelo Island Cultural and Revitalization Society always attracts tourists who eagerly anticipate an encounter with *real* Gullah people and folk culture. Visitors look forward to observing ring shout and Gullah dialect performances, purchasing handwoven sweetgrass baskets and homemade rag dolls, and sampling the Islanders' cuisine on the grounds of the old Farmers' Alliance Hall.

One of the largest barrier islands in the region, Sapelo is comprised of more than fifteen thousand acres of lush landscape, accented by towering trees draped with Spanish moss, expansive marshlands, thick patches of pinewoods, and white sand beaches bordered by billowy sand dunes. The skeletal remains of slave cabins can be found on the grounds of what was once one of the island's smaller plantations, and the mansion that was a seasonal home to the millionaires who occupied the island stands on the exact spot where Thomas Spalding's "big house" stood during slavery days. To date, the island can be reached only by ferry and has just a handful of paved roads, a tiny post office, one gas station, and a small general store nestled in the heart of the island's only surviving black settlement—Hog Hammock. Fewer than fifty descendants of the blacks enslaved on the island continue to live, year round, in Hog Hammock. They share Sapelo Island with transient groups of researchers stationed at the Marine Institute on the island's south end and with tourists and regular weekend visitors.

When Cultural Day visitors arrive on the island and walk the dock's rickety planks as the balmy air engulfs them, they frequently report feelings of being transported back in time. Many of Sapelo's visitors are lured to the island by stories about a place and a people that remain unchanged despite the passing years.[1]

The belief that the Islanders have nurtured their African ancestors' mystical arts and folk traditions for generations ignites their imaginations. This view—initiated by sensational voodoo-filled stories that 1920s and 1930s Sapelo researchers published in books and magazines—obscures the actual history of the blacks who lived on the island. Their characterizations of Sapelo have been echoed in popular tourist literature that describes the island as home to an unspoiled, nearly extinct African American culture that, in the words of one guidebook for tourists, thrived "due to generations of isolation."[2] As a result, a good number of Sapelo's visitors hope to catch a glimpse of a specter of the mystical-magical blacks who, in their relative isolation, managed to exist suspended in time.

But Sapelo Islanders' history is not the tale of an unchanging, time-forgotten folk. In fact, every aspect of life on the island has been shaped by the dynamic convergence of a host of shifts and events. The island's "undeveloped" landscape, the fact that the island has fewer than fifty year-round black residents, and the very notion that Sapelo Islanders are unique Gullah folk can all be attributed to transformations in social, economic, and political realities. However, these less romantic truths are largely absent from the picture of Sapelo Islanders that most visitors imagine. Even though so much of the way that Sapelo Islanders are envisioned is focused on the "past" and on their African ancestors, very little attention is paid to the way that the long history of blacks on the island has shaped the present.

If the scores of tourists who approach Sapelo's shores each year knew the history of Sapelo Islanders, their view of the people and the place would likely change. To start, their fantasies about a nebulous mass of enchanted African ancestors whose traditions have been cited as evidence of heightened retention of African cultural traits among their descendants would quickly fade, and images of hundreds of defiant captives enslaved on the island would take their place. From the first group of Africans brought to the island by Patrick Mackay in 1762 and those who slaved for John McQueen, to the Africans brought to the island in 1791 by the wealth-seeking partners of the French Sapelo Company; from the hundreds of blacks enslaved by famed cotton planter Thomas Spalding to the Africans who came to the island as property of ship captain and slaver Edward Swarbeck and those brought from St. Domingo by their master John Montalet in the wake of the Haitian Revolution in 1805—Sapelo Islanders' ancestors had always been engaged in temporal struggles for their freedom and autonomy.[3] As they labored in the fields making rice, sugar, and cotton, or toiled while gathering timber, their minds were set on freedom.[4]

Most of the stories that attract Sapelo's tourists divorce the Islanders' history from the horrors of chattel slavery. But the island that is now considered a veritable paradise was once the site of incredible suffering. The first groups of blacks enslaved on Sapelo endured whippings, iron collars, weighted ankles, and punishments that included being exiled on the uninhabited neighboring Blackbeard Island, without shelter or rations.[5] But these cruel measures did not kill their will to fight or their desire to be free. Instead, Sapelo's early captives devised plots to run away, and one of the French Sapelo Company's slaves exacted revenge by destroying the company's corn crop by setting fire to the hay barn.[6] When the French Sapelo Company's eighty captives and island holdings were sold to Thomas Spalding in 1802, the numbers of enslaved blacks on Sapelo increased, and the number of their documented attempts to become free did too.[7]

Some Sapelo tourists are familiar with Spalding's captive Bilali Mohammed and are taken by tales about the Muslim from Futa Jallon who is said to have held tight to his fez, prayer rug, and leather-bound journal and was rumored to have been buried with a Koran on his breast. In their imaginations, Mohammed's commitment to Islam simply serves to color the African character of the island.[8] But the fact that Mohammed—Spalding's head driver—did not surrender his religion is in and of itself an act of resistance. He used his knowledge of cotton production to negotiate with Spalding, combining spiritual defiance and cooperation to secure a modicum of autonomy.[9] But several of Mohammed's spiritual brothers chose not to follow his example. These men chose the uncertainty and dangers inherent in crossing the waters that separated the island from the mainland over Mohammed's strategy. Runaway notices for Sapelo fugitives Alik and Abdali were issued in 1802, and again for Toney, Jacob, and Musa in 1807.[10]

Romantic accounts that describe Sapelo during the antebellum years highlight the fact that Spalding—a descendant of Georgia settlers who protested the introduction of slavery to the colony—encouraged his captives to establish independent slave communities as evidence of his benevolent spirit.[11] But documented acts of slave resistance tell a different story. Several of Spalding's slaves decided to face the perils of fugitive and maroon life over the supposed comforts of Spalding's slave villages. The island's cemetery—Behavior Cemetery—is said to stand as testament to a group of captives who made this choice. A local legend describes a standoff between Spalding and several slaves who ran away and took refuge in the woods in order to force Spalding to negotiate with them. Instead of yielding to their demands, those who tell the story say that he left them in the woods until they learned to "behave."[12] Spalding had other slaves who refused to behave. In 1807 Spalding issued a runaway notice for Landua—a French- and English-speaking slave—who he believed was hiding on Sapelo or in Savannah.[13]

When Spalding died, many of the hundreds of captives that he deeded to his children took advantage of the sectional conflict that threatened to destroy the empire that he built to secure their freedom.[14] The mounting tensions caused by the impending war and Sapelo's captives' yearnings for freedom struck so much fear in Charles Spalding—one of the heirs to Thomas Spalding's empire—that he sent a letter to the Georgia militia requesting that naval troops patrol local waters to quell slaveholders' anxieties about slave revolts.[15] Charles Spalding's letter was never answered, and soon Union ships were patrolling the waters off of Sapelo's coast. Islanders remember stories that were passed down about several of the island's enslaved who began hiding in the marshes— waiting for an opportunity to flee to the Union boats.[16] They recall that some of the Sapelo captives were successful in their escape, but one was shot and killed by his master in pursuit of the vessel that he hoped would carry him to freedom.[17]

Most of Sapelo's tourists do not know this history, and their sojourns are not inspired by accounts of captivity, violence, resistance, and triumph. Heroes like March Wilson and James Lemon—Sapelo fugitives who joined the Union forces during the Civil War—are not main characters in the stories that attract most Sapelo tourists to the island.[18] The fact that Sapelo Islanders were likely among the group of courageous black Union soldiers who took up arms against their slave masters and cried out, "Oh mas'r, my wife and chillen lib dere," as they traveled through Sapelo River headed for battle, is little known to the island's visitors.[19] Chronicles of the island's newly freedmen and freedwomen who joined forces with black Union officer Tunis Campbell and used General William T. Sherman's Special Field Order No. 15 to resettle the island is not the main draw that attracts visitors.[20] The story of Fergus Wilson and the fourteen other Islanders who registered for Sherman's plan and, as a result, took possession of 390 acres of land that had previously belonged to the Spaldings is also not commonly known.[21] Likewise, the history of the Islanders who celebrated their status as free people after the Civil War by registering to vote and by building the First African Baptist Church and two schools that educated adults and children are not featured in the tourism literature that invites travelers to the island's shores.[22]

So much of Sapelo Islanders' past has been sanitized and reimagined so that it is easily digested and attractive to those who nurture a nostalgic view of the region and the people who live there. For example, Sapelo Islanders' long struggle for land has been overshadowed by their "quaint" culture. One guidebook claimed that after the Civil War, "the Spaldings deeded . . . their former slaves" over four hundred acres of land.[23] But Sapelo Islanders did not acquire their family properties from benevolent whites, they secured land despite the

Spaldings' efforts to make them landless tenants. For a time Tunis Campbell—the free black man from New Jersey and Freedman's Bureau agent appointed to oversee the settlement of more than four hundred blacks on Sapelo Island and St. Catherines Island—protected the freedmen under his charge from predatory sharecropping schemes and contract work and brokered land grants that would provide them with arable land.[24] When Campbell was removed from his post following accusations of misconduct and criminal charges were levied against him, he was sentenced to serve time on the chain gang. For Sapelo Islanders and other blacks in the region, Campbell's incarceration signaled that challenges to their freedom and autonomy would soon follow. It is likely that Sapelo Islanders were not surprised when Spalding's heirs sent representatives to take back the land from their former slaves. But Sapelo Islanders were not willing to give up the free community that they had built with their hearts and souls. They declared that the land was theirs and threatened to kill the representatives and anyone else who dared to take their land away.[25] Their impassioned stalemate with the Spaldings would not last long; President Andrew Johnson had returned Confederate lands, and when Spalding's heirs returned to once again stake claims to the land, they had the federal government and troops on their side.[26]

Even though it was clear to Sapelo Islanders that the tide had, once again, turned against them, they continued to press for autonomy and freedom. When the Spaldings reclaimed their Sapelo holdings in the 1870s, and took up residence among the fifty-nine black families who lived there—more than three hundred blacks—they successfully took possession of the land, but not the people. Many Islanders refused to work for the Spaldings and instead subsisted on gardens, small farms, domestic livestock, wild game, and the bounty of fish that lived in the ocean waters that surrounded them.[27] Those who worked for the Spaldings demanded their pay and refused to sign unfavorable contracts.[28] Sensing that—like many white southerners—the whites in their midst sought to make them landless laborers, Sapelo Islanders made moves to secure land. In 1871, a group of freedmen—William Hillery, John Grovenor, and Belali Bell—organized the William Hillery Company and deposited five hundred dollars on nearly a thousand acres of land in the Raccoon Bluff hammock and then divided and resold tracts of their holdings to newly freedmen and freedwomen.[29] The company had secured high, dry, arable land for Sapelo Islanders. They grew peas, rice, potatoes, and sugarcane and traded their crops in markets on the mainland, and were able to hold on to their freedom for a little while longer.

But even their most prudent efforts, clever strategies, and their communities' distance from the mainland could not keep the burgeoning Jim Crow racial hierarchy from dashing Sapelo Islanders' dreams of creating a refuge from racial oppression. By 1906, all of the blacks in the region were legally disenfranchised. And just forty-one years after the William Hillery Company was formed—nearly two generations after freedom—a white patriarch emerged on Sapelo, and the island was returned to a virtual plantation state. When a white automobile tycoon, Howard Coffin, first visited coastal Georgia while attending an automobile race in Savannah in 1910, 539 blacks lived on the island.[30] Captivated by the island's beauty, and perhaps inspired by the fact that rich whites had taken to black islands all along the southeastern seaboard to act out their own imperial conquests like those executed by the United States government in the Caribbean and Pacific, Coffin set out to purchase as much of Sapelo as he could in 1912.[31] He convinced the island's white landowners, who benefited from the repeal of Field Order No. 15, to sell him their land, and he even managed to get hold of several tracts of land owned by black families in Raccoon Bluff.[32] Sapelo Islander Allen Green—the island's most famous basketmaker—was a little boy when Coffin first occupied the island, but he remembered that when Coffin came, their lives changed. His own family lost some of their land because of "people selling to Coffin."[33] After Coffin finalized the purchase of a large portion of the island for $150,000, almost all of those blacks who lived there would be forced to act as supporting characters in Coffin's occupation fantasy.[34]

The moment when Howard Coffin used his money and power to take over Sapelo Island marks the most significant chapter in the history of Sapelo Islanders' Gullah identity, yet it is largely forgotten and has never been told. Right away Coffin laid the foundation for Sapelo to function as his private moneymaking oasis. He cleared the land for crops, established a cattle ranch, built a sawmill and an oyster and shrimp cannery, and set up armed guards on neighboring Blackbeard Island—which belonged to the federal government— to protect his seasonal home and investments. He also hired whites who acted as "island managers" to watch the island when he was away and to watch the island blacks to ensure that they were not engaged in subversive or illegal activities.[35] Coffin built the Cloister Hotel and Resort on nearby Sea Island. He also built an elaborate mansion that would serve as his seasonal home on the very site where Thomas Spalding's "big house" once stood; he imported tropical birds from Guatemala for his pleasure; and he built shell roads and artesian wells to be used by livestock and Islanders alike.[36]

When Coffin finished renovations and opened the door for the world to marvel over his palatial mansion and private paradise, he also invited the media to observe the blacks who lived in small communities scattered around the island. As a result, the Sapelo Islanders who lived in Hog Hammock, Raccoon

Bluff, Belle Marsh, Shell Hammock, and Lumber Landing became as exotic and intriguing as the birds that Coffin imported from Guatemala. Not only did Islanders have to contend with the fact that Coffin now seemed to rule their ancestral home, but they would soon have to suffer the curiosities of researchers and writers consumed by questions about black people's racial inheritance and swept up in larger 1920s and 1930s race fantasies. By and large, the first group of Sapelo researchers would twist and distort the Islanders' ancestral legacies. In their writings, the men and women of Sapelo who pursued voting rights, education, Christianity, and landownership as tools through which they could shape their destiny were depicted as childlike and superstitious primitives who put their faith in gris-gris bags and root doctors to secure their future.

These stories about Sapelo Islanders would be made, remade, and made again. They would pass through the hands of black and white researchers, journalists, and writers, and each time the stories were passed something new was added or subtracted or reenvisioned. Even today, stories about Sapelo Islanders' cultural origins and African inheritances either obscure or are enmeshed in reports about the Islanders' daily lives.

Sapelo's "African Feel"

On May 4, 2008, the New York Times reported that the residents of Sapelo Island, Georgia's Gullah/Geechee community, were engaged in a fierce struggle to keep their land. The headline read, "A Georgia Community with an African Feel Fights a Wave of Change." A question emerges from the article's title: what about Sapelo Island gave it an "African feel"? The answer to this question was not found in the reporting of details about land struggles between real estate developers, state officials, and Hog Hammock residents. Nor were the origins of the Islanders' "African feel" fully explained by the author's vague description of the Gullah/Geechee as people who "in the days before air-conditioning and bug repellent had the Sea Islands virtually to themselves and whose speech and ways, as a result, retained a distinctly African flavor."[37] Casual readers of this article may have missed the reporter's veiled reference to Sapelo's "African feel" embedded in stories passed down through the generations, like the eerie one Wevonneda Minis told: "When Wevonneda Minis first came to this marshy barrier island where her ancestors had been ... slaves, she learned of the dream her great-great-grandfather ... had the night before he died. In a dream, people told her, a black cat scratched him."[38]

The Times reporter did not invent the idea that Sapelo Islanders have an African feel. Since outsiders discovered the Islanders during the 1920s and 1930s, voodoo-styled superstitions, a distinct dialect, and stories about ancestors from slavery days have been perceived as essential elements in their murky African connection. Since slavery, white authors and folklore collectors noted coastal Georgia blacks' "uniqueness."[39] They wrote about coastal Georgia blacks' dialect, folktales, and spiritual practices and superstitions, yet they were not explicitly concerned with establishing and verifying their African origins.

Not until the 1920s and 1930s did the meaning and value of these folk practices begin to change as a new body of literature featuring coastal Georgia blacks' folk culture appeared. Coastal South Carolina blacks had, for decades before the interwar years, been known as peculiar "Gullah" folk. Coastal Georgia blacks had not. And while South Carolina communities would also attract more attention during these years, following the rise of Sapelo Islanders and coastal Georgia blacks within the expanding regional narrative about authentic Gullah folk culture presents a unique opportunity to chart the *making* of their "African feel."[40] Beginning in the 1930s, the *National Geographic Magazine* article "The Golden Isles of Guale," the Georgia Writers' Project study *Drums and Shadows: Survival Studies among the Georgia Coastal Negroes* (1940), Lydia Parrish's book *Slave Songs of the Georgia Sea Islands* (1942), and Lorenzo Dow Turner's linguistic study *Africanisms in the Gullah Dialect* (1949) established the foundation of Sapelo Islanders' African aura. Lydia Parrish, wife of famed artist Maxfield Parrish, discovered black Sapelo Islanders while wintering on St. Simon Island during the 1920s and shortly thereafter began collecting slave songs in the region and organizing ring shout performances for white audiences. W. Robert Moore, an adventure-seeking writer/photographer for *National Geographic Magazine*, introduced black Sapelo Islanders and their African essence to the magazine's readership in 1934. Distinguished scholar Lorenzo D. Turner, the only black person to research black Sapelo Islanders during the period, began researching the Gullah dialect in 1930 and spent more than fifteen years in pursuit of its African roots. Mary Granger, an aspiring writer, native of Savannah, Georgia, and supervisor of the Federal Writers' Project's Savannah unit, produced the most consulted of all the works about coastal Georgia blacks written during the period. This pioneering troop of mostly white writers and researchers included Sapelo Islanders in their work, which characterized and described coastal Georgia blacks as the guardians of African-derived traditions and practices that "survived" the Middle Passage and chattel slavery.

The work of the writers and researchers of the period, colored by the assumptions and theories about black cultural life of the 1920s and 1930s, gained significance over time. Although Parrish and Granger were amateur collectors, anthropologist Melville Herskovits—a scholar who could easily be called the father of African survivals theories—took an interest in their research and was a consultant on their projects. Granger's reading of coastal Georgia blacks' culture was so controversial that several scholars were consulted about the

Savannah unit study. Sterling Brown, E. Franklin Frazier, Guy B. Johnson, W. O. Brown, and Benjamin A. Botkin are among the intellectuals who came to the project as either advisers or adversaries. By the 1970s, 1980s, and 1990s, long after the disputes surrounding these works had faded, black women fiction writers and scholars looked to accounts of Gullah life published in the 1920s and 1930s and began to tell new stories about Gullah folks' African connection. They too were influenced by trends inside and outside of the academy. Black Feminism, the new black arts movement, the rise of the Black Studies movement, and the compelling new theories about black folk culture and history that emerged in this moment are evident in their works. Amid this revival, Sapelo Islanders' ancestors such as Bilali Mohammed came forth in black women writers' fantasies, inspiring the creation of fictional Gullah characters like the Muslim making prayer in the opening scene of Julie Dash's acclaimed film *Daughters of the Dust* (1991). Paule Marshall's, Julie Dash's, and Gloria Naylor's writings transformed the popular perception of the "Gullah," creating new possibilities for the identity as a source of pride in the African, slave, and black past. The dawn of the new millennium found the National Park Service, politicians, and Low Country blacks—including Sapelo Islanders—becoming important curators of Gullah folk culture, each group positing their own interpretations of how best to preserve these communities' heritage and African feel at a critical point in their generation's long fight for land.

All of the fascination surrounding survivals in black coastal communities has eclipsed the most compelling aspect of Sapelo Islanders' history and the history of the Gullah identity—the *how* and *why* of their famed African connection. When Sapelo Islanders' folk culture first became a subject of interest to researchers and writers during the 1920s and 1930s, the black women, men, and children who lived on the island faced insurmountable odds. An island that had once been a haven for freedmen and freedwomen had been returned to a plantation state ruled by a white millionaire. The Islanders were poor, and they had to do whatever they could to survive and hold on to their family homesteads. Living in the heart of Jim Crow America, their very blackness was used to justify their degradation and oppression. Like other black Americans, their African ancestry was the assumed root of their supposed inferiority. Antiblack violence was customary in the region, and the realities of their lives were anything but picturesque. It would seem that serious inquiries into their heritage, and new theories about its value, would be unlikely.

Why, then, during the 1920s and 1930s did "Africa" and all that she bestowed on her descendants, become important and noteworthy? What drove the quest to find rare strains of black culture during these years, and why did this quest seem to fixate on African-born superstitions, roots, hoodoo, and conjure? How did the Islanders respond to the inquisitive outsiders who showed up at their doorsteps during the interwar years? How did these blacks understand their own culture, which was increasingly classified under a banner ("Gullah") that they had not, until recently, used to identify themselves? How has the Islanders' view of their culture evolved as a result of the attention that their traditions attracted over the years? And most importantly, what is Gullah and Geechee? From the moment of the first explosion of interest, through the revival, and into the present, what needs have the "Gullah" fulfilled? Together, these questions map the contours of a new Gullah story, a history that turns the observational lens from coastal Georgia blacks, and fixes the lens on the people and forces that *made* them Gullah.

In answering the questions at the heart of this study, I got to know Sapelo Islanders differently from how I have known them. All of my life, Sapelo Islanders were simply family—mother, grandparents, aunts, uncles, and cousins. But the Sapelo Islanders that I discovered in books, news reports, and magazine articles, fictionalized in films and featured in documentaries, had a legacy and importance that extended far beyond the one that I had conceived. In these media, the Islanders were a one-of-a-kind, quasi-African, near-extinct Gullah population. Not long after I began searching for the origins of Sapelo Islanders' Gullah identity, I discovered that from the hunt for African survivals during the 1920s and 1930s, to the fight for their community's survival in recent decades, the meaning of their African and slave past has been debated, negotiated, and invoked to bolster a variety of theories and to promote many different agendas. The tension between Sapelo Islanders' actual past and experiences, and the imagined and theorized versions of their world that have appeared in published works, presented a stark contrast that begged for contextualization. Filled with tensions, contradictions, misappropriation, romanticism, erasures, racial fantasies, and racism, the history recounted in these pages is much more than a simple history about Sapelo Islanders or Gullah folk, it is a much larger story about race and the American imagination.

Collecting the Collectors

Writing the history of how Sapelo Islanders and their Low Country counterparts were made "Gullah" required that I draw on critical analytical frameworks to detect the motives and phenomena central to the notion of "cultural uniqueness." As David E. Whisnant asserts and demonstrates in his study *All That Is Native and Fine: The Politics of Culture in an American Region* (1983), cultural preservation and collection efforts are not "benign incidents," and are only mistakenly categorized as such because the "politics of culture"—the intimate yet politically and socially significant effects of, and inspirations for, a "fixation upon a romantically conceived 'culture'"—are ignored.[41] In his examination of the forces that aroused interest in Appalachian folk beginning in the late nineteenth century, Whisnant interprets the interplay between the political, social, and economic history of the region and the cultural interventions that followed key events. He concludes that while "cultural interventions" are "a little understood feature of every cultural past," they are "an evitable component of every cultural present and future."[42] Re-reading the cultural interventions through which Sapelo Islanders and other coastal Georgia blacks were made Gullah as products of broader social, political, economic, intellectual, and cultural forces, as opposed to reading curiosity about their traditions as separate from these forces, transforms all that has been written about them. The coastal Georgia Gullah researchers of the 1920s and 1930s discussed in this study surely had intimate and divergent reasons for exploring the culture of coastal Georgia blacks, but this does not mitigate the fact that, as they observed the Islanders and their neighbors in the region, their conclusions were shaped by contemporary sentiments and events. This is also true for the Gullah revival of the 1970s, 1980s, and 1990s—a time when the long-anticipated fear of Gullah folk's "extinction" that consumed Gullah observers for decades seemed to finally be at hand. The revival, and the preservation efforts that followed, owe much of their vibrancy and intensity to new theories about black history in the academy, black land loss in the region, and cries for land protections from activists in black coastal communities in the Low Country. Consequently, when all of these interventions are placed in historical context, they tell us as much about American cultural and intellectual life during these years as they tell us about Gullah folk culture.

Situating both the reintroduction of the Gullah during the interwar years and the Gullah revival during the 1970s, 1980s, and 1990s within the American imagination requires that we recognize that these Low Country blacks were represented as links to the past. Particularly during the interwar years, the idea that Gullah folk were relics of the past was a manifestation of a sort of primitivism that lingers in the shadows of all the stories that were, and are, told about them. Because these stories (whether they are in the form of academic studies, fictional literature, or plays and movies) are not incidental, it is important to consider why the storytellers need the Gullah. In *Imagining Indians in the Southwest: Persistent Visions of a Primitive Past* (1996), Leah Dilworth deciphers the "uses of the primitive," emphasizing that designating a group as primitive "depends on a comparison between some standard of 'civilization' and 'others' thought to be somehow simpler and has traditionally functioned as a kind of field on which 'we' write fantasies about 'them.'"[43] Dilworth further explains that fantasies about the primitive, ideas about their authenticity, and the representations through which they are mythologized, are at their core, responses and reactions to anxieties born from contemporary conditions.[44] This, too, is true for Gullah makers. The waves of romantic interest in Sapelo Islanders has been, in part, a reaction to a host of anxieties—tensions that the thousands of black southern migrants engendered in cities in the North and West during the twenties and thirties, anxieties about modernity and industrialization, and, in recent years, anxieties about black land loss along the coast.

Given the fascination with Sapelo Islanders' connection to Africa, this study is especially concerned with examining how "Africa" lived in the American imagination during the Gullah reintroduction and revival. Just as Philip Deloria finds "Indianness" playing a unique role in Americans' self-imagination stretching as far back as the Revolutionary period in Playing Indian, I find Africanness, and by extension Gullahness, being used to shore up an interesting mix of narratives about race and identity.[45] This focus is a decisive move away from debates about the authenticity and accuracy of African survivals in the region that have consumed scholars for decades, and instead grapples with why uncovering, collecting, and documenting black people's connections to Africa first became urgent, and why preserving and reimagining these connections continues to fill an important need in American intellectual and cultural life.

Critical assessments of cultural interventions, collecting and preservation missions, and identity are central to this study, but questions like the ones that anthropologist J. Lorand Matory raises about the Gullah also encouraged my conceptualization of the Gullah identity as a historical subject. Challenging bedrock assumptions about Gullah folks' "isolation," Matory encourages those who seek to understand the meaning of Gullah culture to employ what he has termed the "dialogue model" to make sense of how this folk identity took shape: "Whatever is culturally distinctive about any population on the Atlantic perimeter or anywhere else in the world has resulted not from isolation but from local conditions of trans-oceanic and multicultural interaction across the centuries."[46] When Matory's dialogue model is applied to the Gullah identity, it serves to unmask the many influences that have contributed to various theories about their uniqueness. Heeding Matory's call, and using Sapelo Islanders as a case study, this book attempts to reconnect seemingly disparate phenomena that inspired waves of interest in Gullah folk. By weaving together a history where Jim Crow, the advent of modernism, primitivism, the Great Migration, fantasies about Africa, the voodoo craze of the twenties and thirties, imperialism, the Black Studies movement, racism, the advent of the social sciences, and black land loss are all critical threads, Making Gullah introduces a new way to think about the Gullah. Ultimately, I find that the evolution of the Gullah identity is as tied to these phenomena and events as it is tied to the slave past and Africa.

This history also offers strategies for decoding stories about race and culture. Notions of racial difference are built on stories. And narratives about race and culture can only be understood by examining the larger context from which they emerge. Consequently, all race-culture stories, like the ones that have been told about the Gullah, wittingly or unwittingly engage the racial construct, making larger claims about its merits. When Mary Granger asserts that coastal Georgia blacks possess an African impulse that retards logic, and when Lydia Parrish declares that all that is beautiful about Sea Islanders' traditions were nurtured on idyllic antebellum plantations, they bolster white supremacist logic. But Lorenzo Turner's epic search for the African roots of the Gullah dialect was a mission that was, at its core, a rebuttal against stories about black inferiority. The black women writers who mythologized Gullah folk according to new interpretations of old interwar-era studies penned triumphant black narratives. When blacks in coastal communities in the Low Country joined in and began to embrace the Gullah label during the seventies, eighties, and nineties and celebrated Africanisms in their traditions as signs that slavery and Jim Crow had not defeated their ancestors and as evidence that their land and communities were sacred, their story also engaged the larger racial construct. Their survival story refutes ideas about black weakness and absolute white domination. However race-culture stories are crafted, they are inextricably linked to broader debates about race.

Because of its analytical focus and mission to recover the intellectual and cultural trends that led researchers and writers to the Gullah, *Making Gullah* is unlike other histories that Sapelo Islanders appear in. The Islanders can be found making brief appearances, along with other groups of black southerners, in historical monographs such as Steven Hahn's *A Nation Under Our Feet: Black Political Struggles in the Rural South from Slavery to the Great Migration* (2003) and J. William Harris's *Deep Souths: Delta, Piedmont, and Sea Island Society in the Age of Segregation* (2003), negotiating the terms of their freedom after the Civil War. But historian William McFeely's book *Sapelo's People: A Long Walk Into Freedom* (1994) is the most complete history of Sapelo Islanders to date. *Sapelo's People* charts the experiences of African slaves and their descendants on the island from the antebellum period through Reconstruction, while infusing his reflections of the time he spent in the community. McFeely does not engage the popular notion that Sapelo Islanders were and are distinct because they retained an African essence. But other historians whose works include references to the Sapelo Islanders have found new and creative ways to use the exhaustive research conducted on the island during the 1930s to support various arguments about the past. Among the most recent are: Allan Austin's *Muslim Slaves in Antebellum America: Transatlantic Stories and Spiritual Struggles* (1997), Michael Gomez's *Exchanging Our Country's Marks: The Transformation of African Identities in the Colonial and Antebellum South* (1998), and Philip Morgan's edited collection *African American Life in the Georgia Lowcountry: The Atlantic World and the Gullah Geechee* (2010). For all that these important works uncover about coastal Georgia blacks' past, which to varying degrees includes Sapelo Islanders, none considers the progression of the Islanders' legendary cultural identity.

Retelling the Story

Recognizing the imagination as an essential tool in the production of knowledge and art, *Making Gullah* examines how evolving ideas and fantasies about Africanness, blackness, and southernness have shaped the construction of the Gullah identity. By mapping the flow of discourses about black people's African past inside and outside the academy, this history reveals the complex roots of an identity famous for its simplicity. This study closely follows the published work of Moore, Parrish, Turner, and the Georgia Writers' Project—and the debates and controversy surrounding their work—and juxtaposes these details with larger trends and Sapelo Islanders' experiences. *Making Gullah* also tracks the legacies of these works from their revival in the seventies, eighties, and nineties through the 2006 Gullah/Geechee Cultural Heritage Corridor Act and beyond.

This history does not owe its newness to a shortage of sources. Aside from the published works in which Sapleo Islanders are featured, I use an array of letters, editorial memos, news reports, published studies, stories and interviews, films, and other cultural materials to reconstruct the influences that encouraged individual researchers and writers to study and imagine Gullah folks' heritage. In these sources, I located prominent scholars such as Melville Herskovits, E. Franklin Frazer, and Sterling Brown, hundreds of voodoo news reports, films such as *Harlem's Black Magic*, and Julia Peterkin's novels within the rich tapestry that was the backdrop for Gullah folks' reintroduction. These sources also foreground the Gullah revival, where I find black women writers such as Julie Dash, Paule Marshall, and a group of contemporary scholars, rereading and finding new meanings in Granger's and Parrish's studies.

Because questions about the tension between the imagined Gullah world and the realities of black life in coastal communities and on islands in the Low Country are so important to this study, I made every attempt to recover Sapelo Islanders' experiences and their interpretations of life in the region from the 1930s onward. Oral history interviews with Islanders who were, or whose parents were, featured in interwar-era publications are interwoven throughout the study. Their memories create compelling counternarratives that, until recent years, have been smothered by romantic depictions of life on the island. The voices of the blacks who live in coastal communities and on islands along the section of Interstate 95 recently designated the "Gullah Geechee Cultural Heritage Corridor" are also audible in this book. I used transcripts from Gullah Geechee Cultural Heritage Corridor community input meetings to relay their views on their culture and history and to articulate their conception of "preservation." And when Sapelo Islanders' voices and the voices of their comrades along the coast are added to the chorus of voices that have theorized and described their world for decades, the region that they live in seems less exotic, quaint, and unfamiliar, and resembles a much more familiar and troubling South.

Book Overview

The first two chapters set the stage for Gullah folks' reintroduction during the twenties and thirties. In chapter 1, the successes of Julia Peterkin's Gullah novels are used as a lens through which to view the milieu of countervailing influences from which a new strand of primitivism, and the reimagining of the value of black people's African heritage, emerged. The convergence of the shift from Victorian thought to modernist thought during the World War I era; the advent of the social sciences; the Harlem Renaissance; and the Great Migration are examined here. Chapter 2 explores a moment in America's race-making history that I call the "voodoo craze" of the twenties and thirties. Although Western thinkers held many negative ideas about "Africa" and "Africans" during these years, the common association between Africa and spiritual primitivism (superstitions, the belief in black magic, and dark rituals) was a prominent theme in assessments of Gullah folk's African connection. And stories about black-African spiritual primitivism were abundant in American popular culture during the interwar years. This synchronicity is not a coincidence. Using newspapers that circulated in popular migration destinations, films, plays, and travel writers' accounts to trace popular ideas about African survivals, this chapter charts a mounting obsession with southern black voodoo and superstition that reenergizes the debate over African survivals in academe. From Broadway to Zora Neale Hurston's folklore studies, this chapter grapples with how and why "voodoo" became a nebulous, yet loaded, assumed feature of southern black folklife.

Chapters 3 and 4 follow the production of 1920s and 1930s Sapelo reports, illustrating how ideas about African survivals and the Gullah—inside and outside the academy—came to the island and the region. Chapter 3 investigates the work of Moore, Parrish, and Turner in coastal Georgia and on Sapelo; the interactions of these writers with the Islanders and their theories of African survivals are also analyzed. The production of Mary Granger's study, *Drums and Shadows*, is the focus of chapter 4. This chapter chronicles the feud that ensued between Granger, national Federal Writers' Project administrators, and the scholars who were consulted about the study.

The final chapters discuss the legacies of the studies of the twenties and thirties within the Gullah revival and the land battles raging throughout the region. Chapter 5 excavates the origins of the revival, analyzes the lull that precedes it, and explores the new meaning of "Gullah" that takes shape during the 1970s, 1980s, and 1990s. The last chapter recounts the marriage of Low Country blacks' newly embraced Gullah identity and their fight for the survival of coastal black communities like Sapelo. The final chapter also finds cultural preservation and historic preservation becoming deeply contested categories as Gullah Geechee Cultural Heritage Corridor commissioners and Gullah communities attempt to define their past and plan their future.

Making Gullah examines the unexamined history of the making of a quaint culture and community. It is an account of a remembered, forgotten, overlooked, misunderstood, sanitized, and reclaimed past. It is a tale of Jim Crow, race fantasies, land battles, battles to define racial identity, and the long black freedom struggle. For all that Sapelo Island's contemporary visitors believe that they know about the island, its people, and its past, the history of how they were made Gullah has never been told—until now.

From Wild Savages to Beloved Primitives

No veils of civilization hide the stark realities of love, birth, death, from their eyes, but they find happiness in the present instead of looking for it always in tomorrow and again tomorrow or in something still to be discovered. . . .

On large plantations, where Negroes are in tremendous majority, the field hands have few contacts with white people and no need to amend their speech or give up the customs and traditions of their African ancestry.

—Julia Peterkin, Roll, Jordan, Roll

Four days after Christmas in 1928, dozens of Sapelo Islanders gathered around an oxcart on a dirt road that snaked through live oaks covered in Spanish moss and waited for the white man who was filming them to tell them what to do next. They had already sung "Old Time Religion," "Steal Away to Jesus," and performed a rendition of the minstrel tune that was named the Kentucky state song that year—"My Old Kentucky Home."[1] Each time the camera rolled, the filmmaker directed the Islanders to sing while riding in, or walking alongside, the oxcart. The solemn choral group likely included some of the men Howard Coffin hired to build roads, prepare crops, man his sawmill, tend his cattle, work in his greenhouse, or build boats and other structures. Likewise, several of the women in the chorus were either paid by Coffin to work in his shrimp and oyster cannery or in his fields, or were members of the domestic staff who cooked his meals and cleaned his mansion.[2] Even though the filmmaker captured several "takes" designed to look like mundane and typical Sapelo scenes, that day was anything but ordinary. That day, Sapelo Islanders found themselves in front of cameras, recording equipment, and in the presence of a small crowd of newspaper reporters because their boss had recruited them to entertain the most powerful white man in Jim Crow America, President Calvin Coolidge.

Of course President Coolidge's sojourn to the island made headlines in national newspapers, but articles chronicling the details of his trip also introduced Sapelo Islanders to the nation. Reports described the men, women, and children, who were descendants of the freedmen and freedwomen who fought for land on the island, as the 250 "negroes who" gratefully showed "their allegiance" to Coffin—the man who "permitted" them to remain on the "romantic and picturesque" island when he purchased it in 1912.[3] News stories recounted the president's and the millionaire's hunting excursions led by "'Old Pete' Morgan, native black guide" during which "negro beaters" flushed birds from the brush so that Coolidge and Coffin could easily shoot their prey.[4] Reporters wrote about Mrs. Coolidge's attempts to befriend the island's black children so that she could record them with her motion picture camera.[5] And several papers featured the "sea island rodeo" that the island's blacks performed on the beach to amuse the president and his entourage as one of the trip's highlights. Articles announced that during the rodeo "excited negroes," "the youthful descendants of African slaves" rode wild steers "bareback" on the beach, while "groups of negro girls . . . vied with each other in singing the spirituals of their race and gospel hymns."[6] Together, these brief descriptions presented Sapelo Islanders as a unique population of simple and exotic southern black folk.

It is no surprise that Howard Coffin, who loved slave songs, arranged for Sapelo Islanders to sing for his guests.[7] In 1928, many Americans believed that primitive musical exuberance was a distinct racial trait bequeathed to American blacks by their African ancestors. All of the newspapers that reported on Coolidge's trip wrote about Sapelo's singing blacks: they sang for the president after a luncheon, they sang at the rodeo, they sang "work-songs" that "roused the President before 6 o'clock," and they sang for "the President's entertainment while a speaking motion picture film was made."[8] Surely, many of the Islanders who performed for Coolidge and his entourage were pleased to have the president in the audience of onlookers observing their craft, but their willingness to perform should not be interpreted as a sign that they were content with Coffin's domination and impressed by his wealth, status, and power. In fact, evidence of their discontent can be found in the same musical tradition that was exploited during Coolidge's visit. "Pay Me Money Down" was a popular work song among coastal Georgia blacks by the 1920s.[9] The song's refrain, "Pay me, Oh pay me, Pay me or go to jail," echoed the anxieties that blacks who "owed" debts to wealthy whites suffered. Sapelo Islanders added a very telling verse to the work song as it traveled throughout the region: "Wish't I was Mr. Coffin's son . . . Stay in the house an' drink good rum." Blacks on nearby St. Simon's Island contributed a verse that featured their "big boss." "Wish't I Mr. Foster's son . . . I'd sit on the bank an' see the work done."[10] These lyrics are a clear critique of the raciai hierarchy that limited their life chances. When Islanders sang that they wished they were Coffin's or Foster's son, they were acknowledging freedoms, wealth, luxuries, and power that Jim Crow denied them; they were articulating their frustration with the social structure that forced them into grueling work routines and debt that threatened their freedom.[11]

Unquestionably, Sapelo's singers entertained the president in part, because they had to, but a larger question looms. Why did the reporters and filmmakers who accompanied the president find them so intriguing? Idealized romantic southern plantation scenes featuring happy blacks—like the ones described in "My Old Kentucky Home" verses—were familiar by 1928.[12] This trope could have easily encouraged the reporters and filmmakers in the president's entourage to paint Sapelo Islanders as essential accessories to Coffin's plantation oasis. But by 1928, the American cultural landscape was overflowing with new stories about black southerners like Sapelo Islanders that could have easily contributed to Coffin's guests' fascination with the black people who lived on the island. In fact, one white fiction writer's stories about blacks who lived on a coastal plantation in the Low Country were so popular that she emerged as the first southern writer to win a Pulitzer Prize. The same year that Coolidge visited Sapelo, Julia Peterkin's third book featuring "Gullah" characters—*Scarlet Sister Mary* (1928)—was published. The book was a best seller by June 1929, and a Pulitzer Prize–winning novel a few months later. In as much as Julia Peterkin's novels offered the nation a way to imagine southern blacks like Sapelo Islanders—populations who became known as "Gullah folk"—the stories that she wrote gained popularity partly because of larger shifts in the way that Africanness, blackness, and southernness were imagined.

The 1920s and 1930s marked major transitions in America's racial landscape. Racial segregation was at an all-time high, but the post–World War I era was also witness to a variety of countervailing cultural influences. The period saw the mass migration of southern blacks to northern cities; a shift from Victorianism to modernism; and heightened exploration of black spaces encouraged by the New Negro Black Arts movement. These phenomena cultivated fantasies among white and black Americans about blacks and their Africanness, justified racism, encouraged exoticism, spurred American modernists, and were central to the black arts movement. Understanding these trends and examining Julia Peterkin's reintroduction of Gullah folk within the context of the period is crucial in order to make sense of Sapelo Islanders' emergence as a population whose culture was worthy of collection, documentation, examination, and exploitation.

Julia Peterkin Introduces Gullah Folk to the Nation

No one researcher or writer did more to push "Gullah folk" to the center of the nation's consciousness during the 1920s and 1930s than Julia Mood Peterkin. She was born on Halloween in 1880 in Laurens, South Carolina, and was raised by her father, who was a doctor, and her black nurse Maum Patsy, after her mother died.[13] It was Maum Patsy who taught Peterkin how to speak "Gullah" and ignited in her a spark of curiosity about the inner world of the blacks around her.[14] After she graduated from Converse College in Spartanburg, South Carolina, and married William George Peterkin a short time after in 1903, she became the mistress of her husband's Lang Syne plantation.[15] There, she transformed her fantasies about the five hundred blacks who lived and worked on their two-thousand-acre plantation into characters in the fictional works that made her a historic literary figure.[16]

Playing the role of a caged, delicate plantation mistress did not satisfy Julia Peterkin. For twenty years she focused her energies on becoming a good plantation mistress, which involved acquainting herself with the life habits of the black people who worked for her.[17] The task left her empty. When she was forty years old, she found herself trying to fill the void that the "stillness" of country life left her nursing with piano lessons.[18] But busying herself with piano did not fill the void because she was not good at it. She was, however, good at telling her instructor Henry Bellamann — the dean of the School of Fine Arts — stories about her black charges at Lang Syne. Her stories were so entertaining that Bellamann decided to teach her how to write instead of how to play chords.[19] And right away she found relief from the gnawing abyss. The time that she spent with Bellamann and his aspiring bohemian friends sealed Peterkin's commitment to trying her hand at writing stories.[20] Giving vent, in writing, to the agonies of decades of plantation life, was cathartic. Peterkin explained that "Among the Negroes" on Lang Syne she "saw sickness and death and superstition and frenzy and desire," her eyes looked "on horror and misery," and "the things stayed with" her and she "had to get rid of them."[21] Believing that she had penetrated the veil that separated white life from black life in the South, and convinced that she could channel black people's thoughts and emotions, Peterkin wrote their stories, and literally took on their voice (her short stories and novels were all composed using what she understood to be an authentic Gullah dialect).

The tales that Peterkin wrote about the blacks who lived on the fictional "Blue Brook Plantation" in *Green Thursday* (1924), *Black April* (1927), *Scarlet Sister Mary* (1928), *Bright Skin* (1932), and — her attempt at ethnography — *Roll, Jordan, Roll* (1933) codified the cultural world of Gullah folk. The Gullahs of Blue Brook were imaginary composites of the blacks she encountered on Lang Syne and on Murrells Inlet and Waccamaw Neck — the South Carolina seaside communities where she spent her summers.[22] Peterkin's Gullah folk were isolated from the outside world and had a unique connection to their African ancestors that she described in her books: "The black people who live in the Quarters at Blue Brook Plantation believe they are far the best black people living on the whole 'Neck'. . . . They are no Guinea negroes . . . or Dinkas. . . . They are Gullahs with tall straight bodies, and high heads filed with sense."[23] Blue Brook's Gullahs were artifacts of the antebellum era; they remained on the old plantation and worked its soil long after their ancestors' masters and their white descendants had abandoned the "big house" and moved on. Suspicious of modernity and opposed to "Book-learning" because it "takes people's minds off more important things," Peterkin's Gullah folk consumed themselves with work, pleasure, and daily survival.[24] The main characters in Peterkin's stories struggled through epic personal conflicts (love, death, sickness, and loss). But their lives were ruled by supernatural phenomena: "God" or "conjure" (voodoo) was responsible for everything that happened to them. Blue Brook folk like Killdee and Rose in *Green Thursday*, Si May-e in *Scarlet Sister Mary*, and characters such as Maum Hannah (an elderly midwife) and Old Daddy Cudjoe (the plantation's conjure man) who appeared in several Peterkin stories, navigated life's challenges by working with or struggling against prevailing supernatural forces. Peterkin's Gullah can be found performing ring shouts after prayer services, or "seekin'" a sign in their dreams after a period of prayer signaling their preparedness for baptism—all customs that were once prevalent in black Low Country communities. But just as easily as distraught Blue Brook blacks found themselves crossing Heaven's Gate Church's threshold searching for God's favor, they could also find themselves making the long trek deep into the woods to Daddy Cudjoe's doorstep looking for a magical conjure bag to ease their troubles.

Aside from a few of the Christian traditions Peterkin wrote into her tales, some of the folk practices she fictionalized, and the fact that her Gullah folk still lived on a coastal plantation, Blue Brook bears little resemblance to Low Country black districts during the interwar years. She all but erased white people, Jim Crow racism, and oppression from Blue Brook and from the lives of the Gullah folk she imagined. Peterkin rarely wrote about encounters between Blue Brook's blacks and whites. When she did, these infrequent brushes were depicted as slight inconveniences and annoyances. For example, when a white man forcibly purchased Maum Hannah's land and built his house on her lot, she simply prayed for a sign and discerned that God instructed her to burn his house down. After burning down the white man's house, Maum Hannah sought the white sheriff for help. Playing the part of a submissive "auntie," Maum Hannah identified herself as "one o' ol' Mass Richard Jeems' niggers" and confessed to the divinely inspired crime. She won the sheriff's favor by explaining that she had always been told that "De sheriff is de bes' frien' de niggers is got een dis worl," so he embraced the role and covered up the arson.[25]

Peterkin did not have to rely on her imagination to conceive the predicament that Maum Hannah found herself in; securing and keeping land had always been a difficult undertaking for blacks in the South. But the resolution was a perfect fictional ending—one that was highly unlikely in the Jim Crow South.

In the majority of her Blue Brook stories, "white folk" were more of an idea, and not an actual group of people with whom blacks had to contend. When her characters scoffed at whites' efforts to curtail boll weevils with poisons or to impose regulations on midwives or promote education and literacy, her Gullahs laughed at the very notion that man, and more specifically "the white man," could use his mind and technological innovations to control events dictated by otherworldly powers.[26] In the imaginary world that Peterkin depicted in her first three novels, Blue Brook blacks' poverty and their struggle to survive, and the fact that they were relegated to tenant farming on the old plantation, had nothing to do with the structures of racism; her characters did not detect oppression in their world. Bright Skin (1932), the last novel that she published, was the only work that strayed from this formula. In this final novel, Peterkin attempted to craft a Blue Brook that was less isolated; ideas and people from the mainland awaken Gullah perceptions of racial prejudice and poverty near the end of Peterkin's publishing career.

Ultimately, Peterkin's Gullah folk are a blend of racial myth and published folklore material.[27] Their quasi-African primitiveness freed them to express themselves sexually, but their childlike nature, which predisposed them to give into base impulses, and their tendency toward emotionalism, was the reason why superstition, fear, and "frenzy" seemed to dictate their lives. Blue Brook blacks' passions always ran high. Fierce fights and conflicts between residents; their inclination toward either extreme pleasure or religiosity; their adherence to terrifying superstitions; and their liaisons that resulted in illegitimate children gifted with healing powers because they "nebber see e' daddy, fo-true," were staples in her stories.[28] Even though the imprint of racial caricatures is easily detected in her writings, Peterkin saw herself as one of a few white writers who tried to capture the complexity of black southerners' inner psychology.[29]

Peterkin's characterizations of Gullah folk were certainly rooted in race fantasies that had dominated the nation's imaginary long before she began to write. Joel Chandler Harris, an early explorer of Sea Island folk culture who fictionalized Sapelo's Bilali Mohammed in his writings, discussed the connection between "the Gullah" and prevalent race fantasies in 1894.[30] Reporting on the devastation and relief efforts that followed the Sea Island storm of 1893, Harris explained that black southerners, and Sea Islanders, in particular, had been "wofully [sic] exaggerated by hasty writers for the press . . . and their personal appearance has been caricatured by artists."[31] Harris traced these distortions, and the belief that "Sea Island negroes" were "relapsing into a state of barbarism and savagery," back to the years after the Civil War.[32] However, he wrote, "It is impossible to say precisely what this theory was based on" and concluded that the perception had "no basis."[33] Surely, the savage Sea Islanders theory that perplexed Harris was a product of white southerners' fear of free, autonomous blacks. The idea that blacks in Low Country locales like Sapelo had become barbaric and savage *because* they were free was a myth derived from white southerners' anxieties about this significant change in the racial order. This myth also reveals just how precarious white observations of black southern life were during the period. But Harris rebuked the theory and instead argued that "the Gullah element is nearly wiped out, and the Congo type is rapidly disappearing."[34] Which populations constitute the Gullah and Congo types in Harris's imagination is unclear. However, he did attribute the fact that they were being "wiped out" to vague and unnamed improvements among blacks. The fact that Peterkin primarily organized a host of racial stereotypes under the "Gullah" banner and constructed a cultural type from scraps of older understandings of the label raises more questions. Who were the "Gullah" *really*? And what exactly distinguished the Gullahs from other black southerners?

The term "Gullah" has been loosely used to describe linguistic and cultural patterns among blacks living in coastal South Carolina and Georgia, and the precise origins of the label are hard to pin down. Evidence suggests that the use of the term originated in the slave trade. Variations of the term "Golla" were used as a prefix in numerous slave advertisements in South Carolina dating back to 1742.[35] Notices like the one posted in the *South Carolina Gazette* in 1783 announcing the capture of a fugitive "Negro girl of the Gola country" often appeared in the state's newspapers.[36] In 1850, T. J. Bowen, an American Baptist missionary visited Liberia and assumed that the "Gola" people of Liberia were the progenitors of "Gullah negroes": "The Golah people inhabit both sides of St. Paul's River, back of Monrovia. . . . These are the 'Gula negroes' of the Southern States." Bowen described them as "degraded and superstitious . . . one of the meanest tribes in Africa."[37] During the 1920s, South Carolina folklorists Ambrose Gonzales and John Bennett—both purveyors of Gullah material—disagreed about Gullah folks' African origins. Bennett believed that their roots were in Liberia, but Gonzales pointed out that an 1822 report about Denmark Vessey's insurrection plot described Vessey's co-conspirator "Gullah Jack" (a feared "conjurer") in terms that suggested the word "Gullah" may have been a corruption of the name "Angola." Because Liberia and Angola were so far apart, Gonzales concluded that "these two opinions seem to be in hopeless conflict."[38] Contemporary scholars have also tried to track down exactly where the name came from. Historian Margaret Washington Creel revisited older theories in her study *"A Peculiar People": Slave Religion and Community-Culture Among the Gullahs* (1988) and synthesized newer material, adding more ideas to the list of possibilities, including one that cites slave importation patterns as the source of the label. For example, she writes that the importation of large numbers of slaves from Winward Coast (modern-day Sierra Leone and Liberia) where "Golas" and "Gizzis" lived may account for the origin of the term, as well as the alternate term "Geechee" that some blacks from coastal regions have come to use to describe themselves.[39]

More important than where the Gullah label came from is how it has been used and what it means in the American context. Low Country blacks' historic relationship to the label points to an interesting trend that has been, for the most part, ignored. In coastal Georgia during the 1930s a few blacks remembered that old slaves who came from Africa were called "Gullah" (a prefix to their given names) by their overseers and described them as a group who had long since passed away, but they did not use the label to describe themselves.[40] Blacks in coastal Georgia, until recent years, did not use the term "Gullah" to describe themselves and generally rejected the Geechee label because it was commonly used as an insult that carried a host of negative associations born from delusions and myths about black inferiority and backwardness that have roots that stretch all the way back to slavery days.[41] Only in the last forty years have coastal Georgia blacks embraced and begun to use the label; before that point, the word "Gullah" was primarily relegated to published works written about them.

Slave importation patterns and subsequent labeling of enslaved Africans may account for the presence of the word "Gullah" in the American vocabulary, but isolating and defining the qualities and people associated with the label in published works reveals a fascinating historical progression. Soldiers who fought in the Civil War noted the strange dialect prevalent among blacks in coastal South Carolina.[42] During the later years of the nineteenth century, southern writers Joel Chandler Harris and Charles Colcock Jones Jr. introduced coastal Georgia blacks' dialect and folklore to Americans in their works. But these works, aside from the use of dialect writing, offered little that would definitively set Low Country blacks apart from other black southerners. Harris did, in his report on the hurricane of 1893, attempt to provide the article's readers with a description of the Gullah. He pointed to their speech as an important distinguishing characteristic, a "talk" that he described as "half African and less English."[43] Harris also surmised that Sea Island blacks "belong essentially to the slave type of the African"—peaceful tribes, content to raise cattle and farm[44]—traits that lived on in their descendants who were "gentle, unobtrusive, and friendly" and most of all, "uncomplaining."[45] The only group of Sea Islanders that Harris presented as exceptions to this Negro "type" were Sapelo Islanders and coastal Georgia blacks. He explained that in coastal Georgia, the most noticeable "type" was not Gullah or Congo, but "the Arabian."[46] He presented "Old Ben Ali" (Bilali of Sapelo Island) as an example of the Arab type and wrote briefly about his diary to underscore that this group of Sea Islanders, Bilali's descendants, were particularly intelligent and enterprising.[47] Clearly, speculation about African ethnicities and generalizations about blacks and their inherited peculiarities are at the heart of the messy imaginary from which the Gullah label has emerged. Even as John Bennett took on the Gullah dialect in 1908 in his essay "Gullah: A Negro Patois," and Ambrose Gonzales published his Gullah folklore collection, *The Black Border: Gullah Stories of the Carolina Coast* (1922), neither author could clarify the origins of the term or the characteristics associated with the people it described.[48]

The use of "Gullah" in published works that preceded Peterkin's short stories and novels reveals two clear patterns. The first pattern is that these works were largely about blacks living in coastal South Carolina. The second discernible pattern pertains to the nature of the way that the Gullah were categorized: the identity was assigned according to region, race, and dialect. But that would change during the 1920s and 1930s, and Julia Peterkin's fictional works would be influential in the transformation of the identity. During these years, writers and researchers assigned new interpretations to characteristics connected to the Gullah identity. They expanded Gullah territory to include coastal Georgia blacks and placed greater emphasis on African-derived spiritual practices, crafts, and other primitive traits that they believed were African, and featured them as central elements of the traditions that made the people included under this banner unique from other blacks in the South.

Clearly, the qualities associated with the term "Gullah" evolved over time. More important still is the fact that white "outsiders" like Peterkin initiated the construction of the Gullah identity according to the way that they imagined these black southerners. However, the mere existence of Peterkin's stories does not explain why Gullah folk attracted so much interest during the 1920s and 1930s, and why the identity underwent such a significant recharacterization during these years. The answers to these questions will not be found in the pages of Peterkin's stories because they are rooted in phenomena that swept the nation and consumed cultural and intellectual communities far away from Lang Syne and South Carolina.

From African Savages to Beloved Primitives

The literary musings of a self-professed tortured white plantation mistress from South Carolina would have fallen flat, and failed to capture the attention of the nation's littérateurs, had it not been for the nation's growing obsession with "primitives" in the 1920s and 1930s. The nation's imagination was ripe for Peterkin's tales. The carnage that took place during World War I critically ruptured white Victorian thinkers' assumptions about the superiority of European civilization, inspiring new interest in people once deemed backward and savage among Modernist writers, artists, and intellectuals searching for new ways to understand human society after the Great War. Because race was at the heart of white Victorian thinkers' conceptualization of civilization, it is not surprising that blacks, and more specifically southern blacks, became central to American modernists' quest to recover the experiences and emotions that civilization had deprived them.[49] From the 1830s onward, white Victorian writers and intellectuals had bolstered their claims of white supremacy by constructing theories that characterized civilization as an explicitly racial concept denoting a specific stage in human racial evolution.[50] According to their calculations, nonwhites inherited, and were relegated to, the ranks of barbaric savages, and only white races had evolved to the civilized stage.[51] They also understood culture in racial terms. Since culture was the mark of civilized peoples, the concept was an exclusively white trait. Morality, prosperity, self-restraint, discipline, and formal education were the core elements of civilized culture.[52] Because these Victorians believed that nonwhites occupied the lowest ranks of the evolutionary scale, they characterized them as irrational, immoral, nonproductive savages who could not control their animalistic impulses.

Africa, and her descendants, held a particularly low place in the Victorians' view of human evolution. Even though some white-skinned ethnic peoples were excluded from the Victorians' conceptualization of civilized society, they believed that blacks were the world's most savage primitives.[53] The 1893 World's Columbian Exposition held in Chicago provides a perfect example of how whites used fantasies about black savagery to shore up their image of white civilization. The exposition featured two racially specific exhibits: one highlighted the successes of white civilization and the other ("The Midway") portrayed the dark barbarism of nonwhites.[54] The latter featured primitives in a variety of settings, including a replica of a "Dahomey village" with huts and black people beating tom-toms in the Midway, which offered visitors a quintessential African scene. Guidebooks underscored the racial dichotomies on display by advising visitors to tour the Midway after visiting the White City so that they would better appreciate the difference between the civilized White City and the uncivilized native villages.[55] Hubert Howe Bancroft's description of the fair's exhibits in The Book of the Fair (1893) proclaimed: "All the continents are here represented, and many nations of each continent, civilized, semicivilized, and barbarous, from the Caucasian to the African black, with head in the shape of a cocoa-nut and with barely enough of clothing to serve for the wadding of a gun."[56]

From popular literature to scholarly works, white Victorians' assessment of Africa, African peoples, and African descendants was a prominent theme that colored the American imagination. The enduring popularity of Edgar Rice Burroughs's best-selling novel *Tarzan of the Apes* (1914), set in a primal African jungle populated with man-eating cannibals, is just one example of the American taste for fictions about black savagery.[57] But even scholarly works relied on ideas about black savagery to make sense of the world. The same year that Burroughs's *Tarzan of the Apes* was published, historian John Daniels published a study about blacks in Boston in which he wrote: "It is of course undeniable that the precedent conditions out of which the Negro population is derived, have, from the earliest period down to the present, been of a peculiarly inferior kind." Daniels explained that Boston blacks' ancestors came from an "African jungle where from time immemorial their ancestors had lived in a stage of primitive savagery." Echoing Victorians' bedrock assumptions about civilization, Daniels concluded that Africans were "savages themselves, utterly ignorant of civilization, having no religion above fear-born superstition, and lacking all conception of reasoned morality."[58] Daniels was not alone; many scholars described black-Africans as childlike, superstitious, and uninhibited, with strong sexual instincts and the tendency to express themselves through music and dancing as opposed to civilized forms of communication.[59]

Julia Peterkin lived most of her life in a world in which Victorian virtues and ideas shaped the way that racial difference was understood—and by the time she felt the pangs that sent her searching for a more meaningful life, so much had begun to change. Victorian values could not stand against the tide of disillusionment that swept the nation after the First World War. The disenchantment with Western civilization that followed the war gave way to a sort of liberation and sense of newness that inspired many (but not all) of the nation's black and white writers, artists, and scholars to break away from old conventions.[60] Julia Peterkin's own nonfiction writings bear witness to the dramatic effect that World War I and the advent of modernist thought had on American artists, writers, and intellectuals. In a 1937 book review, while reflecting on the evolution of southern literature and the way that blacks were depicted by southern writers, Peterkin wrote, "It is as if the World War opened men's eyes, ears, minds.... The younger generation in the south seemed suddenly to see that in order to survive, it must liberate itself from the past. The opinions of the preceding generation were discarded, new opinion formed." For southern writers in particular, Peterkin explained that casting off Victorian logic offered a "freedom from formulas" that allowed them to develop a more truthful examination of their region's civilization: "Readers and writers began to face harsh facts without blinking, and resolved to quit exaggerating and pretending."[61]

Peterkin was right. After the war, from Europe to America, artists and intellectuals posed questions that challenged the neat and predictable universe that the Victorians imagined. French symbolist poets, impressionist painters, new turns in the physical sciences, and the advent of the social sciences were all part of the "constellation of related ideas, beliefs, values and modes of perception" that mark modernism.[62] Although American modernism took many different forms, the ideological tendency of modernists can be described in general terms; they wanted to reclaim everything that Victorian moralists excluded from their conception of culture and tried to craft new truths to replace old dogma.[63] But the rebellion against Victorian logic was not limited to the world of arts and letters. New technology and inventions, and the rise of consumer culture, ushered in by expanding industrial development, replaced "Victorian values" (work, order, and restraint) with "consumer values" (consumption, leisure, and free expression).[64] And all of these changes inspired an upheaval of racial thought among black and white thinkers, along with new calls for racial equality among blacks.[65]

The new social scientific theories threatened the very thing that Victorian truths sought to protect: white supremacy. Some social scientists, and more specifically anthropologists like Franz Boas, rejected the Victorian view of race and culture.[66] He argued that "races" could not be ranked because they were impossible to classify. He also maintained that "culture" was not a racial or biological phenomenon.[67] Anthropologists who embraced Boas's approach disputed Victorians' conceptualization of "civilized" and "savage" peoples by consistently proving that "savage" life was not so different from "civilized" life.[68]

At the same time that scholars began to take apart "race" and redefine culture, a new strand of primitivism gained momentum among American artists and writers. Even though Victorian ideas had lost their grip on the American psyche, the racial dichotomy that Victorians had built remained intact. Consequently, many white artists, writers, and scholars seeking to free themselves from the strictures of Victorianism tried to reconcile their *civilized* enculturation with what they believed to be their deeper human instincts by breaking down the barrier between the white civilized world and the nonwhite savage world.[69] Among them was Julia Peterkin who encouraged white southern writers to take advantage of their newfound freedom by exploring the South's complicated and painful racial terrain in their writings and by crafting more authentic portrayals of their "dark-skinned neighbors."[70] Peterkin's certainty that blacks could be useful in whites' quest to understand themselves was not simply a reflection of her own obsession, it was an expression of this primitivist tendency.

Obsessed with the very people that the Victorians had considered savages, primitivists of the modernist era like Peterkin looked to people they believed to be free from the constraints of the civilized world, people who remained close to the earth despite rapid industrialization, and people who were not bound by sophisticated thought to recover the freedoms that civilized life denied them. For Peterkin, Gullah folk were the perfect primitives because, as she explained, "No veils of civilization hide the stark realities of love, birth, death, from their eyes, but they find happiness in the present instead of always in tomorrow and again tomorrow or in something still to be discovered."[71] This fascination with the carefree, unfettered, primitive black "other" was not a departure from racist civilization discourse, but instead was an adjustment of the discourse. Peterkin, and others like her, projected their fantasies onto nonwhite primitives—like their ideological predecessors did their savages—and used them to settle their own inner turmoil and clarify their humanity similar to the way that Victorians used their savages to bolster their sense of racial superiority.[72]

The fact that Africans and their descendants were among primitivists' favorite subjects makes perfect sense. Reaching out to the other side of the veil to recover and encounter all that Victorianism had deprived them of, white primitivists of the 1920s and 1930s would find new meaning in black expressions. Authentically "black-African" elements turned up in Pablo Picasso's artwork, in Julia Peterkin's writings, and made artists like Josephine Baker popular during these years.[73] From this vantage point, the use of black subjects or the incorporation of black-African forms in art, music, novels, and in social scientific studies was a vehicle for rebellion and was, at times, a form of romantic racism.[74]

Much like their predecessors, 1920s and 1930s primitivists made little distinction between Atlantic World blacks and their African ancestors. They too believed that the essence of the African was present in Atlantic World blacks. So, they did not need to travel to Africa to encounter authentic free peoples because they believed that the mystique and allure of the primitive was within reach—their dark-skinned neighbors promised to satisfy all of their curiosities and needs.

Discovering America's Black Primitive and the Negro Vogue

Whereas Peterkin crossed a figurative line in the twenties and thirties in her fictional exploration of the black world, whites in search of authentic experiences in New York, Chicago, and big cities throughout the nation crossed literal boundaries that segregation had created between whites and blacks. Primitivism was not simply a fixation among America's artists and writers. During the twenties and thirties, the "black spaces" created by customs and laws that mandated separation between blacks and whites attracted the attention of adventurous and rebellious whites who wanted to explore the exotic world inhabited by the nation's own primitives. Segregation made black residential zones and leisure and consumer centers easy to find, and the growing vogue of black culture, partly fueled by the popularity of jazz and blues during Prohibition, added to the appeal of black communities.[75] This fad was especially pronounced in metropolises like New York during the 1920s where black communities like Harlem became sites of leisure where whites could go "slumming" and escape the constraints of civilized life.[76]

Rebellious and bohemian adventure-seeking whites looking for interracial encounters in black communities were not alone in their curiosities about black life during the 1920s and 1930s. White scholars such as sociologist Robert Park and anthropologist Franz Boas engaged in academic slumming during the interwar period. Historian Davarian Baldwin explains: "Plantation cafes (or Cotton Clubs), bricolage art pieces and cultural relativisms all derived a direct sense of inspiration and profit as early 'samplers' of what many white people perceived as the unique primitivism of African and southern folk cultures."[77] Although Park's and Boas's motivations and intellectual orientations were quite different, both men's careers included intellectual projects that tackled the race question. In fact, even though blacks were not the only group to which Boas dedicated intellectual energy, he is credited for significantly transforming the way that scholars understood Africa, which inspired black and white academics alike to take a second look at both African "things" and African people and history.[78] For example, the 1923 Primitive Negro Art exhibit showcased at the Brooklyn Museum, featuring objects made in Africa that were subsequently categorized as "art," was inspired by the larger exploration of black people and calls made by black intellectuals and scholars like Boas to recast Africanness.[79]

Intensified white interest in black people and black culture may explain many black-white encounters during the 1920s and 1930s, but it does not explain them all. Interracial contact between whites and blacks during the 1920s was not always the result of exoticism or primitivism, and blacks were not completely powerless in these encounters. In fact, blacks played a significant role in the glorification of "authentic" black culture during these years.[80] The New Negro movement led by the new generation of American blacks who shared experiences with segregation and who pushed for equality and economic opportunities to combat oppression took shape in the years after World War I. The New Negro leaders who organized the Harlem Renaissance were plugged into modernist discourses and tried to tackle racial inequality through the arts; they often branded "black art" according to popular beliefs about authentic black-African folk expressions.[81] For these New Negroes, their primitive past served two purposes: first, their African and black folk past was a symbol of their shared history, which they hoped would become a source of true race pride; and second, the fact that they could point to a primitive past marked their station within modernity.[82]

More importantly, the leaders of the Harlem Renaissance interpreted white rebellion against Victorianism as an opportunity to press for racial equality. From their vantage point, the birth of the modernist consciousness was an irreparable crack in the wall of white supremacy. The ideological shift appeared to be an opportunity to rethink race and recast blackness in the larger American social psyche. Harlem Renaissance organizers, such as Charles S. Johnson, surmised that challenging racial oppression through the arts was relatively safe in light of the rash of antiblack violence that was prevalent during the period, because the arts were the only arena from which blacks had not been barred.[83] Furthermore, the quest for racial equality through the arts promised to reveal black people's complexity when they were depicted as artistic subjects, as well as demonstrate black people's ability to make valuable contributions to the world of art and literature as artists and writers.

However, Harlem Renaissance writers' and leaders' desire to transcend racial boundaries was at times muddied by the fact that they too relied on essentialist ideas about blackness to attract patrons and audiences and to resolve their own misgivings about their African heritage.[84] When Langston Hughes spoke of the connection between black Americans and their African past in his 1921 poem "The Negro Speaks of Rivers" and wrote lines such as "I built my hut near the Congo and it lulled me to sleep" and Countee Cullen wrote "What is Africa to Me" in his 1925 poem "Heritage," they drew inspiration from the primitivist impulse and, as black men, wrestled with their own understanding of their connection to Africa.[85] Indeed, black-African themes had become trendy, but black thinkers disagreed on how to best take advantage of the Negro vogue. Some members of the New Negro intelligentsia worried that slumming and other interracial encounters of the same nature would have little positive impact on their civil rights agenda.[86]

When white primitivist writers of the period fictionalized their encounters with black people in black communities, they tended to typify blacks and inadvertently presented a picture of black life that confirmed some Harlem Renaissance leaders' fears and suspicions. For example, stage works by white writers—such as Eugene O'Neill's *Emperor Jones*—appealed to black and white audiences by attracting whites caught up in racial fantasies and blacks who longed for works that reflected their lives and experiences.[87] But O'Neill's writings were not racially transcendent and instead played up "black attributes" that Victorians damned: he associated blackness with "natural release" and whiteness with "internalized restraint."[88] Similarly, white writer Carl Van Vechten's 1926 novel *Nigger Heaven* made the New Negro intelligentsia leery about the transformative power of white interest in black culture. Van Vechten's novel depicted Harlem's upwardly mobile and educated blacks as barely able to suppress their primitive tendencies.[89] Writings like Van Vechten's and O'Neill's made the dangers of white primitivism to the New Negro agenda clear. Ann Douglas explains: "It is one thing to be in search of the 'primitive' . . . another thing to be told . . . that you *are* the primitive, the savage 'id' of Freud's new psychoanalytical discourse, trailing clouds of barbaric, prehistoric, preliterate 'folk' culture wherever you go."[90]

Even though playing to the Negro vogue, and advancing the idea that blacks had a unique essence that distinguished them from whites, had proven to be a dubious strategy for cultivating racial equality, Harlem Renaissance leaders continued to call for the creation of black art and black books. Charles S. Johnson, a black sociologist and editor of one of the leading black periodicals of the period, specifically called for the production of black stories by black authors. He explained that he wanted to "encourage the reading of literature both by Negro authors and about Negro life, not merely because they are Negro authors but because what they write is literature and because the literature is interesting." Johnson also indicated that he hoped efforts to generate black stories would "foster a market for the Negro writer and for literature about Negroes."[91] Johnson's intentions were good, but the belief that there was a distinct "Negro life," or a common "black" experience marked by something that extended beyond the socially constructed boundaries of racial difference paved the way for white and black writers to formulate ideas about authentic blackness. And most writers looked to southern blacks for the most authentic performances.

Julia Peterkin and Her Beloved Gullah Primitives

The vogue of Negro themes heightened America's readers' interest in stories like the ones that Peterkin wrote, but the mass exodus of blacks from the South guaranteed that her stories would hook the attention of the nation's readers. More than one million blacks moved from the South to the North by the mid-1930s. This historic change in America's racial geography resulted in dramatic demographic shifts in various regions but also produced a significant interest in black southerners and ex-southerners. White and black northerners alike "noticed" the arrival of black ex-southerners who commanded their attention as they continuously showed up at work sites, in neighborhoods, and in public spaces in cities throughout the North.[92] Racial tensions crested between white residents and black migrants competing for jobs, and black northerners expressed anxiety over the arrival of their southern counterparts. The black migrants' rustic habits, and the way they seemed to acquiescence to whites, antagonized black northerners.[93] And residential segregation created a ready-made spectacle in neighborhoods where migrants settled. Soon, white and black social scientists turned their gaze to black migrants and southerners and began to probe their cultural worlds and trace the origins of their pathologies.[94] In fact, one study, *Sea Island to City: A Study of St. Helena Islanders in Harlem and Other Urban Centers* (1932), specifically examined the migration experiences of a group of South Carolina Gullah folk described as "Negroes, unusually pure in stock and culturally distinct because of the homogeneity of the population and geographic isolation" and compared their lives in a "distant primitive 'Gullah' community" to their experiences in the city.[95]

The tensions, curiosity, and angst that surrounded black southerners' arrival in northern and western cities ensured that black migrants, and the world they left behind, would occupy a new place in the nation's imagination. Categorized as foreign, and depicted as mysterious "others," everything about black migrants was read as profoundly different. Their speech, style of religious worship, mannerisms, and musical performances signaled their distinctiveness. But for artists and writers enchanted by primitive peoples, these traits were evidence that black migrants — people who came from close-to-the-earth rural settings tucked deep in the South where their African ancestors were enslaved — had retained something that other blacks had lost. Educated blacks were among those who migrated to the North, but primitivists considered them less exotic than their poorer and less educated comrades because they believed schooling smothered their innate racial impulses. Consequently, white and black writers, artists, and social scientists looked to poor blacks living in the South for authentic black folk.[96] The call of New Negro leaders, like Alain Locke, for a serious examination of black folklore made southern blacks even more attractive subjects.[97] The use of black southern dialects on the part of black writers such as Sterling Brown and Zora Neale Hurston, and Langston Hughes's declaration that common folk were the key to art, reflects the growing importance of black southerners to the New Negro literary movement.[98]

When Julia Peterkin began to write stories about Blue Brook's Gullah folk, she was aware of the popularity of black themes and the burgeoning interest in black southerners. In fact, she was introduced to one of her first contacts in the literary community outside of the South (Carl Sandburg) because a mutual acquaintance thought that he would take a special interest in the "negro material" abundant among the blacks who lived on her plantation.[99] So, she mined Lang Syne's black community for material, collected information about black folk beliefs in the region, and wrote stories that spoke to so many of the prevalent assumptions about black southern folklife, furnishing primitivists with exactly the type of "Negro material" they longed for. For instance, among other representations is the unique connection of Blue Brook Gullahs to their African ancestors: Daddy Cudjoe's voodoo amulets and cures, and midwife Maum Hannah's charm beads, were all brought to Blue Brook from Africa.[100] Written in Gullah dialect, Peterkin's stories painted a picture of black southern life that readily captured popular interest. Several leaders of the New Negro movement found inspiration in her writings; she offered them black stories about black characters living in an all-black community struggling with epic internal conflicts that revealed their humanity. Black and white literary reviewers praised Peterkin's work, and she quickly became known for her "realistic" portrayals of black southern folklife and was considered a Gullah expert.[101]

Peterkin's first book of short stories won the respect of the New Negro intelligentsia and white literary critics in the North, and some in the South.[102] Her work and her Gullah subjects soon gained the national spotlight. One white *New York Times* reviewer noted that few whites had penetrated "evasive negro shyness," or "taken the trouble to consider the blacks as . . . human as we are human" and praised Peterkin for having written "a book unaffectedly about negroes without conscious or unconscious belittling mockery in view of superior white advancement."[103] Peterkin's former piano instructor published a review in South Carolina's leading newspaper, the *Columbia Record*, applauding *Green Thursday* (1924) and celebrating Peterkin for the "manner in which she has penetrated the curious and sometimes very indirect processes" of black people's "mental machinery." Bellamann declared that channeling black people's motivations, desires, and thoughts was an "incredible feat when one considers how remote from us this primitive psychology really is."[104] H. L. Mencken, the literary dynamo who was an important influence on the writers of the Southern Renaissance of the 1920s and 1930s, wrote to Peterkin and commended her for making "these darkeys real."[105] A review for *Green Thursday* written by a black reviewer and published in the *Chicago Defender* was not as enthusiastic, but the reviewer did conclude that aside "from the dialect she puts into their mouths" Blue Brook's Gullah are "real flesh and blood."[106]

The fact that Peterkin's Blue Brook Gullahs were not the same simple stock black characters that had previously dominated white southern writers' fiction was, in and of itself, enough to earn the praise of the New Negro intelligentsia. They, too, affirmed that Peterkin's black characters were "real." W. E. B. Du Bois, Alain Locke, Countée Cullen, James Weldon Johnson, Paul Robeson, Langston Hughes, and Walter White praised Peterkin's work for what they considered to be an authentic portrayal of black southern life.[107] Walter White—the leader of the NAACP—took a special interest in Peterkin's writings. White and Peterkin shared a publisher, so when H. L. Mencken reached out to him and asked

White to help *Green Thursday* achieve "the circulation it so richly" deserved, he did.[108] Surely, Mencken did not use the term "darkeys" to describe Blue Brook's blacks to White as he had in his letter to Peterkin. However he described the book to the leader of the NAACP, his efforts inspired White to have a review of the short story collection sent to two hundred and fifty black newspapers.[109] The review—written by Mary White Ovington, the white NAACP activist who played an important role in the development of the organization—declared that *Green Thursday* was a "reverent portrayal of Negro life" that featured the residents of a "remote plantation" who were "not dressed up" and added that "there is nothing self-conscious about them."[110] Ovington highlighted the appeal of Blue Brook's blacks when she wrote that they were "pathetically poor in material possessions" but were "rich in the things of the spirit."[111] Ovington also wrote that it was good that these stories were written by a white woman because "the Negro author is still too near to his material to use it with perfect naturalness" and explained that the fact that *Green Thursday* was "the work of a Southern woman is a happy sign."[112] When Peterkin visited Harlem in 1929, she was welcomed with open arms.[113] She reported that she was so famous and well known in New York that even "Negro porters know who I am."[114]

Not long after Peterkin's novel *Black April* (1927) was published, a *New York Times* headline that read "Peterkin Writes Again of Gullah Negroes" announced her third book *Scarlet Sister Mary* (1928) as if she were writing fact instead of fiction. The article presumed that Peterkin did much more than imagine Gullah folk and explained that she "is busy with the negro before he loses his simple estate in the South Side of Chicago or Harlem. She is busy setting methods of life on paper that must soon pass away forever."[115] The reviewer's conclusion clearly marks the blurred line between fact and fiction. The mystical, hardliving and hard-loving, unfettered, and earthy southern blacks with special ties to their African ancestors who lived in Peterkin's imagination were gradually becoming real.

By the time that Peterkin's beloved primitives won her the Pulitzer Prize in 1929 for *Scarlet Sister Mary*, the black press had also started describing Blue Brook as if it were a real place populated by real black people. One discussion of Peterkin's work published in the *Chicago Defender* described "Miss Peterkin's novel" as a book "about a certain class of people in South Carolina who have managed to keep pretty close to nature in spite of the march of civilization and American missionaries."[116] Peterkin's audiences did not arrive at the conclusion that she was writing about "real" people on their own, she was also responsible for creating the illusion that the characters that she invented were factually patterned after the people who worked on her plantation. Peterkin frequently boasted that she did not have to rely on her imagination.[117] She insisted that her "writing is not as much a creative thing," her characters were people that she knew and admired.[118] She was so captivated by these blacks that she said that she would never write about white people because "their lives are so drab compared with others."[119]

Some black journalists and some members of the New Negro intelligentsia mistook Peterkin's primitivism as a statement of her commitment to racial equality and interpreted Peterkin's Pulitzer Prize as a triumph for the black arts movement against white supremacy. When the *Chicago Defender* announced that Peterkin won the Pulitzer Prize, the article celebrated the fact that "men and women are being encouraged to uncover facts and figures on the race subject and present them to the reading world" and concluded that this was "a sure sign of a revolution in the making."[120] Believing that Peterkin was a champion for interracial cooperation, an anonymous donor from New York pledged to contribute one dollar to pay membership dues for a hundred blacks on Peterkin's plantation in support of the NAACP's "penny-a-head" campaign.[121] Walter White even trusted Peterkin with confidential files on the NAACP's investigation into V. H. "Pink" Whaley's lynching in South Carolina in 1928.[122] By 1934, the charitable organization, Mobilization for Human Needs, decided that Peterkin was the only white public figure who could write something that would encourage whites to donate money for "negro services" because she had "always been a tremendous factor" in helping people to "understand the negro" and in "making him human."[123]

But the idea that Peterkin's race views were progressive was overstated and exaggerated. Peterkin did not intend to use her writings to challenge the South's racial hierarchy. She worried about provoking the Ku Klux Klan and attracting the scorn of southern whites.[124] And while she was at times privately critical of white supremacy and its adherents, when in South Carolina, she lived her life like other affluent white conservative southern women did.[125] For instance, in 1923, Peterkin was the chapter historian for the United Daughters of the Confederacy.[126] When *Scarlet Sister Mary* was transformed into a play, starring white actress Ethel Barrymore and a cast of all-white actors who donned black face, Peterkin showed no outrage and did not demand that black actors depict Blue Brook blacks—even though she preferred it.[127] In a letter she sent to her lover, Peterkin wrote about Lang Syne's black residents in terms that reduced them to childlike and inferior caricatures: "Would the negroes amuse you with their happy-go-lucky manner or would their pitiful dependence make you sad?"[128] Peterkin may have felt at home with the black literati in Harlem, but rumors swirled about her acquiescence to South Carolina's race codes and her refusal to accept Langston Hughes as a guest in her home when he showed up unannounced at her doorstep at Lang Syne.[129] And even though Peterkin had requested information about Whaley's murder, she never committed to any actions to halt lynchings in her home state.[130] Peterkin's own words best explain her racial politics: she said that she did not care about "the race question": "I'm not a propagandist and the race question means nothing to me."[131]

More than anything else, Peterkin's writings make clear how problematic her racial politics were and underscore the limits of primitivism as a tool for racial progress. While black and white reviewers embraced Peterkin's stories, some readers took offense at the way that she characterized Blue Brook's blacks. On June 8, 1929, the *Chicago Defender* published an article about a talk that Peterkin gave during a trip to New York.[132] The article was a satirical endorsement of her work that poked fun at the fact that Peterkin claimed to have "admired" blacks. Within the article's satire, one finds an alternative reading of the work that so many New Negro literati had applauded. After parodying all of the compliments that Peterkin paid blacks in her speech, the article's author wrote, "And all the time you were under the impression that Miss Peterkin was turning out books . . . with the main sight of showing to the world that we are so near to the beasts that we don't know the difference between incest and immorality."[133] Honing in on the primitivism that pervaded her work, the author quipped, "We thought she was trying to prove that we were first cousins to the wildest wild animal that ever tramped the woods, and here she is writing about us because we are her friends and she likes us."[134] This comedic rendition of Peterkin's work was no laughing matter for the Lang Syne blacks who served as inspiration for her Blue Brook characters. Peterkin often told people that *Scarlet Sister Mary*'s main character—a young woman torn between her lusts and her desire to live a virtuous life—was modeled after Mary Weeks, a black woman who worked for her at Lang Syne.[135] Mary Weeks's children were so outraged when they saw a picture of their mother with a washtub on her head printed next to an article about Peterkin's work in the *Columbia Record*, that they quickly moved their mother off Lang Syne and considered filing a lawsuit against Julia Peterkin.[136]

By the time the New Negro poet and scholar Sterling Brown publicly contradicted the NAACP's glowing endorsement of Peterkin's work by challenging the realness of the Gullah world that she created in 1934, her fantasies about Gullah life were already deeply rooted, and the Gullah explosion was in full swing.[137] Almost ten years earlier, University of South Carolina literature professor Reed Smith wrote, "Recently there has been a marked reawakening of interest in the Gullah," reflected in a host of new publications about blacks living along South Carolina's coast.[138] This reawakening inspired more than the publication of folklore collections and novels. It may have even encouraged a group of affluent Charleston whites to start a singing club in 1922—the Society for the Preservation of Spirituals—that gathered and performed songs in the Gullah dialect that they learned from their black "maums" or nursemaids and other black domestic workers as children.[139]

Brown's review of Peterkin's quasi ethnography *Roll Jordan Roll* was cutting.[140] He pointed out the nebulous geographical boundaries of the Gullah world that she wrote about, territory that seemed to flow back and forth between South Carolina and her imagination: "At times she mentions a 'county,' and one imagines her to be writing again of Blue Brook plantation."[141] Despite the fact that the work is supposed to focus on the Gullah, Brown asserts that her formulations are loose and unreliable: "At other times she speaks generically of the Southern Negro. Perhaps for 'Southern' Mrs. Peterkin wishes 'South Carolina.'"[142] He slammed her "incomplete" depiction of southern blacks and argued that when she looked at blacks, she either saw "loyal" and "fatalistically resigned Uncles and Aunties" who mistrusted "civilization," an "old sharecropper who had thirty 'yard' children with an indeterminate number of others," a servant who "worships his chivalrous master," or "wild bucks" and "girls who slash or conjure their . . . lovers."[143] Brown admitted that these folk may have existed, but emphasized that Peterkin's picture of black life in the region was skewed.[144] The connections that Peterkin made between Gullah folk and Africa also struck Brown as being embellished: "The book jacket promises a tale of Uncle Mose, 'well over ninety years old, captured in the African bush . . . brought to America . . . on the stinking hold of a slave ship.' My Copy of the book must be defective, for I cannot find Uncle Mose. Instead I find another Uncle, one hundred and eleven years old, archetype of all hat-in-hand Uncle Toms."[145] He was especially critical of the fact that, for the most part, Peterkin's portrayal of Gullah folk had purged from their daily lives racial violence, economic inequality, and all of the suffering that Jim Crow caused blacks in the South: "Occasionally, Mrs. Peterkin mentions the hard lot of Negro life in the South. But the cause of hardship is always left vague. . . . Life alone, or the moon, is to blame; never exploitation, never injustice. There is hope, but only in the bright mansions above."[146]

Fact and Fiction

The first widespread reconceptualization of Gullah people was literally rooted in fiction. The people described in Peterkin's Gullah tales, whose stories had been interpreted as ethnographic reports, gained even more relevance in the years after Peterkin won the Pulitzer Prize. The voodoo craze of the 1920s and 1930s had begun. And social scientists had seriously taken up questions about African retentions and looked for verifiable phenomenon through which they could prove that black folk culture and voodoo, roots, and conjure practices among southern blacks originated in Africa—just as Peterkin delivered to the reading world a population of black southerners whose authentic Africanness appeared to be unquestionable.

The hunt for authentic Gullah people, and the search for a *real life* Blue Brook and *real life* equivalents of Blue Brook's Daddy Cudjoe and Maum Hannah and her African beads, would eventually lead researchers to Sapelo Island, Georgia. When the filmmakers and photographers in President Coolidge's entourage fixed their cameras on Sapelo Islanders, they could have easily surmised that they were having a firsthand encounter with the sort of black southerner who had become so admired. And the stories they wrote, and the images they captured, would lure others to come, collect, and explore the black people who lived in the hammock communities through the woods, beyond Howard Coffin's mansion.

2 The 1920s and 1930s Voodoo Craze

AFRICAN SURVIVALS IN AMERICAN POPULAR
CULTURE AND THE IVORY TOWER

*Black magic, voodooism, the evil eye and sundry other terms indicative of "devil"
worship when called to the attention of the average citizen in many instances conjure
up a mental picture of some lonesome spot in the African bush where the chief
medicine man attired in weird garb, gibberingly calls on the powers of darkness to
ward off impending evil. It is not generally known that in the heart of Washington
there is a certain class of citizens, who while they do not dance around a totem pole
attired as was "gunga Din" and striped with multicolored muds, still cling to many
superstitious beliefs that were brought here with the first shipload of slaves landed at
Jamestown, Va.*
—Washington Post, October 6, 1921

"I dunno wut she do wid duh blood an fedduhs," Shad Hall, an elderly Sapelo Islander, told a researcher who came to the island searching for African survivals during the 1930s.[1] His words, *I don't know what she do with the blood and feathers,* dangle at the end of a long quote about old funeral traditions on the island, and about the time that his grandmother Hester killed a white chicken to appease her friend's tormented ghost. The bulk of the interview focused on Hall's memories of his Muslim ancestors, and the stories that they passed down about Africa. But, the unwritten question that he responded to—*What did she do with the blood and feathers?*—is loaded with assumptions that can only be deciphered by examining popular ideas about African spiritual survivals during the twenties and thirties. When this question is set in historical context, a larger trend comes into view.

By the time researchers descended on Sapelo, stories about bloodletting black voodooists saturated the American cultural landscape, and a full-blown voodoo craze was under way. The voodoo craze was born from U.S. imperial conquests; the backlash against crossing racial boundaries; the vogue of Negro themes; and anxieties about the masses of black southerners who flocked to northern cities. Headlines about black voodooists in newspapers in migration metropolises like New York, Chicago, and Washington, DC, appeared in white papers like the *New York*

Times, the *Chicago Tribune,* and the *Washington Post,* and in black papers like the *Amsterdam News,* the *Pittsburgh Courier,* and the *Chicago Defender.* Voodoo-themed books, stage works, and films were all the rage during these years, and, as a result, the social scientists engaged in an intense debate over black people's cultural inheritance relative to their African past wrangled with the notion that voodoo was the quintessential African survival.

The voodoo craze, and all of the assumptions and stories about black people and Africa that energized it, significantly shaped Sapelo researchers' impressions of Gullah folk culture and black life on the island. They had good reason to believe that elderly black southerners like Shad Hall—a man who was born in slavery and lived on the island his whole life serving its residents as a trusted herbalist and healer—retained vestiges of their ancestors' African culture.[2] Surely, during the 1920s and 1930s there were other elderly black southerners like Hall who remembered stories about their African ancestors and could recall their African ancestors' names, repeat stories that they shared, and describe practices and traditions that they learned outside of the American context.[3] But, almost all of the researchers and writers who came to Sapelo's shores maintained a view of black people's African past and African survivals that was tainted by popular stories about black voodoo cults on tropical islands, clandestine rituals led by "rootworkers," hexes, zombies, and black southerners who venerated macabre charms. Although reports about black life on Sapelo produced during the period did not consistently pair their spiritual practices with the term "voodoo," and tended to use words like "roots," "hoodoo," and "conjure" instead, these terms were little more than nicknames for the vague complex of activities associated with "voodoo." Sapelo researchers were certainly influenced by the popularity of African-born dark mysticism. That is why Hall was asked about witches, good luck charms made from animal skins, mojo bags, and "conjuh" practices on the island.[4] All that he could have told researchers about his African ancestors, slavery, and botanical medicines was passed over for the sort of thrilling material at the heart of popular voodoo tales, and what he did tell them about his Muslim ancestors was woven into a repository that was largely about black people's black "magic."

When popular voodoo-themed material and researchers' reports about Sapelo Islanders are read side by side, the connection between the burgeoning characterizations of Gullah folk culture in the twenties and thirties and the voodoo craze of the same period is clear. This was a crucial moment in America's race-making history that deserves much more exploration.[5] Paying attention to the way that racial fantasies shaped voodoo news reports, voodoo entertainment, and social scientists' pursuit of African spiritual survivals unearths the context in which the Gullah were remade during the period. From migration metropolis news stories to the voodoo theories of anthropologists Melville Herskovits and Zora Neale Hurston, the voodoo craze colored how researchers and writers interpreted black culture in the South and obscured actual remnants of African traditions in the region.

Black Savagery Abroad: Voodoo Reports from U.S. Occupied Territories

The expansion of America's domestic policy of white supremacy through imperial projects set the stage for epic encounters between "civilized" whites and "savage" nonwhites that helped birth the nation's renewed interest in black voodoo. Whereas many modernist artists, writers, and intellectuals romanticized nonwhite primitives, stories about the black and brown people who lived in U.S.-occupied territories featured in newspapers played on Victorian ideas about race to justify U.S. occupation. In the case of Haiti, news stories pointed to Haitians' *Africanness* as the root cause of the black republic's backwardness and savagery—and "voodoo" was the primary evidence presented to prove it.[6] The journalists who carried stories about the savage nonwhite world beyond U.S. borders contributed to the more than thirty articles published in migration metropolis newspapers between 1915 and 1935 that depicted black subjects in U.S.-occupied territories as dangerous voodooists. Even though the term "voodoo" was plastered on headlines, readers would not find substantive discussions about voodoo in these reports. Instead, readers found journalists' depictions of a vague African-derived spiritual practice used to work magic by appeasing and conjuring African spirits with spells, blood sacrifices, and wild drum rhythms.

Tales of Haitian voodoo that trickled back to the American mainland initiated an upsurge of voodoo reports in the nation's newspapers. Almost as soon as U.S. military forces set foot on Haitian soil, reports about the black republic's bloodthirsty voodooists began. In 1915 the *Washington Post* published an article announcing that in Haiti "superstition flourishes with politics, and one is not much better than the other. . . .Voodooism with all its horrible barbaric rites still flourishes among the people and its priests have always exerted considerable influence on the government."[7] A month later, the *Chicago Daily Tribune* printed an article that followed the trend of linking turbulent Haitian politics to Africa by underscoring that Haitians residing in remote districts live "much as [they] lived in Africa."[8] By 1920 white eyewitness reports of black savagery in Haiti fueled voodoo headlines. The *Chicago Daily Tribune* ran an article titled "Voodooism Is Faith of Haiti, Admiral Says; Kill Humans, Drink Blood, Knapp Reports," which explained "that 95 percent of the natives of Haiti believe in the African jungle faith of voodooism which requires the sacrifice of human beings and the drinking of human blood."[9] The articles explored everything from U.S.

intervention strategies to Haiti's political history to the challenges that voodoo practitioners presented to America's imperial projects.[10]

American journalists' imaginations ran wild with tales of Haitian voodoo. One *New York Times* report declared that a fifty-seven-year-old Haitian immigrant, Jean Joseph Ysneod Dauphin, took voodoo pills that turned him white, which attracted the attention of American scientists who wanted to study him.[11] The *New York Times* left its readers with the impression that the Dauphin story was genuine, but ten days after the story first made headlines, Harlem's black paper, the *New York Amsterdam News*, ran a counterreport in which the author announced that Dauphin's claims were misleading.[12] The *Amsterdam News* article also delivered a scathing critique of sensational Haitian voodoo reports and the occupation: "Haitians are sensitive people ... especially resentful of the scores of white writers who have distorted the superstitions of the ignorant, stressed the exoticism of tropic existence, and deliberately or unconsciously furnished propaganda for the establishment of marine rule in the island."[13] The apparent frustration in the *Amsterdam News* article was a characteristic response of the black press to both the occupation of Haiti and representations of black voodoo. Black newspapers, like white newspapers, associated voodooism with pathology and dysfunction, but unlike white newspapers, the black press generally considered "superstitious" practices to be expressions of ignorance. Conversely, white newspapers consistently presented voodooism as an inherited racial trait.

Haiti was not the only focus of voodoo reports. Black populations in the Caribbean were also described as contenders in the contest between white civilization and black savagery and were tied to shocking voodoo reports in American papers. Voodoo reports from Cuba related murders, human sacrifice plots, and other forms of ritual abuse.[14] Headlines announced Cuban cannibals, ceremonies involving hearts torn from living bodies, human sacrifices of black babies, and human sacrifices involving white victims. For example, a 1916 report broadcast that three black Cuban voodooists were executed for sacrificing a white man for his blood, and in 1927, the *New York Times* and the *Washington Post* printed the same article about a white American girl who was saved from a Cuban voodooist who tried to abduct her so that her blood could be used to save a sick "Negress."[15] The dangers of voodoo in black communities in Trinidad, Panama, and Brazil made headlines too.[16] Although more common in white newspapers, Caribbean voodoo reports occasionally appeared in the black press. The *Chicago Defender* reported a voodoo murder in Panama in which the reporter described the eerie scene during the suspect's capture: "As he gave himself up to the police he broke into a singsong patois of the voodoo death chant."[17]

Because the dramatic and astonishing voodoo reports published in American papers during the twenties and thirties were racially specific and loosely defined, it is not surprising that newspapers also featured American black voodooists. As one article from the period states, the belief that "traces of voodooism are likely to be found in negro rural communities in any part of the world" was a foregone conclusion.[18]

Black Savagery at Home: Voodoo-Related Murders on U.S. Soil

Since the time of slavery, whites advanced the idea that blacks nurtured a secret love for African-born voodoo and superstition as if they were racial traits. This degrading conclusion is a perversion of a very complicated truth. Enslaved blacks constructed complex spiritual philosophies and practices from remnants of West African beliefs and the spiritual traditions that they encountered in the New World. These New World black spiritual practices could be found inside and outside of formal black religious institutions.[19] The complexity of black spirituality was lost on whites who concluded that black spiritual practices were inferior, satanic, pure evil, and born from ignorance. What appeared in the nation's leading papers during the twenties and the thirties says little of substance about New World black spiritual practices. Instead, articles about black voodooists published during the craze speak to the forces that inspired a ratcheting up of interest in and the demonization and criminalization of "voodoo." By reducing "voodoo" to a mélange of African spells, magical charms, ritual sacrifice, and drumming, and by publicizing and embellishing violent crimes assumed to be linked to voodoo, this new wave of antivoodoo rhetoric published in the nation's newspapers cast whatever African spiritual practices that survived slavery as a disturbing racial caricature.

Aside from degrading potential African spiritual survivals, voodoo murder reports suggested to whites that blacks were inherently savage and dangerous. The numerous newspaper accounts of voodoo murders and voodoo-related violence reported in New York, Chicago, and Washington, DC, between 1915 and 1935 that described heinous crimes, gruesome ritual scenes, and violence provoked by "voodoo curses," undoubtedly reminded whites that their domination was justified.[20] In fact, voodoo reports in white papers painted blacks as the perpetrators of savage ritualistic murders at the very moment when the resurgence of the Ku Klux Klan caused its membership to soar and when white lynch mobs transformed racial violence into ritualized entertainment.[21] White anxieties were high during the period. The New Negro movement, the advent of modernism, "slumming" and racial boundary crossing, the mass exodus of blacks from the rural South, and the perceived encroachment of blacks on northern cities stoked the flames of racial hatred.[22] Even though members of white lynch mobs regularly scrambled to collect their black victims' dismembered body parts in the hope of securing an ear, finger, or penis to keep as trophies and relics and created and sold photographs and stereographs of mob members posing next to black corpses, blacks were depicted as the sole perpetrators of ritual mutilations and violence in voodoo reports.[23] This inversion obscured the reality that whites literally, consistently, and ritualistically sacrificed black people in order to maintain the white power structure.

Yet newspaper reports generally presented black voodooists as the primary culprits of ritual murder and desecration. Americans who read newspapers during the 1920s and 1930s found reports of black American voodooists engaged in the type of African savagery described in Edgar Rice Burroughs's *Tarzan of the Apes* (1914). Burroughs's novel, filled with African cannibals who kept remains of human sacrifices as souvenirs, sold 750,000 copies by 1934 — a clear indication of the popular appeal of these tales.[24] But Americans did not need to look to fiction for thrilling voodoo tales, nor did they have to look to distant continents like Africa or countries like Haiti for these accounts. News stories like the one printed in the *Chicago Daily Tribune* in 1916 verified the persistence of African spiritual savagery in America. The front-page article recounted the series of events surrounding the separate discoveries of a human torso and a skull found between Jennie L. Smith's mattress — "an old Negress who pretended to be a witch and 'voodooist.'"[25] In 1925, a *New York Times* headline read, "Human Bones Found in Voodoo Man's Cave: Negro Chambers of Horror Beneath His House Killed Woman, His Daughter Says."[26] Similarly, the arrest of a thirty-seven-year-old black Cleveland man referred to as a "negro voodoo doctor" found in possession of a decapitated head made headlines in the *New York Times*, the *Washington Post*, and the *Chicago Defender* in 1928.[27] In all of these cases, voodoo was the only explanation presented for the presence of the human remains.

Murder mysteries involving black people were sometimes linked to voodoo during the period even when no evidence of "voodoo" was found at the scene of the crime. In April 1923, the *Washington Post* and the *Chicago Daily Tribune* reported the discovery of infant bones in a pond in Crisfield, Maryland.[28] The *Washington Post* article began: "The discovery of handfuls of human bones, unquestionably those of infants, in the bed of a pond ... followed the finding of headless bodies of two colored children in the same pond yesterday afternoon."[29] Even though authorities had no clues in the case, the writer explained that police "share the belief of some residents that the children were sacrifices of voodooism."[30] Papers described the community's residents as secretive blacks, complicit in voodooism: "The negroes on this point of Eastern Shore are taciturn. They never tell on one another ... no matter what they are accused of doing."[31]

The *Chicago Daily Tribune* article goes further in assuming that local black residents possessed knowledge of African-born voodoo rites: "Negroes throughout the city are being questioned closely to learn if the dead infants had been human sacrifices to the relic of barbarism of darkest Africa and the West Indies, voodooism."[32] Almost a month after the first reports were published, the mystery of the infant bones had been solved. The *Amsterdam News* was the only paper to run an article announcing that voodoo did not play a role in the death of infants and the desecration of their remains. The *Amsterdam News* front-page headline read, "Voodoo Tale Shown to Be Absurd," and the article criticized the prejudiced whites who assumed the infants' remains were linked to "voodoo rites of Africa." The report explained that an unsavory undertaker contracted to bury the bodies of stillborn infants of unwed mothers saved himself a few dollars by disposing of the bodies in the pond.[33]

In the case of the Crisfield voodoo mystery, the black press played its usual role and used its platform to disprove voodoo tales—but that was not always the case. The allure and popularity of racy voodoo stories that helped to sensationalize otherwise mundane tragedies touched the black press too. The *Chicago Defender*'s front-page report about the puzzling murder of three young Harlem women illustrates this point. There were no clues that explained why the killer slashed one woman's throat, asphyxiated the second woman with an indoor laundry line, and strangled the third woman, but the article's writer offered voodoo as a possible motive: "Whether the slayings were the result of the policy racket or the workings of some voodoo cult detectives are unable to say. No policy slips were found."[34]

The 1920s and 1930s found whites crossing racial boundaries to explore black communities, black music, and black bodies, but American voodoo crime reports warned of the dangers inherent in interracial contact.[35] Reports like the one about the black voodooist in Chicago who killed her white common-law husband, and the white Atlantic City shop owner burned to death by the black voodooist he hired underscored the dangers of crossing racial borders.[36] Those news stories were shocking, but the most widely reported voodoo murder was the murder of a white woman at the hands of a black male voodooist. The 1923 murder of white nurse Elise Barthell made news in all of the major cities. Headlines announced that Barthell was murdered by Alonzo Savage, "a negro voodoo doctor."[37] According to reports, Barthell and Savage worked together: he was a butler and she was a nurse at the home of an affluent physician. Barthell asked Savage to help her resolve a romantic issue. Reports explained that Savage killed Barthell during a secret meeting at an abandoned mansion during which she refused to pay for his voodoo services. The *New York Times* wrote that Savage confessed that he "struck the nurse in the face when she grabbed the money out of his hand, felled her with a brick and then dropped a seventy pound block of marble on her head."[38] The *Washington Post* described Barthell's murder using more graphic language to emphasize the fact that Barthell's skull had been crushed.[39] A black newspaper, the *Pittsburgh Courier*, was the only paper that ran an article that revealed discrepancies in the Barthell murder story.[40] The *Courier* questioned the "voodoo" motive and reported that Barthell was pregnant and was involved in a love triangle that may have involved the same white man who drove her to meet Savage the night of her murder. Yet the most important detail in the report was that Savage's friends had never known he was a "voodoo doctor."[41] In the end, Savage was executed in April 1924, and in reporting the event the *Washington Post* maintained that Barthell was killed because she refused to pay $395.00 for a "love charm."[42]

The black press vacillated between rejecting murderous voodoo tales and condemning practitioners, even as it profited from burgeoning voodoo industries. For instance, reports of a murder described as a "human sacrifice" by a Moorish Scientist (Moorish Scientist is a Muslim sect commonly associated with "voodoo" during the period) in 1932 in Detroit, Michigan, declared northern black leaders' opposition to voodoo and its equivalents: "A concentrated effort on the part of ministers, organizations and individuals has been launched to wipe out the evil influence of the 'religious cult,' which includes certain aspects of voodooism and 'Mohammedanism.'"[43] Editorials that appeared in black papers, such as the one written by West Indies–born journalist Edgar M. Grey, tried to balance the discussion of voodoo by exploring the African roots of black folk superstition, describing white racism relative to black superstitions, and by condemning voodoo charlatans who exploited poor, desperate black migrants.[44] And articles like the one that the *Amsterdam News* published in 1927 on high black mortality rates cited black people's belief in superstitions and voodoo among the list of sources of health problems in black communities.[45]

On some level, these articles speak to the tensions between black northerners and black southern migrants and other black immigrants. Even though the New Negro intelligentsia celebrated black-African folk culture through the arts, black newspapers condemned the persistence of these practices in modern cities.[46] These reports also indicate that the black press, like white papers, was caught up in the voodoo-reporting craze. And while black journalists tended to discourage voodooism in black metropolises, black newspapers readily accepted sponsorship through advertising dollars that they received from black men who called themselves "Professors" or "Doctors," claimed African origins, and professed to be magicians, healers, and occultists specializing in "African and Oriental Occultism" and "Black magic Native of Africa."[47] They also published advertisements for some white-owned companies that made popular "authentic" voodoo products like Lucky hand charms, voodoo bags, mo-jo incense, dream books, New Orleans Van Van Oil, and New Orleans Lucky Powder.[48]

Black and white papers triumphantly announced the incarceration of black voodooists and charlatans—especially when their cures killed their patients. While some white and black Americans may have believed in the power of voodoo cures before the 1920s and 1930s, surely the increased attention paid to African "magic" in the media—coverage that was largely shaped by racial fantasies—enhanced the perception that its power was real. When a seventy-three-year-old Alabama man named William Carpenter accidently killed a woman he was trying to rid of evil spirits in 1927, and when voodoo "Doctor" Alphonso Rojansen of New York was accused of killing a three-year-old Harlem boy who suffered from tetanus in 1928, reports of the incidents in black and white papers lamented the naiveté of the poor clients who sought out the services of these voodoo doctors.[49] Even when they did not kill their customers, voodoo doctors landed in jail because they were caught in legal traps created by antiquackery laws, mail fraud prohibitions, and sting operations led by postmasters while selling voodoo cures through the mail.[50] One headline that read "Post Office Stops Voodoo Practice" was followed by a story about a Mississippi voodoo doctor—Prince Hough—who was the subject of a sting operation for soliciting money from clients who he promised to cure if they "just spit on a piece of white cloth, [and] send it [with] $14."[51] Black newspapers reported the arrest of voodoo practitioners like Prince Hough with greater frequency than did white papers.[52] This trend was likely inspired by the fact that educated black northerners were anxious about the negative impact that voodoo stories and stereotypes about superstitious blacks could have on perceptions of black culture. Black papers editorialized and poked fun at "voodoo doctors" while reporting their demise. This was certainly the case when black newspapers discussed "Doctor" Samuel Kojoe Pearce's incarceration. One *Chicago Defender* writer remarked that Pearce was "unable to furnish bond, despite the fact that he" had "a black cat's wishbone in his pocket."[53]

Clearly, news reports about voodoo violence and voodoo crimes bolstered a view of black pathology and inferiority that was, at its core, supposed to be a manifestation of black people's essential African nature and backwardness. Whether Americans believed that voodoo was an expression of innate savagery, or thought it was a tendency toward ignorance and superstition, the "survival" of negative African traits among blacks despite generations in white "civilization" was yet another racial flaw that marred the race. Even so, the black voo-dooist racial caricature was perfect fodder for American entertainment.

Caught in the Spell: Voodoo Entertainment and American Popular Culture

The sensational, horrifying, and thrilling character of voodoo-related news-paper reports ensured that voodoo would emerge as a popular arts and enter-tainment theme during the 1920s and 1930s. Radio shows, films, plays, books, and musicals fictionalized and enlivened the chilling scenes described in voodoo reports. The thrilling discovery of the strange African rites acted out across the nation quickly became a cultural obsession.

The allure of voodoo grew out of "true" stories published in the nation's newspapers, so, naturally, books and stories that featured voodoo were all the rage because they mirrored and reinvigorated its appeal. William Seabrook's *The Magic Island* (1929) is a good example of how profitable and successful voodoo books were during the twenties and thirties. When Seabrook, a journal-ist and travel writer, published his account of the time he spent in Haiti among voodooists, literary audiences were captivated by his tales of voodoo rituals in which African gods and goddesses possessed their devotees, the dead were re-animated and forced to toil in fields, and animals and people swapped souls.[54] Seabrook's bizarre scenes—in which "in the red light of torches," "writhing black bodies, blood-maddened, sex-maddened, god-maddened, drunken, whirled and danced"—fascinated readers and reviewers.[55] At the very moment when travel to exotic locales emerged as a white middle-class pastime, primi-tivist travel memoirs like Seabrook's and travel guides like Harry L. Foster's *Combing the Caribbees* (1929), made the prospects of visiting places inhabited by authentic voodooists exciting.[56]

Seabrook's book sold nearly one hundred thousand copies in the first year that it was published, and reviewers praised him for penetrating the secret world of black voodooists.[57] One reviewer wrote, "Even when he describes the blood rites of Voodoo, you feel that he is reporting things as he found them without exaggeration or self-glorification."[58] Another reviewer admired Sea-brook's descriptions of the "ecstasies of voodoo" and "the ceremonies of necromancers . . . without seeming melodramatic or sensational."[59] Even the black press celebrated *The Magic Island*. The *New York Amsterdam News* applauded Seabrook for suspending his racial prejudices in order to "achieve a moral bal-ance" that freed him from the need to collect "propaganda either for or against the Negroes," and for clarifying that "voodooism is not mere superstition or diabolism . . . it is as much a religion as Christianity."[60] But good reviews in white and black publications did not mitigate the fact that some blacks were annoyed by stories like the ones Seabrook told. The *Chicago Defender* published an article that explained that Haitian officials were fed up and had denounced stories about "voodooistic cannibalism" as a "mere fantasy" that exaggerated practices that in reality only existed in "remote villages."[61]

Whatever redeeming and valuable contribution Seabrook's memoir may have made on the popular view of voodoo and African spiritual survivals, when Hollywood filmmakers read his book, they nonetheless created clichéd stories about black-African savagery. In fact, Hollywood should credit Seabrook and the voodoo craze for birthing the first American "zombie" film because, as a *New York Times* article explained, *White Zombie* was inspired by Haitian voodoo stories that had "been trickling back to these shores for years."[62] Two years after Seabrook's book was published, Edward and Victor Hugo Halperin began working on the film *White Zombie*.[63] Bela Lugosi, Madge Bellamy, and Robert Frazer starred in the voodoo-zombie plot set in Haiti.[64] After *White Zombie* was released in 1932, Roy William Neill and Wells Root transformed Clement Ripley's fiction series *Haiti Moon* (1933) into a film titled *Black Moon* that starred Jack Holt and Fay Wray. *White Zombie* and *Black Moon* shared essential elements — both films' plots centered on white damsels in distress who needed to be saved from the clutches of black voodoo and dramatized the danger that whites encountered when confronted with African-born black savagery. And, in 1920s and 1930s America, both films were guaranteed success because, as one film reviewer explained, "Voodoo ceremonies of Haiti, harking back to the primitive savages of Africa, are fascinating to everyone."[65]

The extent to which *White Zombie* and *Black Moon* speak to 1930s racial fantasies and tensions is not limited to their voodoo plots. Clearly, both films played on racial fictions. But these films also created unprecedented opportunities for black actors. The same longing for representation and inclusion that encouraged some blacks to embrace Julia Peterkin's novels, Eugene O'Neill's plays, and Carl Van Vechten's books also encouraged some blacks to celebrate the fact that *White Zombie* and *Black Moon* brought their favorite black actors to the big screen in movie theaters across the country. Black papers acknowledged the negative stereotypes at the heart of voodoo tales, and they recognized the shortcomings of these films. But even if Clarence Muse only had an "insignificant speaking role" in *White Zombie*, and even if black actors like Billy McClain, Madame Sul-te-wan, Ada Penn, Anna Lee Johnson, John Manning, and the 256 black extras in *Black Moon* only appeared in "bits and parts" of the film or were used to depict a human sacrifice ritual, the black press still cheered them on.[66]

White Zombie's and *Black Moon's* voodoo plot frightened and thrilled large audiences, but their audiences were not the first groups of Americans to enjoy dramatized voodoo tales. Voodoo plays and musicals were performed on stages in theater districts in New York and Chicago as early as 1926, the year when

Columbia University–educated and classically trained black baritone Julius Bledsoe played the role of "Voodoo King" in the opera *Deep River*.[67] *White Zombie* was transformed into a play titled *Zombie* that opened in Chicago in 1932—it followed several other voodoo productions.[68] A host of voodoo stage works created and produced by black and white writers and musicians and acted out by white and black casts appeared on playbills, but they did not receive equally favorable reviews. In fact, the lone all-black production created by a black musician quickly shut down and endured bad reviews while white voodoo stage works experienced greater success.

Surely, when Harlem's own celebrated black composer, H. Lawrence Freeman, conceived a groundbreaking all-black jazz opera about voodoo in antebellum New Orleans, he hoped that his creation would one day draw large audiences. Freeman wrote the opera before the 1920s, but having combined so many popular elements—jazz, voodoo, and an "authentic" southern dialect—one would expect that when *Voodoo* opened at the Palm Garden Theater in New York in 1928, it would have attracted large crowds of black and white patrons, but it did not.[69] Reviewers slammed Freeman for mixing primitive jazz and opera, and when the production ran out of money and closed just nine days after opening, one black reporter remarked, "It was perhaps too much to expect that white music patrons would look with favor on Negro music that aspired to something beyond jazz or ragtime."[70] It is likely that the *Amsterdam News* reviewer was right. America's white music aficionados had decided that jazz was inspired by a quasi-biological racial trait—a trait that they also tied to "voodoo": one critic said that jazz composers used "the same formula as the voodoo chants which Ethiopian cotton pickers used to hymn in the Mississippi swamps"; another remarked that "jazz is the victim of its wild modern devotees who are as bad as voodoo worshippers in darkest Africa."[71]

Where Freeman's opera failed, white-produced voodoo stage works excelled. Reviewers loved *Zombie* and declared that it was "several cuts above the many shrieking pieces of hocus-pocus with which it is allied."[72] Reviewers also applauded *Savage Rhythm*, a voodoo musical set in Mississippi that featured an all-black cast, who acted out the story of a black migrant who left Harlem and returned home to find her "granny" and "mammy" still practicing the voodoo arts handed down to them . . . from African ancestors."[73] The *New York Times* commended *Savage Rhythm*'s white creators for bringing forth an "intelligent drama of Negro sorcery."[74] Two more plays, *Louisiana* (1933) and *Dance with Your Gods* (1934), followed the formula set by the theatrical voodoo works that preceded them and used a combination of black actors, wild drum beats, and voodoo chants to attract audiences and profits.

During the twenties and thirties, Americans did not have to leave their homes or go to theater to experience voodoo entertainment at its best. In 1928, NBC Radio broadcast African drumming featuring voodoo drums that Seabrook acquired in Africa while gathering material for a follow-up book to *The Magic Island*.[75] The *Washington Post* described the drums used in the segment as "worn and polished wood . . . rich natural color, has a luster as though still reflecting the flickering lights and shadows of a council fire before the voodoo doctor's tent."[76] And even though voodoo drums were regarded as dangerous, and were known for being "used to incite dancers to a dangerous state of savagery," NBC broadcast them to entertain their listeners.[77]

Dangerous and compelling, frightening and irresistible, voodoo entertainment indulged the notion that blacks were just one drumbeat away from unveiling their savage selves. That was precisely the message American moviegoers who gathered around Radio City Music Hall's big screen in 1937 were given when they watched a short film titled *Harlem's Black Magic*. The film was a segment in a dramatized newsreel produced by the docudrama series *The March of Time* that announced that more than one hundred thousand New York City blacks were engaged in secret voodoo rites and worship.[78] As was customary during the period, the newsreel was included on theater bills that featured films like *The Soldier and the Lady* and *Off for the Races*.[79] *Harlem's Black Magic* was a sideshow to the main attraction, and it was less than six minutes long, but in that short time, its creators orchestrated the dramatization of the bulk of the voodoo reports published in migration metropolis newspapers.

The audiences of *Harlem's Black Magic* were guided through a series of staged scenes and images that represented voodoo in Harlem. In the opening scene, pictures of the skyscrapers that accented New York's skyline accompanied the narrator's introduction of Harlem as an axis of black primitivism and savagery: "In the shadow of Manhattan's towering skyscrapers lies black sprawling Harlem."[80] "Shadow" is a metaphor for the literal blackness of the film's subjects and prefigures the "dark" spiritual realm of voodoo; the film located black Harlem in the "shadow" of white civilization. Even though Harlem was the capital of the New Negro arts and intellectual movements, *The March of Time* creators mapped it as just another black space where primitives acted out their barbaric rites.

The film focused on Harlem's "uncivilized" spiritual landscape, turning all of Harlem's black religious activities into voodoo. The narrator pointed to the great assortment of churches in Harlem as evidence of black religiosity enlivened by "spirits": "In addition to their religious beliefs, Harlem's people have a childlike faith in spirits and spiritualism."[81] A series of storefront signs for spiritualist churches, incense, and dream-book advertisements scrolled across the screen. Even though the spiritualist movement was initiated in the late

1840s by two white sisters—Katie and Margaret Fox—and was largely populated by whites, by the 1920s and 1930s, it was almost exclusively tied to Africa-
born voodoo.[82] Footage of a staged scene in which a black woman standing
at a makeshift alter in a storefront church singing a black Christian spiritual
standard ("Every time I feel the spirit moving in my heart I will pray") was presented as evidence of blacks' childlike faith in spirits.[83] The narrator continued
and explained that the Great Depression had inspired a resurgence of African
practices among Harlem's black residents and claimed that they viewed the
occult as a viable tool through which they could acquire money or "numbers"
that would help them win the policy racket.[84]

If viewers had questions about the origins of Harlem's voodoo, the narrator
and subtitles pointed to Africa as the source. One scene invited audiences to
observe one of many secret meetings of an "exotic, barbaric" voodoo cult whose
roots "go back to darkest Africa."[85] The "secret meeting" was re-created by
black actors crammed into a small, dark room, beating drums, dancing wildly,
flailing their arms and making unintelligible sounds around an alter decorated
with bones and a human skull encircled with candles. Subtitles informed viewers that the "purest form of African Voodoo in the Western World" was found
"not in Harlem but in the black Republic of Haiti," where blacks "worship and
fear devil gods," and "indulge in wild orgies to cleanse themselves."[86]

The remainder of the film re-created voodoo headlines from newspapers.
Successive scenes depicted gullible blacks being swindled by "racketeers" and
spiritualist mediums; police officers and their attempts to capture root doctors for practicing medicine without a license; white healthcare workers finding voodoo charms on black patients; and black patients who refused medical
treatment and opted instead to consult voodoo doctors.[87] Near the film's end
the narrator disclosed that "nearly one third of Harlem's Negroes have become
voodoo worshippers."[88] In the final scene, the narrator delivered a warning to
the audience and said that "Harlem mystics" have devised a new strategy to
maintain their profitable practices: they "give themselves fancy ecclesiastical
titles and masquerade as Christian clergyman." Images of storefront churches
and signs that had been changed from "Prof. Payanga Devasso: Metaphysician
and Spiritual Adviser" to "Bishop Payango Devasso" accompanied this warning, so even black Christianity becomes suspect. After consuming images of
voodoo dolls, magical incense, and gris-gris bags, audiences were left with
these final words paired with the imagery of the secret voodoo cult dancing
with sacrificial chickens: "And in back rooms in Harlem continues in all its
primitive savagery and superstition, the witchcraft of the African Congo."[89]

The NAACP protested the film and demanded that it be pulled from theaters.
Black papers reported that a reviewer called the film "a dangerous libel on an

entire race" and published reports that condemned the film because it reduced Harlem to a "voodoo heaven" and "veritable jungle" occupied by "a group of primitive, ignorant savages, devoid of any knowledge of the civilization surrounding them."[90] The *Pittsburgh Courier* bashed the film, writing, "Rather strange, isn't it that these people can find little to describe about Negroes except dancing and voodooism."[91] The outrage of the black press over *Harlem's Black Magic* was also a response to the voodoo craze. Even though some black artists and writers had embraced the craze, others were enraged by the racial degradation at the heart of so many of the voodoo tales and stories that made headlines. In articles like the one published in the *Amsterdam News* in 1928, black journalists tried to combat black voodoo tales ("The Negro has been despised and mocked by other races because of his superstition. He alone, in Harlem, in the West Indies, or in Africa, is supposed to live under the spell of voodoo and witch doctors."), but their objections had no impact on the nation's fascination with voodoo.[92]

Despite protests from organizations like the NAACP, *Harlem's Black Magic* was not pulled from theaters. Like the newspaper reports that preceded the film, and the voodoo entertainment that American audiences had grown to love, *Harlem's Black Magic* continued to blur an unclear line between African spiritual survivals and racial stereotypes. Indeed, the popular view of African spiritual survivals during the 1920s and 1930s was more racial stereotype than anything else—a fact that posed a real problem for researchers and writers interested in seriously tackling "survivals" in their works. Untangling all that was conflated in the popular view of African spiritual survivals (racial stereotypes; the activities of charlatan occultists; white travel writers' encounters with voodoo; news reports about crimes linked to African savagery; and authentic black New World spiritual expressions) was nearly impossible. As a result, getting to the bottom of what African traits actually survived in the Americas and in black communities in the South like Sapelo would be both a difficult and contentious undertaking.

Voodoo, African Survivals in the Ivory Tower, and the Gullah

The fact that the American media had reduced the survival of African traits in black communities across the diaspora to "savage" practices like voodoo angered anthropologists like Melville Herskovits. Herskovits, a white Jewish man who dedicated much of his career to finding African survivals, had many times come forth to refute mischaracterizations of voodoo in the nation's newspapers. He was quoted in a *Chicago Tribune* article on Haiti in 1935 saying, "As pictured in fiction and in the movies . . . voodooism includes blood rites and terrors. In reality the religion is most peaceful. The cult followers go to the ceremony regularly every Saturday night, and human sacrifice is unknown."[93] That same year, he told a *Washington Post* reporter that "human sacrifice" was "as much a crime to believers in voodoo as elsewhere."[94]

Believing that voodoo was one of the most genuine African survivals, Herskovits had a vested interest in eradicating negative associations between blacks and voodoo. The pervasiveness of voodoo tales in American culture during the twenties and thirties likely invigorated his interest in the practice, and he responded by formulating theories about voodoo and black cultural inheritance. In 1927, Herskovits clarified his theory on voodoo as an African survival in his review of Newbell Niles Puckett's study on black southerners' voodoo superstitions and folklore, *Folk Beliefs of the Southern Negro* (1926). The volume did not impress Herskovits. Puckett, a white Mississippi native and Yale University PhD, had, according to Herskovits, failed to refer to important sources and employ rigorous methods in his attempt to uncover the African roots of black southerners' "mental antiques." But Herskovits decided that Puckett's voodoo section was the one place where he "makes a case that is less open to attack than elsewhere in the book."[95] He explained: "The history of the voodoo cult is reasonably well known ... and, in the form it has flourished in the West Indian islands, a form not unlike that of the South of this country, many African survivals have been established as being present." Herskovits argued that "voodoo" was the purest African survival: "Voodoo has, from its inception, been under the ban, and has been practised in the greatest secrecy. Is it strange, that here the purest form of African customs, those which have been tampered with least by the white man, should survive?"[96] His positive view of voodoo was not echoed in popular voodoo material, but it did influence his colleague and mentee, African American anthropologist Zora Neale Hurston. Not only did Hurston share Herskovits's view of the scholarly value of voodoo, she wrote that "shreds of hoodoo beliefs and practices are found wherever any number of Negroes are found in America."[97]

Herskovits and Hurston did not conceive their theories about African survivals and voodoo in a vacuum. Their views may have been a reaction to the voodoo craze, but their theories were also rebuttals to arguments against African survivals posited by American sociologists, such as prominent black scholar E. Franklin Frazier. The debate over the racial inheritance of black Americans that raged in the academy during the 1920s and 1930s began with Herskovits's and Hurston's teacher Franz Boas and E. Franklin Frazier's teacher Robert E. Park.[98] On one side of the debate sociologists argued that slavery destroyed all vestiges of African culture among New World blacks. On the other side of the debate, anthropologists contended that blacks had retained traces of African culture and traditions.

Race had always been a central topic in American anthropology and sociology. From the first American sociological study, W. E. B. Du Bois's *The Philadelphia Negro: A Social Study* (1899), to the American ethnologists and folklore collectors who pioneered what became the field of American anthropology, notions of racial distinction shaped theories in these fields.[99] By the 1920s, both fields were moving toward a common view of race that looked beyond biology to explain differences between groups.[100] During the twenties, these burgeoning disciplines also gained prestige as they offered explanations for social and cultural patterns at home and abroad, and their theories and methods overlapped.[101] For instance, Du Bois was a sociologist, but he promoted African survivals theories.[102] But the differences between the fields fueled the tensions at the heart of the African survivals debate.

The stakes in the survivals debate were high. At stake on both sides was the possibility that either position (the idea that blacks are culturally distinct, or the idea that black cultural life is the absolute product of slavery and racism) would bolster notions of black inferiority used to justify racism and segregation. The New Negro intelligentsia was deeply invested in this debate, precisely because they embraced the idea that the social sciences could be a powerful weapon in their fight against racism. Black intellectuals such as Carter G. Woodson, Alain Locke, and James Weldon Johnson hoped that if anthropologists turned their attention from Native Americans to blacks, they could help paint a new positive picture of black folklife in the academy. They encouraged anthropological studies that would overturn the racist assumptions of white folklore collectors of the 1890s concerning black spirituals, folktales, dialect patterns, and non-Christian spiritual practices (voodoo, roots, and conjuh).[103] They also looked to sociology to prove that social, historical, and economic factors shaped what was commonly perceived as "racial difference" and innate "black pathology."[104] But ultimately the struggle to determine which influences—cultural or social—had the greatest impact on black life became contentious. Frazier's and Herskovits's debate is a prime example of this contention.

Another reason why the debate between the two scholars was so hard fought is that it picked up on earlier ideological tensions between their intellectual predecessors.[105] Park, a white sociologist, and Boas, a white Jewish anthropologist, can easily be credited with ushering in modern sociology and anthropology. Although Boas's cultural determinism theory influenced Robert Park's social conditioning thesis, and traces of primitivism can be detected in both their works, the two men had very different readings of black American culture.[106]

Franz Boas challenged the way that Victorians imagined race and culture. Born in Germany on July 9, 1858, Boas studied geography and physics and earned his PhD in Germany before coming to America. He conducted field-work with Eskimos prior to lecturing at Columbia University in 1896 and set out to answer questions about race. Appointed Columbia University's first professor of anthropology, Boas's work broke with early American anthropology's racist tradition. His cultural determinism theory contradicted notions of white superiority, by contending that historical particularism accounted for differences observed between "races."[107]

Boas's view on race attracted the interest and admiration of members of the New Negro intelligentsia. Like most early anthropologists, Boas maintained an interest in Native Americans, but by 1910, he had begun to apply cultural determinism theory to blacks and the American "race problem" — a move that caught the attention of black leaders like W. E. B. Du Bois.[108] The New Negro intelligentsia seemed to forgive the fact that Boas suffered episodic reversions and suggested that blacks were inferior to whites and continued to promote his work in the black press.[109] For the black intelligentsia, Boas's occasional slights were trumped by the fact that he slammed white anthropologists like Guy B. Johnson and Howard Odum for racial biases in their writings about black life, he called for the training of more black anthropologists, and he championed a positive view of Africa.[110] Boas believed that positive portrayals of African history and culture were necessary to eradicate the idea that blacks had inherited their inferior status from their ancestors: "To those unfamiliar with the products of native African art and industry, a walk through one of the large museums of Europe would be a revelation." The "revelation," Boas wrote, would arise from an encounter with "the blacksmith, the wood-carver, the weaver, the potter — these all produce ware original in form, executed with great care, and exhibiting that love of labor, and interest in the results of work, which are apparently so often lacking among the Negroes in our American surroundings." He insisted that "all different kinds of activities that we consider valuable in the citizens of our country may be found in aboriginal Africa."[111]

Boas emphasized the importance of changing the way Americans viewed blacks' African background, but he did not at first believe that remnants of African culture could be found in America.[112] More and more, he became convinced that if any African culture survived American slavery, it would be found in the South: "the amalgamation of African and European tradition which is so important for understanding historically the character of American Negro life, with its strong African background in the West Indies, the importance of which diminishes with increasing distance from the south."[113] The possibility that African traditions survived in the South, presented Boas, and the anthropologists that he trained, with an opportunity to link American blacks to a new vision of Africa—a vision that promised to elevate the value of black culture in the eyes of whites and erode racism.

Robert Park, and the sociologists that he led, championed a different view of black American culture and its connection to Africa. Born in Pennsylvania in 1864, Park eventually studied at the University of Michigan.[114] He spent more than a decade working as a journalist before changing course and going to graduate school at Harvard University.[115] He fine-tuned his analytical skills in the emerging field of sociology in Germany, and not long after, found himself working for the Congo Reform Association (CRA). As a writer for the CRA—an organization dedicated to exposing colonial authority abuses in the Congo—Park became enthralled with the race question.[116]

Park's work with the CRA shaped his belief that black people needed to assimilate in order to eliminate the pathologies that he believed encouraged anti-black racism. Even as his work with the CRA helped him understand structural racism, Park believed black oppression in the Congo, and wherever it existed in the world, was an unintended consequence—"wherever a European people invaded the territory of a more primitive folk in order to uplift, civilize and incidentally exploit them."[117] The fact that Park believed that black Africans were "primitives" who needed to be "civilized" when Park met Booker T. Washington through the CRA did not stop Washington from inviting him to work as a publicist at Tuskegee in 1905. Park further refined his view of the transformative power of assimilation at Tuskegee, and the school's self-improvement ethos encouraged his belief that assimilation—which, according to Park, required that one group in a society incorporate another group's "language, characteristic attitudes, habits and modes of behavior"—was the answer to the race question.[118]

Park's theories would influence his view of urban sociology, which dominated academic life at the University of Chicago.[119] He believed that social environment and conditioning had the greatest impact on human nature and that cultural evolution was the product of sociohistorical conditions, and he used black people to prove his point.[120] Relying on ideas about civilization to frame his understanding of race, Park viewed lower-class black culture as pathological products of slavery and racism.[121] He rejected the idea that African culture survived slavery and explained why in an article that he published at the height of racial unrest in Chicago in 1919 titled "The Conflict and Fusion of Cultures with Special Reference to the Negro."

Although Park declared an anti-African survivals position, the logic that he presented to support his thesis wavered. In the article, Park wrote, "There is every reason to believe ... that the Negro, when he landed in the United States, left behind him almost everything but his dark complexion and his tropical temperament."[122] Even though Park conceded that "race" was not a biological phenomenon, he argued that "racial temperaments" exist, and races are derived from quasi-biological, noncultural differences between the races that "manifest themselves especially in the objects of attention, in tastes and in talents."[123] That Park assumed a connection between blacks' "tropical temperament" and Africa is undeniable, but he insisted that Africa did not play a significant role in black culture: "It is very difficult to find in the South today anything that can be traced directly back to Africa."[124] He embraced the idea that blacks were inclined to adhere to superstitions but insisted that this too, had nothing to do with Africa and instead argued that "superstition, conjuring, 'root doctoring' and magic" in black communities were products of economic and social forces that "grow up anywhere among an imaginative people, living in an intellectual twilight such as exists on the isolated plantations of the Southern States."[125]

As Park made his historic argument against African survivals, he simultaneously presented Sea Islanders, like Sapelo Islanders, as the only populations in which African culture survived—and painted them as exotic racial oddities. Employing sociological analysis, Park argued that the social environment in which Sea Islanders were enslaved, and their geographic isolation, facilitated the reproduction of the African temperament. Park explained that while it was rare, African religious forms did survive in America among Sea Island populations "where the slaves were and still are more completely isolated than elsewhere in the South." These populations, which Park claimed "approached more closely to the cultural status of the native African," nurtured a "distinct dialect" and retained "certain customs which are supposed to be of African origin." He even suggests that these vague, rare survivals were most evident "in their religious practices," which are closest to "anything positively African."[126] It was Sea Islanders' Christian practices that Park believed revealed their nearness to the "African temperament," not actual African traditions. He explained that their style of worship was an expression of something "new and original" and "not the revival of an older more barbaric religion."[127] Even though he rejected sweeping theories that assumed Africa's influence on black culture, Park advanced the idea that authentic African spiritual primitivism likely thrived on the Sea Islands, and the notion that an amorphous spiritual quality was perhaps the most reliable African trait to be found in these communities.

Boas's redemptive view of black people's African past, and Park's declaration that black people's African heritage was meaningless in the American context, made them intellectual adversaries of sorts. Their scholarly differences were never reconciled, and starting in the 1920s the two men's students—Melville

Herskovits, who worked with Boas at Columbia University, and E. Franklin Frazier, who trained with Park in Chicago—initiated their own battle over the origins of black culture relative to African influences. Herskovits's and Frazier's differences extended beyond their intellectual orientation. E. Franklin Frazier was born in Maryland in 1894 to a father who was a bank messenger and a mother who worked at home caring for their children.[128] Melville Herskovits was born in 1895, the son of immigrants; he lived during his youth in Ohio, Texas, and Pennsylvania.[129] Frazier's path to the ivory tower began at Howard University in 1912 and involved several years of teaching before he pursued graduate degrees at Clark University and the University of Chicago, while Herskovits's college education was interrupted by a tour of duty in France during World War I. Herskovits had to wait until he returned home to complete a degree in history at the University of Chicago before heading to New York in 1920 to attend graduate school.[130]

Despite the obvious differences between them, Herskovits and Frazier both saw their scholarship as a way to attack racism, and they shared a common network of friends and mentors who were also grappling with "the race question." They were both deeply involved in the New Negro movement, and their writings were featured in Alain Locke's edited collection *The New Negro: An Interpretation* (1925). And, like Frazier, Herskovits spent a great deal of time interacting with the New Negro intelligentsia. During the early 1920s, Herskovits gave talks at the 135th Street branch of the New York Public Library, attended NAACP and Urban League meetings, and a few meetings at the *Crisis* magazine.[131] Herskovits and Frazier were both influenced by W. E. B. Du Bois, had connections to Alain Locke, and maintained relationships with black sociologist Charles S. Johnson.[132] They disagreed, but the fact that Herskovits recommended Frazier for a fellowship to support his research is a sure sign that the two men respected each other as scholars and were cordial.[133]

Herskovits's and Frazier's relationships with their mentors—Park and Boas—also reveal similarities. The two men embraced and modified their mentors' theories. Herskovits shared many of Boas's perspectives. Like Boas, Herskovits was committed to attracting more black anthropologists to the field and had trained black anthropologists and hired black assistants while conducting research.[134] But during the course of his career, Herskovits built on Boas's theory of cultural determinism and adopted a more complicated reading of black culture that included African survivals.[135] Similarly, Frazier accepted the essential elements of Park's brand of urban sociology, but he was also one of Park's greatest critics.[136] Frazier and his colleague Charles S. Johnson— members of the second wave of black sociologists trained at the University of Chicago—patterned their work after the work of W. E. B. Du Bois; they read "black pathology" within the context of race and class struggles and denounced Park's theory on "racial temperament" as "pseudoscientific nonsense."[137]

For all that Herskovits and Frazier shared, their respective views of black culture could not be more distinct.[138] Frazier insisted that blacks had lost all ties to Africa during the Middle Passage and slavery.[139] As a black man, Frazier understood that black people's connection to Africa had always been used to establish their inferiority, and he saw no benefit in emphasizing the connection between blacks and Africa. In fact, he was annoyed by New Negroes fixated on their folk and African past and had shamed black artists and writers like Countee Cullen who dared ask, "What is Africa to me?"[140] He answered Cullen's question by explaining that the New Negroes' nostalgic view of Africa was nothing more than "the voice of a new race consciousness in a world of conflict and frustration rather than the past speaking through traditions that have become refined and hallowed as they have been transmitted ... generation to generation."[141] Like his mentor, Frazier argued that authentic survivals were few and far between, with the most reliable showing up in the West Indies, and almost never in the United States.[142] He denied the possibility that African culture impacted the black family structure, except in very rare cases where shreds of the African past survived.[143] In describing the way that slavery destroyed African religions, Frazier inadvertently countered popular voodoo tales when he wrote, "Other conquered races have continued to worship their household gods" but "American slavery destroyed household gods."[144] Here, he pointed out that slavery also destroyed "bonds of sympathy and affection between men and women of the same household."[145] From Frazier's vantage point, black pathology began when slavery destroyed blacks' connection to African culture.

For Herskovits, slavery and the Middle Passage did not sever blacks' ties to African culture. He believed that "Africa" survived in black people's spiritual practices, their storytelling, their dialects, their hairstyles, their walk, their laugh, their sitting postures, their dances, their singing, in the way they planted things, and in many other daily activities throughout the diaspora.[146] He spent over twenty years looking for proof that blacks had retained African traits and for evidence that would prove Brazilian anthropologist Arthur Ramos's syncretism theory true. Syncretism, as interpreted by Herskovits and applied to blacks in the Atlantic World, was the process through which cultural practices from two different cultures were combined. Herskovits traveled to Suriname, Dahomey, Haiti, Trinidad, and in the United States on this quest. Like Boas, Herskovits believed that eradicating ideas about African inferiority and linking blacks to the sophisticated traditions, cultures, and cosmology of their African ancestors was important antiracism work. He wrote, "With better knowledge of the African cultures we shall have an adequate basis to investigate the affiliation of those cultural traits the American Negro has retained in his contact with white and Indian civilizations."[147] He even believed that "Africa" had left her imprint on white American culture too.[148] The modernist energy that animated the social sciences, his own primitivist tendencies, and the increase of Africa's allure encouraged Herskovits's hunt for survivals.

Herskovits also decided that Gullah folk—the blacks who lived on South Carolina's and Georgia's coast, and on islands like Sapelo—were ideal populations to examine for African survivals. One year after Julia Peterkin's novel Scarlet Sister Mary won the Pulitzer Prize, Melville Herskovits championed the search for African survivals among the Gullah: "Next on our table we should place such isolated groups living in the United States as the Negroes of the Savannahs of southern Georgia, or those of the Gullah islands off the Carolina coast where African elements of culture are still more tenuous."[149] Had Park's conclusion about Sea Islanders inspired Herskovits's curiosity about Gullah folk? Or did the popularity of Peterkin's work make the relationship between Gullah people and African culture a common assumption? Herskovits more than admired Peterkin's work; like many Americans who read Julia Peterkin's novels, he interpreted her fiction as fact. He even cited a folk superstition that she described in her book Green Thursday in his landmark study Myth of the Negro Past (1941) as evidence. The fact that Peterkin's fiction appears alongside a long list of scholarly studies included in Herskovits's bibliography is, in itself, evidence of his own tendency to lapse into, and be seduced by, racial fantasy.[150] Although Peterkin's book was one among many sources that Herskovits looked to for confirmation that Low Country blacks were promising subjects in his quest for African survivals, once the Gullah identity was consolidated in the ivory tower, Peterkin's fiction began to look more like "fact." Two Sapelo Island researchers called on Herskovits to guide their studies, and Frazier was also asked to review one of these works, which placed coastal Georgia blacks and Sapelo Islanders in the middle of their debate.[151] Whereas Herskovits took great interest in both studies, Frazier believed that the idea that the Gullah were a quasi-African ethnic group was preposterous, and he completely rejected the notion when he was asked to review the writings of one Sapelo Island researcher.

While Herskovits and Frazier were locked in their disagreement, Herskovits had helped groom an ally uniquely positioned to infiltrate black districts in the South like Gullah communities and examine voodoo as an African survival. His ally, Zora Neale Hurston, a black woman from Eatonville, Florida, was exactly what Boas hoped for when he called for the training of black anthropologists. Although she is famous for her fictional works, Hurston made her mark as an anthropologist too. Her anthropological studies, in many ways, laid the foundation for the research that was conducted on Sapelo. Certainly, the voodoo focus of Hurston's studies shaped Sapelo researchers' view of their task and of the Islanders. Through voodoo, Hurston also helped enhance the popularity of anthropological studies and increase black folklore's appeal among primitivists.

Born sometime between 1891 and 1901, Hurston emerged from humble beginnings in the Deep South.[152] A series of tragedies and triumphs took her from her hometown in Florida to Morgan Academy in Baltimore and finally to Howard University in Washington, DC, in 1918.[153] At Howard, Hurston struggled with her studies and, at one point, worked as a manicurist to support herself and pay tuition.[154] Hurston met Alain Locke at Howard; he noticed her writing talents early on and referred her writing to Charles S. Johnson—the cofounder of *Opportunity: A Journal of Negro Life*.[155] Hurston's fiction so expertly blended black folklife and her experiences in all-black Eatonville, that two out of her three submissions won prizes. She was beckoned to New York to attend an award dinner for the shining stars of the Harlem Renaissance, where she rubbed elbows with New York's littérateurs.[156] What happened next changed the course of Hurston's life. Fannie Hurst, a famous white Jewish novelist, offered her a job, and Annie Nathan Meyer—one of the founders of Barnard (Columbia University's women's college)—gave her a scholarship to enroll in the fall of 1925; and while enrolled at Barnard, Hurston met Franz Boas.[157]

While at Barnard, "Papa Franz" helped Hurston channel her gift for writing folklore into an academic career as an anthropologist. She studied with Boas, and learned from Herskovits, and two weeks before she graduated in 1927, Boas secured a fellowship for Hurston and sent her south to collect black folklore.[158] Hurston took the $1,400 fellowship and headed to Florida in pursuit of black folk material. She arrived first in Jacksonville, Florida, sixty-six miles south of Sapelo Island, full of excitement and enthusiasm.

Hurston's mission to collect black southern folklore took an interesting and dramatic turn that sent her searching for southern voodoo. Voodoo had not always been Hurston's folklife calling. Initially, Hurston set out to use the research funds that Boas secured for her from Carter G. Woodson's organization, the Association for the Study of Negro Life and History, to collect folklore in her home state of Florida.[159] Once in Florida, she began to doubt that her position as a race "insider" would grant her easy access to black folktales. She explained: "The glamour of Barnard College was still upon me. . . . I went about asking, in carefully accented Barnardese, 'Pardon me, but do you know any folk tales or folk songs?'" The curt responses that she received from the men and women whom she believed "had whole treasuries of material seeping through their pores" made her believe that the time she spent in the academy had driven a wedge between her and the black folk from whom she emerged.[160] What she did manage to collect did not impress Papa Franz—he remarked that her submission mirrored much of the material that had already been collected by whites.[161]

It was clear to Hurston that if she was going to make her mark in the field of anthropology she needed to devise a new strategy. She later claimed that when she reviewed the folklore that she collected during early fieldwork a clear and consistent link between voodoo (or "hoodoo") and black folklife became apparent. She concluded that hoodoo doctors "took the place of the medical man, the priest, and the lawyer, with the added fear-power that none of the others have" in black southern communities.[162] According to Hurston, it was this discovery that set the course for her voodoo studies. It is highly probable that Hurston adopted the voodoo focus because Herskovits had estimated pure survivals could be found in the tradition. And certainly, the sheer abundance of voodoo material that saturated the media and popular culture, and the troubling and condescending assumptions that framed Puckett's voodoo study *Folk Beliefs of the Southern Negro*, could have easily encouraged the shift in her focus. She spent the next several years collecting more black southern folk material, which included running the voodoo down; she took part in secret initiations, sacrifices, and sat at the feet of a host of voodoo doctors and clairvoyants, and documented their craft.

By 1931, she had collected enough voodoo data to publish an article. "Hoodoo in America" was featured in the *Journal of American Folklore*, a journal published by the American Folklore Society, an organization that dedicated its interests to exploring the primitive world of nonwhites since 1888. The article consisted of over one hundred pages of magical formulas, mystical charms, and dark rites used by blacks in New Orleans, Louisiana, Florida, Alabama, and occasionally Georgia.[163] In the article, she defined voodoo as "the European term for African magic practices and beliefs," and explained that blacks called it "hoodoo," but "both terms being related to the West African term juju." She wrote that blacks also used other terms to describe African magic practices like "conjure." She did not distinguish herbal medicine from African magic; instead, she conflated the two practices and presented them as one in the same: "'Roots' is the Southern Negro's term for folk-doctoring by herbs and prescriptions, and by extension, and because of all hoodoo doctor's cure by roots, it may be used as a synonym for hoodoo."[164]

While readers of "Hoodoo in America" may have found that Hurston's writings illuminated the inner world of a dark practice, what they encountered in the article may have actually distorted the image of voodoo instead of clarifying it. While Hurston's messy definition of voodoo is one of the most concise descriptions of the practice to appear in scholarly literature during the period, the vague distinction between "conjure," "hoodoo," "roots," and her conflation of these terms with Africa did little to explain or elevate "African" cosmology above its common association with savagery. She gathered compelling material and documented significant practices, but the study was set against an incomplete picture of black southern life. Hurston did not contextualize her findings at all. For example, she concluded that all herbal medicine was "root doctoring," or a manifestation of voodoo, which obscured the reason why herbal remedies were pervasive in black southern communities. While Hurston acknowledged that most of her subjects were poor, she did not consider the economic realities that may have encouraged what she assumed to be black southerners' preference for herbal medicine. Similarly, the rest of the study follows no specific pattern of academic inquiry, but instead describes her tutelage under hoodoo doctors; recounts stories, specific rites, and rituals; and provides "how to" instructions for everything from human sacrifice to punishing unkind landlords.[165] Ultimately, Hurston's most stunning assessment was that hoodoo beliefs and practices were pervasive in black communities, a declaration that confirmed what the nation's newspapers had been reporting for years.[166]

The culmination of Hurston's voodoo research in the South was the publication of *Mules and Men* (1935). Ten chapters of the book were dedicated to black folklore, and seven chapters were dedicated to voodoo. In letters she wrote to friends and mentors, Hurston complained that her editors insisted on presenting her voodoo research in a casual format: "The last half of the book is hoodoo material and they are insisting now that I make it more suitable for the general reading public."[167] Hurston scoffed at Broadway's and popular fiction's "voodoo ritualistic orgies," but *Mules and Men* was edited to attract readers who loved the voodoo entertainment that she claimed to despise.[168] She worried that Boas would, once again, be disappointed by her folk material, so she begged Boas to write the introduction in a private letter that she sent him in 1934: "So I hope that the unscientific matter that must be there for the sake of the average reader will not keep you from writing the introduction." She promised Boas that the conversations and incidents that she reported were true, but admitted that the work was not acceptable for academic audiences: "But of course I never would have set them down for scientists to read.... But the man in the street is different."[169] If Boas was disturbed by Hurston's book, the introduction that he wrote did not show it, and despite the fact that *Mules and Men* was not a scholarly text, her voodoo studies continued to garner prestige. Her voodoo research won her a Guggenheim Fellowship in 1936 and 1937, and she used the award money to explore voodoo and folk magic in Jamaica and Haiti.[170]

At the same time that Hurston resented collectors whom she described as "cheap white folks," who were "grabbing our stuff and ruining it," and believed that their racial blind spots guaranteed that "they never do it right" (she may have been referring to white voodoo practitioners or folklore collectors), she also approached black southerners as a collector and observed them—even those in her own home community—through a primitivist gaze.[171] She imagined black southerners, whom she described as both beautiful and "Negroes ... disfigured by ignorance ... a slinking shrinkiness"—as primitive retainers of an older black African folk culture and a core racial essence.[172] Like many whites who collected folk material, she ignored other aspects of their lives such as the travails of Jim Crow and crushing poverty, and instead focused on cultural characteristics.

An astute critic of American race relations, Hurston probably anticipated that her voodoo research would not receive a warm reception by all who encountered it. In 1938, a newspaper report about Hurston's voodoo research in Haiti described her as being as primitive and savage as her subjects, and her work was reduced to absurdity. The article reported that "after eleven months in the dark jungles back of Port-au-Prince, chanting voodoo chants, drinking the blood of the sacrificial goat ... Hurston 'returns a believer in voodooism.' The journalist jested, 'Despite her degree from Barnard, the books she has written, the Columbia and Guggenheim Fellowships which she has won, Miss Hurston is a happy-go-lucky pagan.'"[173] Hurston's work also inspired controversy among the New Negro intelligentsia. Her black critics were troubled by *Mules and Men* because the book closely mirrored the stories about superstitious and primitive blacks that whites had produced.[174] These tensions are evident in a joke that one reviewer made at the end of an assessment of *Mules and Men* published in the *Journal of Negro History*: "Certainly the writer, if she has not convinced all readers of the power of Voodooism, has offered new evidence of widespread ignorance and superstition."[175]

Sapelo's Black Magic

If Harlem's blacks—people who resided in one of the nation's most vibrant modern metropolises—could not escape being reduced to a group of primitive voodooists disguised in fancy clothes that helped them hide in plain sight, how would the researchers and writers who came to Sapelo perceive the Islanders? From the horrific voodoo tales reported in black and white papers and told in American popular culture, to the scholarly studies written by Boasian anthropologists, rural blacks like Sapelo Islanders had all the makings of a perfect population to examine for scraps of African spiritual survivals. But if Zora Neale Hurston, an anthropologist trained by Franz Boas, could not disentangle legitimate African spiritual survivals from the racial fictions that were fodder for voodoo books, stage works, and films, how could two white amateur folklore collectors and a white, adventure-seeking journalist parse racial fiction from authentic expressions derived from African folklife on Sapelo?

When Sapelo's researchers traveled across the water and trekked through marsh and pinewoods in search of authentic Gullah folk and African survivals, they brought a hodgepodge of Julia Peterkin's stories, stereotypes about black folk and voodoo, and Melville Herskovits's and Zora Neale Hurston's theories with them. And overwhelmingly, the characterizations of Sapelo Islanders and their black coastal Georgia neighbors could be traced back to these influences with more certainty than they could be traced back to Africa.

Hunting Survivals

W. ROBERT MOORE, LYDIA PARRISH,

AND LORENZO D. TURNER DISCOVER

GULLAH FOLK ON SAPELO ISLAND

On Sapelo Island, I found in the Johnson family a combination of the old dance form
with rather more modern steps than the original African pantomime warranted. . . .

Negroes can put themselves into very peculiar physical-mental states with
extraordinary ease. They will go into trances, or throw fits at the slightest provocation.
Even a Negro beating a tom-tom quickly becomes very strange; his pupils dilate and do
not focus, he seems to become a rhythmic and unconscious automation. From first-hand
experience, I know that this characteristic survives to a surprising degree among our
rural Negroes of the Georgia Coast.

—Lydia Parrish, *Slave Songs of the Georgia Sea Islands*

It must have taken Emma and Emmitt Johnson hours to dress their eleven children in the fine clothes they wore on that bright day in 1933 when they posed for a family portrait.[1] The entire family stood in front of towering oaks draped with Spanish moss just steps from their small wooden house on Sapelo Island. Despite having little money and many mouths to feed, Emma and Emmitt Johnson always made sure that their children had "good clothes" and "proper shoes" to wear to Sunday church services, as well as on their infrequent trips to the mainland, and on special occasions, such as the one they prepared for on that morning. On that day, W. Robert Moore, a writer and photographer for *National Geographic Magazine*, came to Hog Hammock to take their photograph.[2]

The Johnsons wore their pride on that sunny day, as though defying the Jim Crow era's characterization of southern blacks as backward and inferior. They used their clothes, shoes, and hairstyles to define themselves as respectable, dignified, and modern. The girls wore newly pressed dresses with sashes and belts wrapped around their tiny waists, ankle socks draped over their shoes, and they all sported freshly straightened hair tied down in braids, or secured with ribbons. Surely their mother had instructed them to stand like perfect ladies, which is evident in the several pairs of tiny brown hands clasped at their laps. The Johnsons' older daughter wore a Sunday dress too, but her more mature legs were covered with stockings, her hair was pressed in a style appropriate to her age, a delicate necklace adorned her neck, and dainty teardrop earrings dangled from her ears. The Johnson boys were dressed in suits or slacks matched with vests or cardigans, and all of the boys wore button-down shirts with starched collars and dress shoes. While Emma Johnson undoubtedly spent a great deal of time that day dressing her children, she took extra time to ready herself too. She not only wore an outfit that she had likely set aside for occasions when she was not toiling through her daily tasks, but she also put on a dress coat accented with an ornate puffy collar and cuffs. Emmitt Johnson dressed to complement his handsome family. The island's most prominent boat builder and carpenter took off his workaday brogan shoes and overalls and put on a suit and tie for Moore's photograph.

In the end, however, the Johnsons' fine attire and formal presentation would do little to refute the popular stereotypes and fantasies W. Robert Moore and other white researchers and writers brought to Sapelo. Moore arrived convinced that the Johnsons were authentic primitives, whose daily lives and beliefs mirrored those of their African ancestors. Moreover, W. Robert Moore was not the only writer and researcher who would paint the Johnson family in this way. Lydia Parrish visited the Johnsons in search of slave songs that she believed to be the key to coastal Georgia blacks' African past. While black scholar Lorenzo Dow Turner conducted studies in coastal Georgia, and on Sapelo Island, to restore dignity to black Americans by exploring the African roots of their linguistic culture, the other Gullah researchers who came to the island did not share his affirmative vision of African peoples. In fact, Sapelo's white researchers' writings on African survivals in the region largely reiterated popular stereotypes about superstitious, ignorant, impulsive, childlike, and backward blacks. Consequently, the Johnsons' desire to be interpreted as a respectable upstanding Christian family clashed with mainstream white America's fantasies that imagined these black Sea Islanders as primitives who put their faith in African-born superstitions. The Johnsons' "proper" presentation could not mute the pounding tom-toms and African essence that white Sapelo researchers believed pulsated just under the surface of their polished demeanor.

Uncovering Sapelo researchers' racial politics and examining the racial fantasies that dictated the way that potential survivals among the Islanders were contrived and conceptualized reveals how popular ideas about African survivals and blacks' racial inheritance shaped the works produced by the first group of researchers who came to the island in search of authentic Gullah folk. W. Robert Moore's *National Geographic* article, Lydia Parrish's slave song collection, and Lorenzo D. Turner's *Africanisms in the Gullah Dialect* (1949) embody both the individual perspectives of Sapelo researchers and reflect the larger intellectual and cultural discourses that touched down on Sapelo Island during the 1930s. The encounter between Sapelo Islanders and the fantasies that the nation, and these individual researchers, had about blacks who lived on tropical islands and in the rural South, did not wane in the face of the less than sensational realities of Sapelo Islanders' daily lives in the shadow of Jim Crow. Instead, these fantasies overshadowed the realities of the Islanders' lives, obscured the long history of their fight for freedom and autonomy, and became the basis of the longstanding view of magical, mystical, quasi-African Sapelo folk.

National Geographic Magazine *Discovers Africa on Georgia's Coast*

When they posed for W. Robert Moore, Emma and Emmitt Johnson may or may not have known about the popularity of black voodoo themes in Hollywood films, plays, newspaper reports, and in travel novels of the 1920s and 1930s; and they were probably unaware of the widespread popularity of Julia Peterkin's Gullah tales that depicted the exotic world of the black folk who lived along South Carolina's coast. It is also unlikely that the Johnsons knew about the burgeoning desire among some anthropologists to uncover the significance of blacks' African heritage. But either way, the Johnsons did not see themselves as primitive blacks who retained a unique connection to their African past. In fact, the only thing about their lives that they believed set them apart from mainland blacks was that they lived on an island that was dominated by one of the wealthiest and most powerful white men in the nation.[3] Howard Coffin hosted a long list of dignitaries and famous people at his Sapelo Island mansion—a list that included Presidents Coolidge and Hoover.[4] As far as the Johnsons were concerned, it was solely Coffin and his well-appointed guests who attracted journalists and writers to the island. For instance, in 1928, during President Coolidge's visit, one of the Johnsons' sons, Fred Johnson, was photographed with the president and Coffin while driving the two men in his father's oxcart on a hunting excursion.[5] The Johnsons, and the other blacks who lived on the island, had come to expect the strange mix of animus and curiosity that their blackness inspired in Coffin's visitors, so no one thought it odd when a parade of researchers and collectors began marching through their communities asking questions and taking pictures.

Aside from their proximity to Howard Coffin and their encounters with his influential guests, the Johnsons believed themselves to be rather average. They had married in 1905, and, after that, like most of the other young couples on the island, Emma and Emmitt set up their homestead on land bequeathed to

Young Fred Johnson, Howard Coffin, and President Coolidge.
Courtesy of the University of Georgia Marine Institute Library.

them by their families.[6] Emma Johnson was a descendant of Sapelo's slaves, people who fought to secure land on the island after the Civil War, and Emmitt Johnson's family came to the island from nearby Effingham County, Georgia, some time between 1870 and 1880, long before Howard Coffin purchased most of the island.[7] Emmitt Johnson inherited his father's gift; he too was a master carpenter who built high-quality boats for his boss Howard Coffin and, later, R. J. Reynolds, and used his meager pay to provide for his wife and children.[8] Land that Emmitt's father and mother owned also comprised the small land trust that the Johnsons would eventually pass down to their children.

Even Emma and Emmitt Johnson's children described their parents' daily lives on Sapelo as being relatively ordinary. Each morning, before the first rays of sunlight staggered through the Spanish moss, Emmitt Johnson drove his ox-cart to the island's south end, which served as the command center for Howard Coffin's operations. Once on Coffin's compound, Emmitt began whatever task he was assigned that day. Even though, as Islanders recall, the pay that Coffin offered "wasn't anything to talk about . . . it wasn't nothing to cause nothing," many Islanders worked for him instead of working on the mainland.[9] Like Coffin's other black employees who worked in the greenhouse, maintained the grounds surrounding the mansion, cooked and cleaned in the mansion,

Sapelo road builders. Courtesy of the University of Georgia Marine Institute Library.

worked his fields, tended to his livestock, and worked at Coffin's other island projects, Emmitt worked under the scrutiny of the white island managers Coffin hired to watch the island's blacks and guard his interests.

Emma Johnson also started her workday during the predawn hours, but she worked at home. She cared for the children every day while working her way through a variety of tasks that she assigned to each day of the week.[10] Tuesdays were "washdays," during which she gathered her family's clothes that had been soiled by the island's thick grainy sand and scrubbed them clean in a large cast iron wash pot in the yard. On Wednesdays she ironed, and on other days she managed the family's food supply—an arduous responsibility that varied depending on the season. Tending to her vegetable garden, hulling rice, making preserves, canning vegetables during harvest season, and supervising her husband while he ground corn to make grits or meal, required great skill and kept Emma Johnson very busy.[11] Her son Fred Johnson remembered how she preserved okras: "My mama used to dry them over in front of the housetop. . . . Dry okra and put it in the package and when you ready to cook you some okra, still be just as good as it's bought."[12] Emma also made sure that the pigs and chickens that she kept yielded meat and eggs for her family. Like other Sapelo Islanders, and most rural black southerners of their day, the Johnsons' days were filled with backbreaking work.[13]

On Saturdays and Sundays, the Johnsons and the other families on the island tried to push their work routines out of their minds. For adults, Satur-

day was set aside for relaxation. Women and men on the island gathered to share fried or smoked fish and made social calls to one another's homes. The women visited with each other and swapped remedies for common ailments, made plans to prepare meals for sick or elderly community members, browsed catalogues, and shared gossip about "so-and-so" who was headed to the mainland, or moving north in search of better jobs and other opportunities. The men headed out to the beach and used large handwoven fishing nets to collect the bounty of fish that settled near the island's shore. After the men finished "dragging-the-net," they returned home with scores of fish and shared a strong drink of local brewed liquor around a log fire in the cooler fall and

Sapelo women and girls. Courtesy of the University of Georgia Marine Institute Library.

winter months or sat close to a mosquito smoke (made from burning Spanish moss and pine needles) in the spring and summer.[14] Saturday was still a workday for Sapelo's children. One Islander recalled that when he was young, "We didn't have no time through the week, but on Saturdays when school out . . . we get up . . . first thing . . . go out there and chop [wood]" and "some would go to grinding grits, and some would go beating rice and that stuff."[15] Occasionally, Saturday nights found Islanders gathered for a meeting or a dance at the Farmers' Alliance Hall, which was the gathering place for meetings of the island's Freemasons and Farmers' Alliance members.

Almost everyone attended church on Sundays. Allen Green and his wife, Annie Mae Green, remembered that when they were growing up on the island during the early 1900s, no one dared work, or do anything on Sunday other than go to church: "They ain't a lick a cut a stick of wood on Sunday, not on Sunday, [because] they were very Christian."[16] The only other time when all work came to a halt on the island was when someone died: "If anybody die in the community, nobody don't work."[17] On Sundays, many Islanders walked for miles or piled into a kind neighbors' oxcart or mule-drawn wagon to get to one of the two churches, and those who did not were the focus of harsh criticism and strong condemnation.[18] The Johnsons, most of their extended family members, and other families who lived in Hog Hammock went to St. Luke Baptist

Church. The island's other church, First African Baptist Church, was the spiritual home to the Islanders who lived in, or near, Raccoon Bluff.

This was the "island life" that Emma and Emmitt Johnson knew. Their world was not filled with the beating tom-toms, African ancestors, and hoodoo rituals that some 1930s Sapelo researchers imagined and searched for. The fact that the Islanders used techniques like drying okras, smoking fish, weaving fishing nets and baskets, and adhered to traditions like passing children over the graves of their loved ones at burials, looking for messages in their dreams, and using words, phrases, and baptismal ceremonies passed down from their ancestors is unquestionable. However, most Sapelo researchers and collectors who came to the island during the 1920s and 1930s had their sights set on collecting much more dramatic material. In the end, the Johnsons and other Sapelo Islanders who were featured subjects in the works published by 1930s researchers were immortalized not for the island life that they knew and lived, but for the island life that dominated the intellectual and cultural landscape of the American imagination during the period.

At the point when W. Robert Moore came to Sapelo, fantastical tales of black island life that filled Americans' imaginations with voodoo drums, clandestine African rituals, and black primitives were all the rage. However, when Moore, the white Michigan farm boy–turned–world explorer, packed his clunky Recomar camera and other photography equipment, bound for Sapelo Island, he may have done so at Coffin's request.[19] Despite the fact that by 1932 the Great Depression had ravaged Coffin's assets, he continued to promote his Sea Island Cloister Hotel in the hopes that the venture would help to restore his wealth.[20] While Coffin maintained Sapelo Island as his private paradise, and as the headquarters of a few profit-yielding enterprises, the resort that he built on nearby Sea Island was open to the white middle-class public to enjoy, and he was likely aware of the growing middle-class interest in exotic islands stocked with nonwhite natives.[21] The culture of U.S. imperialism had transformed the appeal of tropical islands—all of Georgia's coastal islands had been purchased by wealthy whites in the wake of the 1930s "island fad" during which wealthy white men like Coffin took over Georgia's coastal islands and acted out their own imperial occupation fantasies.[22] Having his private island, and the region, featured in the nation's leading publication that charted geographical and racial distinction may have promised to attract tourists to his resort, but the venture also afforded Moore yet another opportunity to distinguish himself as one of *National Geographic*'s most prominent explorers.[23]

Even before Moore came to Georgia's coast, he had already crafted a successful career as a journalist and explorer amid the charged racial ideologies of the period. While sojourns to distant lands and encounters with primitives were essential elements of a popular adventure fantasy among his white male age-mates, Moore haphazardly stumbled into his position as a *National Geographic* "staff man." He was on his way to teach in Bangkok after graduating from Hillsdale College when he took a prize-winning photograph with the first Kodak camera he had ever purchased.[24] Moore's career with the magazine took off from that point, and his untrained eye quickly transformed into a skilled one that expertly captured photographs of distant places and foreign peoples. By the time he retired, Moore had published 69 articles and 2,000 photographs in the magazine and had traveled a total of 633,000 miles in pursuit of viable stories.[25] Throughout the 1930s, he was many times the featured lecturer at talks hosted by the National Geographic Society. He described his adventures to National Geographic Society members, local teachers, and general audiences eager to hear firsthand accounts of Moore's foreign excursions among the world's most exotic peoples.[26]

National Geographic Magazine's readership had no reason to doubt the accuracy of Moore's interpretation of black life on Georgia's coast. Long before W. Robert Moore began working for the magazine, the publication had taken up the task of mapping racial and geographical difference and had long since established itself as the preeminent authority on such matters.[27] The publication attracted a large readership because it specialized in telling Victorian-style adventure stories about encounters between heroic civilized whites and non-white primitives—especially Africans.[28] Each issue of the magazine, which is estimated to have reached 37 million people, conveyed to its largely white middle-class readership a highly specific worldview masked as a mix of scientific fact, cultural artifact, entertainment, and educational material.[29] Predictably, Moore's article did not stray from that formula.

Despite the fact that Moore's depiction of Sapelo Islanders may have encouraged the researchers who came after him to visit Sapelo, and bolstered their belief that there was a viable market for works about the island's black residents, he did not count the trip among the most memorable of his career. In his memoir, Moore matter-of-factly described his encounter on Georgia's coast: "Among other home assignments, I photographed and prepared articles on Maryland, and Nevada, and the islands along the Georgia coast."[30] However, when Howard Coffin opened the door for Moore to tour his private oasis, what resulted was the first published work in which the link between Sapelo Islanders and a mystical African essence was coded as fact.

Moore visited the Georgia coast while taking a break from his global travels sometime in 1933.[31] He toured Sapelo Island, Cumberland Island, St. Catherines Island, Jekyll Island, Ossabaw Island, St. Simons, and Sea Island.[32] During Moore's visit, he spent time on Sea Island's beach and resort; he photographed white vacationers skeet shooting, bathing on the beach, and biking in the sun; he toured Coffin's opulent Sapelo Island mansion and captured scenes of coastal Georgia's vast marshlands and sand dunes.[33]

He did not envision coastal Georgia as a modern landscape. Instead, Moore presented it as a place where visitors could get away from the modern world and experience the past. The region's towering pines, haunting Spanish moss–covered trees, billowing marshes, expansive beaches, and largely "undeveloped" landscape all signaled to Moore that modernity had not found its way to Georgia's coast. And if coastal Georgia's mainland communities were decisively premodern places, the islands beyond the shoreline—separated from mainland America by a vast waterway—were surely stuck in an earlier time.[34] In Moore's article, the region's timelessness was its central attraction, and his preoccupation with the coast's ever-present past allowed him to conveniently divorce the region from its place in the modern Jim Crow South, and from all of the contemporary dramas and struggles that Jim Crow produced. So in each locale, Moore focused on reconstructing a romantic past and unearthing local history as far back as the colonial period and the antebellum years and toured the ruins of old plantation houses, slave quarters, and Native American structures.[35]

In the article, coastal Georgia blacks served as living relics of the region's past. As a result, golfing, hunting, fishing, and boating were no longer the only activities to be enjoyed by vacationers—exploring living black relics of the region's African past now ranked high among the list of things to do while visiting Georgia's coast. Moore photographed blacks near tabby slave cottages on Ossabaw and black men participating in boat races, an activity that he explained as "a favorite sport of slavery days."[36] He noted that on resorts, "Negro boys now caddy over a superb golf course where their ancestors picked the fluffy bolls of luxuriant cotton."[37] On St. Simons, Moore visited a "praise house" used by black residents for religious gatherings and observed the performance of spirituals. Moore wrote, "Negroes of the island gather to sing their spirituals, plantation and works songs that have come down from ante-bellum days."[38] He described these songs as "stirring" and "naïve rhythmic spirituals" and linked the songs musical form back to African origins— "in the rhythm of these accompaniments to their labor, the muffled beat of African tom-toms seems to sound dimly in the background"—echoing a popular, loaded simplistic conclusion about the link between black music and Africa.[39] In fact, in a draft of the article, Moore dedicated a section to "Songs with African-born

Rhythm," but the subsection did not survive the editorial process.[40] Like many social scientists who tend to cultures they consider "primitive" with nostalgia, Moore did not assume that cultural retentions were marked by complex and sophisticated social processes, but instead represented them as a sort of retardation of the evolutionary impulse toward progress. His description of a "naïve" musical form is a critical assessment of the retention process, and the conclusion that the songs "stirred" something in him testified to his belief that blacks could rouse emotions that civilized whites worked hard to suppress.

For Moore, and most white Americans during the 1920s and 1930s, the connection between blacks and primitive African "traits" was a foregone conclusion. But unlike most white Americans, Moore had actually encountered African "primitives" on the continent in Ethiopia during Haile Selassie's coronation: "Ethiopia surpasses the wildest dreams of fantasy a man can have ... a country of elephants — ornamented with bizarre trappings, ridden by proud men. It is a nation of lions, a primitive nation of many tongues, a nation in which time has stood still."[41] Moore's primitivist assessment of Ethiopia's people is clear: "As for the natives ... they are docile and peaceful. They become only aroused at such events as coronations and impending wars."[42]

Moore's description of Ethiopians echoes the dominant view of "primitive man," which was rooted in a set of assumptions about nonwhite people. Primitives were believed to express a quality of "timelessness" that was a consequence of their lack of evolutionary progress. Primitives were assumed to be close to the earth and maintained a special relationship with nature and its creatures. Whereas "civilized" whites were thought to posses innate intellectual abilities, "primitives" displayed only simple emotions and uncomplicated dispositions. Although Victorian thinkers had dismissed primitive people's traditions and cultural practices because they surmised they were inferior and unimportant, during the 1920s and 1930s, primitivist artists, writers, and scholars — Moore among them — fetishized nonwhite primitives and rebelliously explored their culture. This is the lens through which Moore read Sapelo Islanders and all of the blacks that he met in coastal Georgia.

While Moore was intrigued by all of the blacks he encountered on the coast, he presented Sapelo Islanders as the most captivating "artifacts" in the region. After Moore admired Howard Coffin's mansion, the artesian wells that he built on the island, and the island's picturesque beaches, he turned his attention to black life beyond the island's south end. Perhaps Moore had become curious about blacks who lived in coastal rural regions through Julia Peterkin's successful novels about the Gullah, which first appeared in the 1920s and created a permanent place in the American imaginary for Sea Island blacks. Moreover, he may have encountered Peterkin's first attempt to write an ethnographic report of the Gullah people in South Carolina, which was first published during the same year that Moore traveled to the coast.[43] However, Peterkin's fictional and nonfictional Gullah works focused on blacks in South Carolina. Moore's discovery of Georgia's black Sea Islanders would reintroduce a new population to the world that Peterkin created. Accompanied by one of Howard Coffin's island managers, Moore explored Raccoon Bluff, Hog Hammock, and Shell Hammock, with his camera in one hand, and his notepad in the other, ready to document all that he discovered.

Moore's mission to document and discover Sapelo's black relics blinded him to the realities of black life on the island. He did not detect tensions between Islanders and Howard Coffin and Coffin's white island managers. Some Islanders described Coffin as a good man, but others remember him ruling the island with a power that surpassed county authorities and local courts.[44] Islanders who lived on Sapelo during Coffin's days remember him as the ultimate authority. Stories about Coffin and his hired white help arbitrating conflicts between the Islanders, forcing them to embrace their remedies "or else," and stories like the one Fred Johnson told about the fate of an Islander accused of murder who he believed was turned over to Coffin for punishment, are prime examples of this perception. Johnson believed that Coffin was so powerful that the millionaire, not a judge or court, assigned the murderer to a chain gang.[45] Moore missed these dynamics and the poverty that resulted from the low wages that Coffin paid Islanders in exchange for their labor. He did not make connections between the Jim Crow racial hierarchy and the subservient and accommodating role that Islanders were forced to assume in the presence of whites (a dynamic he took full advantage of while photographing and interviewing the island's residents). Moore overlooked all of these realities, and in their place, he inserted fantasies in which Africanisms were the governing forces that dictated Sapelo Islanders' daily life and shaped their culture.

In each of his descriptions of the Islanders, Moore connected almost every aspect of black life on the island to African traits. While it is likely that vestiges of African practices had survived among Islanders, it is unlikely that Moore accurately depicted or recorded any of them. Instead, his research was guided by popular American fantasies about Africa. The subtitle of one of the sections of the article exclusively dedicated to black cultural life on the coast and on the island, "Clocks, Lamps, and Dishes Adorn Negro Graves," hints at this preoccupation. He began by stating that the island's graveyard reveals among Sapelo Islanders, "Ancient practices mingled with their religion to-day."[46] When covering the burial practices at the island's Behavior Cemetery, Moore concluded that "strange customs prevail in negro cemeteries."[47] He photographed and wrote about a grave where "short posts are planted at either end of the grave, and upon the mounds of earth are placed cups and dishes, oil lamps, and alarm clocks. On one I also saw a broken thermos bottle; on another a small coin bank! The oil lamps are to furnish light through the unknown paths, the alarms are to sound on Judgment Day and the dishes—the banks, too I assume!—are for the personal use of their former owner."[48]

Undoubtedly the gravesite had historical and cultural significance. Moore did not explain how he learned the meaning of the grave decorations, and the fact that he simply assumed that the practice was evidence of some "strange" ancient rite reveals that he did not estimate that the practice had any meaning beyond superstition. When situated within the cultural landscape of the 1920s and 1930s, this "strange" rite was characterized by Moore—not as a complex New World tradition—but in a way that appealed to the growing fascination with black spiritual primitivism. Moore followed the discussion of "strange" rites involving the dead with a line describing Sapelo's Muslim past, further emphasizing the exotic spiritual tapestry on the island. Perhaps acknowledging that he had played to the thrilling character of black southern spirituality that was so popular, Moore ended his review of black spiritual life on the island by pointing out that Sapelo Islanders "are all good Baptists now," and by describing the Christian baptisms performed in creeks and the praise houses on the island.[49]

Moore next turned his attention to what he called "pleasure" outlets.[50] He wrote: "There are several 'to do' halls, where the secret societies hold their meetings and Terpsichorean devotees give vent to their African-born rhythm."[51] One of the halls that Moore referred to was the Farmers' Alliance Hall, which was first built to host meetings for the Sapelo Island branch of the Colored Farmers' Alliance and Cooperative Union. Originally founded in Texas in 1886, the alliance was created to organize and promote the economic interests of black farmers during the turbulent years following Reconstruction. Yet Moore's lack of interest in race and power dynamics in the region blinded him to the hall's original function, leading him to conclude that the Farmers' Alliance Hall was dedicated to meetings of a secretive African nature.

As far as Moore was concerned, Sapelo Islanders had been under the graceful protection and care of good white paternalistic figures since slavery days.[52] He wrote about his investigation into the island's antebellum past, a period when the blacks enslaved there (Thomas Spalding's "helpers") had it so good that the island was known as "Nigger Heaven."[53] Nowhere in the historical record that Moore used to paint the picture of Sapelo's past did he uncover the host of runaway slave notices that recorded the Islanders' discontent, nor did he unearth the long battle that Sapelo Islanders waged to retain the land that Special Field Order No. 15 helped them to secure as a reparation for their bondage. Moore could not imagine that the secrecy surrounding black Sapelo Islanders' gatherings at the hall was perhaps designed to protect and shield them from the watchful eyes of the island's white managers and to protect meeting participants from the consequences associated with gathering to discuss matters that might usurp Howard Coffin's authority. In fact, Freddie Wilson, a Sapelo Islander who was more than twenty years old when Moore came to the island, said that the hall was primarily used for meetings: "You got something to say, or I got something to say, or anything you want to change, you go to your group and have a meeting and change something or do something." [54]

While it is true that the Farmers' Alliance Hall also hosted dances and socials, Moore's characterizations of these dances were also distorted by his belief in popular ideas about African survivals among blacks. His conviction that black dances arose from the primal need to "give vent" to "African-born rhythm" was derived from the primitivist view of black people's uncontrollable impulses that were provoked by music. Moore described black Sapelo Islanders as if everything about them was exotic and innately African; his sensational descriptions of gravesite decorations, Islanders' Muslim heritage, and indiscriminate references to Africa easily aroused voodoo-tinged fantasies in 1930s America.

Moore's next stop was to Sapelo Island's Hog Hammock community. Here, he staged a chance encounter with Emmitt and Emma Johnson and their "fifteen children" at their home. According to Emmitt and Emma's youngest son, Joe Johnson, Moore likely made arrangements to photograph the island's largest family prior to showing up at their doorstep.[55] He probably knew of the family through the white island manager that Coffin designated to chauffeur Moore around the island. Yet Moore wrote about the episode as if it were a chance encounter. In the section titled "Fifteen 'Head' of Children," Moore quoted the exchange between himself and Emmitt Johnson: "'Yes, suh,' said Emmett proudly. 'We have fifteen head of children. They's all here to-day.'"[56] Moore continued: "Emmett beamed at my immediate request to photograph his kinky-headed group."[57]

Joe Johnson tells a different story of what happened that day. He explained that all of his siblings were not there. Several of his siblings had already left Sapelo and taken up residence on the mainland, and his younger sister Eldora had died before Moore came to photograph his family.[58] But Moore was so desperate to take a picture featuring fifteen black children that he recruited a few

The Johnsons in National Geographic Magazine.
W. Robert Moore / National Geographic Creative.

of the neighbors' children and cousins to replace the Johnson siblings who were not there.[59] Joe Johnson's account reveals that Moore not only misrepresented Emmitt Johnson with a fictitious quotation but also deliberately constructed a fraudulent picture of the family. Photographs not only were essential to *National Geographic Magazine*'s charge to document geographic and racial difference but were also an essential element of documentary journalism during the 1930s.[60] These works relied on photographs as much as they did text in order to create a sense of authenticity and truthfulness. For Moore, the photograph of the Johnson family was necessary in order to give his readers a visual representation of authentic Sea Island folk.

In the article, Moore also further degraded the Johnson family by making a joke based on what Joe Johnson identified as a lie: "'We had better count them up to see if they are all here,' remarked my companion just before I was ready to 'shoot.' There were sixteen! We counted again; sure enough there was one too many. Then Emmitt checked his family. One of the youngsters belonging to a neighbor had joined the group."[61]

According to Moore's report, after the picture was taken, Emma and Emmitt Johnson's nine-year-old son, Isaac, rolled up his pants and spontaneously began to dance.[62] He took a photograph of Isaac in action and titled it "Ball-

Isaac and Naomi Johnson in National Geographic Magazine.
W. Robert Moore / National Geographic Creative.

ing The Jack." The caption read: "Young Isaac exhibits a pair of agile feet burning with African rhythm, while his sister provides the cadence by clapping her
hands."[63] Again, Moore found one of Sapelo's blacks spontaneously "giving
vent" to an inner African musical impulse. For W. Robert Moore, and many
white Americans during the period, one mark of blackness was an irrepressible
primitive African essence—a racial trait that Moore determined was heightened among the human artifacts that he discovered on Sapelo Island.

Moore included three more photographs of Sapelo Islanders in the article.
One was a photograph of Emma and Emmitt Johnson's son, Fred Johnson, driving Calvin Coolidge and Howard Coffin in Emmitt's oxcart taken in 1928. He
described Fred Johnson as a "small and dusky coachman."[64] Another featured a
group of Sapelo Islanders riding in an oxcart. Moore described this group, and
the function of the cart, in the photograph's caption: "Sapelo Island has several
Negro settlements, descendants of the old slave population. Besides serving as
transport, the ox is used to plow and cultivate the small parcel of land which
provides the family sustenance."[65] Moore included an additional photograph
of a Sapelo Islander titled "Descendants of Plantation Workers," that featured
a young unidentified black woman who was "returning home after a four-mile
walk, carrying her youngster and balancing a bag of yams on her head."[66]

Hettie Walker and Ada in National Geographic Magazine.
W. Robert Moore / National Geographic Creative.

Moore's nameless subject was Hettie Walker. Her daughter, Cornelia Walker Bailey, author of *God, Dr. Buzzard, and the Bolito Man: A Saltwater Geechee Talks About Life on Sapelo Island, Georgia* (2000) recognized her mother in the photograph and remembered her parents talking about the conditions under which the picture was taken. She explained that her mother was walking from Raccoon Bluff, carrying her sister Ada, to their home in a section of the island known as Belle Marsh.[67] Bailey said that a despised island manager, whom she called "Cap'n Frank," drove Moore around the island that day.[68] They encountered Hettie Walker on the road, talked to her for a while, and asked to take her picture. Hettie Walker, powerless to refuse or protest, posed for Moore's photograph. Later the family learned that the picture was published in *National Geographic Magazine*.

Had Hettie Walker or Emma and Emmitt Johnson refused to pose for Moore's photographs, they would have surely offended Howard Coffin's guest and risked being counted among the small group of Islanders who Coffin determined could not be trusted.[69] For Emmitt Johnson, such an infraction could have resulted in the loss of his job. Virtually all of Howard Coffin's guests were "important people," and the Islanders had no reason to believe that Moore was not equally important. After all, Coffin's previous guests included Presidents Coolidge and Hoover, Henry Ford, and Charles Lindbergh. Joe Johnson described Moore as a "big shot" and explained that when the "big boss'[s]" guests approached Sapelo Islanders, blacks were obligated to comply with their requests.[70] In the case of Emmitt and Emma Johnson, Hettie Walker, and the other Sapelo Islanders captured in Moore's lens, the consequence of their acquiescence was that they were either depicted as relics, painted as exotic, or mocked.

Nonetheless, the *National Geographic Magazine* subscribers who opened the February 1934 edition, and the readers who paid fifty cents to purchase the publication at shops and newsstands, eager to encounter the "other" in dramatic text and rich photos, were undoubtedly satisfied. The edition featured an article on Ecuador and an essay titled "A Native Son's Rambles in Oregon": both displayed numerous photographs of "Indians" and descriptions of their lifestyles and rituals. In the last article, readers discovered authentic Sea Island folk and their strange African rites among the thirty-six photographs in W. Robert Moore's article. Although a copy of the family portrait that Moore photographed hung in the Johnsons' home, their children do not know if their parents ever saw the magazine, or if they ever read the article in which they were immortalized.

The Sapelo Islanders featured in Moore's article had no control over how they were represented. While they posed for photographs, they had, at best, a vague understanding of the fact that the photographs might be published. But they were completely unaware of Moore's intent to characterize them as exotic, primitive oddities. The ability to represent oneself (or engage in impression management) and the ability to represent others is a form of power. Even though the Johnsons had tried to represent themselves as a respectable, modern family, they were ultimately powerless against Moore's written interpretation of them and their community. During the 1920s and 1930s, American racism took many forms. The Sapelo Islanders featured in Moore's article fell prey to an American racist tradition of whites representing blacks in ways that reinforced popular ideas about black inferiority.

"Miz Parrish's Negroes": Hunting Slave Songs of the Georgia Sea Islands

The Johnsons also had to endure the curiosities of another one of Howard Coffin's guests, Lydia Parrish, who featured them in yet another published work that depicted them according to the dictates of an outsider's imagination. When Lydia Parrish, the wife of famed artist Maxfield Parrish, showed up on their doorstep hunting for slave songs, the Johnsons never imagined that the encounter would result in their being discussed in Parrish's book *Slave Songs of the Georgia Sea Islands* (1942).[71] Indeed, they never saw the book.

Lydia Parrish spent more than twenty-five years collecting slave songs and organizing slave song performances throughout coastal Georgia.[72] She used her friendship with Howard Coffin to gain access to the blacks who lived on Sapelo Island.[73] One of Emma and Emmitt Johnson's sons, Ronister Johnson, remembered Lydia Parrish and recalled an occasion when she organized a group of elderly black Sapelo men to sing for Howard Coffin at the "big house," but he did not know about his family's presence in her book.[74] Yet they were included in Parrish's study — a study that she hoped would definitively connect black musical performance on the Georgia coast to African religious, cultural, and musical traditions.

Lydia Parrish's interest in uncovering connections between coastal Georgia blacks and their African progenitors was more complex than was W. Robert Moore's fascination with black living relics. Whereas Moore's exploration of blacks in the region was an extension of his larger mission as a *National Geographic Magazine* staff man, Parrish hoped to uncover and preserve familiar expressions of what she believed to be black-African culture. Her initial attraction to "slave songs" was ignited during her childhood in a Quaker community south of Philadelphia, where ex-slaves and their descendants outnumbered whites "19-to-1."[75] Parrish had fond memories of the "descendants of slaves and ex-slaves" who "were the only singers" in the community.[76] Quaker abolitionists had attracted a community of blacks, whom Parrish described as "a singing race," into their midst, which animated their otherwise quiet community with music.[77] The slave songs that Parrish heard echoing from the kitchen and the fields in her home community touched a part of her that she believed Victorian strictures had suppressed. She remembered that the Quakers did not try to "curb" what she understood as blacks' innate "musical exuberance" because "perhaps, with them as with me, the Negro's music filled a real need."[78] From the earliest years in Parrish's racial socialization, she learned that the black people who operated on the periphery of her world served whites literally and figuratively: they held the key to a musical gift that brought them a joy that civilized culture denied them. So, when she first visited Georgia's coast in 1909 and heard the slave songs again, she vowed to capture as much of her childhood joy as she could.[79]

In 1912, three years after Lydia Parrish's first visit to Georgia's coast, she began wintering on St. Simons Island.[80] Despite the fact that her famous husband Maxfield Parrish did not often join his wife during her trips to St. Simons Island, her status as the wife of a prolific American artist put her in social proximity to Howard Coffin and the other rich whites who wintered and lived on Georgia's coast.[81] And as Lydia Parrish acquainted herself with whites in the area, she remained curious about the black people who lived there.

At first she was disturbed by their "stillness."[82] The lack of musical exuberance among St. Simons' blacks troubled her because it seemed that the natural link between blacks and their inherited African essence, which was most clearly articulated in musical expression, had been artificially disrupted. Parrish quickly uncovered the disruptive influence responsible for the "stillness": "the island was a summer resort, and contact with city whites and their black servants had had its numbing influence" on local blacks.[83] After what Parrish described as "three musically barren winters," she discovered a few older blacks who remembered "the old songs," and she found that if she offered enough money, they would sing them for her.[84]

By 1915, Lydia Parrish had begun her career as an amateur folklorist and cultural preservationist. She busied herself collecting slave songs and organizing slave song performances. She spent hours listening to local blacks singing and wrote out each song's lyrics and recorded their melodies by hand.[85] Parrish was the first white woman to collect slave songs in coastal Georgia, but she was not the first white American who attempted to document this type of American music. Her work would contribute to a large repository of slave songs that had been collected by whites.[86] Even though whites initiated the first wave of interest in collecting slave songs in the 1850s, by 1925, New Negroes, such as James Weldon Johnson and J. Rosamond Johnson, inspired by Alain Locke's call to record "black folk" traditions, took up the task of documenting slave songs.[87]

Lydia Parrish and Susyanna. From Lydia Parrish,
Slave Songs of the Georgia Sea Islands
© 1992 *University of Georgia Press.*

Parrish was inspired by the black intelligentsia who called for researchers and writers to dig up the black African past, and she cites a talk that Carter G. Woodson gave as a source of inspiration.[88] Her slave song collection was influenced by both the old tradition of white sentimentalism about the "glorious plantation days" and the new interest expressed by whites and blacks in black folklife, black folk music, and its African roots. As a result, both of these influences are evident in her descriptions of people and the songs she collected.

As Lydia Parrish's tenure as a slave song collector and cultural preservationist progressed, she crafted new meanings for the slave songs that she loved within the context of the African survivals discourse of the 1930s. While Lydia Parrish acknowledged that many of the slave songs that she adored were grounded in the American Christian tradition, her fascination with Melville Herskovits's theories on African survivals inspired her to examine the African character of the slave songs that she collected.[89] Fifteen years into her career as a preservationist, folklorist, and collector, Lydia Parrish began a relentless quest to prove that the slave songs she collected and the ring shout performances she observed were definitive evidence of African survivals in America. However, like Moore's, Parrish's view of the Islanders' African background and its continuing influence on black life mirrored popular characterizations of southern black folklife.

But Parrish claimed to disavow such influences, choosing instead to see herself as one of few whites who hunted for scientific proof of black people's connection to African culture. Parrish scorned white "self-seeking collectors" who simply gathered black cultural material for its exotic commercial appeal.[90] She aggressively pursued a relationship with Melville Herskovits and sought out his advice in order to avoid being counted among the list of collectors who presented blacks as primitive oddities to be exploited and explored.

Lydia Parrish and Melville Herskovits exchanged more than one hundred and fifty pages of correspondences between 1936 and 1942.[91] She relied heavily on Herskovits's formulations about African survivals and syncretism to make sense of the slave songs she collected, and Herskovits sent Parrish literature, graduate students, and advice about how she should approach establishing a connection between Africa and coastal Georgia blacks.[92] Parrish considered Herskovits to be an invaluable resource. While she had studied and taught art, she was "not a scientist" and had no background in anthropology or music, and prior to beginning her collection of slave songs she was only "vaguely aware" of a connection between black and African culture.[93]

Even though Parrish was admittedly insecure about her lack of knowledge about anthropology, Africa, and black history, she took pride in the fact that she knew "Negroes." In fact, she believed that *knowing* blacks gave her a unique advantage over other whites who collected black folk music. She was outraged when Laura Boulton, a seasoned white folk music collector who had collected in Africa, suggested that she was not well suited to study the African roots of black music because she had little knowledge of Africa. She was insulted by the fact that Boulton "could not imagine that I knew anything about Afro-American music."[94] But Parrish believed that her lifelong proximity to blacks provided her insights into black life and culture that superseded even the way that blacks understood their own folkways. Parrish admired Herskovits's work because she believed, as a result of her own encounters with blacks, that his conclusions were accurate: "The greater part of my life I have lived as close to Negroes as white people.... Your work ... rings true according to my experience."[95]

Her experience remained paramount to her research on Georgia's coast and shaped the way that she imagined African survivals. Even with Herskovits's influence and advice, Parrish contrived a view of black culture and African survivals that was largely the product of her own perceptions about black people. Her conceptualization of African survivals hinged on discounting black people's understandings of their traditions and privileging her own assessment of a persistent, undying African essence in black communities. This tendency is best illustrated in Parrish's quest to establish antebellum "slave night funerals" as a survival of an older African tradition. Even though Parrish focused her energies on collecting slave songs, she also took interest in all aspects of black folklife on the coast. When Parrish inquired about the prevalence of night funerals among slaves in coastal Georgia, a local historian told her that slaves' night funerals "grew out of conditions arising from epidemics," and local blacks said slaves had night funerals "because their masters would not let them use daylight-work time" to bury their dead.[96] But Parrish did not accept these explanations because she recalled reading somewhere that "negro funerals" were held at night and that pine knots were thrown in graves, so that "the dead man . . . could not find his way home in the dark." Even though she could not recall exactly where she read it, she was sure "such a notion prevailed among certain African tribes."[97]

In this instance Herskovits encouraged Parrish's loose assertion. He admitted that he did not "know about night funerals," but also remembered that he had read something similar in a "passage somewhere" and told Parrish that his "feeling would be that they are African."[98] He pointed to the fact that West African funerals were held at sundown to connect the practice to Africa.[99] Parrish was not satisfied with the explanation that ex-slaves gave her: "Our masters wouldn't let us take daylight from our work."[100] She dismissed black informants' explanations and concluded that it was "pure nonsense."[101] She discounted their explanation because she believed that it was "too much like the information the abolitionists swallowed whole" about cruel slave masters.[102]

Parrish's insistence that "night funerals" were derived from an African practice despite all evidence to the contrary reveals the flimsiness of her African survivals formulations. Like Moore, Parrish inserted African characteristics into black practices with or without evidence of any kind. While vestiges of African cultural traits could be found in black communities throughout the nation, African survivals hunters like Parrish fixated on a version of African folklife that was the substance of popular films, novels, and other stories about primitive blackness.

For example, Parrish's characterization of slave songs was consistent with the eerie, haunting quality of black voodoo that permeated popular culture during the period. She believed that the songs themselves had an "almost human will to live."[103] She explained, "Frequently persons, who have heard the singers the night before, telephone for the words of a song. The tune haunts them, but without the verses they cannot give it expression." She claimed to have "suffered in the same fashion, and been obliged in self-defense to learn the songs." When she complained to her black cook Julia about the way that slave songs tormented her, Julia told Parrish that "they do us that way too, until we learn them."[104] Even though Parrish believed that blacks were most susceptible to the powerful influence of slave songs, the African spiritual power that lived in black music could possess even whites: "These songs have no regard for color."[105]

Parrish also believed that African survivals were both biologically and spiritually bound to black bodies. Throughout her writings, she articulates a very specific calculation of black "musical exuberance." She maintains that Africans (and blacks) posses an innate understanding of rhythm and music, whereas white music was taught and cultivated, and concentrated on melody and musicality.[106] According to Parrish's logic, blacks' musicality was akin to a natural emotional release, while white musical expression was the product of conscious intellectual effort and hard work. To some extent, Parrish appears to have believed that enslaved people's ability to fuse African musical styles with the music of colonial planters reflected great skill and sophistication.[107] Yet she concluded that this feat was achieved because of enslaved Africans innate "remarkable musical gift and deeply religious nature."[108]

While Parrish concluded that African survivals were most pronounced among blacks on Georgia's coast, she believed that they could be found in the music and dances of black people across the nation. In her slave song study, she instructed whites interested in observing African survivals to look to "a Negro community on or near your property." "All you need do (provided you live in a remote district and are generous with your silver)," she explained, "is to let it be known that you wish to see such solo dances as the 'Buzzard Lope,' 'Juba' ... (accompanied by an occasional exclamation of 'Slap 'em! Slap 'em')—and they may be forthcoming."[109] Her instructions reveal her assumptions about the power that whites have over blacks: she assumed a landlord-tenant relationship between whites and blacks who live close to one another and was confident that if the right amount of money were offered, blacks would freely perform for whites.

Similarly, racial assumptions also structured the way Parrish understood, identified, and characterized African practices. In exploring the origin of the ring shout tradition among coastal Georgia blacks, Parrish rationalized her theory that ring shouts were derived from African practices with sweeping generalizations about the continent's peoples, which cast all Africans as a homogeneous, static group. "Those who have traveled in Africa, and have seen native dancing, are convinced that the shout of the American Negro is nothing more than a survival of an African tribal dance," she wrote, before explaining "that the accompanying chants in their form and melody are quite as typical of Africa as the dance itself."[110] Ironically, although underlain with ill-informed generalizations about Africa, Parrish's writings about the ring shout may prove to be the most significant documentation of the ring shout tradition (a potential African survival) on the Georgia coast.[111]

Despite her ignorance about African cultures and stereotypical readings of black life, Lydia Parrish managed to preserve and capture a noteworthy repository of the black folk music of coastal Georgia. Parrish did not consider her whiteness to be an obstacle in her mission to collect and preserve; instead she embraced the notion that her whiteness positioned her to achieve her goal. Parrish's romantic racialist tendencies encouraged her to believe that the very racial hierarchy that determined that whites were superior to blacks could be invoked to encourage blacks to embrace their African past. Parrish romanticized "slavery days" and despised abolitionists who, she argued, "did the Negroes no good service when they taught them to believe that they had been unjustly treated."[112] Believing that slaves where better off than poor whites, she held a fantasy of slave life that was populated by kind, generous, paternalistic masters and blacks who looked to their masters for approval. Consequently, Parrish argued that restoring esteem to the performance of slave songs required that blacks and whites assume the roles that they would have occupied as masters and slaves in the antebellum South.

She explained that "the rural Negro has always taken his cue from the white folks at the 'Big House.'"[113] "If they favor and enjoy the slave songs, it may be that he is not so far wrong after all, in cherishing his heritage in the face of jeers from the style leaders of his community."[114] Parrish insisted that all whites had to do in order to help save slave songs from extinction was follow the example set by whites like Howard Coffin, the "Big Boss of Sapelo Island," and "allow the Negroes to provide entertainment in the manner that was usual on many antebellum estates."[115] (Coffin frequently hosted slave song performances for white audiences at his Cloister Hotel.) Parrish also suggested that affluent whites could use their economic power over poor blacks and offer money in exchange for the performance of slave songs to avert the extinction of the performance style.[116] During the Great Depression, this particular strategy worked well for Parrish's purposes when "some of the singers literally sang for their supper."[117]

Lydia Parrish had devised, according to her logic, a perfect system for collecting slave songs and promoting their performance, but she complained that her intervention efforts were frequently threatened and undermined. One of the greatest obstacles to her collection and preservation efforts was what she understood to be black people's innate "secretiveness." She argued that blacks' secretiveness had caused whites' "ignorance of the race." She declared that blacks' secretive nature was "probably an African survival"; she cited Herskovits's research in Dutch Guiana—during which he was told by a "Bush Negro" that "our ancestors taught us that it is unwise to tell anyone more than half of what he knows about anything"—as evidence of the trait's African origin.[118] Parrish's own cook Julia hid her knowledge of slave songs from Parrish for fifteen years before she discovered that Julia knew many of the songs that she had hunted since the two first met.[119] Parrish concluded that Julia, like all of the other blacks she encountered on Georgia's coast, took pleasure in "knowing something that the white man does not," and contrary to dominant white opinion, blacks were not ignorant, but were smart tricksters, and "like their African cousins," they were "born actors."[120]

While coastal Georgia blacks' "secretiveness" constantly stifled Parrish's efforts, she considered "Negro school teachers" to be the greatest threat to the survival of slave songs. She wrote, "Negro school teachers . . . do their utmost to discredit and uproot every trace of it. Instead of being proud of their race's contribution to the world . . . too many of them treat it like a family skeleton."[121] As far as Parrish was concerned, "Negro school teachers" undermined coastal Georgia blacks' potential role in American popular culture. She pointed to comments that Carter G. Woodson made in a talk he gave to strengthen her condemnation of black educators. She recalled that Woodson had said that the "American Negro is the victim of traditional teaching in Northern white schools" and as a result has become "a race of imitators" who need study their African background "to come into their own."[122] She was also inspired by the fact that the trends of the 1930s had brought "authentic" black southern musical performance and culture to mainstream audiences. She explained that "the fact [that] Broadway features Negro actors, dancers, and musicians as never before, and that the producers of a Negro opera attempted to teach the Harlem blacks to speak and sing like their primitive Southern cousins," made "clear that this is no time for the race to be disdainful of its African Heritage."[123] The fact that black actors, dancers, and musicians who performed in stage works such as H. Lawrence Freeman's 1928 opera *Voodoo*, had learned to "sing and speak like their primitive Southern cousins," signaled to Parrish that the moment had arrived for black coastal Georgians to declare their uniqueness, to cash in on, and embrace, their innate racial talents—not treat them like family skeletons.

Parrish also worried that self-seeking collectors would steal her black performers and their songs from her. Yes, other folk song collectors hunted black music on Georgia's coast. Robert Winslow Gordon, the now celebrated folk song collector who maintained a post at the Library of Congress, spent several years in Darien, the city on the mainland across from Sapelo, collecting folk songs during the 1920s.[124] Parrish and Gordon probably crossed paths.[125] She never mentioned Gordon in her letters to Herskovits, and there is no indication that he spent time on Sapelo, but his nearness to the music and people that she claimed ownership of validates her paranoia. She was livid when Zora Neale Hurston and her traveling and collecting companion, Alan Lomax, came to Georgia's coast in pursuit of folklore material. She complained to Herskovits about their invasion of her territory and wrote that they "tried to swipe my material from under my very eyes" when they attempted to get a hold of a young St. Simons singer whom she had trained for years.[126]

Even in Lydia Parrish's perception of the obstacles that she faced, a great deal is revealed about the racial views that shaped her understanding of the material and people she collected. Like Moore, who imagined a romantic world on Georgia's coast, Parrish saw the region as a site of peaceful and harmonious black-white encounters. The Jim Crow hierarchy, and all of the oppression and violence that bolstered it, were not realities in her vision of coastal Georgia. Instead, Parrish read black people's "secretiveness" and reluctance to talk to and sing for her as evidence of an inner African impulse. She was wholly unaware that, for blacks, "secrets" and limited communication with whites functioned as a defense mechanism against white violence. One Sapelo Islander remembered that while growing up on the island during the 1930s, she had been all too aware that "getting involved" with white people was dangerous. She said: "Back in them days they'll kill you if you get involved with white people."[127] Interracial interaction, she explained, could lead black people to "forget their place," and trouble was sure to follow. Incidents like the lynchings of George Grant in 1930 and Curtis James in 1934 in nearby Darien, Georgia, the mainland community just across the water from Sapelo Island, no doubt fostered blacks' fears about the dangers of interracial mingling.[128]

Parrish's disdain for "Negro school teachers" also speaks to the extent to which she misunderstood the people and the cultural world that she so desperately wanted to preserve. While New Negro intellectuals called for studies on black folk culture, and Carter G. Woodson most certainly advocated for blacks to gain greater knowledge of their history, New Negro intelligentsia also advocated for academic achievement among blacks as a tool to challenge dominant ideas about black inferiority. Parrish embraced the New Negro call for the collection and preservation of black folk material and African history, but she did not understand that this material was important to the New Negroes because it provided a basis on which they could identify themselves as "modern" relative to their folk past and foster race pride. Contrary to New Negroes' goals, Parrish's cultural preservation interventions hoped to revive antebellum black-white relationships relative to slave songs and their performances.

Parrish's paranoia about collectors like Zora Neale Hurston and Alan Lomax encroaching on her research can be partially attributed to tensions between competing collectors, but the ownership claims that Parrish staked on the black singers who performed for her can also be understood in racial terms. To some extent, Parrish's continuous declaration that the groups of singers that she directed, recorded, and booked for performances belonged to her was a natural outgrowth of the fact that she was their manager. Yet, when Parrish's constant iterations that the black singers were "her Negroes" is read in the context of her idealized view of slave masters' relationships with their slaves, a more troubling picture of their relationship emerges.

Ultimately, Lydia Parrish's shaky African survivals formulations, her fantasies about the good old plantation days, and her fascination with primitive blacks shaped the way she interpreted the people and folk culture that she encountered on Georgia's coast. In each black community that she frequented over the course of two decades, Parrish believed that she found confirmation of her theories about the continuity of African culture in black communities in the region. Like Moore, Parrish chose Sapelo Island as one of her favorite African survivals hunting sites. St. Simons Island—the place where Parrish spent winters—had been connected to the mainland by a four-mile causeway since 1924. But Sapelo Island remained reachable only by ferry, which added to the illusion of the Islanders' distance from modernity. The fact that Coffin restricted access to his private seasonal paradise also intensified the air of mystery that shrouded the island's black residents. And Parrish reveled in the fact that she could examine and interrogate the descendants of Thomas Spalding's slaves, especially because she had been told that Spalding had many "green hands from Africa," some of whom "were cannibals" who sometimes escaped and "made trouble."[129] For Parrish, the possibility that wild Africans—just like the Africans who filled the jungles in Edgar Rice Burroughs's Tarzan novels—had left an imprint on the blacks who lived on Sapelo represented a rare opportunity to explore authentic African survivals.

Over the years, Parrish cultivated relationships with two elderly black Sapelo Islanders who gave her just the sort of information that she dreamed would be uncovered on the island. Despite the fact that Parrish complained to Herskovits that a "veneer of sophistication" had settled on the island in the years since Coffin first "took it," disguising the island's and the people's primitive orientation, the time that she spent with Katie Brown and Shad Hall made her confident that "if the surface is scratched you get the real material."[130] Katie Brown was one of the island's midwives, and Shad Hall was a trusted herbalist, and the two were cousins. Believing that older blacks were more attached to the "old ways," Parrish eagerly asked Hall and Brown to sing old slave songs, but she also asked them about voodoo, roots, and conjure practices. Brown admitted she knew little of the practices Parrish inquired about, but she offered Parrish cemetery rituals designed to ward off ghosts and remedies for fighting off "hags" who tormented sleepers.[131] Parrish wrote about Brown and Hall many times in letters to Herskovits, and she even told him that Brown had said something about "dyin'-bed makers" that made her theory about the African origins of slave night funerals more plausible.[132]

But it was Brown's and Hall's memories of their African-born ancestor, the famed Muslim Bilali Mohammed, that captured Parrish's interest, distracted her from her song-collecting mission, and sent her on a quest to track down his Arabic diary for transcription. Almost as soon as Parrish began writing Melville Herskovits, she told him about Brown's and Hall's stories about "Old Bilaly," his prayer rug and beads, and the way that Bilali and his wife "got down flat" during prayers and prepared rice balls to eat after fasting. She promised to secure a photostatic copy of parts of the diary so that Herskovits could transcribe it.[133] Herskovits agreed to help Parrish unearth the diary's origin and content, and assigned a doctoral student, Joseph Greenberg, to the task.[134] Herskovits valued the diary as a potential source of important details about African slaves and Africa, but Parrish prized it for Bilali Mohammed himself—whose African religion and Sapelo Island descendants lent an undeniable African authenticity to the region.

To Parrish's credit, her push to have Mohammed's journal transcribed resulted in the first published translation of the diary. After consulting scholars on both sides of the Atlantic, and taking copies of the diary to Nigeria where it was shown to native scholars, Greenberg concluded that previous theories that claimed the book contained the slave driver's plantation records were wrong.[135] Greenberg discovered that Bilali Mohammed had tried to reproduce what he remembered of the religious instruction he received as a young student somewhere in northwest Africa and wrote it in the leather-bound book.[136] Misspellings, errors, and unreadable passages in Mohammed's diary did not hide the fact that the book had meaning that extended far beyond the silly "pothooks" that Joel Chandler Harris fantasized about in his fictional representation of the journal.

Lydia Parrish's interest in Katie Brown, Shad Hall, and their African ancestors is clear, but understanding why Brown and Hall entertained Parrish's curiosities is less self-evident. In America in the twenties and thirties, anyone acquainted with Julia Peterkin's fiction would have assumed Sapelo's midwife and herbalist, similar to Blue Brook Plantation's Maum Hannah and Daddy Cudjoe, were the guardians of genuine folk practices. But Brown and Hall had their own reasons for entertaining Lydia Parrish's and other researchers' inquiries. Sapelo Islanders had always sought Brown and Hall out for information and advice. For years, black women on Sapelo Island looked to Katie Brown to provide prenatal care, deliver their children, and help them tend to their newborn babies. Similarly, Islanders consulted Shad Hall for healing remedies and

herbal medicines largely because they had little money for, and limited access to, mainland doctors.[137] Brown and Hall had always served as repositories of knowledge, and even though they were confronted with new white and black visitors from the mainland during the 1930s—visitors who asked Hall and Brown different questions from the ones that they had grown accustomed to— they remained poised to perform their usual duties. Brown and Hall may have even interpreted the new interest that Coffin's guests and other researchers and writers expressed in their knowledge of the past and the stories that they told as recognition of their position as respected elders among the Islanders. More-over, the interactions between these two elderly black informants and Lydia Parrish were, of course, shaped by Jim Crow customs. Even if they did not want to answer Parrish's questions, they would have had to carefully craft their response to her inquiries so as not to offend her. They could have used the same strategy that Parrish's cook Julia employed and pretended not to have known the answers to her questions. But this strategy would have required Hall and Brown to deny the very source of their esteem in the community—their knowledge. Instead, they became the most documented Sapelo Islanders featured in published works.

Not all Sapelo Islanders volunteered to participate in Parrish's survival study. The Johnson family can be counted among the list of unsuspecting coastal Georgia folk who unknowingly became research subjects featured in Parrish's book. Like the other coastal Georgia blacks discussed in Parrish's study, the Johnsons, and the songs that they shared, would be presented as evidence used to bolster her tenuous African survival theories. During Parrish's first visit to the Johnson home, she convinced Emma and Emmitt Johnson's twins, Naomi and Isaac, to perform what Parrish called an "African pantomime."[138] Naomi and Isaac performed "Throw Me Anywhere," a children's song-dance game during which "one lay on the floor . . . representing a dead cow," and another participant "called out cues in a sharp staccato," and the other participant mimics a buzzard.[139] Parrish noted that Naomi "did the patting while Isaac did the dancing." Parrish recorded the song:

> March aroun' (the cow)
> Jump across! (see if she's daid)
> Get the eye! (always go for that first)
> So glad! (cow daid)
> Get the guts! (they like 'em next best)
> Go to eatin'! (on the meat)
> All right-cow mos' gone!
> Dog comin'!
> Scare the dog!
> Look aroun' for mo' meat!
> All right!—Belly full!
> Goin to tell the res.[140]

Parrish did not explain how Naomi and Isaac's song and dance qualified as an African survival, but, like Moore, she ascribed African characteristics to it anyway. While there is no direct link between the song and Africa, there is a link between the song and slavery. It is likely that the song/dance was a "survival" of a black critique of race-power dynamics from the antebellum era. Sapelo Islander Cornelia Bailey presents a compelling analysis of the meaning and performance of buzzard-prey song/dances—an interpretation that varies greatly from Parrish's conclusion that the song was simply an "African pantomime." In her book *God, Dr. Buzzard, and the Bolito Man* (2000), Bailey linked the "Buzzard Lope" dance and similar song/dance performances to racial oppression.[141] When writing about the time that she witnessed her father and his friends performing the mournful dance, she explains, "There's a story that goes with the dance and it's from the days of slavery." She writes, "When the people who were enslaved had a hard taskmaster ... and they were working in the fields, in the sun, in the summertime, and the heat got to someone ... and he fell over dead in the field.... The master wouldn't let the workers stop.... But a whole day in August was a lifetime, and the buzzards came, and they circled around, and the head buzzard came in and checked out the prey and the other buzzards joined him, and they started their natural thing of cleaning up the earth."[142]

Bailey's story about slaves worked to death and eaten by buzzards as they lay dead in the field because cruel slave masters would not allow blacks to bury their dead before the work was done is jarring. Bailey's version of plantation life bears no resemblance to the romantic plantation that Lydia Parrish imagined. Furthermore, Parrish outright rejected the idea that most slave masters were cruel, and even argued that the idea was a fiction created by abolitionists. Bailey concludes that the Sapelo men performing the dance "might take turns acting the part of the buzzard in that dance but they weren't the buzzard. They were the prey. Black people had been bossed around ... and picked on ever since we got here."[143] According to Bailey's interpretation, Isaac and Naomi had learned more than a children's song/dance, they had learned the grim realities of black life and death and had been introduced to the relationship between the "prey" and "the hunter"—a dynamic that was all too present in the lives of black Sapelo Islanders. Lydia Parrish, the survivals hunter, never attempted to analyze the metaphors and symbolism of the song lyrics that she collected. Instead, she clung to her fantasies about black primitive life and presented the Johnson twins' performance as evidence of an enduring African character among Sapelo Islanders. In the same way that she missed the true meaning of "Throw Me Anywhere," she also missed the critical message about Coffin and the power that he and his comrades had over blacks in "Pay Me My Money Down."

Parrish visited the Johnson house a second time and also wrote about it in her book. While Parrish's description of her second visit to the Johnsons was not used to prove the black-African connection, it does underscore the way that her fantasies skewed her perception of her research subjects and the realities of their lives. In describing the cause for her second visit, she wrote: "In hunting up Emma Johnson's twins, I came upon such a picture as must have been common in plantation days."[144] Parrish romantically described the scene that took her imagination back to the antebellum days: "Under the immense live oaks, two boys were beating rice in a home-made mortar. Chickens were all about, picking up stray grains. A couple of fanners were on the ground ready to fan rice as soon as the hulls were loosened in the mortar. Emma was thrifty, and the rice hulls—which looked like bran—fell on oilcloth laid on the ground. She told me they were to be fed to the pigs."[145]

Parrish's sentimental view of "plantation days" relative to Emma Johnson's and her children's performance of taxing mundane chores reflects the way that she completely imagined her subjects according to her own fantasies. During the 1920s and 1930s, the poverty and hardships that plagued black rural life was exotic and intriguing. For Emma Johnson, the "picture" that Parrish encountered at the Johnson house was a snapshot into her daily struggle to feed her family, and what Parrish noted as Emma Johnson's thriftiness was an essential survival strategy. Parrish's description of Emma Johnson and her children's work reflects the bourgeois luxury of "appreciating" the simple life of those who live "close to nature." During this visit to the Johnson family, the Johnson boys were "shamed" and stopped singing when Parrish arrived, so Emma Johnson, steeped in work, sang for her. It would have been hard for Emma Johnson to refuse Parrish's request. Parrish, like other guests of Howard Coffin who toured the island's black hammock communities, was most likely escorted by one of Coffin's island managers—this likelihood was even greater for a white woman traveling alone. The Johnsons depended on Coffin for work, and shunning one of his guests' requests could cause trouble for the couple. So, Emma Johnson sang for Parrish as she pounded rice in a pestle and unwittingly contributed three songs to Lydia Parrish's slave song collection.[146] One of the songs she sang for Parrish, "Hard Time in Ole Virginny," recalled the agonies of bondage and yearnings for freedom, realities that Parrish had discounted as inauthentic among blacks enslaved on picturesque antebellum plantations: "My ole missus promise me ... when she die she set me free.... She live so long ... her head got bald."[147]

In the end, Parrish's misconceptions about black culture and life in coastal Georgia, and elsewhere, did not stop one of the most influential black intellectuals during the period from praising her efforts. Carter G. Woodson published a glowing review of Slave Songs in the Journal of Negro History when the manuscript was published in 1942.[148] In the same way that so many members of the New Negro intelligentsia praised Peterkin's stories, overlooking troubling racial characterizations and focusing instead on more promising elements of her tales, Woodson commended every hopeful feature of Parrish's book. He wrote that she had made great strides in sincerely examining coastal Georgia blacks' connection to their African forebears, a feat that was impressive because American scholars "know less about Negroes at their doors than they do about the Brahmins of India."[149] He admired her commitment to earnestly search for clues to the African past and applauded her methods. He wrote, "She lived among these Negroes. . . . She won their confidence by entering into the spirit of what they were doing."[150] Woodson gave Parrish credit for uncovering and making sense of material that other whites had unappreciated, and identified her study as a template for "showing an unwilling world what is necessary to be done to understand these people and their contributions."[151] Predicting that scientists would reject the book's African survival thesis because "White Americans have produced such a little in this sphere that they are anxious to take credit for Negro music since it is now regarded as an outstanding contribution" and because "Negroes cannot achieve great things," he claimed Parrish's study as a triumph.[152] Woodson did not comment on Parrish's formula for restoring slave songs' value among blacks (which involved replicating plantation performances), nor did he address any of Parrish's other thorny assumptions about blacks and Africans in his review. Instead, he sifted through the work, elevating its potential as a source of race pride and appreciating it as an invaluable treasury of black culture.

Lorenzo Dow Turner: The Father of Africanisms in the Gullah Dialect Comes to Sapelo

After many years of collecting folk culture material in coastal Georgia, Lydia Parrish came to think of herself as the gatekeeper to the region, so she carefully monitored all who desired access to "her Negroes." In letters she wrote to Melville Herskovits, she took full credit for granting Lorenzo Dow Turner, a black scholar who studied the Gullah dialect, access to the most authentic subjects that the region had to offer his research efforts. "I know where the more primitive Negroes live," she wrote, and boasted that she saved Turner a great deal of time by locating them for him.[153] Parrish also used her close ties with Howard Coffin and other whites in the area to help Turner gain access to coastal Georgia blacks without arousing suspicion that he had come to agitate "their Negroes."[154]

Yet Parrish remained suspicious about the quality of Turner's work. She considered him "an honest scientist" and found him to be a "reliable person to work with."[155] The two would work together, and she reached out to Turner for help with her own research.[156] She admitted that the Gullah vocabulary that he developed filled a real need for African survivals researchers in the region, but she remarked that his "will-to-believe" was "the only loose screw in his outfit."

She explained that Turner did not know Negroes as well as she did because he did "not recognize that the Negroes closest to Africa tell you what they believe you want to hear."[157]

However, it was Parrish's mistrust of her subjects, and her refusal to accept their explanations for, and understandings of, their cultural life, coupled with her pet theories about black-African primitives, that made her interpretations of African survivals in the region unreliable. She simply did not understand or believe in the fact of black oppression. For example, in a letter to Turner, Parrish described Sapelo's Shad Hall as being "bitter" about his experiences as a slave because "his mistress required 2 tas's [tasks] when only one was customary."[158] The possibility that Hall's bitterness derived from his being held captive never occurred to Parrish. When Parrish's criticisms of Turner are read within the context of her racial views, it is not surprising that she thought herself to be—to some extent—superior to a man who outranked her in scholarly training.

While Parrish may have opened the door for Turner in coastal Georgia, her vague characterization of African survivals in the region did not influence his study. In fact, Turner's research took a dramatic turn away from many of the racial fantasies that permeated Moore's article and Parrish's song collection. His research would produce the only Gullah study involving Sapelo Islanders that presented substantial evidence of links between coastal Georgia blacks and their African progenitors. Turner's book, *Africanisms in the Gullah Dialect* (1949), revolutionized the way that the Gullah dialect was imagined, elevating it from a mark of ignorance and backwardness to profound evidence that African words and linguistic patterns had survived the Middle Passage and slavery.

The fact that Lorenzo Dow Turner was the only black researcher to explore African survivals among coastal Georgia's blacks is significant, and for him, questions of slavery and African survivals took on a different set of meanings than they did for white Gullah researchers.[159] Whereas Moore and Parrish searched for confirmations of the racial characteristics that they had been told were biologically coded in Africans and black Americans, Turner looked to Africa to overturn assumptions about black people's racial character.

Like many other members of the New Negro intelligentsia, Turner struggled to break into the academy. He worked as a waiter and porter to fund his studies and graduated from Howard University in 1910.[160] Turner went on to complete graduate studies at Howard University and the University of Chicago before returning to Howard to take a position as an English professor. While at Howard University, Turner worked closely with Carter G. Woodson.[161] Woodson, the father of black historical studies, encouraged the rescue, reconstruction, and preservation of black history.[162] Naturally, when Turner expressed an interest

Lorenzo Dow Turner. Lorenzo Dow Turner Papers, Anacostia Community Museum Archives, Smithsonian Institution, Gift of Lois Turner Williams.

in exploring the dialect that he heard his students from South Carolina speak to one another to his mentor, Woodson encouraged his curiosity and helped support Turner's first research trip to St. Helena Island, South Carolina.[163]

Turner's preliminary research on St. Helena reinforced his resolve to tackle the Gullah dialect. Shortly after visiting coastal South Carolina, Turner began in-depth training in the field of linguistics. He knew that he had to arm himself with expert linguistics skills in order to refute the prevailing view of the Gullah dialect that dominated scholarly discourse since the publication of the first study about the dialect in 1908. John Bennett, Guy B. Johnson, Ambrose E. Gonzales, H. P. Johnson, Mason Crum, and George Philip Krapp had all argued that the Gullah dialect was a simple form of "baby talk" that developed between white plantation owners and their slaves.[164] These researchers concluded that the distinct speech patterns used by coastal blacks was a mark of their primitiveness and intellectual inferiority. This view is evident in Ambrose Gonzales's writings on Gullah folklore: "Slovenly and careless of speech," the "Gullah seized upon the peasant English used by some of the early settlers and by the white servants of the wealthier colonists, wrapped their clumsy tongues about it as well as they could, and enriched it with certain African words." Gonzales surmised that black people's "flat noses and thick lips" were equally responsible for "Negro speech of the lower districts of South Carolina and Georgia."[165] He insisted that coastal blacks "seem to have picked from the mouths of their African brothers not a single jungle-word for the enrichment of their own speech."[166]

Turner, by contrast, was convinced that the Gullah dialect included a vocabulary drawn from several West African languages. To prove this, he studied at a linguistics institute at the City University of New York during the 1930s, during the months when he did not have to teach classes at Fisk University.[167] There he learned the phonetic alphabet and transcription methods and gained research skills that transformed him from an English professor to linguistics expert. Despite the fact that Turner had trouble securing funding for his study, he was eventually awarded research funds from a linguistics award that enabled him to begin fieldwork in coastal Georgia and South Carolina in the spring of 1932.[168]

While Lydia Parrish's and Lorenzo Dow Turner's interest in and view of African survivals were very different, Turner shared Parrish's anxiety about the time-sensitive nature of Gullah research. Both researchers wanted to capture the essence of a people they believed were vanishing. Whereas Parrish worried that education would erode her subjects' authenticity, Turner feared that the dialect would soon become extinct as a result of Islanders' and coastal blacks' increased contact with the "modern world." He explained the urgency of his work in a research proposal: "Even though their speech, which is unique among the dialects of the country, has undergone little or no change since the seventeenth century, such a condition cannot long obtain, for contact with the outside world [facilitated by] modern means of transportation" ensured that the "distinctive characteristics of these people and their speech" would gradually disappear.[169] Even though Turner rejected many of the primitivist ideas about the black-African connection that Moore and Parrish embraced, he shared their belief that the Gullah were a relic of the past. He also shared their belief that coastal blacks were isolated and cut off from the modern world. Turner's conclusion that Islanders' speech had "undergone little or no change since the seventeenth century" is evidence of his belief that Gullah folk were stuck in an earlier time. He was convinced that modernity threatened to destroy the Gullah. Yet he hoped that if he moved quickly, his study would reveal a significant connection between the Gullah dialect and several West African languages.

Since Turner believed that the sole quality that made coastal South Carolina and Georgia blacks unique was endangered, he aggressively pursued funding for his research from several organizations. The urgency of Turner's proposal won him an award. He spent the spring of 1932 and the summer of 1933 and 1934 in South Carolina and Georgia. In South Carolina, he collected linguistic samples from Edisto Island, Johns Island, St. Helena Island, Hilton Head, Wadmalaw Island, Bluffton, Cordesville, Pinckney Island, Sandy Island, and Georgetown.[170] In Georgia, he collected samples from Harris Neck and Brewer's Neck, St. Simons Island, St. Marys, Darien, and Sapelo Island.[171] Turner traveled with a thirty-pound electric recorder and, in most locations, he sought out black community leaders to act as intermediaries.[172]

True to his charge as a trained scholar, Turner attempted to devise a research strategy that would avoid the biases and sentimentality regarding race that plagued most Gullah researchers. To ensure that he gathered the most "pure" linguistic samples, Turner had very specific criteria for his informants in each locale: "At least three informants," two of whom had to be "above sixty years of age and one between forty and sixty. Both sexes represented, with one exception all of the informants were natives of their respective communities. Their parents were also natives."[173] For the interviews, Turner developed a highly systematic method of gathering Gullah linguistic samples: he organized a worksheet patterned after those used by the Linguistic Atlas of the United States and Canada.[174]

At first glance, Turner's plan appeared to be devoid of the cultural motivations that tainted most Gullah studies. But Turner could not avoid the allure of the kind of folk material that had become so trendy during the 1920s and 1930s. The phonograph recordings that he made included samples in which subjects gave autobiographical sketches, narratives of religious experiences (prayers and sermons), religious and secular songs, folktales, proverbs, superstitions, descriptions of living conditions on the Sea Islands, recollections of slavery, systems of counting, methods of planting and harvesting crops, and cooking.[175] And he dedicated a section in the summary of his findings to Gullah words for "religion, magic, and superstition," like "vudu" and "hudu."[176] Perhaps Turner surmised that if the Gullah had in fact retained their African progenitors' spiritual and cultural traditions, then a discussion of these practices would yield the greatest number of West African linguistic correlates. Ultimately, he had formulated a system through which he could collect and document the sort of historical and folk material that New Negro scholars like Carter G. Woodson believed to be invaluable, while also gathering dialect samples that might actually verify the presence of African retentions.

Clearly, Turner's scholarly training gave him an advantage over the other African survivals researchers who came to Sapelo, but the fact that he was black also aided his research. Turner believed that his blackness helped him elicit raw material from his subjects. In his study, he wrote about the negative reaction that one of his subjects had when he brought a white colleague along on an interview. He recalled that his colleague "unintentionally used a tone of voice which the informant resented" and explained that "instantly, the interview ended. Apologies were of no avail. The informant refused to utter another word."[177] When Turner returned to the Sea Islands several weeks later, he reported: "I was confronted on every hand with this question . . . 'Why did you bring the white man?'"[178] It is likely that many coastal Georgia blacks subverted the Jim Crow hierarchy and avoided Parrish's and Moore's inquiries by feigning ignorance or responding with silence. But, perhaps, for the first time in his life, the racial tension that Jim Crow fueled had helped Turner, and not hindered him.

Even though Turner felt that the Gullah were generally reluctant to talk to white strangers, and wrote that they had become annoyed with people's curiosities about their speech and their lives, he found that his subjects became more comfortable with him over time, and, as a result, they used more African words in his presence.[179] Even though Turner's blackness had helped him earn his subjects' trust, the fact that he was an outsider to their community did present a barrier that he had to work through. Yet his visit to Sapelo Island stood out in Islanders' memories. While most elderly Sapelo Islanders today do not remember Lydia Parrish's visits or her name, they recall that a "learned black man" had come to their community to ask them questions. Sapelo Islander Cornelia Bailey remembered the "old folks" talking about Turner's visit to the island.[180]

When Turner came to Georgia's coast in 1933, he depended on Lydia Parrish for support. Little is known about how the two met, but once they became acquainted, Parrish made arrangements for Turner to conduct interviews and collect shout songs in the building that she built for slave song performances on St. Simons Island.[181] Turner's recording device required reliable electricity, a commodity that few black homes on the Georgia Sea Islands had during the 1930s. For this reason, it is likely that Parrish accompanied Turner on his visit to Sapelo Island and made arrangements for him to use one of Coffin's outbuildings to conduct and record interviews there as well.

Turner recorded interviews with five Sapelo Islanders: Katie Brown, Shad Hall, Tom Lemon, Balaam Walker, and Reverend John Dunham.[182] In addition to the audio recordings that he collected, Turner made biographical notes about each Sapelo informant that documented details about their lives and communities that do not appear in any published work that they were featured in during the 1930s. Turner's notes reveal that Shad Hall was eighty-five when they met; he was twelve or thirteen when the Civil War started; his grandmother spoke French; and unlike many of the Islanders who attended one of the island's two schools after the war, Hall never went to school.[183] His notes on Katie Brown covered similar ground but also included comments on her behavior as a research subject. He wrote that Brown was "quite intelligent," she "attended school until fourth or fifth grade," and she was "serious." Turner's notes also expose the fact that Brown was a clever informant who code-switched and adjusted her demeanor when interacting with researchers: "During interviews her speech is less spontaneous and natural than at other times and she seems inclined to prefer recently acquired pronunciations to those she always used and heard on the Island."[184] He described all of the Sapelo subjects as "fairly intelligent" and wrote that most were "reticent"—none were eager subjects.[185] The idea that "change" was coming to the island, the very anxiety that drove his study, was repeated in Turner's notes. At the end of each biographical sketch, he wrote about the toll that the Great Migration had exacted on the island's communities: "During the past twenty years," the island's "population has steadily decreased."[186]

Brown, Hall, Lemon, Walker, and Dunham told Turner what they remembered about slavery and shared transformative Christian religious experiences; they sang songs and made Christian prayers for Turner's recordings and told Brer Rabbit and Brer Wolf stories.[187] One of the more compelling Sapelo recordings is of Katie Brown sharing her memory of the newly freedmen and freedwomen's return to Sapelo near the end of the Civil War. Brown told Turner that hoards of newly emancipated slaves walked to Savannah, Georgia, to Union headquarters and requested that they be allowed to return to their island homes. Brown said: "And they get a great large boat and put all the people in it and bring them, and put them on the sea coast all along, until they got back to they different homes. And they did promise to give the people they homes, but afterward it was turn back to the owner-master."[188] Brown's memory of General Sherman's failed land distribution plan was keen. All of her life, Katie Brown witnessed black land loss on Sapelo Island.

Islanders did not directly describe the impact of racism on their daily lives during Turner's recording sessions, nor did they talk specifically about the island's white patriarch. But Rev. John Dunham did talk about the "change" that occurred on Sapelo Island from the time the newly freed men and women returned to the island after the war to the period of Coffin's occupation of the island. Reverend Dunham said: "Things are very different now from what it used to be. . . . The time has been when we made plenty of cotton, plenty of corn, plenty potatoes, plenty peas, plenty beans." "Everything was plentiful. . . . Money was plentiful. Now it get to the place where there is nothing, everything become hard." From Dunham's perspective, the hope that the Islanders had for a new life as free people when their "northern friends" helped to emancipate them during the Civil War gave way to disappointments. Although he recalled that "in the first of freedom when we landed on Sapelo Island (I think it was about '65)" the Islanders faced hard times, he testified that "the Lord take care of us and feed us just like he feed the birds and the ravens in the field, and we thank God."[189]

The change that Reverend Dunham described as a transformation from a time when everything was "plentiful" to the time when "there is nothing" was a clear statement of Sapelo Islanders' poverty. According to Dunham, when Islanders were newly free and completely independent, they had everything they needed. However, the reinstatement of the plantation state on the island made things "hard" for blacks because now they were poor wage laborers.

Whereas other researchers asked Shad Hall about voodoo, conjuh, shadows (ghosts), and African ancestors, Turner asked Hall to recite a prayer. In fact, Turner asked all of his Sapelo subjects to pray. Hall prayed for Turner's recording and delivered a heartfelt Christian prayer of thanksgiving. Hall began: "Everlasting God, we come to thee o' father to render thanks unto thee for the saving grace that you have given from the early rising . . . ," and Hall ended the prayer asking for deliverance from earthly suffering "through Jesus Christ and our Lord, Amen."[190] Turner did not provide editorial comments about the specific content of the recordings beyond a discussion of the relationship between specific words and syntax relative to African linguistic patterns. Yet one might imagine that he must have paused to consider the weight of the stories, prayers, and testimonies that Sapelo Islanders had entrusted him with.

Turner's research in coastal South Carolina and Georgia black communities yielded rich data. By 1934, Turner had managed to acquire an extensive collection of Gullah dialect samples from coastal South Carolina and coastal Georgia. The next step in answering the question about the origins of the Gullah dialect was to establish African linguistic correlates. Even as Turner's linguistic training prepared him to decode patterns in the Gullah dialect, he would have to become proficient in working with West African languages in order to prove his theory. Accordingly, Turner applied to the School of Oriental Studies at the University of London to study West African languages.[191] He competed with other African survivals hunters, like Zora Neale Hurston, for the Guggenheim award in 1936. Even though he did not win the grant, he managed to gather enough financial support to leave for London in October 1936.[192]

The training that Turner received at the School of Oriental Studies at the University of London, and the encounters that he had with Africans in Europe, helped him unearth specific African roots of the Gullah dialect. At the University of London, Turner worked closely with scholars who had extensive training in West African languages. However, Turner's encounters with native African speakers while in Europe proved to be equally valuable to his work. While in Europe, Turner interviewed more than twenty-five African informants. The African informants represented the full array of linguistic families in West Africa: Bambara, Efik, Ewe, Fante, Fula, Ga, Ibibio, Ibo, Kikongo, Mende, Twi, Umbundu, Vai, Wolof, and Yoruba speakers were all represented. One by one, Turner interviewed blacks from French West Africa, Southern Nigeria, Togo and Dahomey, Gold Coast, Sierra Leone, Belgian Congo, Liberia, Gambia, and Senegal.[193] During the interviews, Turner played Gullah recordings from the Georgia and South Carolina coast, and time and time again, connections were made that established a link between the Gullah dialect and its West African progenitor.

After fifteen years of research, Turner concluded that West African linguistic patterns were abundantly evident in the dialect spoken by black people in coastal Georgia and South Carolina. Turner argued that these survivals "were most numerous in the vocabulary of the dialect but can also be observed in its sounds, syntax, morphology, and intonations."[194] Looking closely at patterns of African slave importation to South Carolina and Georgia helped Turner establish the clusters of linguistic concentrations that resulted in the survival of Twi, Dahomean, Mandingo, Yoruba, Ibo, and Ovimbundu words and personal names in the Gullah dialect.[195] He used the more than 165 pages worth of Gullah personal names, words, and their West African correlates to rebut the popular "baby talk" thesis. Turner noted that the Gullah dialect samples collected in coastal Georgia were fruitful in identifying direct West African correlates: "Approximately three-quarters of all Gullah personal names I collected in coastal Georgia, principally on St. Simons Island, Sapelo Island, and Harris Neck, and in the vicinity of Darien."[196] Turner proved that systems of counting recorded in Darien, Georgia, were direct derivatives of Fula numerical marking systems, and songs recorded in Harris Neck, Darien, and St. Simons Island were of Mende origin.[197] Turner found that words used by Sapelo Islanders like "bidi, bidi" (small chicken) used in Kongo linguistic families and "nini" (female breast) shared the same meaning in Mende linguistic families.[198]

Turner's research proved to be the most fruitful of all the inquiries made into the prevalence of African survivals on Georgia's coast. He had effectively proven that West African linguistic patterns had survived chattel slavery. The fact that Turner had identified a survival that could be scientifically verified distinguished his research from Moore's and Parrish's. Moore and Parrish looked for an African essence in coastal Georgia blacks—an "essence" that they assumed animated all black people (but were most pronounced among Gullah people)—which was ultimately unverifiable.

Turner's findings promised to restore dignity to coastal Georgia and South Carolina blacks. The advent of modernism had, at least, attempted to replace this purely denigrating view of blackness with an affirming view of black folk. Franz Boas and his students, Alain Locke and the New Negro vanguard, had pushed for a new imagining of Africa and black people's African heritage. They called for a new view of the black-African connection, and Lorenzo Dow Turner carried out that mission. Turner's Gullah dialect was reflective of a people who had held on to the words and naming practices that gave meaning to the world that their forefathers conceptualized.

A New Sapelo

The perception of Sapelo Islanders that emerged during this moment of "Gullah re-discovery" was largely shaped by the stories that Moore, Parrish, and Turner told about them. Shaped by 1920s and 1930s intellectual and cultural preoccupations, Moore's story about the island's black relics, Parrish's account of African-inspired musical exuberance, and Turner's evidence of the African origins of their speech each contributed to the creation of notions of Sapelo Island's cultural distinction. As the implications of these works were conflated, fact and fantasy became more intertwined. Moreover, the Jim Crow race relations that obligated all of Sapelo's informants to participate in interviews, pose for photographs, and sing and dance has been erased from the published works in which the Islanders were featured. While it is true that personal incentives, and perhaps even personal benefits, encouraged Katie Brown and Shad Hall to sit for hours of interviews and emboldened Islanders to sing for Coffin's guests, Brown and Hall, and other Islanders such as the Johnsons and Hettie Walker had no control over the way they were represented in published works. Although the Johnsons certainly tried to shape their own image, their careful self-presentation in the *National Geographic Magazine* photograph was trumped by the power of Moore's written word—which was bolstered by his racial authority and by the magazine's reputation. In the end, the stories that Sapelo's researchers told about them lived longer than they did and would continue to inspire stories about their lives for generations. Soon, the federal government would fund research that would institutionalize the fantasies and theories that outsiders had about Sapelo Island blacks, making African survivals among them "fact" and a permanent part of America's racial, cultural, and ethnic tapestry.

4 Drums and Shadows

THE FEDERAL WRITERS' PROJECT, SAPELO ISLANDERS, AND THE SPECTER OF AFRICAN SUPERSTITIONS ON GEORGIA'S COAST

The funeral rites of the modern Negro, in so far as they include casket, flowers, music and religious services are obviously borrowed from his civilized environment. But the strange practices that color the coast Negro[e]s' death and burial, barbaric pageantry, and the unrestrained mourning are products of his forgotten years in the deep wilderness of Africa. Ages past, his forefathers accompanied death and burial with superstitious practices taught to them by voodoo priests.

—Federal Writers' Project Savannah unit,
  "Studies of Negro Survival Types in Coastal Georgia"

On a sunny day during the fall of 1937, Katie Brown, one of Sapelo's oldest residents at the time, sat on the back steps of her small wooden house with her dog Flint at her side absorbing the sun's warm rays.[1] Surely, the chugs and creaks of the oxcart that carried Mary Granger, the supervisor of the Federal Writers' Project's Savannah unit, and her research team, caught Brown's attention as it moved closer and closer to her home.[2] By 1937, the road that led to Katie Brown's house had been well traveled by curious visitors—researchers and writers—who showed up at her back door hoping to sift through her memories for evidence that could be used to prove the viability of their African survivals theories.

As the oxcart slowed to a stop on the dirt road at Katie Brown's back steps, and Mary Granger and her small entourage climbed out, Brown must have wondered what this new group of white visitors would ask her to do. Would she be asked to sing slave songs like she had for Lydia Parrish? Would they ask her to talk into a recording machine like she did for Lorenzo D. Turner? She may have asked herself these questions, but as soon as she saw the group move toward her back steps with pens, notepads, and photography equipment in their hands, she must have known that whatever they asked her, it would certainly be about the past. She would not be asked about the young, rich playboy—"R. J." Reynolds—who replaced Howard Coffin as the island's white patriarch and had begun to push black Islanders off their land almost as soon as he purchased Coffin's holdings.[3] Nor would she be asked about the scores of Islanders who abandoned their jobs at the "big house," and at other sites on the island, and migrated to nearby cities on the mainland and in the North searching for economic opportunities and racial equality. Katie Brown's back-step visitors never asked her opinion, they never asked her to comment about contemporary life on Sapelo, and they never asked about her struggles, or the struggles of the Islanders in general. They came to collect her memories.

It is true that Katie Brown could have offered researchers valuable insights into black life, history, and culture on the island stretching back to the Civil War years. She remembered much about the past, and she remembered stories about her African ancestors. She blossomed when she talked about her family's African-born Muslim patriarch—Bilali Mohammed. She recited for researchers what she remembered learning about the prayers that Mohammed and his wife made when they "bow tuh duh sun" and used beads to move through their prayer ritual, saying, "Belambi, Hakabara, Mahamadu," and "Ameen, Ameen" when moving from one bead to the next.[4] She told them about the "funny wuds" that her grandmother used to name everyday objects like "mosojo" instead of "pot" and "diffy" instead of "fire."[5] She always told them about the "saraka" cakes that her grandmother made from rice once a year.[6] Her memories of her ancestors reflected the highest potential for African survivals hunting in the region. But the deep significance of Brown's precious remembrances would be lost on the white woman who walked up to Katie Brown's back step that sunny day.

When Mary Granger approached Katie Brown, and offered her an old pair of shoes that did not fit, and pipe tobacco in exchange for her cooperation, Granger had already decided that coastal Georgia blacks were, and had always been, slaves to a primal African impulse that predisposed them to engage in primitive spiritual rites and superstitions.[7] While Mary Granger included the stories that Brown told about Bilali Mohammed in Drums and Shadows (1940), and marveled at the fact that on Sapelo she had found several interview subjects who remembered their African ancestors, their forebears' "Mohammedean" rituals simply served to color the hidden world of voodoo and conjure that Granger believed existed on Georgia's coast. During the 1920s and 1930s, black Muslims were frequently described as virtual voodooists.[8] Brown's memories of Mohammed's religious practices fit perfectly with the stories about old Africans, flying Ibos, drums, hoodoo, conjure, death rituals, and shadows (ghosts) that the Savannah unit hunted on Georgia's coast. In Mary Granger's fantasies, coastal Georgia black communities were places where "sorcery" was "still practiced" and "modern root doctors" were "visited frequently by their superstitious clients."[9]

Mary Granger had every reason to believe that a study that explored the hidden world of black coastal Georgians' African-born spiritual practices would attract attention and praise. "Voodoo" was all the rave during the 1920s and 1930s. And the emergence of mystical Gullah folk in the national imagination—ushered in by Julia Peterkin's Pulitzer Prize–winning novel, and by other books and theatrical productions like *Porgy and Bess* (1935)—could have also inspired Granger, an aspiring writer, to direct her staff to take a second look at the blacks who populated her home region. Whereas Peterkin's novels and *Porgy and Bess* featured South Carolina's Gullah, W. Robert Moore's *National Geographic Magazine* article had called attention to the folk culture of coastal Georgia blacks. Given all of the attention paid to voodoo, black southerners, and the Gullah during the 1920s and 1930s, it is no surprise that the blacks who moved in the background of white life in Savannah emerged from the shadows of Granger's Jim Crow consciousness as potential subjects for a published work that would earn acclaim. Cloaked in the authority and legitimacy that she garnered as one of the Federal Writers' Project's lead writers, Granger set out on a mission that landed her on Katie Brown's back steps.

A close examination of the construction and evolution of the Savannah unit's book *Drums and Shadows: Survival Studies Among the Georgia Coastal Negroes* (1940) reveals many of the tensions and negotiations that shaped the way that African survivals on Georgia's coast have been characterized and coded as fact. Following the debate that raged between Federal Writers' Project national administrators, Mary Granger, and social scientists over the book casts new light on the work. Prominent scholars such as Melville Herskovits, Guy B. Johnson, E. Franklin Frazier, and Federal Writers' Project administrators Sterling Brown, Henry G. Alsberg, and Benjamin Botkin each presented arguments for and against the Savannah unit's reading of coastal Georgia blacks. Their debate has been overlooked and largely divorced from the legacy of *Drums and Shadows*—a study that is easily one of the most frequently cited and consulted works about Georgia's Gullah folk.[10]

Within their long forgotten debate lies a deep contention about the way racial and cultural difference was codified and established as "fact" in published works. Sapelo Islanders and the other coastal Georgia blacks who sat for interviews with Mary Granger and her staff were pointed to in order to prove various arguments in a larger conversation about race, culture, and the construction of knowledge. Moreover, much of the angst that early drafts of *Drums and Shadows* roused was tied to the disturbing ways that the Savannah unit conflated *race* and *culture* by depicting hoodoo superstition as an inherited trait. Consequently, situating the Savannah unit's portrayal of Sapelo Islanders and other coastal Georgia blacks within these debates and popular influences unveils the negotiations and forces that facilitated the construction of their identity as unique folk, by untangling the compromises that enabled the publication of the study. Even though Sapelo is just one of twenty communities featured in the book, and the Islanders' interviews fill fewer than twenty pages, the fact that their memories were included in a larger repository of African-derived folk magic and superstition would have a lasting impact on how generations of readers of *Drums and Shadows* would envision their cultural world.

Mary Granger, Federal Writer

Mary Granger's journey to Katie Brown's backdoor on Sapelo started long before she left the Georgia Writers' Project office in Savannah. Her journey to Sapelo Island may have even started two decades before, when she left her affluent Savannah family for preparatory school in Peekskill, New York, and postsecondary studies at Barnard College in New York City.[11] By the time Mary Granger earned a bachelor of arts in English in 1921, the vogue of Negro themes had already taken hold in New York City.[12] Living and studying so close to Harlem during the Harlem Renaissance, Mary Granger would have had to fight hard to ward off the mystique of the "Negro world" that had enticed so many young New York City whites into crossing racial boundaries.[13] To be sure, Granger showed all of the signs of developing a modernist-bohemian consciousness. For example, she tried her hand at painting while living in New York City and showcased her artwork in an exhibit there sometime before she began teaching English and "Dramatics" at Hunter College.[14] Her family remembered that she "hung out with the literary crowd and academic crowd . . . in New York" and was entrenched in New York City's vibrant bohemian culture during the 1920s.[15] All of which made her exposure to, and interest in, Negro themes and black culture even more likely.

When Granger was forced to return to Savannah after traveling internationally, and publishing two novels, she brought her new consciousness with her. Her family's money troubles hastened her return to the South. The Great Depression crushed her father's real estate business and brought his plans to build a great subdivision and hotel in Savannah to a screeching halt.[16] Mary Granger was likely dependent on her father for financial support. The two romance novels that she authored—*The Widow of Ephesus* (1926) and *Wife of Pilate* (1929)—got bad reviews, and her writing showed no promise of producing income that she could live on.[17] Unmarried, and without enough money to support her travels and maintain her livelihood, Mary Granger moved back to Georgia.

Mary L. Granger at Barnard, 1921.
Courtesy of Barnard College Archives.

Once she returned to the Jim Crow South, Granger's family noticed the impact that years spent in Manhattan literary circles had had on her: she had developed a distinct liberal attitude about race.[18] Her family's assessment of the notable change in Granger's race politics may not have been an illusion. In December 1932, a package arrived at Mary Granger's home on East 47th Street in Savannah that included a letter, three pages of typed annotated statistics, and a sixteen-page pamphlet from the Commission on Interracial Cooperation (CIC).[19] Granger wrote to the CIC, the Atlanta-based organization created to maintain peaceful race relations between whites and blacks, with a vague request for materials.[20] Whether or not Granger became involved with the CIC is unknown, but R. B. Eleazer, the CIC's educational director, responded to Granger's request and sent her several sets of statistics highlighting racial disparities in the state, a letter, and a pamphlet that he authored titled *America's Tenth Man: A Brief Survey of the Negro's Part in American History.* The pamphlet identified America's "tenth man" as the "one in ten" American blacks whose "ancestors began to arrive hundreds of years ago with the early settlers."[21] The pamphlet was largely dedicated to cataloguing African Americans' accomplishments, but it also posed a question that would attract Granger's attention for years to come.[22] In the pamphlet, Eleazer asked: "Did these slaves come to America empty-handed, or did they bring some heritage of native endowment and skill, and even of civilization?"[23]

The CIC pamphlet answered the question about the impact of African culture and civilization on American blacks by presenting a series of examples that linked black Americans' accomplishments to their African background. *America's Tenth Man* contained exactly the sort of material, and reflected precisely the type of thinking, that Melville Herskovits hoped would be inspired by African survivals studies. In the pamphlet, Eleazer lauded the skill and industriousness of the Africans who were the first humans to master iron smelting and linked the dominance of black blacksmiths during slavery to their legacy. He described black American folklore and music as being connected to a "distinct gift" that Africans brought to America and called white folk writers, like Joel Chandler Harris, appropriators of the gift that blacks had brought to whites "from their African homes."[24] The pamphlet applauded black spirituals, ragtime, and jazz, and noted that these musical forms that originated in Africa were "the only distinct contributions America has made to the music of the world."[25] Although praising black Americans' African-born musical gifts was common during the period, and was often paired with a host of derogatory racial traits, Eleazer's declaration that even African Americans' intellectual achievements could be traced to Africa was a complete departure from common reductive assumptions about blacks' racial characteristics. To prove his point, Eleazer wrote about the Muslim slave Lahmen Kebby, "who, back in Africa had been well educated and trained as a school master."[26] In addition to presenting the positive contributions of Africans to black American and white American society and culture, *America's Tenth Man* also acknowledged black Revolutionary War and Civil War heroes, black teachers and preachers, and leaders of the black intelligentsia like Alain Locke. Despite the fact that the pamphlet's language occasionally betrayed its mission by generalizing "Africa" and by, at times, describing Africans in primitivist terms ("kidnapped from idolatrous parents in Africa"), the publication attempted to redeem black American's African heritage.[27]

Whatever Granger thought about the pamphlet, the only indication that the CIC's publication made an impression on her was her desire to uncover African spiritual survivals on Georgia's coast. Her future writings about coastal Georgia blacks completely ignored the racism that Eleazer cited in his notes on lynchings in the state and in the statistics he used to illustrate the way that Jim Crow simultaneously robbed black Georgians of their tax dollars and educational opportunities.[28] Overlooking or discounting his notes on structural racism, Granger clung to Eleazer's ambiguous discussion of "Africa" and black people's "gifts"—ideas that likely encouraged her burgeoning, nebulous conceptualization of African survivals. Even though Eleazer dedicated a section of the CIC pamphlet to black Americans' commitment to Christianity, and cited multiple statistics to underscore blacks' remarkable religiosity, Granger would imagine black spiritual life in a very different way. Eleazer hoped that readers would be impressed by the fact that, by 1931, blacks had "42,585 churches, with 5,203,487 members, and 36,000 Sunday schools enrolling 2,144,000 pupils," but those figures would not stick with Mary Granger as she led explorations in the black communities on Georgia's coast hunting voodoo, drums, rootworkers, and shadows.[29]

Three years after Granger received *America's Tenth Man* in the mail, she would have the opportunity to channel her intellectual curiosities about black culture and her literary aspirations into her new job overseeing the publication of several works that represented her home state's uniqueness as a supervisor for the Federal Writers' Project (FWP). The fact that Granger was a published author with ties to the literary community and was the eldest daughter of a respected Savannah businessman, undoubtedly helped to secure her post as the leader of the Savannah unit of the FWP. Granger's staff of "Georgia writers," like other FWP teams in the state, likely included newspaper and radio writers, poets, cartographers, law students, clerical workers, and typists who acted as secretaries, writers, editors, abstractors, research assistants, supervising clerks, typists, and research fieldworkers.[30] As the leader of the Savannah unit, Granger was charged with leading her staff of twenty workers in their mission to "document America." While she fulfilled the FWP mission by supervising the creation of books that featured Savannah's history, surveyed the remains of local plantations, and illustrated Chatham County maps, she also tapped into the FWP's mandate to represent the nation's diverse cultural composition and re-imagined this mandate so that it allowed her to engage with popular fantasies about black hoodoo superstitions in her quest to uncover the African roots of black coastal Georgians' folklore and spiritual practices.[31]

Even though FWP administrators would eventually clash with leading social scientists and Granger over the Savannah unit's survival study, the FWP's expressed interest in documenting the lives of common Americans, collecting regional folklore, and its desire to explore the nation's racial terrain in its works gave Granger license to take up hunting for African survivals on Georgia's coast. Eleanor Roosevelt, literary powerhouse Henry G. Alsberg, and the Writers' Union had all called for a relief program for writers akin to the Public Works of Art Project for artists, which ultimately resulted in the birth of the FWP in 1935.[32] Described by one of its writers as a "freak enterprise, a strange creature of the Depression created by a special breed of men and women," the FWP's mission reflected the mixed motives and agendas set by its administrators.[33] The organization was also animated by the modernist intellectual and cultural trends of the period.[34]

On the surface, it may appear that the FWP simply oversaw the production of state guidebooks, local histories, collections of regional folklore, and recorded interviews with ex-slaves. But FWP administrators nurtured a larger vision that they hoped would shape the projects that state writers produced. This group of liberal leftists and social science enthusiasts embraced Boasian anthropology and cultural pluralism.[35] National FWP officials such as Henry G. Alsberg, Sterling Brown, John Lomax, Benjamin Botkin, and Morton Royse saw themselves as much more than high-titled administrators—they saw themselves as leaders of a cultural movement.[36] They were members of an elite literary, artistic, and academic vanguard who wanted to tap into the powerful "common man" vernacular and "documentary expressions" that permeated literature during the 1930s and turned the nation's readers' attention to poor Americans' experiences in rural and urban settings.[37] They were plugged into the new theories that social scientists put forward challenging the racialized view of civilization and savagery that had dominated the previous generation of Victorian thinkers, and the FWP wanted the stories about America that their writers produced to reflect this fresh intellectual orientation. They were also inspired by the vogue and allure of the Negro themes that rocked the literary world during the Harlem Renaissance and sought to incorporate its vibrancy into their publications.[38] And the FWP's most prominent writers tried to achieve the national administrators' vision. The experience of the "common man" was communicated in dramatic photography and descriptive narratives in texts produced by the photographer Dorothea Lange and social scientist W. T. Couch.[39] Similarly, black writers and artists like Richard Wright, Frank Yerby, Katherine Dunham, Willard Motley, and Zora Neale Hurston lent their talents to the FWP's grand vision.[40]

Even though FWP's leadership had a relatively unified view of America with regard to race and class, state writers' views on these subjects often clashed with national administrators' progressive perspective. Historian Jerrold Hirsch explains that "the contrast between the views of the national office and members of the state units indicates that the ideas of the national FWP officials . . . did not represent the variety of views regarding race, ethnicity, and the definition of American nationality that could be found among the general population and that were present among Federal Writers."[41] Managing the race politics of the more than six thousand Federal Writers on FWP payrolls at the height of the program in 1936 would prove to be an impossible task[42]—a task that was made even more difficult by the fact that white supremacy dictated social, political, and economic life in America during these years, and derogatory representations of blackness dominated the nation's cultural landscape. Conflicts between FWP national administrators and state writers over race and representation were exacerbated by the reality that FWP publications carried a "double authority": the FWP was government sanctioned, and its publications were framed as "factual" information.[43] FWP's national administrators struggled to maintain the integrity of their larger vision while combating the bigotry evident in the submissions that they received from state writers.[44] Consequently, disagreements between national administrators and state writers, like the dispute that Mary Granger found herself entrenched in, reflected a high-stakes debate about race.

Mary Granger versus National FWP Officials: Debating and Negotiating the Africanness of Coastal Georgia Blacks

Granger had good reason to think that searching for African survivals on Georgia's coast would be an appropriate project for the FWP's Savannah unit to take up—reasons that extended beyond the popular fascination with voodoo and exotic black southerners. When Granger took leadership of the Savannah unit, she likely received the "folklore and customs" guide that national FWP administrators in DC sent to state writers. The guide could have easily reignited her curiosity about African survivals in the region. It instructed Federal Writers to search out "what is unusual about a city" and "to survey their towns with fresh eyes," in order to detect "lore and customs known to them all their lives."[45] It also advised Federal Writers to avoid "leading citizens of towns" because they were "not always the best sources for lore."[46] Instead, writers were instructed to seek out "an old cook, washerwoman," or "gardener," as well as the "Oldest residents" of communities, especially those who were "close to the soil" because "circumstances ... cut them off from education and progressive enlightenment."[47] "Cultured citizens" were described as being potentially helpful to fieldworkers collecting folklore because they may have conducted "local research" for "their own amusement."[48] The guide offered Federal Writers examples of folk customs, folklore, and superstitions that listed "amulets," "incantations," "supernatural powers," and "conjure bags" among other folk beliefs and practices.[49]

Even as FWP national administrators hoped to transcend reductive presuppositions about race and class, their fixation on the "common man" and "the folk" dangerously teetered the line between scholarly interest and exoticism. The instructional language used in the folklore and customs guide unwittingly reiterated the primitivist fantasies that biased FWP writers already had about "the folk." The guide's author made no attempt to disentangle meaningful explorations of folk traditions from the stories being told about poor and uneducated "backwards" rural "folk" in the broader national culture— narratives that were even more salient and damaging to black southerners. This tension was at the heart of Mary Granger's conflict with FWP administrators. Granger's conceptualization of black folk culture was informed by the depictions of blacks found in William Seabrook's and Julia Peterkin's writings, and in film's like *Harlem's Black Magic* and *Black Moon*—and the FWP folklore guide encouraged her to look for this type of black in coastal Georgia. Even though anthropologists like Melville Herskovits and Zora Neale Hurston attempted to elevate "voodoo" to the ranks of a significant African survival, the voodoo reports published in northern papers captivated the imaginations of Americans, who, like Granger, simply conceived of voodoo as a marker of African spiritual primitivism. Ultimately, the FWP folklore and customs guide offered no corrective remedy for Federal Writers' latent racism and classism that masqueraded as innocent curiosity and friendly fascination.

Encouraged by the convergence of the FWP's vision, popular primitivist fantasies about black southerners and voodoo, burgeoning African survivals theories, and the emergence of "the Gullah" in America's consciousness, Mary Granger conceived an African survivals study that would eventually become *Drums and Shadows*. In fact, Julia Peterkin's attempt at an ethnography of the South Carolina Gullahs—*Roll, Jordan, Roll* (1934)—would prove useful to the Savannah unit study, which cited Peterkin's book throughout its report.[50] With Peterkin's characterization of uninhibited, superstitious, quasi-primitive, and carefree Gullah folk fresh in her mind, Granger followed the path laid by W. Robert Moore, Lydia Parrish, and Lorenzo D. Turner and began inquisitions into coastal Georgia blacks' racial inheritance. Sometime in 1935, Granger and her team began conducting research. They interviewed a few blacks, observed and read about their "ceremonies," and captured glimpses of their lives. At the end of the first round of research, Granger and her crew wrote a manuscript titled "Studies of Negro Survival Types in Coastal Georgia."[51]

This first incarnation of *Drums and Shadows* reveals more about Mary Granger's and the Savannah unit's view of blacks than it does about African survivals in the region. Likewise, the debates that ensued over the draft, and subsequent drafts of the manuscript, expose even more tensions around the African survivals concept. Similar to those of W. Robert Moore and Lydia Parrish, Granger's observations of black life on Georgia's coast were filtered through a racial lens colored by popular stories about primitive blackness. The draft scarcely included specific information about the locales visited and seldom identified interview subjects by name. The blacks described in the manuscript were little more than a nebulous mass of quasi-African, coastal Georgia primitives. The Savannah unit's appraisals of their folklife were largely unmediated by scholarly analysis. Du Bois's writings were consulted three times, but lengthy footnotes largely cited works written by white African missionaries, and writers like Julia Peterkin were offered as "evidence" that coastal Georgia blacks' traditions had come directly from Africa.[52]

At the very beginning of the manuscript, in the introduction, Granger unveiled her conceptualization of African survivals and coastal Georgia blacks. She had told two friends, whom she would later recruit to serve as photographers on the project, about her plan to lead an investigation into "African cultural survivals she believed to be extant along the Georgia coast," and although members of her team contributed to the work, the fact that she had the final say on what should be written guaranteed that her ideas about survivals would heavily influence the study.[53] Acknowledging that many books had been written about "folk customs of the Negro," Granger proclaimed the uniqueness and importance of the study by explaining that "in this section where primitive people have been more or less racially distinct the field is so wide that intensified study in special areas still reveals valuable information."[54] She pointed out that "the Negro of this section is perhaps closer to his native Africa than any other in this country."[55] It was true that during the 1930s, many black communities in the rural South were largely comprised of family groups who had occupied the same areas for generations—going far back into the antebellum period. And surely some older coastal Georgia blacks, like Katie Brown, remembered their African ancestors. But Granger's view of Africa and blacks' Africanness was wildly stereotypical and may have even obscured the very survivals that she perused.

She explained that coastal blacks, "Like his white neighbor," "works for his home, his church, and his country" and is "a generous contributor" to "many movements for the betterment of humanity." But at the same time, she concluded "Yet, despite his social and economic advancement, like members of other races, he responds under excitement to the fundamental racial trait of his African heritage." Conflating *race* and *culture*, she continued, "It is these natural reactions that link the educated Afro-American citizen to his African forbearer and to the humbler type of Negro, still primitive in his outlook."[56] Even though she vacillated between presenting a progressive and favorable image of coastal Georgia blacks, and a distinctly racist primitivist view, her bias is clear. Granger believed that these blacks were different because they possessed a racial trait that could be triggered and arouse their African impulses. Consequently, six sections of the manuscript were dedicated to unveiling evidence that coastal Georgia blacks continued to express this fundamental African trait. Sections of the manuscript were devoted to coastal Georgia blacks' slave background, ceremonies, superstitions, and dialect, and the manuscript also included a catalogue of old songs, common sayings, and interviews with ex-slaves.

Granger and her team pinpointed hoodoo superstitions, unrestrained emotional displays, and musical exuberance as predominant "traits" that coastal Georgia blacks inherited from their African progenitors.[57] The study did assert that coastal blacks' "natural reactions" had been nurtured by the fact that they were largely "untouched by the opportunities" around them, but ultimately concluded that "in spite of his contact with civilization," these blacks continued to cling to beliefs in the power of talismans and charms to direct their fate.[58] This assumption was supported by a long description of coastal Georgia blacks' slave past, and with an exploration of their "ceremonies." Here, the Savannah unit declared that coastal Georgia blacks displayed a hyperconnection to rituals and ceremonies, because when they were "uprooted from" their "jungle environment . . . the Negro brought to his strange new world" traits such as "native African rhythmic sense . . . superstitious beliefs and ceremonial rites."[59] And the Africans' need to cling to superstitions and ceremonies was also interpreted as an "outward expression of the inward awe the Negro felt before forces he did not understand."[60] Granger and her team did not consider the possibility that "black superstitions" were rooted in complex cosmological theories. They simply decided that ignorance was at the heart of African spiritual life. And according to this logic, the slave trade and American slavery exacerbated Africans' ignorance and fearfulness. They also pointed to the "interchange of tribal customs" facilitated by the slave trade to explain the "widening of folk customs" that "intensified the folk urge" in isolated slave communities largely comprised of saltwater Africans smuggled onto Georgia's coast.[61]

In the draft, even Christian rituals in black coastal Georgia communities looked more like voodoo-styled superstition than they did European Protestantism. Melville Herskovits had maintained that the presence of non-European forms of expression in black religious ceremonies reflected a sophisticated negotiation of distinct worldviews, but the Savannah unit study announced that "the Negro unconsciously injected into a Christian service certain ceremonial survivals of a pagan past."[62] The "emotional stress" of religious conversion and "death" were listed as triggers that caused "Coast Negro" to revert to "primitive instincts."[63] They presented "shouting" as evidence of a "common barbaric survival of African heritage."[64] Baptism rituals were also offered as proof that coastal Georgia blacks were still plugged into "his African love of ostentation and pageantry."[65] Even the songs that blacks sung during baptisms further confirmed the African origins of coastal blacks' primitive instincts: "The rhythm of his singing, his loud simple ecstasy, and his unrestrained emotionalism are the pagan heritage of his jungle background."[66]

The study's readers would find that even weddings created yet another opportunity for coastal Georgia blacks' "sharply primitive" instincts to emerge.[67] The "Coastal Negro" retained "good and bad luck voodoo superstitions pertaining to nuptials," according to the Savannah unit's findings.[68] They explained that, while, on the surface, black brides appeared to adhere to traditional customs—white dresses, flowers, and the like—"she probably has a 'lucky dime' tied around her ankle."[69] The same was true for black grooms. They too wore voodoo accessories "guarding against evil with an amulet in the form of a watch or a luck ring."[70] Black wedding receptions also conjured an African ritual scene: "As the musicians cast off the borrowed beat of the white man's music and pour out strange rhythms from the past, the dancers create barbaric steps, jerking their bodies and clapping their hands with hilarity."[71] And after the wedding, the bride "often finds that she must support her husband," a trend that Granger and her team connected to African origins, citing W. D. Weatherford—a white southerner—in his discussion of African polygamy and black immorality in his controversial and poorly reviewed book *The Negro from Africa to America* (1924).[72]

It is no surprise that black funerals revealed even more "African correlates" in the Savannah unit study. The 1920s and 1930s voodoo craze had normalized the idea that black death rituals, voodoo, and Africa were inextricably linked. Salt sprinkled on the stomach of dead corpses; "set ups with the dead" to keep "ju-ju" from stealing the body; children passed over graves to keep them from dying; and salt and ash placed under coffins to prevent the spread of fatal illnesses were all loosely attributed to Africa in the manuscript. Yes, Sapelo Islanders had, for generations, passed children over their loved ones' graves, and "set ups" (the period during which the deceased was laid on a cooling board in the home for final viewing) were common in the days before mainland funeral homes were able to provide these services for the Islanders. Coastal Georgia blacks' funeral rites could have generated compelling evidence of the retention of African cosmological principles, as well as shed light on more practical issues. But when Granger and the researchers under her charge read about or attended black funerals while conducting fieldwork, what they found mirrored the images of primitive blackness that already lived in their imaginations. For example, they stated that "caskets, flowers, music and religious services" at black funerals were "borrowed" from whites' "civilized environment," but the essence of the rite, and blacks' "natural reactions" to death, were "products of his forgotten years in the deep wilderness of Africa.... His forefathers accompanied death and burial with superstitious practices taught to them by voodoo priests."[73]

The section of the manuscript titled "Superstition and Beliefs of the Coastal Negro" parroted exactly the sort of material that sold copies of newspapers that contained voodoo reports and sold voodoo books, plays, and films during the 1920s and 1930s. The manuscript included a list of magical herbal remedies commonly included in advertisements for voodoo supplies published in black newspapers such as the *New York Amsterdam News*, *Chicago Defender*, and the

Pittsburgh Courier during the 1920s and 1930s. Graveyard dirt, lucky hand root, five-finger grass, and Adam and Eve root are just a few of the magical-herbal concoctions identified as common remedies for supernatural problems.[74] The Savannah unit also characterized coastal Georgia blacks as dependent on "root and conjure doctors" who just like Julia Peterkin's character Daddy Cudjoe "lived apart from the others in an isolated or wooded section."[75] Holding "sway over a large percentage of their superstitious fellowmen," they claimed that these "witch doctors in modern guise" ruled coastal Georgia blacks.[76] The manuscript's readers would also find a link between coastal blacks' preoccupation with hoodoo rites and their enslavement. Granger's unit assumed that when blacks were taken from their "native haunts in the jungle" and brought to America, they were terrified and needed "some means of protection, some assurance of good luck," but in the end, the hoodoo traditions documented in the draft were described as being spurred by ignorance inspired by a quasi-biological racial trait.[77]

At the same time that Mary Granger's unit's proposed study unwittingly established hoodoo practices and superstitions as one of the characteristics that defined Georgia's Gullah, she paid little attention to the Gullah label in the manuscript. Aware of the fact that the term "Gullah" had historically been used to describe South Carolina's coastal blacks, she was ambivalent about the use of the term relative to coastal Georgia blacks. The study included statements that challenged the validity of the theories that John Bennett and Ambrose Gonzales put forth about Gullah folk in the footnotes: "No student in the field seems to have given satisfactory explanation of the origin of these Negroes."[78] When discussing the local dialect, she wrote, "As has been stated previously … the Negroes of this section are known as Gullah, and their dialect rightly or wrongly termed Gullah."[79] Lorenzo D. Turner's research was well on the way to proving that coastal Georgia's and South Carolina's blacks' dialect yielded the greatest amount of evidence of African survivals in the region—evidence that might prove that West African grammar, syntax, and personal names had survived chattel slavery. But when Granger and her team grappled with the meaning of the dialect in the manuscript, they sided with the men whose theories Turner hoped to disprove. Like Guy B. Johnson, John Bennett, Reed Smith, George Phillip Krapp (whose work she cited), Granger used the "baby talk" thesis to explain the Gullah dialect. In the manuscript, coastal blacks' dialect was portrayed as nothing more than a garbled form of English that often included words that were remnants of obsolete forms of English words, or words that appeared "to be derived from an entirely alien source."[80]

The entire "Studies of Negro Survival Types in Coastal Georgia" manuscript maintained the same basic thesis about African survivals throughout. Page after page, the manuscript cast coastal Georgia blacks as primitive, super-stitious, and ignorant people bound by an inherited racial trait that retarded their evolution. Even though Granger argued that their disposition was quasi-biological, she shared Lydia Parrish's and Lorenzo D. Turner's anxiety that this "Negro type" was in danger of evolving and vanishing from the nation's cultural landscape forever.

Much to Mary Granger's dismay, her sense of accomplishment and urgency did not guarantee that the manuscript would be pushed to the top of FWP administrators' list of works approved for publication. Her unit's survival study would have to go through the same rigorous evaluation that all manuscripts submitted by state writers endured. National officials mandated that manuscripts first be approved by state FWP administrators before being sent to the national office where they were "checked, verified, and edited."[81] More importantly, projects like Granger's survival study were subject to additional scrutiny because they featured African Americans.

Almost as soon as the FWP was organized, black leaders, including Walter White, John P. Davis, and Ralph Bunche, pressured Henry G. Alsberg to appoint a black scholar who was knowledgeable about black literature and history to oversee projects, and to presumably protect the nation's blacks from being misrepresented in publications commissioned by the federal government.[82] Alsberg appointed Sterling Brown—a black poet and scholar—to the post. In 1936, Brown accepted the appointment as the FWP editor of Negro Affairs, adding this new responsibility to the obligations that he had as an English professor at Howard University.[83] Brown was an ideal candidate for the position. He had graduated from Williams College and received a graduate degree from Harvard University in 1923. He was an avid supporter of folklore studies and was one of the early pioneers of the artistic use of black dialect in literary works. If his scathing review of Julia Peterkin's Roll, Jordan, Roll served as an indicator of how he would handle white writers under his charge, one would expect Brown to fearlessly expose racial fallacies in their writings.[84] As the FWP editor of Negro Affairs, Brown was positioned to both quell black leaders' fears about the ways that blacks would be depicted in FWP publications, and support FWP administrators' larger vision. Although he was more than qualified to fill the role, the job was not easy. Not only did he review manuscripts, but he made sure that black writers were employed by state offices and were treated fairly. However, acting as a racial mediator taxed Brown. Working with a small editorial staff that consisted of two Howard University researchers, he quickly discovered that curtailing the antiblack biases reflected in the manuscripts that state writers submitted would prove to be an almost impossible task.[85]

The Savannah unit's study was one among many manuscripts that tried Sterling Brown's ability to navigate the racial prejudice that pervaded state writers' works. Charged with editing submissions riddled with racial stereotypes, Brown had to direct white state writers to abandon the use of derogatory terms like "darkie" in their writings, and he had to instruct writers to avoid "debatable generalizations" with regard to race.[86] Unlike the tensions that quickly surfaced between Brown and white state writers from the South who resented his authority, trouble between Sterling Brown and Granger unfolded gradually. Oblivious to the manuscript's problems, and confident about the study's merits, Granger sent it off to her state supervisor, Samuel Tupper Jr., in July 1937.[87] She also had Sterling Brown read the manuscript. Brown had traveled to Savannah during the summer of 1937, which afforded Granger the opportunity to personally hand over the study for his review.[88]

Right away, Brown expressed uneasiness about the manuscript. Just three years before, he had bashed Peterkin for writing about the Gullah in much the same way that the Savannah unit had. However, he agreed to approve the project if Granger shifted the study's focus so that the study was more "descriptive" and less "anthropological."[89] This gentle redirection was an acknowledgment of the fact that Granger was clearly in no position to make anthropological claims about African retentions—she did not have a background in anthropology, and she knew nothing about Africa. Yet Brown remained optimistic about the study's potential, despite the fact that the Georgia FWP director was uncomfortable with the project and admitted to Brown that he "did not feel qualified to pass on the work."[90] Whatever Brown thought of the manuscript, he described Granger as "enthusiastic, capable, and energetic."[91] He also wrote that she had been "exceedingly gracious" during his visit.[92] Perhaps the combination of Granger's charm and his own interest in black southern folk culture made him hopeful that she could be coached into changing the orientation of the study and could produce a simple book that described black folk practices in the region.

While Granger graciously agreed to make significant changes to the manuscript during Brown's visit, she was not willing to abandon her African survivals thesis. She told Tupper that she had incorporated "most" of Brown's suggestions in the revisions.[93] She continued to revise the manuscript, submitted updated drafts for review, and she also began to make moves toward gathering a group of white scholars who would support her African survivals theories and advocate for the manuscript to be published. She sent five letters to Brown between September and November inquiring about the status of the project, only to receive apologies for the delay.[94] She grew impatient waiting for Brown's and Alsberg's comments on her revised study. Anticipating Brown's continued insistence that she give up the survivals thesis, and hoping that the University of North Carolina Press would publish the book, Granger solicited white social scientists Howard Odum, Guy B. Johnson, and W. T. Couch at the University of North Carolina's Institute for Research in Social Science, and Melville Herskovits at Northwestern University, in October 1937.[95]

Granger's efforts to gather a group of scholars who would support her study were successful. She spent several days at the University of North Carolina in Chapel Hill discussing the manuscript with Guy B. Johnson and his colleagues.[96] Despite the fact that Guy B. Johnson had gone on record and questioned the plausibility of African survivals theories in his book *Folk Culture on St. Helena Island* (1930) by examining the "white ancestry" of the Gullah dialect and spirituals, he supported Granger's research.[97] After their meeting, Johnson wrote Granger a letter on October 13, 1937, encouraging her to move forward with the project because there had not yet been a thorough study of African survivals in the United States, which in and of itself, made the project significant.[98] He also explained that even though "African survivals are relatively insignificant" compared to "the total culture which Negroes have borrowed from us," investigating their existence "would still be interesting" to "know exactly what has survived from Africa and how it functions in Negro life."[99] Johnson's use of the word "us" is revealing. Johnson believed that he and Granger—two whites—shared a common culture that largely dominated and replaced African culture. He also wrote that the project took advantage of a "rare opportunity" to gather "first hand" descriptions of "revivals, baptisms, weddings, funerals and conjuring practices."[100] The popularity of southern voodoo themes made Johnson's next statement more fact than opinion: "I have no doubt that there will be sufficient usable material to form the basis of a publication which should have quite wide appeal. I think that there will not be a great deal of difficulty in getting a publisher for such a volume."[101] W. T. Couch's endorsement of Granger's study was not as enthusiastic. Acting as a representative of the University of North Carolina Press, Couch cautioned her to "pay careful attention" to Johnson's suggestions but ultimately decided that "some material in this manuscript is valuable" and, "if properly prepared," should be published.[102]

Johnson's and Couch's validation of Granger's study probably quelled her anxiety as she waited for Melville Herskovits—the emerging expert on African survivals—to respond to her request for advice on the project. In the letter she sent to him on October 4, 1937, Granger wrote, "We are not trying to prove anything by these studies." Yet she did make a claim: "We believe that the introduction of slavery into this section at a comparatively late date, the favorable conditions for illegal slave trading and the isolation of our Coastal and Island plantations provided unusually favorable conditions in which inherited beliefs might survive." And she declared that African survivals were abundant in coastal Georgia black communities: "In fact, it is a question whether it would be more accurate to call the work Studies of African Survival Types in Coastal Georgia."[103] She credited Guy Johnson for directing her to him in the hope that Herskovits would identify literature that she could read on the topic, so she asked him to send whatever materials he believed would suit her purposes.[104]

In the letter, Granger tried to pique Herskovits's interest in coastal Georgia black communities. But she did not need to: he had already encouraged survivals research in the region. Before Granger wrote him, Herskovits had already begun exchanging correspondence with Lydia Parrish about slave songs and ring shouts and their possible African origins[105] Parrish—a woman who was very protective of "her Negroes"—would, several times, caution Herskovits against getting involved with Granger because she believed Granger was nothing more than a self-interested collector in pursuit of Bilali Mohammed's diary and its transcription for her book. Parrish also told Herskovits that Granger was an "expert at 'picking' other peoples [sic] brains." But Parrish's warnings did not discourage Herskovits.[106] When Herskovits responded to Granger in November 1937, he complimented her "interesting" study and apologized for the fact that he was abroad and could not send her the materials she requested.[107] He suggested that she read his work on blacks in Dutch Guiana because he believed they were "not very different" from the "Gullas [sic]."[108] While this sweeping generalization—that coastal Georgia blacks and blacks in Dutch Guiana were essentially the same—pointed to weaknesses in Herskovits's estimations of black culture, it nonetheless leant support to Granger's working thesis regarding African survivals in coastal Georgia.

Emboldened by the support of her new allies, Granger pushed Sterling Brown to deliver final approval for her study. She did not hide the fact that she had found well-known social scientists to endorse her work.[109] And she did not attempt to mask her annoyance with Brown in a letter that she sent him in late October 1937: "We still have received no general criticism from you on the manuscript. . . . Please let me know if you have another address . . . at which I can reach you more directly."[110] When she learned that he would be spending less time on FWP projects because he was awarded a Guggenheim fellowship from 1937 to 1938, she grew even more concerned that FWP national administrators would never read and approve her revised draft.[111] He was, however, apologetic for his delayed action on her manuscript; he vowed to "send down full comments shortly" and wrote, "Although I am technically freelance . . . I do intend to keep in touch with you about the manuscript."[112]

Granger did not wait for Brown's comments, or approval from the national FWP office, to continue fieldwork. She continued to hunt African survivals on Georgia's coast. Although she and her team visited numerous black communities in coastal Georgia, Sapelo Island struck her as one of the more fascinating places she had been. She was so taken with the island and the Islanders that she mentioned her experience there in a letter that she wrote to Brown: "I have just returned from three days at Sapeloe Island. I regret more than ever that you were not able to get there on your Darien trip. It is simply unbelievable, even to me. I do hope sometime . . . you will get down here again."[113] What exactly had Mary Granger found to be "unbelievable" on Sapelo Island? Perhaps she was taken back by the scenic landscape, or more likely, she was shocked by the island's relative isolation. Whatever the cause of Granger's awe, she would make every attempt to feature Sapelo Islanders prominently in her work. Sterling Brown echoed Granger's interest in the island in his reply to her letter: "I hope that I shall see the coastal sections again, and this time really get to Sapeloe."[114]

In the same letter in which Brown expressed the desire to visit Sapelo, he granted Granger permission to proceed with her study.[115] He explained that he and Alsberg were slow to respond to her correspondence because they were busy with other manuscripts, and wrote, "Go right ahead with your plans as your letter indicates you have done."[116] He knew that Granger was determined to finish the project with or without permission from the national office. But Granger's determination was probably not the only factor that contributed to Brown's decision. He promised to give the manuscript as much attention as he could, because he too was "anxious for the book to be first-rate." Perhaps Brown was being professional and polite. Or maybe his own interest in the artistic and intellectual potential of black folklore overpowered his reservations about the manuscript.[117] He may have even been hopeful that out-of-the-way black communities like Sapelo Island contained a repository of valuable folklore that needed to be mined, or he may have been optimistic that Granger could be corralled and steered away from the pitfalls that marred many white folklorists' depictions of black culture. He may have even believed that the intrinsic value of these folk treasures would overshadow the fact that the person who discovered them linked their origins to "jungle rites" and "ignorant primitives." It is also possible that he felt pressured to approve Granger's continued fieldwork because she had gathered notable supporters. Surely all of these factors contributed to Brown's decision to encourage the completion of Granger's study, but the likelihood that he had not finished reading her revisions before giving her clearance to proceed may have also played a role. Almost two months after Brown told Granger to continue her fieldwork, he sent a letter to the Georgia FWP director, Samuel Tupper Jr., admitting that he had not had time to prepare comments on the manuscript.[118] By February, it was clear that neither Brown nor Alsberg had given Granger's manuscript a close read. But

Brown did give Granger's manuscript to two of his colleagues at Howard University, and when their scathing reviews arrived at national headquarters, FWP administrators' view of the project quickly shifted from "promising" to "problematic."

When Howard University sociologists E. Franklin Frazier and William Oscar Brown read "Studies of Negro Survival Types in Coastal Georgia," they found no merit in the manuscript. Both men decided that the Savannah unit study revealed nothing about the culture of coastal Georgia blacks and instead concluded that it merely regurgitated dominant racial stereotypes disguised as African survivals. While much of Frazier's and W. O. Brown's negative reviews of the study were inspired by its shaky formulations, unreliable evidence, and clear dependence on racial stereotypes, it is worth noting that both men had been Robert E. Park's students and, like their mentor, they had denied the existence of significant African cultural retentions long before they read Granger's work. Surely, Sterling Brown knew that he had given Granger's survival study to skeptics when he handed it to Frazier and Brown for review. But the critical problems that they uncovered in the manuscript far surpassed their resistance to African survivals theories.

By the time E. Franklin Frazier read Granger's manuscript in 1938, he had argued against the validity of African survival theories for a decade. Frazier's position on this issue had been clearly articulated in his debate with Melville Herskovits and was well known in the academic world.[119] Herskovits's work had not managed to convince Frazier of the existence of African retentions, and Mary Granger's study only confirmed Frazier's suspicion that African survival hunters relied on simple, reductive, essentialist notions about racial distinctions in order to make wild declarations. Predictably, Frazier's fundamental criticism of Granger's manuscript was that its thesis was false; he did not believe that her study, or any study, could yield reliable evidence to prove that African cultural traits had been transmitted to America. On this he wrote, "It has been extremely difficult for specialists in the field of anthropology to secure evidence which would substantiate such a thesis"; he concluded that "the authors of this manuscript seemingly have no conception of the problems involved in this type of research."[120] To prove his point, he directed Sterling Brown's attention to the suspicious African parallels with black superstitions that Granger referenced in footnotes—citations that presented missionary reports and "amateur anthropologists" as "competent observers." On this, he wrote, "Of course such a procedure is nonsensical. Many of the superstitious practices found among these people are characteristic of folk people all over the world."[121] He insisted that whites held similar beliefs and suggested that Granger read a study titled "Social Origins and Social Continuities" because it included a discussion about the superstitious beliefs and practices of white college students.[122] More importantly, Frazier argued that the study should be conducted by a real social scientist: "If money is going to be spent for the purposes of determining African 'survivals' among Negroes in America, it should be given to competent anthropologists."[123] Ultimately, Frazier concluded that "this type of work merely tends to emphasize certain stereotypes which have grown up in America concerning the Negro."[124] According to Frazier, everything about the manuscript was troubling, even Granger's attempt to re-create the dialect of coastal Georgia blacks: "I have a feeling that the dialect is not authentic."[125]

W. O. Brown's review of the manuscript was more caustic than Frazier's. W. O. Brown, a white southerner, echoed most of Frazier's critiques. Like Frazier, he believed that Granger was not qualified to conduct survivals research. "The problem is technical and complex, beset with pitfalls even for the scholar and highly hazardous for the lay student."[126] He argued that any researcher hoping to make such a discovery should be well read and trained in history, anthropology, and African cultures.[127] He also noted that the obvious projection of racial stereotypes in the manuscript signaled a larger problem with the way that coastal Georgia blacks were characterized in the work. He pointed out that the Savannah unit's use of the phrases "innate primitive instincts," "primitive emotion," "unrestrained emotionalism," "frenzied emotions," "jungle fervor," "jungle background," and "pagan heritage" were problematic.[128] Brown contended that Granger used "myths to explain facts" and concluded that her observations of coastal Georgia blacks revealed more about her than they did about her subjects: "Her 'thinking' is a strange mixture of traditional stereotypes about Africa, primitive people and Negroes, with a dash of Southern sentimentality. This thinking is itself a fine example of 'survivals.'"[129] Noticing that "when the writer has no historical evidence she appeals to race," W. O. Brown called attention to the fact that "there is a constant confusion of race and culture. . . . But Miss Granger does not seem to have the slightest notion of the distinction."[130] He further argued that if one believes Granger's logic, "coastal Negroes turn out to be Africans in an American setting."[131] Brown challenged Granger to consider the "American context of the coastal Negro" and insisted that there were social and economic realities that figure more prominently in their lives than Africa.[132] This was certainly the case for "set-ups" with the dead and the use of herbal remedies, or "roots," as medicine. Sapelo Islanders reported that bodies of the deceased were kept at home because they did not have undertakers and funeral homes, and that the expense involved with seeing a doctor, as well as the time it took to travel to the mainland, made herbal remedies and "set-ups" popular.[133] He suggested that if Granger studied poor rural white folk, "she might be less impressed by the uniquely African nature of the coastal Negroes."[134] Finally, W. O. Brown told Sterling Brown that either the project needed a new focus or a new supervisor because it "inclines toward the preposterous."[135]

After Henry G. Alsberg read Granger's work and E. Franklin Frazier's and W. O. Brown's criticisms, he refused to endorse the study in its current form. On February 16, 1938, Alsberg sent Sterling Brown a memo in which he stated that he completely agreed with W. O. Brown: "I think the attempt of this manuscript to trace coastal Georgia Negro Folkways and superstitions back to the African jungle is strained, far-fetched and unscientific."[136] He explained that Granger's "tortured effort" to "connect Coastal Negro Folkways" to "jungle folkways" while ignoring the American context defied logic.[137] Alsberg agreed that Granger needed to abandon the African survivals thesis and instead suggested that the study aim to simply describe folkways. But he also pointed out that the manuscript could not even pass for a folklore study because its descriptions were "done too much from the outside and in a kind of patronizing manner so that you miss the actual life and color that ought to be there."[138] He continued, "It is my opinion that in the attempt to be scientific Miss Granger falls between two stools." Detecting similarities between Granger's descriptions of the superstitions of coastal Georgia blacks and popular works about black superstitions and other similar documented folk material, Alsberg became suspicious. He questioned the "originality" of Granger's study and suggested that she may have borrowed, and not collected, her findings. He asked, "How much of the material included in this study has been actually collected by word of mouth or some living source, and how much has been taken out of books?"[139] At the end of the memo, Alsberg conceded that the manuscript contained some evidence of "thorough and conscientious work" but explained that the type of study that Granger had attempted required "training in anthropology, ethnology, etymology and folklore."[140]

After waiting seven months for national FWP administrators' approval, Mary Granger finally received a package from Washington containing Sterling Brown's letter and the comments of Henry G. Alsberg, E. Franklin Frazier, and W. O. Brown. Sterling Brown carefully crafted a complimentary yet stern letter that he attached to the pages of comments that he sent to the Savannah unit. In the letter, Brown told Granger to read Alsberg's, Frazier's, and Brown's review and directed her to abandon the African survivals thesis and focus on producing a "descriptive account" of the "very interesting isolated" black communities along Georgia's coast.[141] And he emphasized that "vague connections" to Africa "seriously weakened" the work.[142]

Granger was so upset by the comments that she composed a fiery response almost as soon as she received them. She thanked Brown for sending the reviews, but added, "I must say that in a sense, I was very much disturbed by them."[143] First, she attacked Sterling Brown for having misled her to believe that if she made the changes that he suggested and continued to revise the manuscript, the national office would approve the project: "We have been revising the manuscript according to your suggestions along these very lines since last August."[144] Next, she explained that she had already edited out much of the material that W. O. Brown and Frazier objected to. She reminded Brown that she had already agreed to eliminate stereotypical phrases; they were the first things that the Savannah unit red-penciled. Granger challenged W. O. Brown's and Frazier's knowledge about "pure Negro" communities and demanded to know if either scholar had ever traveled to coastal Georgia.[145] Believing the Savannah unit had uncovered legitimate African survivals in the region, Granger resisted eliminating African parallels in the footnotes: "But for this type of study which is not trying to prove anything (as you and I both agreed), I see no reason why travellers' reports, missionaries' diaries, etc., should not be taken as truthful accounts."[146] She was not afraid to attack W. O. Brown's and Frazier's comments, but she respectfully refrained from challenging Alsberg's criticisms. Especially since Alsberg—the director of the FWP—was already skeptical about her work. So, she simply asked Sterling Brown to explain her position to him.[147]

The fact that Granger questioned the validity of W. O. Brown's and Frazier's critiques, and resisted Sterling Brown's directives, were clear signs that she intended to hold on to her view of coastal Georgia blacks and her African survivals thesis. She continued to collect stories and folklore in Georgia's coastal black communities, and she worked closely with her allies Guy B. Johnson and Howard Odum to revise the manuscript so that it addressed Sterling Brown's and Henry Alsberg's larger criticisms, while retaining her core assessment of the primitive nature of coastal Georgia blacks.[148] Whereas earlier versions of Granger's document generalized coastal Georgia blacks' African-born superstitions, the new manuscript featured the same material but presented it within portraits of specific communities and interviews. While she worked with Odum and Johnson to meet national FWP administrators' standards, she also courted another white scholar to vouch for the merits of her survivals study—a sociologist at the University of Chicago—W. F. Ogburn. Eager to prove to Sterling Brown that his Howard University sociologists were wrong about her work, Granger forwarded a copy of Ogburn's endorsement to Brown's office: "It is an excellent piece of work" and "a valuable contribution to our knowledge of folk culture."[149]

Even after moving forward with a new strategy for writing about hoodoo superstitions and conjure on Georgia's coast, Granger was still seething over the critiques that Brown had sent. She continued to challenge Brown's directives and his colleagues' criticism in a letter that she sent him in March 1938.[150] Before launching into a continuation of the rebuttal that she sent to him a month before, Granger updated Brown about changes that she and her staff had made to the manuscript: "As it now stands, it is made up entirely of field reports on the communities with a short introduction and footnotes giving the African parallels."[151] She was sure to include that Guy Johnson believed that the "critical study" that she first attempted "had certain advantages," and he was confident that she and her staff were "quite able " to finish the task.[152] She told Brown that she kept the footnotes that established African parallels with the folk customs that she found, while pretending to be concerned that the move may upset Frazier and W. O. Brown, whom she took every opportunity to discredit. For example, she directly refuted Brown's claims that the work reflected her prejudices and was fueled by stereotypes when she wrote: "Neither Mr. Ogburn, who is certainly one of the most eminent sociologists in the country, nor Mr. Johnson, who is certainly a first ranking folklorist, feel that the manuscript is biased."[153] She even suggested that black sociologist Charles S. Johnson would be a better reviewer because he was "one of the most outstanding and unbiased sociologists in the country."[154] She insisted that some individuals would never be satisfied with her study no matter what she did: "A thing of this kind will not be pleasing to radicals who wish to ignore cultural inheritances."[155] Granger continued and explained that some blacks would welcome the work: "I believe that the group of creative artists who are interested in a cultural African renaissance will be highly interested — so, for the pique of one we could possibly have the approval of the other."[156] She also reminded Sterling Brown that despite the fact that the new manuscript "avoided anthropological and ethnological claims," simply removing the term "African survivals" from the work did not erase the fact that the "very nature of the study itself would suggest a belief in certain Africanisms."[157]

Both of Granger's rebuttals reveal much about the way that she understood (and misunderstood) race. Her insistence that she was not trying to "prove anything," illustrates how little she knew about the way that racial difference had been constructed in America. During the 1930s, the very association between any aspect of black life and Africa automatically conjured a host of racial theories used to "prove" a variety of assumptions about the inherent nature of black people and black culture. The fact that she did not understand that missionary reports could not be taken as authoritative accounts of African life is more evidence that shows that she did not understand the way that race worked. White missionaries' view of the blacks they observed were often tempered by their beliefs and misconceptions about Africans, and what they imagined to be fundamental differences between whites and blacks. Unwilling to entertain the possibility that race prejudices shaped white missionaries' impressions of African life, Granger insisted that they were valid sources partly because she believed in the infallibility of whites' perceptions of blacks. She also trusted missionary reports because Guy B. Johnson encouraged her to. He explained to Granger in a letter that "ethnological literature" was more reliable, but he also wrote that in many cases, "the descriptions given by missionaries and travellers are about as accurate and usable as the descriptions by highly trained anthropologists."[158]

The question that she raised about W. O. Brown's and E. Franklin Frazier's familiarity with "pure Negro communities" also speaks to assumptions made about the impact of education, and more so, "civilization," on blacks like E. Franklin Frazier. Like Lydia Parrish, Mary Granger had come to believe that educated blacks were ashamed of their own Africanness and would stop at nothing to stamp out Africanness in blacks. From this vantage point "pure Negro communities" were imagined to be authentic, and closest to a true black essence—the very thing that a black scholar would have to suppress in order to operate in the civilized world. And what made Frazier and W. O. Brown "radical" was that they rejected the idea that there was a fundamental difference between whites and blacks and embraced the belief that the only difference between blacks and whites was socially constructed, an opinion with which Granger obviously did not agree.

Granger's rebuttals also confirmed that black people's African heritage had taken on new meaning during the 1930s. Granger was right, black artists had demonstrated a marked interest in their African heritage. Zora Neale Hurston, Countee Cullen, and Langston Hughes all invested considerable artistic energy in representing their African ancestry in their works. Eldzier Cortor, a black painter who worked for the Federal Arts Project, was specifically interested in Gullah folk. Cortor won two Rosenwald fellowships to fund his travels to coastal Georgia to paint "Gullah" women and black women in the Caribbean.

Granger pressed forward collecting as many endorsements as she could from additional white scholars who shared her view of blacks' racial inheritance—men she believed outranked E. Franklin Frazier, W. O. Brown, and maybe even Sterling Brown. She added folklorist Newbell Niles Puckett to her list of white advisers and consultants.[159] Puckett had authored a massive compilation of black southern voodoo and superstition titled *Folk Beliefs of the Southern Negro* (1926). He liked Granger's study so much that he wanted to partner with her and expand the project—but she declined the invitation.[160] Melville Herskovits also officially joined her advisory team when he read her manuscript in September 1938.

Of all Granger's advisers, Melville Herskovits's endorsement meant the most because he was the foremost authority on African survivals.[161] She waited until she and her staff had come close to compiling the final manuscript draft before sending it off to Herskovits at Northwestern University. Certainly, Granger was expecting Herskovits to validate her work, but he was reluctant at first. Even though Herskovits had called for scholars to explore the connection between "the Gullahs" and their African progenitors, he was skeptical of the African parallels that the Savannah unit linked to black folk traditions.

Herskovits had only read half of the manuscript when he sent her his comments, but he made nearly one hundred notes on the draft, which was in and of itself a strong testament to the study's problems.[162] Whereas Granger had based her entire conceptualization of African culture on white missionary reports and popular travel books featuring Africans, and had pushed hard to keep their accounts in the footnotes, Herskovits echoed her critics and told her that the section needed "radical revising."[163] He was equally troubled by the fact that she had allowed popular writers like Julia Peterkin, and specifically William Seabrook, to stand in for the research that "real" anthropologists conducted on African culture. On this he wrote: "I would suggest that your bibliography be radically excised of a great many of the popular and semi-popular works of which it is composed."[164] He explained that Seabrook's book on West Africa was "an example of journalistic travel literature at its very worst" and suggested that she reference his research instead.[165] Concerned with how the material discussed in the manuscript had been gathered, and aware of the racial tensions that pervaded southern life, he told Granger to describe her collection process in the text: "The reader will want to know who collected them [the material], whether they were whites or Negroes or both, how did they go about getting to know their informants, and how long they spent in the process."[166] Black folks' voodoo and conjure were popular themes, and were, according to Herskovits, fertile ground for survivals, but he felt that the Savannah unit study overemphasized the topic. Herskovits was very direct when he told Granger that "the religious phases are overstressed" and encouraged her to turn her attention away from hoodoo, roots, and conjure, and look to "work-a-day aspects of life . . . cooperative labor and family organization."[167] If Granger had taken Herskovits's advice and shifted the focus of her study when examining black life on Sapelo, or in any of the other black communities that she visited, she would have had to have contended with the fact that Jim Crow racism and economic discrimination were powerful forces in the lives of coastal Georgia blacks — more powerful than African superstitions.

Granger disagreed with many of Herskovits's suggestions, but she attempted several of the changes that he encouraged her to make to the manuscript. She continued to champion the integrity of the popular sources that Herskovits had dismissed as "unprofessional accounts," and continued to argue that whites who were eye witnesses to black primitives in action were "sometimes more acceptable" than scientific reports "broken down into a complicated analysis," but she ultimately decided to use many of the sources that he pointed her to in order to keep Herskovits as an ally.[168] And Herskovits maintained that Granger had collected "good material" but continued to encourage her to find "more specific references" if she insisted on "tracing African survivals."[169] The two worked together from September 1938 through the completion of the manuscript to salvage Granger's novice survival study.[170] They replaced the descriptions of popular writers and some of the missionaries regarding African practices with Herskovits's writings on African cultural traditions and survivals and other more scholarly sources. Even though Granger did not shift the study's focus away from spiritual survivals and superstitions, Herskovits stood by the work. In the end, he testified that the study should be published because it was a "distinct addition" to existing "literature on Negro life."[171] Herskovits became such a loyal supporter of the Savannah unit study that he would even suggest that Granger ignore Sterling Brown's "far fetched" criticisms on her final draft.[172]

Even though Granger's study had won the support of academia's foremost authority on African survivals, and she had made numerous changes to it—reducing the study to a series of interviews, with African parallels appearing in the appendix—national FWP officials remained reluctant to approve the manuscript for publication. As the chief FWP folklore administrator, Benjamin A. Botkin, explained: "A rereading of the manuscript confirms the impression of a rather disjointed and desultory piece of work in which description, editorial comment, and interview are jumbled together in a feature story fashion."[173] He also complained that Granger's interviewing technique was bad and revealed prejudices.[174] Aside from the fact that the study compiled "data on certain superstitious beliefs and practices in the area," Botkin found almost no value in the work. "At present we have a series of loosely connected local color sketches, each of which is more or less a hodge-podge of chit chat and gossip, with leading questions and often misleading answers."[175] He too suggested that Granger look for European parallels for local superstitions.[176]

Like Botkin, Sterling Brown was skeptical of the study. He maintained that there was merit to Granger's poorly executed survivals thesis, but he did not agree that "superstition" was its strong point. He contended that Granger had been right—African survivals could be found in the region—but rejected voodoo as evidence of a unique regional survival. He wrote, "Conjure, herb-doctoring, etc., can be found in Harlem, Chicago, Los Angeles.... Luck charms are worn by Americans of different races."[177] Brown was worried that the manuscript presented a distorted picture of life in the region: "By concentrating on the primitive aspects of a few people interviewed, a whole section and a large number of people who have many more things of equal and greater importance in their lives are really done injustice."[178] For these reasons and more, Brown suggested that the manuscript not be rushed to press.[179]

National FWP officials agreed that the manuscript was inherently flawed, but they each had different ideas about what those flaws were. One FWP national reviewer even suggested that Granger needed to revise the manuscript so that it read more like Zora Neale Hurston's *Mules and Men*.[180] In the end, they were forced to compromise. The FWP needed to publish books in order to justify the agency's existence. FWP administrators' decision to approve the Savannah unit study for publication was a response to bureaucratic and political pressure, and not an affirmation of Granger's work. One of the final editorial reports acknowledged that the work maintained "a highly questionable thesis," but it ultimately declared that "if there is still disagreement among the various editors and consultants as to these technical details, they should and, we believe, can be settled by compromising differences in the interest of a successful book."[181]

Drums and Shadows *and* Sapelo Island

After nearly three years of offering coastal Georgia blacks sweet rolls, tobacco, and old clothes in exchange for interviews, and debating with state and national FWP officials and consultants, *Drums and Shadows* was finally made available to America's reading public in December 1940.[182] After all of Granger's campaigning at the University of North Carolina, the University of Georgia ended up publishing the study, but Guy Johnson did write the foreword.[183] The book featured interviews conducted in Old Fort, Tin City, Yamacraw, Frogtown and Currytown, Springfield, Brownville, Tatemville, White Bluff, Pin Point, Sandfly, Sunbury, Grimball's Point, Wilmington Island, Harris Neck, Pine Barren, Darien, St. Simons Island, St. Marys, and Sapelo Island. *Drums and Shadows* introduces the blacks who lived in these communities to its readers as people "sometimes called Gullah," while noting that "in general parlance the term is applied only to the Negroes of coastal South Carolina." The book explains that similarities in "type and speech" have resulted in their inclusion under the label, and clarifies that "Geechee," a term derived from the name of the nearby Ogeechee River, is "also used locally to designate the Negroes of this district."[184] In an attempt to re-create the dramatic documentary photography that Doris Ulmann produced for Julia Peterkin's *Roll, Jordan, Roll*, Mary Granger's longtime friends Muriel and Malcolm Bell Jr. staged and captured haunting images depicting coastal Georgia blacks and their crafts.[185]

Consistent with national office FWP guidelines for collecting folklore, each community portrait generally featured interviews of the oldest and least educated residents in each locale. Granger explained that she preferred this group because "young and middle aged persons, reticent before strangers, appear dubious and suspicious." She wrote that younger coastal Georgia blacks "profess great knowledge of conjure and superstitions, but they hasten to say that they 'sho ain't gonuh tell nobody' what they know about these things." Granger found older blacks, like Shad Hall and Katie Brown, to be "more loquacious, [and] enjoy relating their beliefs and customs to a willing listener."[186]

In many of the communities featured in the book, Granger and her staff asked local residents about hoodoo and conjuh, roots, drums, ghosts, animal sacrifices, burial rituals, witches, charms, amulets, African and slave ancestors, and folktales. Readers could find parallels for these practices among the Ibo, Tshi, Dahomean, Yoruba, Bantu, Ewe, Ibibio, Ashanti, Mandingo, Hausa, and Bakongo peoples of West Africa and even Ethiopia in the appendix.[187] Not all of the practices were linked to Africa. The cultures of Haiti, Jamaica, Suriname, and the Bahamas were listed as having similar beliefs, practices, and folklore.[188] Granger was right when she told Sterling Brown that removing the term "African survivals" from the work did not distance the study from the underlying assumption that coastal Georgia blacks' superstitions were ultimately African. Her unstated thesis was clearly transmitted in the book.

Even though Granger heeded national FWP administrators' warnings and did not directly describe the "survivals" named in the book's title as "African," she did not alter her imaginings of coastal Georgia Gullah folks. In the introduction, she described coastal Georgia blacks as being superstitious and fearful: "Many coastal Negroes view adversity not as the workings of fate but as the revenge of a personal enemy brought about by the mystic working of the conjure doctor." She wrote, "His imagination continues to crowd his world with spirits, both good and evil. Spirits of the departed are still believed to make frequent visitations to the earth and are as real to this type of Negro as his next-door neighbor."[189]

Flouting Melville Herskovits's advisements, Granger's writing shows little acceptance of the idea that voodoo practices were survivals of a valuable West African cosmology. To the contrary, *Drums and Shadows* seemed to draw more inspiration from popular voodoo entertainment than it did Herskovits's scholarly formulations. For example, in Old Fort, Granger and her research team asked residents if they believed in witches and "conjuh": "At the mention of 'cunjuh' the old woman lit her pipe, smiled pathetically, and shook her head. As the blue smoke curled upward, she told of having been conjured and of how it changed her whole life in a few short weeks."[190] Like Parrish, Granger painted Georgia's Gullah as secretive, a trait that frequently veiled the dark activities of voodoo doctors who further concealed themselves underneath an unassuming demeanor. Invoking the same dramatic feel communicated in newspaper voodoo reports, Granger wrote about Evan Brown—a secret rootworker: "To see him going daily about his duties as janitor of the West Broad Street Negro School, no one would suspect unusual powers at work beneath his good-natured exterior." She continued, "Yet he not only said that he believed absolutely in the supernatural but proudly asserted that he could work magic himself."[191] The sensational voodoo superstitions reported in *Drums and Shadows* contained all of the elements found in popular voodoo tales. The study contained the testimonies of interviewees born with the "caul" who could see the dead and the future; of midnight harvest ceremonies guided by mystical drums; of stories of conjure specialists who could transform themselves into animals; and of animals sacrificed to rid the living of the dead. It also included tales about witch doctors who made conjure bags who could cast spells as well as conjure victims. The reports even described the dangers lurking around voodooists. Granger wrote about a warning she and her research team received while conducting fieldwork and described it as one of the most memorable exchanges. Mr. Jones "sternly forbade us to discuss conjure." He asked, "Dohn yuh know . . . dat yuh might bring trouble on yuhsef?"[192] Jones's warning did not deter them. When stories like these featured in *Drums and Shadows* are read in the context of the 1920s and 1930s voodoo craze, coastal Georgia blacks seem less exceptional, and more like figments of the nation's imagination. But, more significant, and less popular, material appeared in the book too.

Documentation of important traditions, folk tales, and beliefs, and powerful memories of slavery days, Africa, and African-born ancestors are jumbled together with sensational caricatures of superstitious black folk in the book. *Drums and Shadows* retold stories about Africans who took flight to escape enslavement, and stories that African ancestors of coastal blacks told about their captivity, their religions, and about their homes in Africa. The study also features local blacks' recollections of African words, baptismal rituals, ring shouts, and gravesite decorations and shrines in the text. However, these recorded treasures were not contextualized, and their deeper meanings were not investigated.

A close examination of the way that Sapelo Islanders were characterized and featured in *Drums and Shadows* provides several examples of the troubling assumptions that contaminated the study and highlights the fact that the Savannah unit missed many opportunities to truly contextualize and examine coastal Georgia blacks' past and present. On Sapelo, Granger wrote, many Islanders "lead an easy carefree life which consists chiefly of fishing, crabbing, and cultivating a small patch of garden, while others engage in regular employment at the sawmill or in the company offices."[193] Had Granger taken Herskovits's advice and explored the Islanders' work life and routines, or if she had done as W. O. Brown suggested and considered the social context that shaped coastal Georgia blacks' lives, she would have noticed the tensions and stresses that made Sapelo Islanders' lives anything but carefree. The fact that Granger concluded that Islanders' constant struggle with poverty was a carefree existence reveals her primitivist orientation. The primitivist did not view primitives as being concerned with anything beyond their base desires. In the minds of white primitivists like Mary Granger, the aspiration to accumulate wealth, obtain meaningful work, and the desire to secure land, property, and rights were aspirations far beyond the primitives' mental grasp. She could not imagine that Sapelo Islanders, like other coastal Georgia blacks, were consumed by anything except rootwork and superstitions.

As far as Granger and her researchers could tell, black-white relations on Sapelo Island were peaceful and in their proper order. They were oblivious to the fact that when R. J. Reynolds purchased the island from Howard Coffin in 1934, his vision for his private opulent island paradise would ultimately dispossess many of the Islanders of their land. Sapelo Islanders' lives were anything but "carefree" under Reynolds's rule. Reynolds enjoyed the privacy that island life afforded him, especially since just five years before he purchased Coffin's holdings, he had served five months in jail in Britain on a manslaughter charge after killing a man while driving drunk.[194] Even though he retained many of Coffin's island industries, he planned to make changes that would effect the Islanders' lives for generations.

Reynolds was determined to consolidate black landholdings on the island, and he used threats and coercion to force blacks into "land swaps" designed to push them all into one hammock community—Hog Hammock—giving him ownership over the rest of the island.[195] Because most Sapelo Islanders worked for Reynolds as maids and cooks in his mansion, or as laborers for his various island enterprises, he was able to threaten their livelihoods in exchange for their land.[196] Joe Johnson said that some Islanders had offered land to Reynolds in exchange for loans and cash advances, and they lost their land because Reynolds was savvy and originated terms for the loans that borrowers could not meet.[197] Some Islanders willingly sold their land or interest in Sapelo family properties during the Great Depression to fund their relocation to cities on the mainland. But others say that their families lost land in unequal swaps.

Sapelo Islander Ruth Hillery Johnson tells a story about how her parents lost their Shell Hammock property in a land swap with Reynolds. She remembered the day that her father marked a contract that one of Reynolds's island managers presented to him with an "x." She said that her father was told that he could move back to Shell Hammock once renovations to the area were made, but the verbal agreement between R. J. Reynolds and Gibb Hillery was not honored.[198] When asked why all the Islanders abandoned Raccoon Bluff, Allen Green, Sapelo's renowned basket weaver, replied, "Reynolds want the people to move from there. He said to get all the people in one settlement, he could do more for them. That was a trap set."[199] Cornelia Walker Bailey, the daughter of the woman that W. Robert Moore photographed—Hettie Walker—also remembered stories about how Reynolds coaxed Islanders into land swaps: "He offered to build new houses in the community for a few families in Shell Hammock . . . they turned out to be cheap, little preassembled-type wooden houses with a very inferior grade of wood that didn't hold up well."[200] Bailey had first-hand experience with Reynolds's land swaps. She remembers how the white island manager "Cap'n Frank Durant," gradually pressured her father to leave their land in Belle Marsh and move to Hog Hammock.[201] First, Cap'n Frank suggested that Hicks and Hettie Walker's children would fare better in Hog Hammock because they would not have to walk so far to school. Then he promised Hicks Walker free lumber if he built a new house in Hog Hammock and even told him that R. J. Reynolds would continue to pay him on the days that he took off from work to build the house. When Hicks Walker declined Reynolds's offer, the island manager responded, "Well Hicks, you know it'd be too bad if you lose your job and have to go to the mainland and your family have to fend for themselves."[202] The prospects of economic banishment from the island and leaving his family behind was too horrible for Hicks Walker to consider, so he moved his family to Hog Hammock.

After spending three days on the island that doubled as R. J. Reynolds's private hideaway, and blinded by her hoodoo superstition obsession, Granger missed the land struggle that was unfolding in front of her. This is perhaps ironic, because Granger noted in the book, possibly in awe, that an old Sapelo Islander who sat for an interview, Nero Jones, lived on sixty-five acres of land with his daughter—land that he owned.[203] But, her fantasies about Sapelo Islanders' "isolated existence" that helped them to preserve "many customs and beliefs of their ancestors, as well as the dialect of the older coastal Negro" clouded her perception of their actual lives.[204] So, she sought out the island's oldest residents for evidence that confirmed her singular impression.

And she found some willing informants who offered little challenge to her views. By the time Mary Granger came to Sapelo, Katie Brown and Shad Hall

Katie Brown in Drums and Shadows. *Courtesy Muriel and Malcolm Bell Jr.*

Shad Hall in *Drums and Shadows. Courtesy Muriel and Malcolm Bell Jr.*

had become veteran Gullah informants. They were among the first elderly Sapelo Islanders she sought and were featured in her book. Photographs of Katie Brown and Shad Hall were included among the other documentary scenes from coastal Georgia. Granger and her team asked Sapelo residents the usual set of voodoo questions, and Katie Brown responded, "I an know bout cunjuh ... I heahs bout spells on people, but I ain seen um."[205] Shad Hall, on the other hand, told Granger and her entourage that he had seen people bury conjure bags under their doorsteps and tie rags on gates to protect their homes.[206] He even told Granger that during his grandmother's time, animals were killed during "set-ups": "Dey kill a wite chicken wen de hab set-ups tuh keep duh spirits away ... she alluz keep wit e chicken fuh dat in yahd."[207] He told them he had not heard much about "cunjuh" on Sapelo.[208] Both Katie Brown and Shad Hall did share stories about "shadows" (ghosts) with their curious visitors.[209]

While Katie Brown and Shad Hall had given Savannah unit researchers a few supernatural tales, one elderly Sapelo Islander refused to fuel their fantasies about superstitious blacks. Julia Grovernor snubbed Granger's voodoo questions and refused the pipe tobacco she offered. Granger described Grovernor: "Julia, very black, tall, and gaunt, was slightly hostile and suspicious and disinclined to talk."[210] Grovernor told Granger, "No'm, I ain know nuttun. Ise feeble-minded. I bin weak in head sence I small chile. No'm, I ain know nuttun bout witches. I ain know nuttn bout root doctuhs. No'm, I ain nebuh heah uh cunjuh. No'm, I ain know nuttun bout spells."[211] Julia Grovernor eventually gave in to Granger's inquiries when she stumbled upon a topic that she liked— her Muslim "Ibo" grandparents.[212] Grovernor had decided that talking about her ancestors was acceptable and told Granger about the two old Ibos, Hannah and Calina, and she repeated the story that her grandmother told about being abducted by slave catchers while digging peanuts with her aunt in Africa when she was a little girl.[213] Grovernor's cousin Phoebe Gilbert told Granger and her team a story about how Calina was trapped by slave catchers when he was a boy. He told his granddaughter that he was playing on the beach when he and a group of children were lured to a boat because they were curious about a piece of red flannel that the men on the boat displayed to attract their attention: "Den duh mens comes off boat an ketch um."[214]

On Sapelo Island, Granger expanded her inquiry to include questions about Muslim slaves. Mary Granger could have easily learned about the Islanders' Muslim ancestry from the *National Geographic Magazine* article. However she learned about the island's Muslim past, it captured her attention. And Herskovits had told Granger how important Mohammed's journal translation would be, because it would likely serve as a "demonstration of how much an educated slave knew and retained of certain formal aspects of one of the complex West African civilizations."[215] But Granger did not include this sort of analysis in *Drums and Shadows*. She asked Katie Brown and Shad Hall about Bilali Mohammed and recorded what Katie Brown and Shad Hall told her about their Muslim ancestor. They told her about Bilali's seven daughters and about his wives.[216] They described his prayer rituals: "Dey wuz bery puticuluh bout duh time dey pray an dey bery reguluh bout dey hour. Wen duh sun come up, wen it straight obuh head an wen it set."[217] Shad also shared with Granger their ancestors' borrowed memories from Africa: "Muh Gran Hestuh say she kin membuh duh house she lib in in Africa."[218] Mohammed's descendants were not the only Islanders who told the Savannah unit about the island's Muslim past. Nero Jones also shared memories of Hannah and Calina's prayers made "on duh bead."[219]

Despite all of the valuable and fascinating things that she had heard about Sapelo Islanders' Muslim ancestors, and other recollections from Africa and slavery days, Granger's summary of her visit focused on the relationship between Sapelo Islanders and mysterious hoodoo. Shad Hall had told Granger that he had been a slave, that he recalled the succession of masters who held him in bondage, and he had even said that he was a "big man wen freedom come," but there is no evidence in the book that suggests that she showed any interest in his experience as chattel.[220] After interviewing Islanders, observing their crafts, and visiting a religious service at one of their praise houses, Granger concluded that the Islanders shared superstitions prevalent among coastal Georgia blacks: "If an owl hoots on top of the house or near a house, it is supposed to be a sign of death. . . . If a rooster comes upon the porch and starts crowing, it is a sign of death in the house. It is also considered bad luck to start on a journey and have to turn back." Granger reported that among the Islanders "the method employed to ward off disaster is to draw a cross where you turned back and spit on it." While these small discoveries confirmed Granger's thesis, the fact that she did not find a voodoo doctor on the island must have been disappointing: "We were told that most of the island Negroes believed in root doctors, but that they imported them from the mainland. There were none on the island."[221] Descendants of the Sapelo Islanders featured in 1930s studies similarly report that there were no "rootworkers" on the island, and said that those practitioners could only be found in mainland cities like Savannah and Charleston.[222] Nonetheless, Granger still pointed out that they all believed in conjuh, and for her, that was a significant piece of evidence of their racial heritage.

Granger may have been disappointed that she did not find an elaborate voodoo scene in the one place that she had determined was most ripe for authentic survivals. Yet she maintained that the people were unique and concluded her Sapelo Island report with a description of its African feel: "The boat neared the mainland. Our trip was over. As we bade goodbye to our guide, we cast a look of farewell at the dim outline of the island. On the journey homeward impressions received during our stay on Sapelo crowded against one another in disturbing sequence. . . . Faintly the echo of shouting rose and fell in the distance. The measured chanting of voices and the pounding of feet seemed to follow us across the water."[223] The "impressions" of Sapelo Island that stayed with Granger, the "shouting," "chanting voices," and "pounding feet" — specters of the Islanders' undeniable African essence — all followed her across the water and would influence the perception of Sapelo Islanders for years to come.

The Shadow

Drums and Shadows was sparsely reviewed and was equally praised and criticized. The New York Times featured a review of the Savannah unit study alongside a book about South Carolina Sea Islanders written by Mason Crum, a professor of religion at Duke University, titled Gullah: Negro Life in the Carolina Sea Islands (1940). Like Granger, Crum was a white southerner who attempted an investigation of the cultural world of the exotic blacks who lived in his home region. Melville Herskovits dismissed Crum's book, citing Crum's nostalgia and the fact that he did not conduct field research as reasons why "it cannot be said of the book as a whole that it contributes anything significant to the understanding of Negro life in the sea islands, its professed objective."[224] But the New York Times review applauded Crum's manuscript and presented Gullah and Drums and Shadows as important, complementary works.[225] Both books were touted as valuable contributions to the study of folklore because they captured and portrayed the essence of blacks living on barrier islands.[226] So much had been written about South Carolina Sea Islanders, so the New York Times reporter further praised the Savannah unit for covering "fresher ground" by including locales like Sapelo Island and capturing its essence before "sophistication" comes to the black people living along the South Carolina and Georgia coast.[227]

Drums and Shadows was criticized too. Columbia University anthropologist George Herzog's review of the book expressed the view that Granger's work was exaggerated and questioned why its author did not attempt to uncover European parallels, an oversight that left the study's readers "with an exaggerated picture of African culture on the Georgia coast." But Herzog concluded that the study's value exceeds its flaws: "Weighed against the wealth of new material the book offers, however, and the immediate glimpses of Africana on United States soil, its weaker points are negligible and the Project may well be complimented on a pleasant volume."[228]

Drums and Shadows became a work of lasting historical and anthropological importance despite mixed reviews. Just one year after Granger's study was published, her work had already been used to bolster scholarly research; and the conflict, controversy, and compromises that shaped *Drums and Shadows'* production were quickly forgotten by researchers who used the book as an authoritative source for information on Georgia's Gullah. In 1941, William R. Bascom, one of Melville Herskovits's first graduate students, published an essay titled "Acculturation Among the Gullah Negroes" in *American Anthropologist*. In the essay, Bascom cited *Drums and Shadows*, referred to Sapelo Islanders as "Gullah," and included them in the short list of locales in the coastal regions where "African elements" are most pronounced.[229] In Bascom's essay, it becomes evident that Granger's amateur and problematic theories had become fact. More shocking is that he cited Julia Peterkin's novel *Black April* (1927) too. It is obvious that Bascom was a good student, because he carefully navigated the fact that most of the African survivals hunting in the region had not involved the type of rigorous investigation methods that Lorenzo Dow Turner employed. Bascom was careful to note at the start of his essay that exact and specific African traits had not been found in coastal regions: "But even among the Gullah in the coastal regions of South Carolina and Georgia, where the Negroes have been as isolated as anywhere in the United States, resemblances to specific African tribes are very rare."[230] Yet Bascom reasoned that there are African survivals in Gullah communities, but that they were general, and not specific: "For the most part the similarities are to those elements which are common to West Africa as a whole—to the common denominators of West African culture."[231] In this way, the authentic Africanness and Gullahness of Sapelo Islanders, and the blacks who lived in other Gullah districts, was at first institutionalized as a vague, yet verifiable fact.

Since the publication of W. Robert Moore's article in 1934, Granger's study in 1940, Parrish's song collection in 1942, and Turner's linguistic study in 1949, Sapelo Islanders have been grouped and identified by a label that many do not use to name themselves—Gullah. When the descendants of Sapelo Islanders featured in 1930s studies were asked about the term "Gullah," they insisted that it is not a word that they use to describe themselves. Paul Walker said that on Sapelo Island, among the blacks who live there, "You never hear talk of Gullah."[232] Similarly, Betty Johnson Cooper said that when she grew up on the island, she never heard anyone use the word.[233] Emmitt and Emma Johnson's son, Joe Johnson, remarked of the term "Gullah," "They makes the name."[234] The "they" that Johnson identified was white people who wanted to sell books. Cornelia Walker Bailey echoed Johnson's sentiment: "It was something thought of by white folks. . . . In South Carolina, they say they always call themselves Gullah. . . . In Georgia it was never Gullah, it was Geechee."[235]

The identification of Sapelo Islanders as Gullah in scholarly literature, and

Sapelo Islanders' views of the label, reflect the gulf between the way that Sapelo Islanders see themselves and the way that outsiders have imagined them. The meanings associated with the Gullah label were constructed through a complex history, one that involved a myriad of influences and motivations. The noble quest for a venerable African ancestry; stereotypical depictions of a primitive people; the rejection of Victorian ideas about race; the voodoo craze; and the institutionalization of the hunt for America's own folk are all factors that contributed to the construction of Sapelo Islanders' Gullah identity. W. Robert Moore, Lydia Parrish, Lorenzo Dow Turner, and Mary Granger each contributed to the collective image of Sapelo Island's Gullah folk. While most of these works presented problems, they at least furnish for Sapelo Islanders' descendants a repository of literature in which they can find their ancestors talking to researchers, dancing for them, remembering slavery days, telling them stories about distant ancestors, and posing for pictures, as well as providing information about their ancestors that would have otherwise been lost.

While outsiders were preoccupied with uncovering Sapelo Islanders' African past, Islanders were consumed with navigating complicated economic and racial terrain. Securing employment, educating their children, amassing wealth, and securing their ancestral land had occupied them for generations. To achieve those ends, they would do whatever was necessary. Eventually, revolutionary changes in the perception of Gullah folk, new African survivals theories and research, and catastrophic trends in their communities would encourage them to re-examine their connection to the Gullah identity and take a long, hard look at the role that stories about their *past* might play in their *future*.

5 Reworking Roots

BLACK WOMEN WRITERS, THE SAPELO INTERVIEWS
IN DRUMS AND SHADOWS, AND THE MAKING OF A
NEW GULLAH FOLK

*Praisesong for the Widow started with a place I came across, this place called Ibo
Landing in a book entitled Drums and Shadows.... That's how Praisesong began,
with that folktale.*
—Paule Marshall

"We want to look ahead. We don't want to remember Geechee or slavery or Africa. We just want to be American citizens like everyone else. And all we need is enough work so we can stay right here on our island."[1] That is what Sapelo Island elder Ben Johnson told James Cerruti, *National Geographic Magazine*'s assistant editor, when Cerruti came to the island in 1971. Thirty-seven years had passed since the first white *National Geographic Magazine* staff man came to Sapelo and introduced Ben Johnson's aunt Emma Johnson, his uncle Emmitt Johnson, his cousins, and the island's other black residents to its readers as American oddities.[2] Like his predecessor, Cerruti came to Sapelo while touring the Low Country's coast, gathering information and taking photographs throughout the region for an article. He described Sapelo Islanders as "unusual" black folk, who descended from people enslaved by a benign slave master, and as a group of blacks whose oldest members held on to old-time ways, "old-time talk," and the remnants of old traditions shunned by younger Islanders—all characteristics that echoed so much of what had been written about them during the 1930s.[3] Even though Cerruti's discussion of the Islanders does hark back to the primitivist formula that shaped the way they were described in the magazine in 1934, this article was different.

When Ben Johnson's comments quoted in the piece are read alongside Cerruti's descriptions of a unique and charming time-forgotten southern black community, a different view of Sapelo Islanders emerges. Johnson's comments are a clear indication that Sapelo Islanders had grown tired of entertaining outsiders' curiosities about African survivals, the past, and "old-time" ways—they were more concerned about their future.

Although Cerruti was aware that tensions were brewing between Sapelo's residents, the Reynolds Foundation, and the state of Georgia over the fate of the island's black community, his view of race relations on the island reflected the same plantation nostalgia that shaped his *National Geographic Magazine* predecessors' observations of Sapelo's people. In the article, Cerruti professed that the "angry winds sweeping black-white relations elsewhere have hardly touched Sapelo."[4] But when Ben Johnson told Cerruti that "Slave days are over" and declared that it was time for Islanders to fight for their ancestral land ("We've got to tell 'em why we ain't gonna go"), it was clear that Cerruti's characterization was more fantasy than fact.[5] Jim Crow had sustained critical blows throughout the South and the nation. Sapelo Islanders were ready to take control of the stories that were told about them and they were going to fight for their home.

So much had changed on Sapelo in the years between World War II and 1971 when *National Geographic Magazine* came back to the island. The Islanders had kissed their menfolk goodbye as they left the island to serve America during World War II, the Korean War, and in Vietnam.[6] They had watched as even more family members and beloved friends packed up their belongings and left Sapelo and headed for nearby cities on the mainland like Savannah, Atlanta, and Jacksonville, or faraway destinations in the North. The steady flow of migrants who left Sapelo in search of good jobs and a better life resulted in dwindling numbers of black residents on the island. By 1970, the island's black population decreased from 345 residents in 1930 to roughly 175 residents.[7] The number of children who attended the Sapelo school that had for decades serviced all of the island's little children ebbed, and so did the number of middle and high school–aged children who took the long ferry ride to the mainland each day to attend secondary school.[8]

Sapelo Islanders had closely followed the war against Jim Crow that took place on the mainland during the 1950s and 1960s. The Islanders who had electricity, televisions, or radios during the civil rights movement huddled around television sets watching protest scenes or gathered around radios listening to the latest reports, while others read about them in newspapers. At the same time that civil rights leaders pushed for racial equality and the death of Jim Crow, R. J. Reynolds continued to use his land swap scheme to push the island's remaining black residents off the land their families had inhabited for generations into Hog Hammock.[9] Even though the world around them was changing, one Islander remembered that R. J. Reynolds and his "henchmen" were "pretending that nothing had changed. . . . The whole island was run like it was his private paradise."[10] Reynolds's own son acknowledged that his father seemed to fantasize that he was the "lord of a well-run kingdom" on Sapelo.[11] So it is not surprising that civil rights victories had no influence on the way that Reynolds ran the island and interacted with its black residents.

Civil rights–era victories were not just slow to come to Sapelo, all of the blacks who lived in McIntosh County, Georgia, found themselves waiting to experience the effects of Jim Crow's legal demise. But as Melissa Fay Greene points out in her journalistic portrait of McIntosh County's delayed civil rights revolution, *Praying for Sheetrock: A Work of Nonfiction* (1991), the death of Jim Crow would be postponed in the county until the mid-to-late 1970s.[12] The McIntosh County that Greene characterizes in *Praying for Sheetrock* was anything but hospitable toward the idea of racial equality. Instead she describes a poor coastal county steeped in a culture of corruption and racism — a place where blacks told stories about blacks who were lynched, about blacks who "got out of control" and disappeared: "'We used to say they took a swim across the river wearing too much chain.'"[13] McIntosh was a coastal county where some blacks remembered the time when black women would hide in the woods while making the long walk to work at shrimp canning factories "because white guys be coming along."[14] It was a county where a corrupt sheriff — a white man to whom R. J. Reynolds had given sizable monetary gifts — took local blacks' land in exchange for making warrants and indictments go away.[15] In this climate, Reynolds had no reason to change course.

But, like black people all over the nation, and the other blacks who lived in McIntosh County, Sapelo Islanders expected change. Tensions on Sapelo worsened when R. J. Reynolds died in 1964. His young widow sold a sizable portion of his Sapelo estate to the state of Georgia, and as a result, the Department of Natural Resources (DNR) replaced the island's white patriarch in the "big house." Reynolds's pet project — the Marine Institute — was a permanent fixture on the island as a University of Georgia research center by 1964, and his dream of creating a hunting and wildlife reserve on the island was well under way.[16] But life for Sapelo Islanders grew more and more uncertain. The jobs that Coffin and Reynolds offered the Islanders were gone, and the few jobs that DNR and the Marine Institute made available were not enough to stop the steady flow of migrants who left the island in search of work. For a period of time during the 1960s, Sapelo's children were banned from using Reynolds's ferry to commute to school, so their parents sent them to live with family and friends on the mainland so that they could continue their education.[17] In the midst of the new challenges that they faced, Sapelo Islanders began to question the future of their community on the island, where many of their ancestors had lived since slavery.

By the 1970s, Sapelo's people agreed with Ben Johnson — it was time to fight for their island. McIntosh County blacks had begun to pose significant challenges to the local white power structure during the 1970s. First, there was the group of two hundred blacks who stormed Darien's city hall demanding answers about a police shooting in 1972.[18] And in the fall of 1975, a group of outraged, anxious, and worried black residents gathered in the annex of St. Luke Baptist Church — one of two churches their ancestors had built on the island in the first decades of freedom — to devise a plan to stop a proposed land sale that was rumored to force them off the island.[19] Among the meeting's organizers were: Ben Lewis, an Islander who lived on the mainland and worked at Savannah State College; Fred Johnson, the son of Emmitt and Emma Johnson described as the "dusky coachmen" and pictured driving President Coolidge and Howard Coffin in the oxcart in *National Geographic Magazine* in 1934; and Cornelia Bailey, Hettie Walker's daughter, the woman whose picture also appeared in that 1934 article balancing yams on her head.[20] Fred Johnson, Cornelia Bailey, and all of the Islanders who attended the meeting were fearful that the whispers and gossip that they heard about the Reynolds Foundation's plans to sell the island's south end to the state, a sale that included Hog Hammock, would drive them off the island forever. So, they gathered at St. Luke and unwittingly reinvigorated their ancestors' more than one-hundred-year-old fight to secure black land on the island.

They had good reason to believe that the rumors about a plan to expel them from Sapelo were true. Some say that Reynolds, while suffering from the debilitating effects of emphysema, had promised his favorite black employees that they would be taken care of when he died. But Sapelo Islanders had little faith in promises made by a man who had disinherited his own sons.[21] Moreover, Reynolds had successfully acquired black landholdings around the island and pushed all of the island's residents into Hog Hammock. He cleared black residents out of Belle Marsh, Lumber Landing, Shell Hammock, and Raccoon Bluff.[22] And when he died, his widow sold the north half of the island to the state of Georgia in 1969 — a transaction that many Islanders suspected included property that Reynolds acquired surreptitiously.[23]

The Sapelo Islanders who attended the meeting that day knew that the Reynolds Foundation had enough money and influence to crush their rebellion, but they were empowered by a new consciousness. Cornelia Bailey explained that "the civil rights movement had made us realize that you *can* oppose someone powerful, and not only that, sometimes you can even win."[24] So they hired a black lawyer and founded the Hog Hammock Community Foundation.[25] Organizing and securing legal counsel would prove wise. Bailey maintained that when the "first set of papers on the proposed sale of the South End" were read aloud at a community meeting, "Hog Hammock actually was included in the proposal," but once the Reynolds Foundation "realized the stink it would cause to uproot us," the "next set of papers read aloud" at a later meeting no longer included Hog Hammock.[26]

The Hog Hammock Community Foundation won their first battle, but their struggle was far from over; it had just begun. Just one year before President Jimmy Carter, a Georgia native, followed in President Coolidge's and President Hoover's footsteps and planned a getaway on Sapelo, the island's school closed in 1978.[27] Hog Hammock was patrolled by DNR workers, and the island was buzzing with groups of tourists who ventured to Sapelo to participate in DNR's sightseeing expeditions.[28] The Islanders were, once again, objects of interest for curious outsiders. New challenges erupted at every turn, and they needed a strong weapon to stake claims to their ancestral home.

A group of black women writers would unknowingly give Sapelo Islanders exactly what they needed for the next phase in their fight. Through their fictional works, black women writers gifted Sapelo Islanders with one of the most powerful weapons they could deploy in the fight to keep their island home. A resurgence of interest in Sea Islanders' cultural lives among scholars and artists during the 1970s, 1980s, and 1990s inspired the women who would give Sapelo Islanders and other coastal Georgia and South Carolina blacks a new way to imagine their identity, and a new way to understand their culture—one that replaced the old primitivist and condescending portraits of their cultural world that pervaded Moore's, Parrish's, and Granger's writings. Black women writers and a new generation of scholars reached back into the imperfect repository of sometimes racist 1930s published works featuring Sapelo Islanders and gave them—and all blacks living in the coastal communities of the Low Country—a reason to remember Gullah, Geechee, and Africa—and reasons why they should never be separated from their land.

Burying and Unearthing Roots

When *National Geographic Magazine* came back to Sapelo in the 1970s, more than three decades had passed since W. Robert Moore, Lydia Parrish, Lorenzo D. Turner, and Mary Granger had come to the island in search of African survivals. In that time, major changes in the nation had briefly quieted interest in the African roots of coastal Georgia blacks. World War II shifted the imagination of many of the nation's scholars, writers, and artists away from the exotic cultural landscapes of America to the war and the world beyond America's borders.[29] Mary Granger complained in a letter she wrote to Melville Herskovits in 1941 that her plans to expand the African survivals research that she conducted in Georgia had been halted by the evolving global conflict: "I have written Washington recommending the extension of the work, but everybody is so taken up with defense that I don't know whether or not anthropology will get a hearing!"[30] Granger would have found the civil rights years even more inhospitable to the search for African survivals, and interest in the African heritage of black Americans would not peak again until the Black Power movement of the 1960s, just before her death.

Outsider interest in Sapelo Islanders' African heritage and the African background of the blacks who lived along South Carolina's and Georgia's coast had always been connected to larger national trends rooted in complicated questions about race. While the marked loss of interest in black southerners' African background during the World War II years can be easily explained by the fact that the war had so completely consumed the imagination of the nation, the continued disinterest in Gullah folks' African heritage during the civil rights years is more complicated. However, one scholar's writings provide insights into why the obsession with the connection between blacks and their African background prevalent during the 1920s and 1930s dwindled during the civil rights years. Charles I. Glicksberg, a white English professor at Brooklyn College, authored several articles during the 1940s that pointed out the condescending and prejudiced white attitudes that stoked the 1920s and 1930s "Negro vogue." He argued that white people's "fascination" with blacks during the interwar years simply "reinforced the role traditionally played by the Negro," and reduced American blacks to "a foreign but picturesque ingredient ... which was made to stand out conspicuously by emphasizing its strangeness, its uniqueness, its sheer primitivism."[31]

Glicksberg directly called for an end to African survivals hunting in the 1947 article "Negro Americans and the African Dream" published in Phylon. He wrote: "If the Negroes in the United States have no intention of 'returning' to Africa, why then this furor about African culture and African Art?"[32] Glicksberg rebuked Melville Herskovits's retention theory and argued that it undermined black efforts to be perceived and treated as equal to whites. He posed pointed questions for survivals enthusiasts to consider, such as: "What are these survivals and how are they to be identified and measured?"; and "Does not such a theory tend to revive the exploded fallacy of 'racial character' and 'racial inheritance'? Such doctrines reinforce the popular stereotypes that the Negro is ... basically African." Glicksberg posed another poignant question: "If he still carries within him the cultural survivals of his racial ancestry, what hope is there of ever assimilating him within the American cultural pattern?"[33]

Glicksberg's opinions did not inform civil rights leaders' views on black people's African heritage, but his sentiments do clarify why inquiries into African survivals diminished during the 1950s. Despite the fact that the New

Negro intelligentsia and New Negro artists hoped that explorations of black folklife and culture and black people's African heritage would reveal black people's humanity, encourage race pride, and undermine the culture of white supremacy, white audiences, white sponsors, and white critics overwhelmingly continued to process "fictional" and "factual" accounts and representations of black folk culture and African retentions through the primitivist lens. The New Negro folk culture project that had in part inspired the surge of Gullah studies during the period had failed to transform the popular view of black culture. And by the 1940s, the rise of colorblind liberalism, a discourse which asserted that there was no difference between races, eclipsed the notion that iterations of blacks' racial and cultural uniqueness was the pathway to equality. Color-blind liberalism instead encouraged the idea that eradicating white-on-black racism would stamp out racial inequality.[34]

Indeed, the shift in discourses about race and racism during these years pushed ideas about racial distinctiveness and African survivals to the back burner. E. Franklin Frazier's insistence that whatever was distinct about black culture was born from systematic racial oppression became more relevant alongside Gunnar Myrdal's landmark study *An American Dilemma: The Negro Problem and Modern Democracy* (1944) — a work that dominated conversations about American race relations after the war. Myrdal, the Swedish scholar who led the Carnegie Foundation–sponsored project, collaborated and consulted with leading American social scientists to gain insight into America's race problem, and for support for the survey.[35] To varying degrees, and with differing levels of enthusiasm, intellectuals such as Guy B. Johnson, Howard Odum, Sterling Brown, W. O. Brown, Ralph Bunche, E. Franklin Frazier, Melville Herskovits, Charles S. Johnson, Alain Locke, W. E. B. Du Bois, Franz Boas, and Robert Park offered Myrdal their reading of American race relations.[36] Although Myrdal consulted with Herskovits and cited his research, and even though the Carnegie Foundation would publish Herskovits's *Myth of the Negro Past* first, Myrdal was not a fan of Herskovits's survivals theories.[37] Myrdal regarded Herskovits as an extremist concerning his interest in African survivals.[38] And in the final study, Myrdal estimated that the 1920s movement to recover black history, folk art, and African survivals was simply a form of protest and described Herskovits's efforts as a "yeoman service" rendered to "Negro History propagandists": "He has not only made excellent field studies of certain African and West Indian Negro groups, but has written a general book to glorify African culture generally and to show how it has survived in the American Negro community. He has avowedly done this to give the Negro confidence in himself and to give the white man less 'reason' to have race prejudice."[39] Identifying the hunt for African survivals as a *symptom* of the nation's larger race drama, Myrdal's comments undercut survivals research by diminishing the significance of blacks' cultural inheritances. *An American Dilemma*, forty-five chapters examining race in America, called attention to the greater conflict at the heart of notions of race and identity in the United States—systematic white oppression.

As the civil rights movement unfolded, color-blind liberalism, the emphasis on cultural "sameness," and structural racism were dominant, but its leaders also posited a new view of a transformed black southerner who was fighting Jim Crow, and whose distinct culture thrived despite racial oppression.[40] This cultural "reconfiguration" found popular elements of black southern culture—such as religious music—morphing into the freedom songs that motivated protestors to press onward; they were no longer simple melodic expressions of an essential racial characteristic.[41] During the civil rights years, there was little room for stories about content, naïve, ignorant, loyal, musical, superstitious, and quaint quasi-African primitive "aunties" and "uncles" like the ones that Julia Peterkin told about Gullah folk. The new black southerner whom the civil rights movement introduced to the nation through its marches and protests were not tucked away in time-forgotten rural communities, separated from one another by distinct regions. The new black southerner lived in one place—the Jim Crow South—and they were anything but content.

But the South's Gullah folk would reemerge as distinct once again amid another wave of dramatic reimagining of the value of black people's racial heritage and African background. The civil rights movement's war on Jim Crow racism during the 1950s and 1960s made great strides in addressing institutional markers of American racism, but blacks continued to face discrimination and oppression. During the mid-to-late 1960s, a new group of black leaders emerged to combat de facto Jim Crow and the racial discrimination that persisted despite the long-fought battle for equality. The young black leaders of the Black Power movement, some of whom were active in the civil rights movement, rejected what they believed to be the failed assimilationist policies of civil rights leaders and initiated a new strategy for black resistance. The Black Power movement and its leaders instigated a new wave of challenges to the white power structure—encouraging black separatism and emphasizing the greatness of black's African ancestry as a tool for dissociating them from their white oppressors and encouraging a nationalist race pride. The Black Power movement leaders' agenda and methods were shaped by a host of complex ideas and phenomena. Decolonization theory and the failures and triumphs of the civil rights movement were among the influences that led Black Power leaders to determine that before blacks could work closely with whites they must first develop a strong internal leadership and sense of nationalism born from the knowledge of black history.[42]

While the leaders of the Black Power movement who represented numerous organizations had distinct political, economic, and social objectives, the movement also inspired cultural changes and intellectual trends among its adherents. For instance, African Americans who subscribed to the Black Power ideology articulated by the leaders of the Black Arts and Black Power movement embraced and enacted this new African-rooted race pride, using their bodies as sites of discourse: they wore natural African hairstyles and African-styled clothing.[43] The black nationalist aesthetic tradition that was born during this period called for a new imagining of black and African people, black history, and black culture. Much like the members of the New Negro intelligentsia, who insisted that restoring black people's pride in their heritage was the key to improving black people's self-esteem and undermining racism during the 1920s and 1930s, Black Power activists looked to their African past for a restored sense of black self-worth and value. Social scientists Daniel P. Moynihan and Nathan Glazer discounted these expressions and strategies, which they viewed as frivolous extremism that would have little consequence on black life in *Beyond the Melting Pot: The Negroes, Puerto Ricans, Jews, Italians, and Irish of New York City* (1963).[44] But the movement would have a lasting impact on the perception of black history—Black Power activists would arouse a campaign that transformed the importance of black history in the academy.

A good example of the importance of history to Black Power activists is the black history study groups from which early chapters of the Black Panthers evolved in California.[45] These study groups read both Melville Herskovits's and E. Franklin Frazier's work. Despite the fact that the two scholars and their theories were largely at odds, young Black Power activists were able to extract from their works ideas and theories that furthered their reconceptualization of the black experience. Most important to these activists were Herskovits's African survivals theories, and Frazier's critique of the black bourgeois, which they combined and added to the array of intellectual influences from which they crafted their ideology.[46]

Black Power also birthed a student movement that demanded that academic institutions on every level of the American educational system begin to fully incorporate black and African history and arts into its curriculum. The Black Studies movement emerged largely as a result of this push. Student protests and sit-ins forced colleges and universities to establish academic programs that explored the black experience in Africa and in the African diaspora.[47] During the late 1960s, scholars, students, and Black Power activists and enthusiasts focused on contemporary issues, but they also combed the annals of African history, black history, and black culture to unearth all that had been written about the black and African past and revived old debates like the one between

Herskovits and Frazier.[48] Even though black educators disagreed about how best to institutionalize and standardize this new field of study, Black Studies activists' insistence that there was a unique black experience that needed to be examined and explored shifted race discourse back to the idea of racial distinctiveness.[49]

The advent of Black Studies, and the revived interest in black folk culture among black and white youth during the 1960s and 1970s, ensured the resurrection of 1920s and 1930s black folklore and survivals studies.[50] Not only did these studies make a comeback, but African survivals research reemerged as a lost treasure that proved that African culture had survived slavery and attracted the interest of scholars, students, and artists who had been excited by the vibrancy of Black Studies. New dynamic inquiries into enslaved people's experiences benefited from the recovery of this material. For instance, John W. Blassingame's *The Slave Community: Plantation Life in the Antebellum South* (1972) included, among other things, African survivals in discussions about slave resistance and in appraisals of cultural life in the South.[51] Also, new works built on 1920s and 1930s folk culture and survival studies appeared in print. One example of the resurgence of interest in black folklore is black writer and scholar Alice Walker's resurrection of Zora Neale Hurston's works in an article published in *Ms. Magazine* in 1975. Walker's "In Search of Zora Neale Hurston" discusses both Hurston's fiction and anthropological work, and the article helped to revive interest in Hurston's writings and the folklore that she documented. Two years after Walker's article was released, white historian Lawrence Levine's landmark study *Black Culture and Black Consciousness: Afro-American Folk Thought From Slavery to Freedom* (1977) was published. *Black Culture and Black Consciousness*—an intellectual history—traces shifts in black folk thought and expressions in order to examine the ways that blacks imagined themselves and the oppressive society in which they lived.

Levine's groundbreaking work revealed that there was a different way to *read* and use much of the problematic material that white observers had recorded about black folk culture. Levine admitted that works like Lydia Parrish's and Mary Granger's were "not perfect sources," but he believed that valuable material could be extracted from these writings.[52] In his study, Levine referenced folklore and practices recorded in Mary Granger's *Drums and Shadows* and Lydia Parrish's *Slave Songs from the Georgia Sea Islands* more than twenty times to bolster his arguments, and he featured Sea Island blacks as proprietors of sophisticated and complex intellectual formulations that articulated resistance to white supremacy. Whereas Granger and Parrish excluded racism from their conceptualizations of coastal Georgia blacks' cultural world and assumed that their traditions and practices were unconscious reproductions of their ancestors' primitive compulsions, Levine put racism at the center of their lives and found Sea Islanders constantly adapting and adjusting their worldview to survive slavery and Jim Crow. For instance, Levine used a song and story told to Parrish to prove that slaves originated lyrics to maintain secret communications that undermined their masters; he cited one of Granger's interviews to underscore the fact that blacks skillfully used scripture to prove "the efficacy of sacred folk beliefs"; and he referenced another interview that Granger recorded to emphasize the connection between slave folk beliefs like "root doctoring" and the strategies that slaves used to preserve their health and survive.[53]

Other scholars followed in Levine's footsteps. By 1980, the academic journal dedicated to Black Studies—the *Journal of Black Studies*—enthroned the Gullah as one of the field's most important subjects.[54] The special issue devoted to "Sea Island Culture" validated the new approach to reading old folklore studies that Levine introduced (embracing the label "Sea Islanders" instead of "Gullah") and attempted to replicate this reimagining in its pages.[55] Contributors to the volume included a mix of academics and Sea Island natives whose writings grappled with the Gullah dialect, folk culture and lore, and other aspects of contemporary life in coastal communities in the Low Country.

Volume editors Mary A. Twining and Keith E. Baird, professors at the State University of New York, acknowledged that early "observers of Afro-American culture were usually negative in their estimation of the moral and cultural integrity of the group." The editors homed in on the eerie and fantastical qualities ascribed to much of the folklore that had been collected, but they concluded that the material preserved in these works is invaluable because it points to "the continuance of African customs in spite of the fact that they may have been seen as bizarre or barbarous."[56] The idea that African customs were *bizarre* and *barbarous* was particularly true for folklore collectors like Granger and Parrish—researchers who conceptualized and conducted studies at the height of the voodoo craze. Despite being problematic, 1920s and 1930s research is the scholarly foundation of the issue—a collection that recast *survivals* as "reaffirmations," re-creations of "traits of a lost culture in an alien land." However, not every contributor was a survivals enthusiast. Guy B. Johnson, Mary Granger's adviser who had rejected African survivals theories but encouraged Granger to focus on the more bizarre elements of black life in her study, contributed an article to the volume that briefly revisited his 1930s account of folk culture on St. Helena Island in South Carolina, and largely reasserted his repudiation of Herskovits's and Turner's emphasis on the African roots of the Gullah dialect.

In the volume, the troubling conceptualizations of Gullah folk that inspired so much controversy among scholars during the 1930s were overshadowed by Sea Islanders' new appeal. Janie Gilliard Moore, a native Sea Islander and contributor to the volume, connected renewed interest in the culture of Low Country blacks to the movements of the 1950s and 1960s during which "Blacks became more concerned about their ethnic roots and authenticity—their African heritage and culture" and developed "the desire to relate to everything which is African."[57] Blacks had developed a renewed curiosity about their ancestry, and widespread interest in Alex Haley's book-turned-film *Roots* (1976) demonstrates the popularity of personal searches for the black-African past. Invoking her Sea Island roots and its African origins with pride, Moore declared, "We are that unique group of people who constitute the remnant which has maintained to the highest degree evidences of ethnic authenticity, of African cultural continuity."[58] Moore was correct, the Sea Island vogue was growing among black Americans. For example, the next *National Geographic* writer who came to the Low Country's coast looking for Gullah folk in the 1980s was a black historian, Charles S. Blockson.[59] And black Low Country natives like Vertamae Grosvenor, the author of a cookbook/memoir titled *Vibration Cooking: Or, The Travel Notes of a Geechee Girl* (1970), also expressed a renewed pride in their heritage. Even though this surge of interest in Gullah culture was very different from the 1920s and 1930s explosion birthed by Julia Peterkin's popular stories, the Gullah revival of the 1970s, 1980s, and 1990s would also have ties to popular fiction. But this time Gullah fictional tales were inspired by a new reading of old folk material that had been transformed into *fact*.

Black Women Writers Discover Sapelo Islanders

Academic studies were responsible for the recovery of old Gullah folk material, but black women fiction writers made the Gullah an important part of black cultural life inside and outside of academia during the 1970s, 1980s, and 1990s. It is only fitting that the Gullah identity, which first gained popularity during the 1920s and 1930s within the fiction genre as a result of Julia Peterkin's writings, lives on in fictional works. But unlike Peterkin, whose fascination with the Gullah in her midst was spurred by the popular fad of exploring America's primitives, the black women writers who picked up the Gullah as fictional subjects did so to restore a sense of race pride and ancestral lineage that they believed black people had lost.

Toni Morrison, Paule Marshall, Gloria Naylor, and Julie Dash reimagined the Gullah folklore material in their fiction, harnessing the dynamism of the Black Studies movement and drawing inspiration from black feminist discourse that compelled them to grapple with their dual subjectivity as both black people and women.[60] Literary scholar Cheryl Wall argues that the fictional works that black women produced after the advent of the Black Studies movement reveals a consistent desire to represent the past four hundred years of black history in the African diaspora, reclaim lost parts of their lineage, as well as reveal black women's unique experience within this history.[61] This preoccupation is certainly evident in the way that Morrison, Marshall, Naylor, and Dash reimagined the Gullah folk material in their writings.

The fact that these black women were entrenched in the academy during the years when the Black Power, Black Studies, and Black Feminist movements had the most significant impact on the ivory tower guaranteed that their writings would reflect the ideologies of these movements. Toni Morrison was a student during the civil rights movement and a professor during the height of the call for Black Studies; she earned a bachelors degree from Howard University in 1953, a masters degree from Cornell University in 1955, before working as an editor and taking up teaching posts at colleges such as the State University of New York and at Yale University during the 1970s. Similarly, Paule Marshall graduated from Brooklyn College in 1953 and had worked intermittently as a journalist, writer, researcher, and professor through the 1970s. While Marshall and Morrison were pursuing literary projects and teaching at universities, Naylor and Dash were students. Gloria Naylor went to Medgar Evers College and Brooklyn College, before beginning graduate studies in literature at Yale University in the 1980s. Likewise, Julie Dash was a film student during the 1970s: she attended both City College and the American Film School before pursuing graduate studies at UCLA during the 1980s. At the very moment when black folklore and African survivals theories were resurrected in the academy, these black women were navigating the complex racial terrain of a turbulent period when questions about race, heritage, oppression, gender, and Africanness were raised for scholars to consider. They wrestled with all of these questions in their fiction, and 1930s Gullah reports—especially Mary Granger's *Drums and Shadows*—played a special role in the way that they responded to emerging ideas about the meaning of their racial and gender identities.

When Mary Granger and her team interviewed coastal Georgia blacks during the 1930s, she did not believe that the practices and beliefs that they described had any positive value within the modern context aside from the excitement that researchers might derive from discovering their African origins. Instead, she noted their superstitions and stories about their ancestors as evidence of their quaint, primitive African impulse and naïve racial character. But when black women writers discovered Granger's conversations with Sapelo Islanders and other coastal Georgia blacks, they used the interviews to interpret and reimagine the Gullah. From Granger's reports of "shadows," rootwork, and conjuh, these black women writers imagined a new mystical, magical, powerful, African-inspired Gullah folk culture that is evident in Toni Morrison's *Song of Solomon* (1977), Paule Marshall's *Praisesong for the Widow* (1983), Gloria Naylor's novel *Mama Day* (1988), and Julie Dash's film *Daughters of the Dust* (1991). The Gullah, as described by most 1920s and 1930s journalists, folklorists, and amateur anthropologists in search of authentic relics of African culture in America, represented an exotic, ignorant, primitive "Negro type" doomed to extinction. Yet, when Morrison, Marshall, Naylor, and Dash mined 1920s and 1930s Gullah studies, sifting through the intellectual debris of a charged moment in America's race-making history, and discovered Mary Granger's study, their imaginations were ignited, and new formulations of Gullah folk surfaced in their fictional works.

Together, black women writers helped to revive the African survivals concept and constructed a fictional context that mirrored the view of Gullah folk culture that was taking shape in the academy. While Granger represented African survivals as a vanishing primitive orientation bred in ignorance and isolation, black women writers interpreted survivals as a triumphant, powerful cultural legacy. This view of African survivals looked at retentions as evidence of black people's resistance to white cultural domination that literally helped them to "survive" slavery—a conviction that closely resembled the conception of survivals that Blassingame described in *The Slave Community*.[62] Levine too, clearly communicates this interpretation of African continuities when he argued against the way that early African survivals enthusiasts characterized survivals as "quaint reminders of an exotic culture sufficiently alive to render the slaves picturesquely different but little more."[63] He contended that slaves brought from West Africa a worldview "capable of withstanding the impact of slavery," and that they used and adjusted this worldview, and the cultural expressions associated with it, to survive slavery and articulate resistance. While 1920s and 1930s academics such as Melville Herskovits and Zora Neale Hurston took African survivals seriously, and Herskovits wrote about slave resistance in *Myth of the Negro Past*, the two coastal Georgia researchers for whom Herskovits served as a consultant never asserted that the traits that they explored had helped blacks to survive oppression and pursue freedom. Rootwork, voodoo, and conjuh for white 1920s and 1930s observers like Mary Granger were nothing more than remnants of an ignorant, unsophisticated, primitive African culture. But when Marshall, Naylor, and Dash reimagined Gullah rootwork, voodoo, and conjuh practices that may not have existed as described in 1920s and 1930s Gullah literature, they found powerful black matriarchs propagating profound African cosmological principles and enduring wisdoms through which true freedom was secured. Likely unaware of how the 1920s and 1930s voodoo craze shaped the descriptions of Gullah life that they reimagined, black women crafted a world where the Gullah and their mystical arts and African ancestors become the sole group of *African* Americans to survive chattel slavery.

Toni Morrison was the first black female writer in the group to incorporate details from *Drums and Shadows* in an imaginative literary work. In *Song of Solomon* (1977), the novel that contributed to Morrison's winning of the Nobel Prize in literature, Morrison uses elements of Gullah folklore and weaves details from *Drums and Shadows* into a larger tale set in the 1950s and 1960s about one black man's quest for his family history that restores pride in his ancestry. Gullah themes from the interwar years are not central to the story that Morrison tells, but her use of research from the period is indicative of how black women writers would use the Gullah in their works. The main character in *Song of Solomon*, Milkman Dead, is introduced to family lore about flying Africans by his estranged magical aunt, Pilate Dead. Milkman's quest sends him on a reverse migration to his family's ancestral homestead in Virginia, where he uncovers his family history that is embodied in the discovery of his great-grandfather's name.

Stories about "flying Africans" can be found in Mary Granger's *Drums and Shadows*. While many 1920s and 1930s Gullah folklore collectors documented stories about Africans that escaped bondage by flying back to Africa, these tales were also recorded in several *Drums and Shadows* reports. The stories that coastal Georgia blacks told about these defiant and magical African captives—legends that might have evolved from accounts of a slave mutiny that took place on a ship off the coast of St. Simons Island—held little relevance in the study beyond typifying coastal blacks' fantastical supernatural lore.[64] Shad Hall, one of Sapelo's most sought after informants, told the Savannah unit a story about Africans who escaped being whipped by their master by flying away.[65] And when Mary Granger's team interviewed Prince Sneed of White Bluff, they heard a different story about "flying Africans":

Muh gran say ole man Waldburg down on St. Catherine own some slabes wut wuzn climatize and he wuk um hahd an one day dey wuz hoein in duh fiel an duh dribuh come out an two ub um wuz unuh a tree in duh shade, an duh hoes wuz wukin by demsef. Duh dribuh say, "Wut dis?" an dey say, "kum buba yali kum buba tambe" . . . quick like. Den dey rise off duh groun an fly away. Nobody ebuh see um no mo. Some say dey fly back tuh Africa. Muh gran see dat wid he own eye. [*My gran say ole man Waldburg down on St. Catherine own some slaves what wasn't climatized and he work them hard and one day they was hoeing in the field and the driver come out and two of them was under a tree in the shade, and the hoes was working by themself. The driver say, "What this?" and they say, kum buba yali kum buba tambe . . . quick like. Then they rise off the ground and fly away. Nobody ever see them no more. Some say they fly back to Africa. My gran see that with he own eye.*][66]

Morrison explained her attraction to this specific lore and the use of flying blacks in *Song of Solomon* in an interview that she gave in March 1981: "There is a certain sense of family I don't have. So the myths get forgotten. Or they may not have been looked at carefully. . . . The flying myth in *Song of Solomon* . . . is about black people who could fly." For Morrison, this myth was an important metaphor in black culture: "That was always part of the folklore of my life; flying was one of our gifts. I don't care how silly it may seem. It is everywhere—people used to talk about it, it's in the spirituals and gospels. Perhaps it was wishful thinking—escape, death, and all that. But suppose it wasn't. What might it mean? I tried to find out in *Song of Solomon*."[67] In the novel, the myth of flying Africans has multiple meanings, but most important is that it was the "gift" of ancestry—Milkman was told that his great-grandfather Solomon could fly, and the story was critical to his transformation.

Naming was an important theme in *Song of Solomon*, and Milkman's discovery of his great-grandfather's name can specifically be traced back to Sapelo Islanders' interviews featured in *Drums and Shadows*. Morrison explains that names play a unique role in the experience of blacks in America: "If you come from Africa, your name is gone. It is particularly problematic because it is not just *your* name but your family, your tribe. When you die, how can you connect with your ancestors if you have lost your name?"[68] She describes the loss of family and tribal names as a source of trauma that produces a psychological scar in the black American psyche. So, in the novel, she uses the process of naming to move through Milkman Dead's story of ancestral discovery: "Most of the names in *Song of Solomon* are real, the names of musicians . . . biblical names. . . . I also used some pre-Christian names to give the sense of a mixture of cosmologies. Milkman Dead has to learn the meaning of his own name and the names of things."[69] It is in Milkman's discovery of his own ancestor's name—which is listed in a song, sung by a group of children—that Mary Granger's report of an interview with Sapelo residents finds its way to the apex of Morrison's novel. When Granger interviewed Katie Brown, she asked Brown what she knew about her Muslim ancestor, Bilali Mohammed. Brown replied: "He hab plenty daughtuhs, Margret, Bentoo, Chaalut, Medina, Yaruba, Fatima an Hestuh."[70] Again, Granger asked Julia Grovernor, the woman who was resistant to Granger's voodoo questions, about her Muslim grandparents, Hannah and Calina Underwood, and Grovernor told Granger that the couple "hab twenty-one chillun."[71] Both Grovernor and Brown described what they knew of their ancestor's African background. And Katie Brown recounted a cake her grandmother made during Muslim holidays: "She make a funny flat cake she call 'saraka.'"[72] Morrison took these Sapelo Islanders' remembrances of their ancestors, immortalized in *Drums and Shadows*, and wove them into Solomon's song:

> Solomon and Ryna Belali Shalut
> Yaruba Medina Muhammet too.
> Nestor Kalina Saraka cake.
> Twenty-one children, the last one Jake![73]

Also in the song is Morrison's variation of the magical words that Prince Sneed said was used to make the Africans fly: "Come konka yalle, come konka tambee."[74] The variations in the spelling of names and words used in Morrison's novel do not obscure the origins of her inspiration. Just as Sapelo Island researcher W. Robert Moore cited what he described as the Islanders' "picturesque names," such as "Julius, Isaac, Ishmael, Caesar, Nero, and Balaam," to verify they were authentic relics of the primitive past, Morrison finds in Sapelo Islanders' names and words a link to a powerful past.[75] Despite the fact that Mary Granger's interest in the Muslim ancestors of Brown, Hall, and Grovernor revolved around establishing the authentic Africanness of the survivals that her subjects described, Morrison found great value in the report. Brown's and Grovernor's memories of their African ancestors were invoked in Morrison's construction of Milkman Dead's ultimate transformation, which was completed when he discovered his ancestors.

Morrison's belief in the restorative power of black folklore and the discovery of black ancestry was, in part, inspired by Gullah remembrances. When Morrison discovered the stories that Brown, Grovernor, and Sneed told Mary Granger, what she read settled in her imagination and was "conjured" in the writing of *Song of Solomon*. This was also true for Paule Marshall. Marshall explained in an interview that her novel *Praisesong for the Widow* (1983) was inspired by Granger's *Drums and Shadows*: "*Praisesong for the Widow* started with a place I came across this place called Ibo Landing in a book entitled *Drums and Shadows*."[76] Although she mischaracterized the Georgia Writers' Project study as "a series of interviews with some very old people who lived on the Sea Islands, off the coast of Georgia and South Carolina," Marshall was clear in explaining that what she read in the book impressed and inspired her: "Nearly everyone spoke of a place on one of the islands called Ibo Landing. According to a story handed down over the years, a group of Ibo slaves decided they didn't like the looks of America" so they "turned around and walked back across the Atlantic Ocean. That's how *Praisesong* began, with that folktale."[77]

Marshall did not simply stumble on Granger's study, she admitted that she had always been "taken with historical material," and she looked to the past for inspiration.[78] However, Marshall's memory of what she read in *Drums and Shadows* was not precise. The study only focused on blacks in coastal Georgia, and while Granger and her staff may have asked residents about "Ibo Landing," many residents talked about "Ibo" slaves, and only one St. Simons resident, Floyd White, talked about Ibo Landing:

> Heahd bout duh Ibo's Landing? Das duh place weah dey bring duh Ibos obuh in a slabe ship an wen dey git yuh, dey ain lak it an so dey all staht singin an dey mahch right down in duh ribbuh tuh mahch back tuh Africa, but dey ain able tuh git deah. Dey gits drown. [*Heard about the Ibo's Landing? That's the place where they bring the Ibos over in a slave ship and when they get here, they ain't like it and so they all start singing and they march right down in the river to march back to Africa, but they ain't able to get there. They gets drown.*][79]

White's Ibo's may have drowned, but in Marshall's imagination, the Ibos, like the flying Africans described in other interviews, made it back to Africa.

Praisesong for the Widow tells the story of an African American woman who was led back to her Gullah ancestral roots by a magical matriarch. The novel's main character, Avey Johnson, a sixty-four-year-old widow, is on a cruise with friends when her great-aunt Cuney comes to her in a dream and encourages her to abandon the cruise ship and embark on a life-changing experience. During her sojourn in the Caribbean, Avey's encounters call up memories of summers that she spent on the fictional Tatem Island in South Carolina. Marshall's fictional Gullah island is populated by blacks who perform ring shouts and seek the help of the island's root doctor—"'Doctor' Benitha Grant."[80] Avey remembers an old Tatem Islander, Shad Dawson, whose house she and her great-aunt Cuney passed on their daily walk to Ibo Landing. Marshall's use of the name "Shad" was likely inspired by Granger's interview with Sapelo's Shad Hall (whose memories featured prominently in Granger's book) in his description of Sapelo Islanders' African ancestors' traditions.[81] On their visits to Ibo Landing, great-aunt Cuney retold the story of the enslaved Africans who escaped captivity and made it home: "They just kept walking right on out over the river. Now you wouldna thought they'd of got very far seeing as it was water they was walking on. Besides they had all that iron on 'em. Iron on they ankles and they wrists and fastened 'round they neck like a dog collar. 'Nuff iron to sink an army. And chains hooking up the iron. But chains didn't stop those Ibo none."[82] Marshall's version of the Ibo Landing story was a triumph that served as a way to link Cuney and Avey to their ancestors in victory instead of through tragedy. And Avey, whose real name was "Avatara," was an "avatar" that embodied the story and legacy of those who made it back home.

Avey's quest to get home, to New York, ultimately took her back "home" to her Gullah roots on Tatem Island. While trying to get home from Grenada, the "patois" she heard around her made her remember the Gullah dialect. She also remembered the power of the "Five Finger Grass" that her great-aunt Cuney "used to hang above the door of the house in Tatem to keep trouble away."[83] Avey remembered that her deceased husband called "her behind Gulla gold" and was reminded by a local Islander that she should pay homage to her ancestors because if she didn't "they'll get vex and cause you nothing but trouble. They can turn your life around in a minute, you know."[84] The ancestral ceremonies that she encountered on the out island made her recall similar ceremonies on Tatem: "She had seen it once at the funeral of an old man her great-aunt had taken her to, a plate prepared with meat, greens and the inevitable rice and side-dish of sweet potato pudding which had been the dead man's favorite, resting on a small flowerstand of a table next to the open coffin in the front room."[85] Marshall could have easily drawn all of these practices from Granger's reports about roots, charms, and practices to placate the dead. Mattie Sampson told Granger, "Dey hang Five Finguh Grass ovuh deah bed aw doeway tuh protec duh whole house" from witches and spirits that visit in the night, and Susan Maxwell told Granger that "ebry night attuh duh fewnul I put food on duh poach fuh duh spirit tuh come git it."[86] In the end, Avey Johnson's journey "home" was not facilitated by a flight on an airplane, but was achieved by journeying back to memories of Ibo Landing and reclaiming her lineage and legacy.

Gloria Naylor's novel *Mama Day* (1988) also centers on a homeward journey that invokes the essence of how the Gullah were imagined during the 1920s and 1930s. Naylor's novel takes place on a fictional Gullah island on the border of Georgia and South Carolina named Willow Springs. Naylor invokes the voice of an omniscient Gullah narrator that uses the Gullah dialect in telling different parts of the plot. In the novel, Ophelia (whose "basket name" [nickname] is Cocoa), a daughter of Willow Spring's Gullah community, left the island to experience life in New York City. Ophelia returns to the island with her "citified" husband George to visit with her grandmother Abigail and grand-aunt Miranda (Mama Day) and is caught in the crossfire of a voodoo war that ultimately results in George's death.

Whereas Morrison and Marshall borrow from documented Gullah folklore of the 1920s and 1930s and *Drums and Shadows*, Naylor does not. She imagines a new myth about an enslaved people who use voodoo powers to escape bondage. Willow Spring's residents are eternally connected to their slave past, which is represented in the enduring myth of their common African ancestor Sapphira Wade. Sapphira is celebrated for using mysterious African magical powers and her sexual prowess to trick the island's plantation owner into freeing his slaves and deeding his plantation to them. Her spirit is immortalized in a local saying—"18 & 23"—which is used to describe situations in which individuals are tricked, swooned, or hexed. Sapphira Wade's legacy in Willow Springs extends beyond tales of her mythical life, but is captured in the resident's continued invocation of voodoo powers. While Mama Day uses voodoo for good, Dr. Buzzard works roots for money, and Ruby works a root that almost claims Ophelia's life.

For Naylor, the essence of the Gullah identity is the connection to their African ancestors and the magical quality of African spiritual survivals. While this assessment may at first glance seem to mirror the 1920s and 1930s reading of the Gullah, showing no trace of evolution, Naylor's work reflects a marked difference from the earlier depictions of Gullah voodooists. Naylor explains in an interview that Mama Day was inspired by the stories that her Mississippi migrant parents told about black women who "not only worked as quasi traditional doctors, but who used roots and herbs and had supernatural kinds of powers."[87] Naylor also had a specific vision for the powerful women rootworkers in the novel: "I wanted as well to look at women in history, especially at women connected to the earth who could affect behavior."[88] The centrality of the relationship between women and power to Naylor's tale clearly echoes the feminist energy that permeated identity discourse during the 1970s and 1980s. Ultimately, Naylor used "voodoo" to reflect her own beliefs: "When I got to Mama Day, I wanted to rest and write about what I believed. And I believe in the power of love and of magic—sometimes I think they are one and the same. Mama is about the fact that the real basic magic is the unfolding of the human potential and that if we reach inside ourselves we can create miracles."[89]

Naylor communicates a very personal understanding of "voodoo," but she also reveals a nearness to 1920s and 1930s African survivals discourse that makes her decision to tell a magical Gullah tale a logical choice. She explained, "When our people came to this country, they brought animism with them, what people used to call paganism. They brought their traditional beliefs, their traditional sense of religion. Then they made a coalition between what they brought and what they found here as far as religion."[90] Zora Neale Hurston's and Melville Herskovits's view of voodoo and African survivals is clearly echoed in Naylor's understanding of spiritual retentions. That Naylor expresses, as a fact, the idea that Africans brought with them to America a spiritual "animism" and made a "coalition" between their native religions and Christianity, suggests that in the wake of the Black Studies movement, Herskovits and Hurston won the survivals debate. E. Franklin Frazier's arguments against African survivals theories lost their potency during the Black Studies movement, when many black scholars, black students, and black writers—longing for their lost heritage—considered the possibility that all African culture had been destroyed during slavery an unfathomable prospect.

More than the personal allure of voodoo magic inspired Naylor to write a novel about the Gullah; she was also attracted to their relative isolation from the white world. For Naylor, Gullah communities represent the perfect black community. Naylor explained that Willow Springs "offers redemption through holding out the basic tenets that have kept the black community strong, which is a sense of history." She continued, "It's a sense of community. It's a sense of family. It's a respect for spirituality."[91] Naylor's imagining of a Gullah community clearly elevates this population of blacks from the position of backward primitives to conscious guardians of a distinctly uplifting black culture. Willow Spring's geographical location was also designed to achieve a higher symbolic meaning: "For me Willow Springs was to be the ideal black community. And that's why it is separated from the mainland. But there is a bridge where people can go back and forth. You know. No one's prisoner there.... But the very island itself was to be a redemptive place."[92] During the 1920s and 1930s, the distance between black Gullah islands and mainland communities was noted as the source of Islanders' ignorance and superstition, but in Naylor's imagination, the distance acts as a buffer against the brutality of white racism and serves to protect the black community.

The "distance" between life on the black Gullah island and life on the white dominated mainland also factors prominently in Julie Dash's 1991 film *Daughters of the Dust*. Like Naylor, Dash conceives of the Gullah island as the place where black heritage, spiritual traditions, and the black family remain intact, while the mainland overwhelmingly represents struggle and strife in the white world. Given that Gullah researchers and writers of the 1920s and 1930s largely ignored the racial power dynamics between Islanders and powerful whites such as Howard Coffin and R. J. Reynolds, it was easy for the black women writers who consulted early Gullah folk culture to imagine that Gullah islands were free from white domination.

In Dash's telling of a Gullah tale that also draws, in part, on Sapelo Islander interviews, several members of the Peazant family make their final preparations to leave their Gullah island homeland in search of a new life on the mainland in 1902. The family's difficult decision to remain rooted in Peazant ancestral land or leave, and the return of two daughters who had already left, sets the stage for the drama that unfolded on film screens in 1991. In this story, the rootwork of the Peazant family matriarch, Nana Peazant, links the family to their ancestral past and protects the family from unseen dangers that threaten them in their uncertain future.

Dash's epic film would become the most celebrated and memorable film about the Gullah, but it was not the first film to feature a Sea Island community. Nearly two decades before Dash's movie was released, one white southern writer, Pat Conroy, tapped into the Peterkin formula and published a memoir titled *The Water Is Wide* (1972) about his encounter with blacks whom he characterized as isolated and backward residents of Daufuskie Island, South Carolina. When Conroy's account was turned into a motion picture (which was actually filmed on Georgia's coast) titled *Conrack* (1974) and was shown in theaters, reviewers bashed the movie for its belittling portrayal of Sea Islanders.[93] One reviewer pointed out that Conroy's story "is not really about the Sea Islanders — it is about the young white liberal" and wrote that the film projected a negative view of Sea Islanders formed by "the total absence of any hint of indigenous Sea Island culture." The reviewer explained that "actually, the Sea Islands have a very rich folk culture, fascinating to folklorists and to laymen who take the trouble to look."[94] The movements of the 1950s and 1960s had guaranteed that *Conrack* would be scrutinized for its condescending and prejudiced portrayal of Sea Island blacks. Where *Conrack* failed to incorporate Sea Island culture, *Daughters of the Dust* triumphed in creating a cinematic masterpiece, whose plot and characters animated folk cultural material and elevated Sea Islanders in the national imagination.

Dash, the daughter of South Carolina migrants raised in Queensbridge Housing Projects in New York, crafted this epic tale in search of her own family's story.[95] Dash explained that "the stories from my own family sparked the idea of *Daughters* and formed the basis for some characters. But when I probed my relatives for information about the family history in South Carolina, or about our migration North to New York, they were often reluctant to discuss it."[96] So, in 1983, Dash took the funds that she was awarded from a Guggenheim grant and began conducting extensive research at the Schomburg Center for Research, the National Archive, the Library of Congress, the Smithsonian Institute, and Penn Center and discovered 1920s and 1930s Gullah studies.[97] Dash wrote that she decided to use the Gullah in her telling of a black migration story because of their unique patterns of African cultural retentions: "The sea islands off the coast of the Carolinas and Georgia became the main drop off point for Africans brought to North America" and "became the region with the strongest retention of African culture, although even to this day the influences of African culture are visible everywhere in America."[98] Dash's conclusion that the Gullah offer "the strongest retention of African culture" is evidence of the evolution of African survivals discourse from controversial "unproven theory" in the 1920s and 1930s, to a commonly accepted "fact" by the 1980s.

To replace the missing stories from her own family's lineage, Dash adopted the Gullah, and made them fictive ancestors of African Americans. Like Morrison and Marshall, Dash mixed details from Granger's book with other research and her own imaginings of the black-African past she longed for. The result was a tale full of dynamic characters and a fascinating plot that was captured in the first feature film with a general theatrical release made by an African American woman.

By 1987, Dash had concluded her research and writing and headed to St. Helena Island, South Carolina, with a production crew to begin filming *Daughters of the Dust*. Dash had plenty of help in her efforts to craft an authentic Gullah tale: she consulted with historian Margaret Washington Creel, author of *A Peculiar People: Slave Religion and Community-Culture Among the Gullahs* (1989), Vertamae Grosvenor appeared on screen, and Gloria Naylor worked as a production assistant on the film.[99] When an interviewer asked Dash to describe the new film that she was working on, her own imagining of the Gullah emerged: "*Daughters of the Dust* is another period piece. It takes place at the turn of the century, and it's about a black family, a Gullah family. It's about the struggle to maintain their own family unity as half of the family wants to migrate North and the other half wants to stay behind and maintain cultural traditions and beliefs. So it has a lot of mysticism in it and magic in it."[100] "Mysticism" and "magic" distinguish Dash's Gullah from other blacks during the period. It is evident in Dash's film that the magical and the mystical nature of the Gullah that was consolidated in 1920s and 1930s Gullah research, and, in particular, in Granger's *Drums and Shadows* study was certainly prominent among other published works that stimulated her imagination.

Dash incorporated the names of people who were interviewed and discussed in *Drums and Shadows* in *Daughters of the Dust*. As with Morrison's discovery of him, Dash's discovery of Bilali Mohammed, Sapelo Island's famous African Muslim ancestor, left an indelible mark on her imagination. "I learned about Bilal Muhammed. . . . He was in the Sea Islands during slavery, but by the turn of the century, his five daughters who were also Muslim, were still carrying on the tradition of Islam. . . . So it was important for me to include him in the story . . . because he meant so much to me."[101] The particulars of "Bilal's" life that Dash shared with the interviewer were jumbled, and were perhaps composites of other details about enslaved Muslims in the region that Dash encountered through research, but the fact that Sapelo Islanders' famed ancestor stuck with her is unquestionable. Drawing from Sapelo Islanders' conversations with Mary Granger about Mohammed, and perhaps Lydia Parrish's descriptions of Bilali too, Dash fashioned her own version of Bilali Mohammed named "Bilal"—a character who clings to his Muslim faith, teaching the younger generation of island residents his African-born spiritual practice. Near the start of the film,

Bilal is performing his morning prayer, and Dash's instructions in the screenplay direct camera technicians to take a close-up shot of "Bilal's homemade KORAN and his hands in prayer."[102]

Shad Hall, the Sapelo Islander whose name is used in Marshall's imagining of the Gullah past, is also invoked in *Daughters of the Dust*. Hall, like Katie Brown, was one of Bilali Mohammed's descendants. While his interview with Mary Granger also revealed interesting details of his ancestor's African past and spiritual practices, it is likely that Shad Hall's portrait featured at the beginning of *Drums and Shadows* may have helped to fix Shad Hall in Dash's and Marshall's imagination. The 1930s documentary motives that influenced photography helped to make Shad Hall one of Granger's most-imagined Sapelo Island subjects. Shad Hall's photograph is one of two photos displayed that resemble intimate portrait photography. Unlike other photographs of research subjects in the book that place black bodies in a larger picture designed to cast them as part of the natural scenery and landscape, Hall's is distinctly a portrait. The close-up shot of Hall's face and features is haunting: his closely cropped gray hair frames his face; his smooth skin, which defies his advanced age, covers his high-set check bones; and his eyes are fixed in a faraway gaze, as if peering into a distant past. Perhaps it was this image of Hall that inspired Dash to name Nana Peazant's husband, "Shad Peazant."[103]

The mystical and magical Gullah essence that Dash creates in the film is also derived from 1920s and 1930s research. Eula Peazant uses a glass of water as a conduit to communicate with her dead mother, and the spirit of Eula's unborn child narrates the film and is present among the Peazant family throughout the movie.[104] Nana Peazant sprinkles rice in order to be granted admission into the family cemetery where she ventures daily to visit her deceased husband.[105] Dash included a handwritten note in the script to remind the reader that the newspaper pasted on the walls of the Peazant home was there "to protect family from evil."[106] The script also includes directions that read: "FRIZZLED CHICKENS scratch their way in front of the shanty looking for conjure bags."[107] All of these elements are included in Granger's study. In Granger's reports, communicating with the dead was represented as a natural part of daily life for blacks in coastal Georgia. Mary Stevens told Granger, "Duh spirits is ebryweah," and Elizatbeth Stevens added, "Dey dohn hurt yuh none, jis walk long wid yuh an talk."[108] Katie Brown, of Sapelo Island, described rituals performed before entering the cemetery: "Dey say, 'Fambly, we come tuh put our brudduh away in mudduh dus. Please leh us go tru the gate.'"[109] Stories about magical newspapers and frizzled chickens' protective intuition are also described in Granger's study.[110]

When Mary Granger unearthed stories about traditions used to honor the dead and folktales about flying Africans among coastal Georgia blacks, she presented them as exotic, primitive local lore. But black women writers found in those same stories a powerful tradition of ancestor veneration and black people's magic. The "bottle tree" that Dash envisions in the Peazant family yard is a good example of this translation. Dash describes the bottle tree in the screenplay: "Protecting the Peazant household from evil and bad luck. The bottles are of various shapes, sizes and colors. Sunlight radiates through the bottles, throwing a rainbow of hues across the Peazant family shanty."[111] Dash's description closely mirrors Granger's account of her observations of a family cemetery in Sunbury: "Most of the graves were decorated with possessions of the departed persons. There were many glasses, bottles, and vases, most of which had been turned a shimmering purple from long exposure to the sun."[112] Dash also weaves the narrative of protective ancestral spirits and ancestral knowledge that is communicated through folklore throughout her story.

As was the case with Marshall, Dash also fantasizes about the mythic group of Ibos that used African magic to escape captivity and transport themselves back to Africa. Dash gives birth to the first visual imaginings of "Ibo Landing" in the opening scene. While Dash may have discovered the story while conducting research, it was Paule Marshall's "Ibo Landing" story that moved Dash. Dash liked it so much that she used Marshall's exact prose as dialogue in the scene where Eula Peazant recounts the story of the Ibos to the Unborn Child.[113]

Nana Peazant's rootwork plays a pivotal role in *Daughters of Dust*. Nana Peazant's mystical charms act as a link between past and present wisdom, and she desperately clings to them despite her children's growing doubts about the power of the talismans she makes. Because Nana Peazant chooses to observe ancestral traditions and wisdom, she is gifted with spiritual insight and knowledge. She is the only Peazant who can sense the Unborn Child's spirit moving among them: "A great wind is blowing, Nana turns her face into the sweet wind and smiles. Nana senses the presence of the Unborn Child."[114] In the climactic scene, when the entire Peazant family is gathered at Ibo Landing and tensions between the Peazants who want to stay and observe the old traditions and those who want to leave and abandon their past crests, it is Nana Peazant's construction of a special "hand" charm that quells the conflict by fusing new gods with old gods to keep the family together. *Drums and Shadows* reports about "hands" identified the protective power of the charm. Clara Smith told a story about a "hand" that her aunt made: "My aunt destroy duh sacks an gie duh woman a good luck han tuh weah so no udduh root wukuh could hahm uh."[115] Peter McQueen said that "hands" were the only protection that one had against curses: "Only ting yuh kin do tuh keep frum bein cunjuhed is tuh carry a han.

... Mos folks tote a han wid um."[116] Granger collected these stories about the power of "hands," hoping to compile the sort of material that had become so entertaining in the popular culture, but Dash's discovery of 1930s reports about "hands" provided her with the perfect symbol through which the central conflict of her story could be resolved. Dash calls the ceremony that Nana Peazant guides the family through to activate the "hand"—a "A Root Revival of Love."[117] With Bilal by her side, her descendants in front of her, and the "hand" placed on top of Viola Peazant's Bible, Nana Peazant says: "We've taken old Gods and given them new names. They saw it all here that day, those Ibo.... This 'Hand,' it's from me, from us, from them (the Ibo).... Just like all of you.... Come children kiss this hand full of me. Take my 'Hand.' I'm the one that can give you strength."[118] One by one the Peazants come, some reluctant and some eager, and kiss the "hand," igniting its power to keep their family from falling apart once they are divided by the waters that separate the island from the mainland.

Reworking Roots

The personal search of Toni Morrison, Paule Marshall, Gloria Naylor, and Julie Dash for a meaningful African American past led them to the Gullah. What they found inspired them to create magical and powerful rootworking black women who reignite the mystical authority of African spiritual practices to heal the wounds of their descendants and instill an understanding of their ancestral lineage. Pilate Dead, great-aunt Cuney, Mama Day, and Nana Peazant give birth, from their mystical wombs, to stories and spiritual knowledge that ultimately saves Milkman Dead, Avey Johnson, Ophelia, and the Peazant family. Through these stories, Morrison, Marshall, Naylor, and Dash declare the power of black women to direct the forces of the universe.

These writers' rootworking women are all gifted with the keen ability to "see": they see the past and the future, the dead and the living and harvest the wisdom that this sight cultivates in order to save their descendants. When one considers the oppression that marked the condition of blacks in America and the influence of both the black nationalist and black feminist discourse on black women writers, it makes sense that they imagined women who have the power to invoke forces that trump the power of American racism and sexism. Despite the fact that 1920s and 1930s Gullah researchers paid little attention to gender distinctions among the people that they studied, black women writers, inspired by the black feminist tradition, create a distinct relationship between black women and their ancestral past, making them guardians of tradition and the most skilled practitioners of mystical arts.

The invocation of Gullah folktales about flying Ibos and Ibo Landing also originates in black women writer's desire to uncover stories of *survival*. Bilali

Mohammed becomes the ancestor of every African American in search of a forebear who resisted white cultural hegemony by passing down to his children sacred beliefs and practices. Each description of charms, rituals, and African ancestors inspires the black imagination to contemplate coastal Georgia and South Carolina blacks moving through an alternative power hierarchy in which they possessed the ability to command the forces of nature, talk to their dead, and dictate the terms of their earthly experience. Stories about Ibos escaping slavery function as both stories that connect blacks to their African past and as testaments to the ability of blacks to escape psychological bondage and return "home." "Home" for the Ibos described in Gullah folklore was literally Africa, but in black women's writings, "home" is the cognitive space in which blacks reconnect with their past and receive their spiritual inheritance and true sense of self, which is defined by knowledge of their ancestors. Black women writers' reimaging of details from *Drums and Shadows* re-creates the Gullah, elevating them from backward isolated research subjects and transforming them into the supernatural bridge that leads all African Americans "home." Evidence of black women writers' and artists' new emphasis on Gullah communities as a mythical home can be found in testimonies like the one that photographer Carrie Mae Weems shared in an interview. In discussing the inspiration for Sea Island photography, Weems said that "Home for me is both mysterious and mythic—the known and the unknown" and remarked that her "search" began "with the *Sea Islands* piece. The initial focus on family folklore was the beginning of my searching out a home place."[119]

Black women fiction writers were not alone in the dramatic reimagining of Gullah folk; historians and anthropologists who published studies during the 1980s, 1990s, and in the new millennium joined them. These scholars looked past the troubling conceptualizations of black life that framed early Gullah studies and probed these works to uncover new ways to think about the past. In particular, Granger's interviews with Sapelo Islanders have captured scholars' attention. Like Lawrence Levine, these scholars, armed with new perspectives and more knowledge about black history and Africa, reread *Drums and Shadows* and found in the interviews and memories of Katie Brown, Shad Hall, and other coastal Georgia blacks so much more than their original collector had looked for. Scholarly investigations into the roots of African American art and ideology; the origins of black nationalism; slave life and culture in the Low Country; and the history of black Muslims in antebellum America all benefited from the material that Granger collected.[120] The wide range of works that cite *Drums and Shadows* illustrate the fact that Mary Granger's study, the most controversial of all of the 1930s Gullah studies, emerged as the most useful source of information about Georgia's Gullah.[121] Each scholars' creative use of Sapelo

Islanders' reports adds value and meaning to Granger's findings—meaning that complicates the heritage of a people whom Granger imagined to be quintessential examples of primitive black people.

Lydia Parrish's and Lorenzo Dow Turner's studies were also used by scholars who investigated Gullah folk culture in recent years. Turner's research is the foundation of countless linguistic studies, but Joseph Opala's discovery of, and investigation into, one of Turner's recordings resulted in a remarkable breakthrough. Opala, an anthropologist who began studying the Gullah during the 1970s, published a pamphlet that links coastal South Carolina and Georgia blacks to Sierra Leone titled *The Gullah: Rice, Slavery and the Sierra Leone–American Connection* (1987). Opala's research attracted the attention of Sierra Leone government officials, and, as a result, the nation's leader, President Joseph Saidu Momoh, organized a visit to the Low Country in 1986 and arranged for a Gullah delegation representing Georgia and South Carolina to visit Sierra Leone in 1989.[122] While conducting research and preparing for the Gullah delegation's homecoming in Sierra Leone, Opala discovered a Mende song that Turner recorded during the 1930s. The song was sung by a coastal Georgia resident named Amelia Dawley who lived in Harris Neck—a mainland community that sits just across the waterway from Sapelo. Turner suspected that the song included Mende words, but he was not able to find anyone who could translate its lyrics. Opala joined with Cynthia Schmidt—an ethnomusicologist—to find someone in Sierra Leone who could help translate the song. They were successful. In 1995, Opala, Schmidt, and their team planned a reunion between Dawley's descendants and Bendu Jabati, the Sierra Leone native whose family had, for generations, sung the same song, and made a documentary film about the song and their meeting titled *The Language You Cry In* (1998).[123]

New Roots at "Home"

As writers and scholars rescued the Gullah from the stereotypical, ahistorical, primitivist gaze that colored 1920s and 1930s Gullah studies, and uncovered specific and verifiable connections between their ancestors and Africa, coastal Georgia and South Carolina blacks began to embrace the new "Gullah" identity and heritage. In 1986, Beaufort, South Carolina, held the first Gullah festival, a multiday event that featured Gullah crafts, cuisine, and cultural performances. Not long after, similar gatherings were organized in communities throughout the Low Country. In 1994, Ron Daise, a St. Helena, South Carolina, native, and his wife, Natalie Daise, partnered with Nickelodeon Network to create the first children's sing-a-long television show centered on a black family. *Gullah Gullah Island* was broadcast for four years and was nominated for numerous awards including a Daytime Emmy Award in 1998. Set on a fictional island in the Low

Country, the show features the Daises, their television family, and their pet pollywog—who sports the Gullah name Binya Binya (meaning "been here")—performing colorful, musical scenes. The new pride that some Low Country blacks found in their Gullah heritage was not only expressed in festivals and entertainment, but was also channeled into endeavors like the project born from a collaboration between a few black St. Helena residents led by Rev. Ervin Greene and a white local couple who had worked for Wycliffe Bible Translators, to translate the Bible into Gullah.[124] By 1994, the translation team that included Penn Center director Emory Campbell published the Gospel of Luke in Gullah titled *De Good Nyews Bout Jedus Christ Wa Luke Write* (1994), and a complete Gullah translation of the New Testament, *De Nyew Testament*, was published in 2005.

Like many of their counterparts in the Low Country, some Sapelo Islanders began staking claims to their uniqueness and revising the story of their community. The Islanders formed a new organization in 1993—the Sapelo Island Cultural and Revitalization Society—and the group held its first Cultural Day festival in 1995. As the island garnered more attention for being one of the last Sea Island communities of its kind—one that is not connected to the mainland by a bridge—Cornelia Bailey stood at the forefront and quickly became the public face of Sapelo Island's newfound pride in its African ancestry. She became a black land retention activist as a result of Hog Hammock's close call with the Reynolds Foundation and developed ties with other community-based organizations in the Low Country who were fighting similar battles. As a result, she was asked to represent Sapelo in the Gullah delegation traveling to Sierra Leone—a trip that changed her life. Bailey wrote, "Everywhere I went in Sierra Leone, I saw similarities to Sapelo. . . . In the faces of people, in the language, the food, the terrain and some of the old traditions."[125] More and more, Low Country blacks like Bailey, people who were exposed to and influenced by the new view of the Gullah born during the Black Studies movement, claimed the Gullah label that had been crafted by outside observers, and the Geechee label that was once used to degrade their dialect and rustic origins. "Gullah" and "Geechee" had become something to be embraced, remembered, and something worth fighting for.

6   Gone but Not Forgotten

SAPELO'S VANISHING FOLK AND THE GULLAH

GEECHEE CULTURAL HERITAGE CORRIDOR

We got more people who want to come back when they're dead than alive.... They want to come back home and be buried.

—Maurice Bailey, Sapelo Islander

On the morning of June 29, 2009, three commissioners representing the newly created Gullah Geechee Cultural Heritage Corridor (GGCHC) gathered a small group of Sapelo residents and a few outsiders on the island for a meeting. GGCHC commissioners—Charles Hall, Jeanne Cryiaque, and Althea Sumpter—officiated the symposium, and like many of the group's commissioners, they were blacks with deep ties to coastal communities in the Low Country. Charles Hall's relationship to Sapelo was special—he grew up there—and his family had called the island home for generations. Hall had presided over many community meetings on Sapelo in recent years, but on this day, he and his colleagues came seeking the community's input on how the GGCHC—a new and unique National Heritage Area—could best preserve Gullah-Geechee folk culture, history, and all of the things that the world had come to love about Sea Islanders.[1]

The gathering on Sapelo was the eighteenth public scoping session in a series of meetings hosted by the GGCHC that had convened in coastal black communities in Florida, South Carolina, and Georgia since February that year. On the surface, questions about how best to preserve local folk culture and history seem innocuous. After all, for nearly one hundred years researchers and writers had tried to capture, collect, and preserve Gullah folk culture in South Carolina and Georgia, and by the 1970s, 1980s, and 1990s, many Low Country blacks had begun to embrace their cultural uniqueness and its African roots. But, by 2009, cultural preservation and historic preservation had become charged concepts in communities like Sapelo—concepts that were riddled with concerns about land retention and fears about permanent displacement.

Aware of the grim prospects for black land retention on Sapelo, the commissioners likely expected what Cornelia Bailey would say when they opened up the floor for comments that Monday morning. Bailey told them, "One of the most precious things we need to preserve is us. . . . When you preserve us, you preserve everything else."[2] Bailey had become the island's foremost land retention activist. More than three decades had passed since she and the other members of the Hog Hammock Community Foundation had formed the island's first organization to protect their land. Since then, she published essays and a memoir, appeared in two documentaries, and had sat for interviews with numerous scholars and journalists.[3] Perhaps all of the time that she dedicated to thinking, writing, and talking about Sapelo helped her to devise a theory about how to preserve Gullah folk culture on the island. She said: "There's so many things to preserve, but we can't do it unless the community itself remains intact, and to remain intact, we have to have a solid land trust base."[4] Bailey explained that a land trust would give Islanders the means to "buy land when it becomes available" in order to "keep the outsiders from invading us, which they are doing now."[5]

Like Bailey, the other black residents in Gullah districts who attended GGCHC public scoping meetings in 2009 homed in on the underlying tension that pervaded the cultural and historic preservation goals of the GGCHC and offered an alternative conceptualization of what *preservation* meant in their communities. GGCHC commissioners—volunteers who devoted their time to the organization's mission—did not have the authority to eliminate the threats that these black communities faced. Land loss, encroaching developers, rising taxes, and scarce economic and employment opportunities exacted a new toll on coastal black communities whose populations began to wane when the first wave of black migrants fled the South during the World War I era. Having a long history of being considered nearly extinct relics of a distant past, blacks who lived in Gullah districts like Sapelo began to articulate a different view of their cultural world—one that was entrenched in the conflicts of the present, and not simply tied to the past. When they raised their voices and told their own stories about their culture and history, the legacy of racism and stunted economic opportunities were as much a defining characteristic of life in their communities as were the survival of African and slave traditions. Their interpretation of preservation focused on economic opportunities and land protections, essential elements needed to foster the longevity of a living Gullah culture, and the very survival of their communities was at stake.

Losing Ground: Sapelo Islanders' Land Fight
on the Eve of a New Millennium

The fact that black land retention in coastal communities in the Low Country had rapidly declined in the decades leading up to the creation of the GGCHC was perhaps the most powerful motivating force that inspired the movement to officially document and preserve Gullah people's history and cultural uniqueness. Like their comrades throughout the region, Sapelo Islanders lost land, but they also lost their people. Sapelo Islander Mildred Grovner told a reporter, "The young people are all leaving, the old people are dying and nobody's having babies."[6] As black land holdings decreased, and the racial and economic composition of these historically black communities began to change, questions swirled about the fate of Gullah culture. This was certainly the case on Sapelo, and in the summer of 1995, concerns about the possible extinction of the island's distinct folk culture caught the attention of state officials and the local media.

On June 25, 1995, the *Atlanta Journal-Constitution* published an article that announced a growing conflict between the DNR, Sapelo Islanders, and whites who had purchased land on the island.[7] The article's author explained that at the center of the conflict were fears that "an influx of white people will dilute Sapelo's Gullah culture."[8] The state of Georgia had already declared Sapelo's black community to be among its most valued and endangered cultural treasures when its legislators formed the Sapelo Island Heritage Authority (SIHA) in 1983 — a council comprised of the governor, the commissioner of the DNR, and other state officials — because it "is important to the citizens of the state of Georgia that this community, which reflects the past culture of this state, be preserved for the benefit of present and future generations."[9] But exactly what the SIHA would do to achieve its goal remained to be seen. However, in 1995, Commissioner Lonice Barrett of the DNR took action and wrote a letter ordering a moratorium on development on Sapelo to slow the influx of outsiders seeking to build homes on the island that was reported widely in the local media. Barrett told one journalist, "We need to decide what to do in terms of management so that beautiful culture doesn't erode away completely."[10] An article published in the *Augusta Chronicle* a few weeks later included quotes from Barrett that further clarified his mission: "I felt like the community over there was feeling so much pressure from outsiders, people who were not the descendants of slaves"; and "Without taking some steps to protect the wonderful black culture of the Hog Hammock community, I think the culture would just cease to exist. The newcomers would push the native people out."[11] Barrett's concerns were echoed by Alan McGregor, the former director of R. J. Reynolds's Sapelo Island Research Foundation: "It's not like we don't want white people over there, but look at the fate of blacks in other coastal communities where whites have come in."[12] McGregor concluded, "There's no way the integrity of the community can withstand what is starting to be a building frenzy."[13]

Barrett's moratorium, as described in newspapers, placed radical restrictions on future development on Sapelo. The *Atlanta Journal-Constitution* reported that the moratorium prohibited "the barging of mobile homes, cars and building materials to the island, but exempted three white landowners" whose construction projects were already under way.[14] Barrett's remedy had been approved by the state attorney general's office, but it was only a temporary measure to give DNR time to develop a long-term plan.[15] When the moratorium expired, newspapers reported, DNR would propose new rules to be voted on that "would allow DNR to deny water hookups, ferry transport, access to island roads and other essential services to anyone who is not a descendant of slaves owned by Thomas Spalding."[16] McIntosh County Commission proposed to "prohibit new homes exceeding one story or 1,400 square feet" and "require a minimum lot size of 20,000 square feet and ban condominiums and multifamily housing," restrictions designed to prevent dramatic shifts in property values, property taxes, and the building of structures that could accommodate large groups of tourists.[17] The county's proposal was timely because property tax hikes had already become a problem for some Sapelo residents. When SICARS's chairman Ben Hall talked to reporters about the DNR's moratorium, he pointed out that the new homes built on Sapelo were assessed at higher values than other Hog Hammock homes and had already generated more costly tax bills for residents: "My taxes have tripled in the last three to four years."[18]

The DNR's moratorium infuriated Sapelo's new white landowners. The *Atlanta Journal-Constitution* reported that one white landowner declared that "Barrett's directive violates his constitutional rights," and a follow-up article published on August 24, 1995, reported that white landowners also argued that the DNR's plan to reserve Sapelo for the "natives," descendants of the slaves who had been held captive there, was "discriminatory."[19] The threat of lawsuits and legal actions was imminent. One editorial letter published in the *Atlanta Journal-Constitution* on July 2, 1995, expressed even more ire: "We are told that the 'beautiful culture' of Hog Hammock is endangered by white influx.... The bottom line is, keep it primitive and keep it black."[20] The letter writer declared, "I don't think it is our government's place to try to manipulate the ethnic complexion of a community," and explained that those worried about the extinction of a "unique culture" should "take note and take pictures because it soon will be subject to technological and societal change like the rest of the country."[21] At the end of the letter, the author suggested that those interested in protecting the island should encourage the National Park Service to buy the land owned by nonresidents—a strategy that the author believed had been employed on nearby Cumberland Island.[22]

Some of Sapelo's black residents were also resistant to, and suspicious of, the DNR's plan. At first glance, the DNR proposal appeared to be a radical move in favor of black land retention on Sapelo, but some Islanders did not see it that way. The *Atlanta Journal-Constitution* reported that the island's black residents were upset because they were not consulted about the plan and believed that the community "should have the final say in any decision the state makes."[23] The DNR's very presence on the island stirred old tensions and anxieties born of the paternalistic authority that Howard Coffin and R. J. Reynolds used to rule Sapelo's people. When news outlets sought Cornelia Bailey for comments on the growing conflict, she linked the Islanders' skepticism about Barrett's plan to their long history of having been forcibly moved around: "We've been moved around so much without our consultation that I think we have a right to be suspicious."[24] She was equally unsure about the SIHA's intentions, a group that she described as "three white men in Atlanta."[25] And the fact that three white landowners had been exempted from Barrett's moratorium exacerbated suspicions. Bailey acknowledged that the future of Hog Hammock's black community was uncertain in light of current trends: "If we get too many outsiders on the island, we'll be another St. Simons Island or Daufuskie Island," islands that, "almost all belonged to black people until the development started."[26] She also told a reporter that Barrett's plan did not simply prohibit whites from building on Sapelo, but would also bar descendants from coming back to the island and building on their family's land.[27] Her own son had been denied access to a permit to put a mobile home on the island so that he could live there as a result of Barrett's moratorium.[28] To be sure, the mobile home ban would likely disproportionately impact landowners who could not afford to build new homes on the island, especially Sapelo's descendants. Bailey was not alone; other Sapelo Islanders expressed their disapproval of the DNR's moratorium. Bernice Banks, a Sapelo Islander identified in a newspaper report as being from the island but living part-time on the mainland, said, "It doesn't seem fair, to people like me who were born on the island, to tell us we can't bring stuff over."[29]

Newspaper articles chronicled black and white Sapelo landowners' reactions to DNR plans, but only one article hinted at a critical factor in black land loss on the island that had not been discussed. The *Augusta Chronicle* pointed out that "the state DNR owns all of Sapelo Island except for about 500 acres, including Hog Hammock. And DNR isn't inclined to release its land to private buyers."[30] Indeed, the state's Sapelo landholdings had been organized into a wildlife reserve and could not be sold for development. Property in Hog Hammock was the only land on Sapelo open to private sale. In fact, one of SICARS's primary objectives was to encourage descendants to hold on to their family properties. Were Sapelo Islanders active partners in the "change" that threatened their island community? Was the simplest solution to the mounting problems that Sapelo residents faced—a population comprised of a little more than 70 people in 1995—to stop selling their land?

Some Sapelo Islanders and island descendants had willingly sold land, but like other blacks in Low Country coastal communities, some lost family properties in sales that were not voluntary. Paul Walker's story about the dilemma that his family faced while trying to hold on to his ancestral property on Sapelo reveals how hard keeping family land on the island was. Walker was born on Sapelo during the 1930s, and was raised in Shell Hammock.[31] He was a teenager when he left the island to work in Savannah before migrating north to Newark, New Jersey, in 1957 in search of better economic opportunities outside of the Jim Crow South.[32] When he arrived in Newark, he lived with a grandaunt from Sapelo who settled there in the 1930s. Walker carved out a good life for himself in the city. He married and started a family with a woman who had moved north from North Carolina. He also turned his natural inclination for building things, solving puzzles, manipulating electronics, and skills he acquired through vocational training, into a career at Lockheed Martin that lasted almost twenty-three years.[33] Walker had done well for himself in the big city, but like many other Sapelo Islanders who migrated to mainland cities in the North and in the South, he visited the island as often as he could and maintained close ties with his family in coastal Georgia.

Walker understood the value of his family's property on Sapelo in terms that far exceeded its economic worth. He remembered when there were multiple black settlements on Sapelo—the time when blacks lived in Belle Marsh, Shell Hammock, Raccoon Bluff, and Lumber Landing before they were all pushed into one settlement at Hog Hammock.[34] Having witnessed the closing of so many of the island's communities, he realized how important it was for Sapelo Islanders to guard what was left of their ancestors' estates. He also recalled how sacred family property was to elders on the island: "All I could hear, you say something about the land, they say 'Don't bother it! Don't touch it.... That's [for the] children!'"[35] This view of landownership was a *survival* of the southern black consciousness born after the Civil War, when blacks began to pursue landownership and as a result acquired millions of acres of land in the South in the first five decades of freedom.[36] Newly freedmen and freedwomen, like the three Sapelo men who purchased one thousand acres of land in Raccoon Bluff in 1871, viewed land as a means of survival and believed property ownership was necessary for freedom.[37] Adhering to this view, Walker's grandfather secured as much property as he could in the hopes that it would one day benefit his children. His holdings were eventually passed down to his seven children, and then again, to their children.

Walker quickly found out that retaining family property that had passed from one generation to the next without a will was not easy. His grandfather probably had one hundred or more descendants who all had shared claims to his property.[38] It was not uncommon for black southerners like Walker's ancestor to die without leaving a will (a possible consequence of limited access to the legal system during the Jim Crow years and limited access to funds for legal services), but when they did, their landholdings were designated heirs' property, land owned in common.[39] At one point, Walker considered suggesting that the family break up the acreage "so that everybody could have their own piece," but there were too many heirs and not enough land for the plan to work. Reaching consensus among so many people about how best to manage the property and pay what eventually amounted to nearly twenty thousand dollars in annual taxes had been almost impossible. An outstanding tax bill was not the only problem the family faced. At some point, Walker said, a "white man come and bought four people's part" of the family estate, and not long after, "his name was on the deed."[40]

For Sapelo Islanders and other blacks who lived in coastal communities in the Low Country, the decision to sell or keep family properties was not easy and was not always within their control. Scholars have examined the difficulties that black southerners and ex-southerners like the Walkers encounter when trying to hold on to family land. Thomas Mitchell's research on black heirs' property in the South reveals why this unstable form of land ownership is more susceptible to forced tax and partition sales. While tax sales are prompted by outstanding debts, forced partition sales can be initiated by heirs desiring to liquidate their holdings, or by outsiders, usually land speculators or lawyers, who surreptitiously acquire interest in heirs' property from an heir in exchange for readily available cash. Because interest in heirs' property is usually held by large numbers of people, and the land they share cannot easily be divided into individual plots, courts tend to order that the land be sold and that heirs split the profits. Mitchell also points out that, in 2001, 41 percent of black landowners in the South were tenants-in-common in land designated as heirs' property, and that their numbers swell as time passes and new generations of heirs are born, a scenario that is complicated by the fact that these heirs are often scattered across the nation.[41]

Holding on to heirs' property has proven to be even more difficult for blacks living in coastal communities in the South. Historian Andrew Kahrl's study *The Land Was Ours: African American Beaches from Jim Crow to the Sunbelt South* (2012) explores the impact of "coastal capitalism" on black communities and argues that real estate developers, investors, and speculators in states like Georgia and South Carolina have taken advantage of the heirs' property crisis in order to carve out profits in the booming coastal economy tied to beach resorts and leisure centers.[42] Equally detrimental is the fact that historic credit and income gaps between whites and blacks in America guaranteed that most Low Country blacks would not be able to take full advantage of the profit-making potential that their properties yielded in the burgeoning coastal leisure economy.[43] Even though blacks living in coastal regions in the Low Country faced unique challenges with regard to land retention, their struggle was similar to other black Americans throughout history, and in other parts of the country, who found themselves entrenched in epic battles for homes and land.[44]

Given the insurmountable odds that blacks who owned coastal lands in communities like Sapelo faced on the eve of the new millennium, the DNR's proposal, which was designed to deter speculators and developers from descending on Hog Hammock, appeared to be the most viable solution. But the plan was too controversial. Both black and white Sapelo landowners challenged its legitimacy, and that was not the only problem the moratorium presented. Surely the very notion that descendants of Sapelo's slaves were owed some special protection and restitution raised more issues than it resolved. How could state DNR officials implement a quasi-reparations plan when the United States government had never seriously entertained the idea that former slaves and their descendants ought to be compensated for their suffering and bondage?

After a long summer of debate and discussion, the *Atlanta Journal-Constitution* reported in September that the state Board of Natural Resources' vote on the proposed rules had been delayed.[45] The short article quoted Barrett, who explained that comments made in public meetings raised concerns "worthy of further consideration," including questions about how Hog Hammock landowners would be treated.[46] Barrett announced: "We'll look and see if we can find compromises or alternatives."[47] When the panel convened again in January 1996, they voted on a revised set of rules designed to simply restrict the free movement of visitors on the island and to verify that all Sapelo landowners complied with McIntosh County construction and zoning codes.[48]

Just as it became clear and ever more certain in 1996 that the numbers of Sapelo's black residents and landowners would continue to dwindle, plans to place historic landmark plaques in Hog Hammock, on First African Baptist Church, and on Behavior Cemetery's gate, were under way.[49] These signs were both celebratory and ominous. They were celebratory because they acknowledged the importance of Sapelo blacks' long history on the barrier island. But they also signaled the transformation from a time when the Islanders told stories about their past to a time when cold slabs of metal, wood, and cement would tell their stories when the last of the island's black residents were gone.

Creating a Gullah Geechee Cultural Heritage Corridor

As the 1990s came to a close, black leaders in Low Country districts identified as authentically Gullah employed various strategies in response to increasing threats of permanent displacement. They continued to organize in their communities and braced for a long battle to hold onto their inheritance. For example, on Sapelo, the Sapelo Island Cultural and Revitalization Society (SICARS) intensified its membership campaign, appealing to the island's descendants far and wide for support, and continued to seek out institutional alliances that would aid their mission. But now more than ever before, the idea that Gullah communities were unique and invaluable cultural resources became particularly crucial. As a result, Gullah leaders invoked the beautiful traditions and heritage that had been fictionalized in black women writers' Gullah stories and pointed to the groundbreaking research that scholars had produced in the wake of the Black Studies movement that confirmed their connections to Africa and chronicled their history to elicit the support of blacks and whites who lived in and outside of the region.

Cornelia Bailey's 1998 account of life on Sapelo published in *Essence* magazine is a good example of this trend. *Essence*, a publication whose target audience is black women, a demographic that likely included many of the people who found inspiration in Morrison's, Marshall's, Naylor's, and Dash's work, featured Bailey's essay titled "Still Gullah." In the essay, Bailey declared she was one of seventy-four Sapelo residents: "I am the last of a generation to be born, raised and schooled on Sapelo. . . . Today my life is a blend of the old and new ways. . . . I live on a dirt road in a wooden house that my husband and I built 24 years ago."[50] "Our old ways are dying," she wrote, explaining that while she relishes "the modern amenities that have come to our island," she felt a "heavy sense of loss at the vanishing ways."[51] Bailey recounted her family's non-American roots, and the roots of the other Islanders and their African background, according to her understanding of their past; Haiti, Sierra Leone, and the "Gola" tribe were each flagged as likely points of origin.[52] Her account of the vanishing Gullah was a much more complicated reading of the convergence of Sapelo Islanders' past and present than were the stories about their endangered culture that dominated 1920s and 1930s Gullah works. She employed the same narrative strategy in composing the *Essence* essay that she would use to formulate future writings about life on Sapelo. She balanced material that reiterated popular descriptions of the Islanders' traditions and history with commentary that boldly pointed out the impact that racism and limited economic opportunities had had on the Islanders.[53]

As Bailey's account unfolds, readers find ornate passages about Sapelo's landscape, the "old ways," and the Islanders' connection to their African ancestors, but they also find thinly veiled references to the negative impact that R. J. Reynolds's domination had on their community, and the tensions that resulted from *changes* in their community culture. Even though in her assessment of the changes that transformed the Islanders' way of life Bailey did not include Coffin's reign on Sapelo, or the closing of so many of the island's communities, she did describe the mounting pressure that weighed on them. She told readers: "If you look beyond the wild natural beauty of the place, you might notice something different in the people. You will see the proud stance as well as the angry walk, the easy smile as well as the hard frown, the serenity of island life as well as the travails." She concluded, "All the contradictions in our lives are visible in the faces and postures of our people." She recounted the tragedy caused by the loss of jobs on the island, and the slow exodus that followed, while painting a picture of an idealized cultural and actual landscape that rivaled the magical scenes in black women's Gullah writings.[54]

Near the essay's end, Bailey offered *Essence* readers the opportunity to help Sapelo Islanders. "We have to tell our young people the old stories, show them our dances and teach them our crafts. . . . That is . . . why we have held an annual festival called Cultural Day. . . . We welcome visitors to the island." The essay was featured in the magazine's travel section, so, accordingly, Bailey announced that tourists could "rent mobile homes," or "stay in a Hog Hammock guest house," and recommended that visitors enjoy the island's landscape or "try an old-fashioned mule tour run by my own son, Maurice Bailey." [55] Next to selling off land piece-by-piece, establishing a small-scale tourism industry was perhaps the most viable option for Islanders of working age who refused to abandon their homes. However, what Bailey offered *Essence* readers was more than a typical tourist attraction. She invited the magazine's black readership to visit Sapelo to reconnect with their own black past. But this strategy raised a critical question: could the admiration of small groups of tourists who visited Low Country locales like Sapelo—casual visitors who might observe locals casting handwoven fishing nets in the ocean, sample native cuisine, and marvel at sweetgrass basketweavers' craftsmanship and the Gullah dialect—help save their communities?

Ultimately, tourism was not the Islanders' only plan. The determined leadership of SICARS developed numerous initiatives. Fred Johnson's son, Ronald Johnson, a vocal Sapelo land retention activist and a man whose father and grandparents were featured in *National Geographic* in 1934, helped shape the organization's mission while serving as the president of its board of directors. With strong leaders like Carolyn Dowse—a retired elementary school principal and Sapelo native who joined the organization's highest ranks as executive director in 1997—SICARS pushed forward.[56] Dowse's commitment to, and love for, the island that her ancestors came back to after the Civil War did not diminish during the years that she lived in Savannah. Under her leadership, the organization continued to host the annual Cultural Day event, but they also envisioned the creation of a "cultural village, an artists' retreat and nature center, affordable housing" and "recreational facilities," in the hope of bringing young people back to the island.[57] Dowse told a reporter, "We hope to attract young people with means, but to do that we need job opportunities."[58] Dowse made inroads toward the organization's goals. She became the first community member to sit on the SIHA and represent the Islanders' interests; she helped create the island's first public library in the old school house; she oversaw the restoration of the old Farmers' Alliance Hall; and she won a $115,000 grant from the Ford Foundation to continue SICARS's preservation efforts.[59] However, SICARS's larger projects, plans designed to reverse the losses that the community suffered, such as the creation of a land trust, remained works in progress.

Some Islanders worried that the land trust, and all of the other innovative projects that SICARS proposed, would come too late. When asked about the changes taking place on Sapelo, resident George Walker—Paul Walker's brother—told a reporter, "Big money coming in. Doctors, lawyers and land speculators."[60] Others believed that the Islanders' multigenerational experience with oppression and racial domination made some Sapelo residents pessimistic about their community's future and reluctant to fight for Hog Hammock's survival. Maurice Bailey explained this to a reporter, saying, "We was never free. We went from Thomas Spalding to Howard Coffin to Richard Reynolds to the DNR.... There was always control. That's what people are used to, and they felt they couldn't do anything."[61]

A Gullah leader from St. Helena, South Carolina, Marquetta L. Goodwine (known as "Queen Quet"), the founder of the Gullah/Geechee Sea Island Coalition organized in 1996, championed an entirely different approach to keeping Gullah communities intact. In 1999, Queen Quet addressed the United Nations on behalf of the Gullah in Geneva, Switzerland.[62] Over and over, Queen Quet had heard blacks from coastal communities in Florida, Georgia, and South Carolina, saying, "Okay, enough is enough. There's too many people moving in. There's too many of us getting moved out. We have to do something that's going to stop this."[63] Queen Quet hoped that the United Nations' international platform would draw widespread attention to the need to preserve Gullah culture, a move that she believes has made more Low Country blacks who live in Gullah districts aware of how their land struggles fit into larger discussions about international law and human rights.[64] Years before she addressed the United Nations, Queen Quet used skills she acquired while studying computer science and mathematics at Fordham University and Columbia University to build a digital network of Gullah residents, descendants, and supporters.[65] As she began to conceptualize "Gullah/Geechee" people as a distinct cultural and ethnic group within the larger tapestry of the world's indigenous peoples, she made efforts to ally with Native American groups such as the Onondaga, Seminole, and Cherokee.[66] By 2000, Queen Quet's multistate Gullah/Geechee Sea Island Coalition became the Gullah/Geechee Nation, comprised of Low Country black residents and descendants who volunteered to join the group. Queen Quet was voted chieftess and head of state of the Gullah/Geechee Nation: "From July 2, 2000, to now, we have been an internationally-recognized nation or state, as you're called at the United Nations."[67]

Despite the fact that Queen Quet and members of the Gullah/Geechee Nation envision themselves as a distinct body politic, they dedicated time and energy to petitioning local and federal officials in the United States to halt black land loss in the Low Country and to preserve their culture. Queen Quet explained, "We do lots of things with petitions and letter-writing to government officials whether they're local, state, federal, wherever."[68] She maintains that her organization's activism was instrumental in the creation of the Gullah Geechee Cultural Heritage Corridor (GGCHC): "That's how come the Gullah/Geechee Cultural Heritage Act got passed.... A lot of our supporters were the ones that wrote letters and called the congresspeople across the country."[69] Michael Allen, a Kingstree, South Carolina, native and the National Park Service (NPS) ranger who led the team who established the GGCHC, identified different origins for the corridor. However, he did describe Queen Quet as a particularly helpful partner to the project: "When we began this journey in 2000, I called upon people who I knew of goodwill up and down the coast to help me.... One of the individuals I called upon was Marquetta Goodwine ... because she's done a lot of work ... in the community, and she's known internationally."[70] He noted that Queen Quet was "very helpful in opening doors and helping us in this process."[71] Acting as a liaison between the NPS and the community, Allen was focused on building community partnerships, so he did not allow his own skepticism about the idea of a sovereign Gullah nation and the phone calls and emails that he received from people bothered by what they interpreted as Queen Quet's determination that she spoke for all Gullah people, to divide his efforts: "I think that's a central sore point because some folks don't want her to project for them.... Some people take issue with the terminology of the use of 'queen' that she calls herself. . . . I have bigger things to deal with, and so a lot of things I'm not going to get into the mud with."[72]

Allen certainly did have bigger things to grapple with. As a longtime NPS ranger assigned to the Charles Pinckney National Historic site in Mount Pleasant, South Carolina, he was keenly aware that critical elements of the black experience in the Low Country were missing from many of the NPS sites in the region, and so during the 1990s, when interest in the Gullah began to grow and fears that the culture would soon be lost forever heightened, Allen helped to facilitate conversations about how to include the culture in the stories told at NPS sites.[73] The conversation intensified and ultimately included the voices of residents in Gullah districts and caught the attention of U.S. congressman James E. Clyburn, the representative for the sixth district of South Carolina.[74] Soon, the conversation was no longer simply about how to include the Gullah story at individual sites in South Carolina; the conversation evolved and produced more substantial questions about where the Gullah fit within the larger narrative of the nation's past. And the NPS, the federal government agency that had curated and interpreted the cultural and historical significance of sites and places since 1916, was uniquely positioned to take up the question.[75]

Congressman Clyburn was also the ideal champion to push this question to the forefront: his connections to South Carolina's Gullah communities were deep. As a young boy, Clyburn accompanied his father, who was a minister, to churches on James Island, Johns Island, and Wadmalaw Island on occasions when he was invited to deliver sermons there.[76] The congressman taught school in Charleston, South Carolina, after graduating from college in the 1960s.[77] When he left teaching in 1965 and went to work as an employment counselor at the Youth Opportunity Center in Charleston, Clyburn continued to interact with the young people in Gullah communities.[78] His wife was raised in Moncks Corner, South Carolina—a community in one of the state's many Gullah districts; and Clyburn had even served on Penn Center's board.[79] It was through his involvement with Penn Center—the historic school established on St. Helena Island for freedmen and freedwomen during the Civil War—that he became more aware of black land loss in Gullah communities, which he described as "unfortunate" but "not illegal": "you see what happened on Hilton Head, it's just that when you start building resorts . . . the tax code took care of the rest, the natives could not afford to pay the new assessments, and a lot of them lost land that way."[80]

In light of all of his encounters and experiences with people who were now being described as "vanishing" and "endangered," Clyburn was troubled by what he heard. Allen explained that the congressman's commitment to introducing legislation that would give the NPS a budget for a special study "which would look at the history, look at the scope, look at the threats, look at the opportunities that Gullah-Geechee people" faced "now and into the future" was pivotal.[81] In 1999, Clyburn secured an earmark that enabled the NPS to conduct a special resource study (SRS) on Low Country Gullah culture.[82] Not long after, Allen and the NPS organized a team of researchers to explore all that had been written about the Gullah and talked to people in Gullah districts, asking them critical questions, such as, "What is Gullah? What is Geechee? What's the history? How do you tie [it in]? What are the threats? What are the opportunities? Where do you see your future?"[83] These were questions no researcher had ever asked blacks who lived in Gullah districts.

Assembling a research team who could effectively engage with black communities in the Low Country who had long since grown tired of outsiders' and researchers' curiosities undoubtedly posed a challenge to the study's organizers. The majority of the SRS team consisted of NPS employees, and Allen served as the project's primary point person. But the study's principal researcher, Cynthia Porcher, the investigator designated to interact with the community and uncover Gullah history, was not an NPS employee.[84] Porcher, a white woman, was described in the SRS final publication as a "low country native" who was a "former community health outreach specialist with more than thirty years experience in the area" whose work with the SRS "returned her to the Sea Islands of Beaufort County ... the site of her first field research study during the late 1960s."[85] Queen Quet believed the NPS should have assigned a principal researcher who was better suited for the task, like Barbara Tagger, a black historian and longtime NPS ranger whose accomplishments include working on the Selma to Montgomery Historic Trail and the Underground Railroad State Park.[86] Queen Quet recalled being stunned when she learned that the NPS hired "an Anglo woman" to do the field research, a woman who she at first thought was hired as administrative help, and said that she received emails and phone calls from her constituents who were "mad" and reluctant to participate in the study because "as far as they were concerned, she's the symbol of those who have exploited them."[87] To be sure, tensions between Queen Quet and Porcher ran high: "She was mad because I wasn't going to take her around in our community."[88]

Unlike Julia Peterkin, Lydia Parrish, and Mary Granger—white women who conducted research in Gullah communities during the interwar years— Porcher acknowledged that she had to overcome a steep learning curve in order to connect with Low Country blacks and make sense of their history. In fact, she talked candidly to news reporters about the revelations that she had during the study. Porcher confessed anxieties about interacting with Low Country blacks: "My first thoughts were how are we going to take our white faces in here and have any kind of success" and recognized that many of the people that she encountered were "cautious with outsiders."[89] She admitted to being "amazed at the depth of . . . Gullah-Geechee culture," and said, "It's something that is difficult for an outside white person like myself to get a sense of. But I'm now truly convinced in my heart that the rest of America needs to hear the Gullah-Geechee's voice."[90] One reporter mentioned that Porcher, a product of South Carolina's segregated school system, "had little personal interactions with Gullahs" prior to the study and had "for years . . . wrongly interpreted" their dialect "as simply bad English grammar," an assumption that she abandoned as she learned more through research.[91] Porcher also told reporters that, like many whites and blacks, "I didn't learn very much in school" about black culture, but she said because of the study she learned more about the black experience: "I learned a great deal about how unhappy slaves were."[92] She discovered that enslaved blacks used "work stoppages and slowdowns and sickouts and all kinds of things on plantations" to resist their captivity. "They were not 'happy-clappy' black faces and mammies with big smiles. . . . For the most part, that was a myth."[93]

One thing that Porcher told reporters that she figured out right away was that Gullah communities were working hard to save themselves "with little time and resources."[94] Whether or not the NPS could do anything to help them remained to be seen, but Porcher and her team moved forward. Tasked with conducting an in-depth examination of the history and cultural life of coastal black communities in Georgia, South Carolina, and Florida to determine if Gullah culture had "national significance" and to ascertain how it might be protected by the NPS, the SRS team went to work.[95] Between May 2000 and August 2000, they hosted community meetings in Charleston, Georgetown, St. Helena Island, and Little River, South Carolina; St. Simons Island and Savannah, Georgia; and Jacksonville, Florida.[96] They also combed through everything that had been written about Gullah folk and about the history of black coastal settlements in the region.

The final SRS report on the Gullah is unquestionably the culmination of the construction of the Gullah identity coded as ethnographic fact. Cynthia Porcher and NPS regional ethnographer Dr. J. Anthony Paredes wrote the report, and regional and national NPS reviewers, along with a panel of experts on Gullah/Geechee and African American history and culture, reviewed the document.[97] Published in July 2005, the final report consisted of 435 pages of narrative, multiple appendices, and supplemental material. Its authors compiled and presented old and new theories about the Gullah and African survivals, historical accounts (informed by the Black Studies movement) of black life in the Low Country, and Gullah folks' testimonies about their contemporary struggles as evidence of their uniqueness and significance. Acknowledging that scholars and experts did not agree on the origins of the terms "Gullah" and "Geechee," the report's authors concluded that the "vernacular use of the terms will suffice for the purpose of this study," and consequently, "Gullah people are ... located in South Carolina and Geechee people are those who live along the Georgia coast and into Florida."[98] The final SRS report also established Gullah territory's geographic boundaries in terms of natural demarcations that cemented the idea that these populations had been isolated and confined "from the Cape Fear River near the North Carolina/South Carolina line to the St. John's River near Jacksonville, Florida and 30 miles inland following estuarine boundaries."[99]

The SRS report went even further and added a new dimension to the old equation used to connect the Gullah to Africa. Believing that the research and theories that anthropologist William Pollitzer presented in *The Gullah People and Their African Heritage* (1999) reflected the most authoritative, contemporary published study on the Gullah, the report's authors noted that Pollitzer's "work demonstrates that the Gullah/Geechee people are a distinctive biological population with less European admixture than other African Americans."[100] Indeed, Pollitzer, a white anthropologist born in Charleston, South Carolina, who, for most of his life, "knew little of the 'darker side' of life there, the black folks," had used his expertise in anthropology and genetics to assert that "in both morphology and serology the Gullah are closer to western Africa and further removed from whites than other African Americans."[101] At the very moment when the power of the human genome to solve criminal, medical, and ancestral mysteries had gained popularity around the world, Pollitzer applied the modish preoccupation with genes to the Gullah, returning the conversation about their cultural distinction to quasi-biological racial origins.[102] While the bulk of his book synthesized what had previously been published about African survivals and the Gullah, Pollitzer presented blood types, physical features, and the rate and frequency of diseases like sickle cell anemia to assert that there was a sort of racial genetic purity among the Gullah despite recognizing that "physical features are too blended, genetic markers too intermediate, and data from Africa too sparse to connect them directly with some specific region of that continent."[103] The report's authors did not rely exclusively on Pollitzer's work to explain and characterize African survivals in Gullah communities, but they did cite his book throughout the report and boasted that he had specially prepared "a condensation of his monumental work . . . for inclusion in this study"—a fifty-page appendix found at the end of the document.[104]

Aside from suggesting that Gullah/Geechee people were biologically distinct, the authors of the SRS report did not strain to illustrate that their subject's history and culture were a unique and important part of America's national heritage.[105] Using much of what scholars had written about black life in the region since the Black Studies movement, they traced the history of the Gullah from the Africans who came to Charleston from Angola, Senegambia, the Winward Coast, the Gold Coast, Sierra Leone, and other places, through slavery, the Civil War, and Reconstruction.[106] They wrote about Charleston's prominence in the slave trade, the plantation economy, and rice production along the coast and also pointed to the slave task system and the fact that the Gullah had largely been separated from mainland communities on barrier island plantations and remote locales along the coast to explain the emergence of their distinctive culture.[107] The study established the importance of Christianity enhanced by African expressions in historic Gullah communities, relegating rootwork, hoodoo, and conjure to the margins of Gullah life—which was a dramatic turn away from what had been written about them during the interwar years.[108] Stories about the Gullah who fought in the Civil War and those who used Special Field Order No. 15 to build all-black enclaves along the coast were included in the report.[109] This was the historical and cultural context that SRS authors provided to explain why and how the Gullah/Geechee dialect had taken root, how Gullah Christian praise houses, ring shout performances, and special funeral rites became customary, and how unique foodways, basketweaving techniques, and fishing styles had become routine.[110]

In recounting the chronology of Gullah folk from slavery to the present, however, the report's authors missed the most important moment in the history of the Gullah identity—the 1920s and 1930s. Nestled between passages about Reconstruction and World War II, one sentence proclaimed: "The early 20th Century brought about the 'discovery' of Gullah/Geechee language and culture by artists and scholars."[111] The declaration was followed by, "During the same timeframe, there was a parallel 'discovery' by those desiring Gullah/Geechee natural resources and lands."[112] Certainly, this critical omission is problematic, but it is also understandable. The study's authors depended on scholarly sources to reconstruct Gullah history and define their culture, but no scholar had taken up the task of contextualizing the construction of the Gullah identity. At the time when the SRS team busied themselves combing through troves of literature about the Gullah, no work had been written that examined the moment when Low Country blacks first became subjects in larger debates about race, heredity, and African survivals and emerged as objects of fascination in a cultural landscape that had learned to exoticize black southerners, voodoo, roots, and conjure. No study had chronicled the tension between Gullah folk and the outsiders who imagined them according to Jim Crow fantasies about black life and the rebirth and redefinition of the identity within black people's new racial consciousness during the 1970s, 1980s, and 1990s. Even so, this glaring gap in the history of Gullah folk is a missed opportunity to explore how Low Country blacks who lived in coastal communities have been entangled in a hundred-year-old struggle over race, heritage, and identity.

In the end, the report's writers concluded: "Gullah/Geechee people are the most African of African Americans in physical type, language, and culture; yet they are a uniquely American cultural type formed by the fusion of African cultural heritage and American experience."[113] Surely this narrative of more than a hundred pages of Gullah history, culture, and contemporary struggles, with written endorsements from William Pollitzer and Professor Richard A. Long—a black historian at Emory University—justified further NPS action.[114] Other organizations also bolstered their call to action: in 2004 the National Trust for Historic Preservation listed the "Gullah/Geechee Coast" on its list of eleven most endangered places, citing widespread change as the nebulous culprit that precipitated its demise.

Confident that they had made a strong case establishing Gullah folks' historical and cultural significance, and sure that they had proven that their subjects' folkways were endangered, the team presented five intervention alternatives for the NPS and the community to consider. However, the alternatives were limited by the fact that the NPS did not have the authority to intercede in the land battles that, according to residents, posed the greatest threat to their way of life. Perhaps because this constraint seemed to run contrary to the project's larger mission, when the final SRS report was drafted, a disclaimer about the land retention issue appeared in the document's introduction: "While the NPS may be able to do a great deal to assist in interpretation of culture, the preservation of land lies largely in the hands of government entities that regulate property taxes and control real estate development, and the Gullah/Geechee people themselves."[115] But the lines that followed optimistically alluded to the possibility that the NPS could serve to connect Gullah communities with organizations that might be able to help them in their land fight.[116]

The NPS could only offer intervention alternatives that were consistent with the traditional role that they played as a government agency. The proposed alternatives included establishing Gullah/Geechee heritage centers on public lands; expanding the Gullah/Geechee story at existing NPS sites; creating a multistate national heritage area connected by a network of historically and culturally significant places; structuring a combination of heritage centers within a national heritage area; and no action at all.[117] Each alternative presented advantages and disadvantages, which included the cost of implementation.[118] The report indicated that focus groups composed of NPS and community members determined that creating a National Heritage Area (NHA) was the best choice. The report's writers described the option as cost-effective because it "can facilitate the leveraging of funds and resources through a working partnership among federal, state and local entities."[119] Federal funding for the NHA "could be up to a maximum of $1 million annually, not to exceed a total of $10 million over the period of NPS involvement."[120] And, ultimately, the NHA "would essentially become the responsibility of the people living within its boundaries," and "the federal government would not assume any ownership of land, impose zoning or land use controls in heritage areas, or take responsibility for permanent funding."[121]

However, the possibility that Gullah districts in the Low Country would be linked in the proposed NHA promised some benefits to these black communities. The NPS describes these areas as locales "designated by Congress as places where natural, cultural, and historic resources combine to form a cohesive, nationally important landscape" and "celebrate our nation's diverse heritage" and as a "grassroots, community-driven" approach to "heritage conservation and economic development."[122] Economic development and heritage conservation had become critical concerns in Gullah districts throughout the Low Country, and some blacks who lived in communities where anxieties about displacement were particularly high imagined that any sort of intervention that the federal government made could only help their plight.

Since Gullah people were ultimately responsible for the NHA, their input was needed to construct the management plan. Throughout the research period, the SRS team sought residents in Gullah districts for their perspectives about contemporary issues and included their opinions and documented community revitalization efforts in the study.[123] At times, the team encountered residents in communities who were apprehensive about participating in the process: "Several speakers at public meetings in 2000 expressed their concerns about the number of outside researchers who have come into Gullah communities to study and write about their culture."[124] When they did open up, researchers learned as much about land battles, revitalization efforts, and other challenges communities faced as they learned about Gullah culture and history.[125] Dr. Michael Davis's rhetorical analysis of the SRS Gullah community meetings held in 2000 revealed that the community members who spoke out at these gatherings used those public forums to shift the conversation from simple conceptualizations about history and culture to more nuanced discussions about the challenges that they faced.[126] This was not lost on the SRS team. When they took the intervention alternatives to the community in the fall of 2002, they reported that some of the community members who participated in the workshop raised concerns that were outside the purview of the NPS, such as "land retention and zoning," "property tax rate controls," and "creating jobs."[127] And surely everyone involved understood that these issues would not be easily remedied and would find their way into every input meeting.

Defining the Gullah/Geechee Experience from the "Inside Out"

After the NPS completed the *Low Country Gullah Culture Special Resource Study and Final Environmental Impact Statement* and it was published in 2005, Congressman Clyburn introduced, revised, and then reintroduced, the Gullah/Geechee Heritage Act so that the NPS's recommendation could be implemented.[128] While North Carolina was not included in the original NPS conceptualization of Gullah territory, a groundswell of requests from North Carolinians who lived on the state's coast demanding to be included resulted in the corridor's boundary line being moved farther north.[129] The bill received overwhelming support and was cosponsored by a bipartisan group of eight representatives from South Carolina, Georgia, Florida, and North Carolina.

The Gullah/Geechee Heritage Act was passed in 2006, and, in 2007, the NPS, and State Historic Preservation offices and community members in North Carolina, South Carolina, Georgia, and Florida recommended commissioners to manage the corridor.[130] The impressive twenty-six-person list of cultural resource experts, state representatives, and alternates included some of the most accomplished and influential blacks from the corridor. Eleven professors and educators whose expertise included history, anthropology, and linguistics, such as Penn Center's former director Emory Campbell, historian John H. Haley, and museum consultant Deborah L. Mack, were chosen to be commissioners.[131] Inspiring local artists and Gullah performers such as Ronald Daise—*Gullah Gullah Island*'s creator and lead actor—and Hilton Head's Gullah storyteller Louise Miller Cohen were also on the list.[132] Community leaders and activists such as Eulis Alexander Willis (the mayor of Vassa, North Carolina), Sapelo Island's Charles Hall (president of SICARS), and Queen Quet were selected to lead the heritage corridor.[133] Lawyers and business people were also named among the list of scholars, community leaders, and activists—almost all black, and almost all from Gullah communities—chosen to set the direction for the GGCHC.[134]

The GGCHC commissioners who had been chosen were likely the most skilled and best-equipped people to achieve the corridor's mission "to recognize and sustain an environment that celebrates the legacy and continuing contributions of Gullah/Geechee people to our American Heritage."[135] Despite their collective expertise and individual accomplishments, the commissioners did not approach the community as all-knowing experts, but instead expressed a desire to work hand in hand with the people to achieve the corridor's goals and to correct the way that outsiders had imagined them. Commissioner Veronica Gerald articulated this aspiration when she addressed the

Atlantic Beach community at an input meeting. She explained, "Outside of the culture," Gullah folk "were considered to have thick lips and lazy tongues and could not speak the King's English.... We ate a lot of rice.... We believed in root work and magic." She concluded, "We had been interpreted from the outside in for so long.... So your presence tonight ... is an attempt to get a look at this culture from the inside out."[136]

Excited by the chance to define their culture "from the inside out," most of the community members who commented at the twenty-one public scoping meetings held between February and August 2009 offered support for the corridor's mission and made suggestions to help the commissioners along the way.[137] At the start of each meeting, the commissioners explained the point and purpose of the corridor and described their role within it. After that, they sat quietly and listened to what the community had to say. And the Gullah folk who attended the meetings had a lot to say. They told family stories, shared memories about growing up in the corridor, and discussed local food traditions; they talked about the Gullah/Geechee dialect and the shame that once came from speaking it; they talked about Africa; they suggested sites for historic preservation such as old school houses and overgrown long-forgotten cemeteries; they identified potential institutional partners for preservation efforts; and they proposed ideas for Gullah/Geechee festivals to attract tourists to the region.[138] The people who attended the meetings were proud of their history, their heritage, and the contributions their ancestors made to America. Pride emanated from their comments. At a meeting held on Johns Island, South Carolina, the son of the island's famous civil rights activist Esau Jenkins reminded the group that Dr. Martin Luther King Jr. had attended workshops at the Progressive Club on the island during the 1960s.[139] And at a meeting in Georgetown, South Carolina, one resident pointed out that the nation's first "first" black family had Gullah roots: "Maybe we need to have a plaque on this house to say that Michelle Obama's grandfather and grandmother lived in this house."[140]

But other comments and stories painted a bleak picture of black life and history in black coastal communities in the Low Country. Several speakers decried American racism, recounted black suffering during Jim Crow, and pointed out the irony in talking about cultural and historic preservation without addressing the land battles raging throughout the region.[141] For these attendees, America's insidious racism and all of the injustice that it produced, was not just a part of the Gullah past, it was a part of their present-day experience. These commenters wanted to know, and in some cases demanded to know, how the GGCHC would address these issues.

Jim Crow necessitated the creation of many of the historic black structures that the GGCHC hoped to preserve, and some community members pointed out that a lingering Jim Crow consciousness may have also hastened the destruction of these important Gullah landmarks. At a meeting held in Savannah, a community member talked about a black theatre that had been demolished: "We don't have anything to say this was a black theatre . . . because urban renewal came through. It just destroyed all of our historic landmarks."[142] In another meeting held in Savannah, a man quipped, "I don't know how we're going to preserve what's already been gentrified."[143] A remark from the meeting held in Mount Pleasant, South Carolina, noted a similar trend in Charleston: "And the thing is, those homes on the Battery, only those big mansions, the folks down there don't pay their tax   they're tax-free because they got a big historical home. But . . . the uptown area, where the minorities is at, these houses are being torn down and being replaced with new homes." Another speaker noted that in Mount Pleasant, "All of these schools that were built specifically for African-Americans are being torn down."[144]

Not even black historic cemeteries were safe from destruction. At a meeting on Johns Island, South Carolina, one speaker talked about how a family cemetery had been included in a land sale. At the Mount Pleasant meeting, a woman named Ms. Carter told a story about how her family cemetery was almost lost. "Those of you that live here know that we just completed the battle about the cemetery. . . . A man bought ten acres and decided to build his dream home on the cemetery." She explained that when Hurricane Hugo hit in 1989, the cemetery was covered by downed trees, and the people could not afford to have them moved: "We needed resources." The community's effort to reclaim the burial ground was aided by an 1870 map that identified the cemetery, so they won the case. Carter said that the first interment in the cemetery after the victory "was my dad"; he "was buried in the cemetery where his grandfather was buried."[145]

Ms. Carter's testimony also revealed how vulnerable black landowners had always been in the Low Country. While fighting to save the cemetery, she said members of the community began exchanging stories about how their families had been victimized by Jim Crow's economic and legal systems: "You told what happened in your family. And you said, 'You think that's something? Here's what happened to my family.' And you had all these stories in one room."[146] Like the story she was told about a family who "walked to the county courthouse in our city to pay their taxes. They were told . . . you'll have to come back next week because the tax books have gone home with a private citizen." When the family came back, "the tax books were returned, 16 pages of records pertaining to our community were gone." She concluded the story by saying, "So these are the kinds of things that are heavy on our minds."[147]

Ms. Carter was not the only community member who attended one of the GGCHC meetings with black land loss on their mind. In Conway, South Carolina, a woman told commissioners, "When we were talking I thought about my great-grandfather. And we were talking about heritage. To him it was land." Another man at the meeting said, "My concern is that we're going to lose a lot of land simply because of taxes. . . . Just like we've lost Kiawah Island and Seabrook Island, John's Island."[148] At a meeting in McClellanville, South Carolina, a sweetgrass basketmaker pointed out the impact that land loss had on Gullah crafts: "When I was a little girl we used to always go at Seabrook Island and Kiawah Island to pull sweetgrass, but after the golf course and the condos come, that's gone. So we have to travel far distance to find sweetgrass and palmetto, now."[149] In Savannah, a community member challenged the commission: "If this commission cannot, or persuade someone to save the land, all we're going to have is a memory. And we know what the history of this country is toward the history of black people. There will be none." He ended his impassioned comment with this statement: "There needs to be something done to preserve this. If we can't preserve land, then we have nothing . . . land is the hope."[150] At the same meeting, a woman's stirring remark about the land loss problem expressed the sadness that many blacks who lived in coastal communities likely felt: "It's heartbreaking. I look at my children and I think about my grandchildren, and we're not going to have a place to call home. . . . I'm going to bring them to some subdivision, not the land that my grandfather plowed, not the cotton that my great-grandmother lost her fingers picking."[151]

Frustrated by the developers encroaching on their communities and rising taxes, some of the residents who attended input meetings expressed criticisms of what they believed to be GGCHC's passive position on their land fight and singular focus on culture and history. At one of the meetings held in Savannah, an attendee declared, "I think the commission has to have serious goals and not frivolous ones. I'm not prepared to have plantation life celebrated, and people coming up and down this corridor to look at people weaving baskets and playing out plantation play."[152] In a meeting held in Darien, Georgia, a city on the mainland across from Sapelo, one person said, "The National Park Service, as far as I'm concerned, really has no business with what we are about as Gullah/Geechee. We are not going to be in a museum, or in a box, a glass cage where you come and look at us, and then you leave and say oh, wasn't that beautiful?"[153] The Darien meeting was intense, and almost as soon as the floor was opened for discussion, the same participant criticized the composition of the GGCHC leadership, asking "where are the plainfolk," and stating, "If you have a grassroot's person . . . speaking on behalf of us Gullah/Geechee they will speak that grassroots perspective."[154]

Others who were frustrated by land loss offered the commissioners actual plans for land retention. A Clemson University professor who spoke at the

Mount Pleasant meeting suggested that the commission develop a "framework to address working with municipalities, with policy, with development" in order to stop "exclusionary planning practices."[155] And a man who commented at the meeting in St. Helena, South Carolina, proposed a strategy to deal with the heir property crisis: "I would like to suggest that if this Commission would be able to request . . . special laws to be set aside on a revolving loan basis . . . that families will be able to go to this fund, request up to $28,000 to get appropriate attorneys . . . to be able to clear the title on the property."[156] Perhaps because Gullah authenticity was tied to slavery, one commenter in Darien, Georgia, recounted the history of General Sherman's Special Field Order No. 15 and said "look at the Geechee/Gullah corridor right now . . . 50% of that corridor is Special Order 15." He next calculated, according to his interpretation of historical events, all of the years that blacks had been enslaved and oppressed in the region and proposed a reparations plan: "So if you go from 1526 roughly to 1865, we're looking at 350 years . . . add 50 years for reconstruction . . . give you 400 years . . . which I don't think is very long, that people who are Gullah culture or heritage, who have land, that their land is preserved tax free for the next 400 years." Near the end of his speech, he talked about Sapelo, and put forth an eerie challenge to the commissioners to emphasize that something drastic needed to be done: "What I would like for this council to do . . . since they will be at Sapelo, count the number of black people you have there. Come back next year and see how many black families you have."[157]

When the commissioners came to Sapelo on June 29, 2009, for the meeting, a gathering that was officiated by Sapelo's own commissioner Charles Hall, they did not need to count black families on the island to know that Hog Hammock was in trouble. The SRS team had been to Sapelo, and they too knew that the Islanders faced overwhelming odds against their community's survival. Despite the fact that the SRS team had botched the summary of Sapelo's history in their final report (they omitted critical details, excluded Coffin from the history, and made assertions like "Balili helped to ensure the survival of African traditions by instilling African customs and teaching the Gullah/Geechee language to slaves on Sapelo"), they did understand that the Islanders' land struggles had been playing out for decades.[158] Even so, the commissioners proceeded as they had in other communities throughout the corridor and asked the Sapelo residents who attended what they wanted to preserve: "They can be physical things like houses, churches, buildings, schools, or they can be what we call intangible things."[159] Despite the fact that Sapelo residents undoubtedly wanted to talk about the land issue, like other people who had participated in the input meetings that year, they too offered a list of things that should be preserved and recalled the old days. They talked about the Farmers'

Alliance Hall and the island's historic churches. They suggested that Emma and Emmitt Johnson's home—the Sapelo family featured in the 1934 *National Geographic Magazine*—be restored as a significant island landmark. They talked about smoked mullet fish, hunting, red peas, butter beans, fishing, and making cast nets and sweetgrass baskets.[160]

Even as Sapelo Islanders reminisced, like other residents who attended meetings up and down the coast, they continuously vocalized an alternative conception of "preservation," one that focused on their community's survival and not just old homes and other artifacts. One of the first comments at the meeting was that Sapelo was "the last intact island-based Gullah/Geechee community in the state" to emphasize that "there needs to be a lot of investment in Hog Hammock. It would be a tragedy to see its demise, and that means we need help."[161] Commissioner Hall's son, Reginald Hall, an emerging young voice in Sapelo's land fight, who had attended an input meeting in South Carolina the month before, explained that the group needed to "cover some basics"—"Number one being land retention, there should be something set up for the Gullah/Geechee as a whole to get what I know is education of land retention."[162] Others made comments that revealed friction between the Islanders about land sales. One Islander remarked that retirees, people who had "lived their life," were guilty of selling off land: "We lose more land through the older generation than the younger generation. . . . We got people in this room that have sold land and are trying to sell land." He continued, "You come here and preach to us, come sit under the tree and laugh and talk with us and you sold your land."[163]

As was the case during other input meetings in the corridor, the Sapelo Islanders at the meeting offered solutions and presented plans to revive their community and hold on to their family properties. Cornelia Bailey proposed the development of a land trust, but other Islanders focused on economic development. Reginald Hall spelled out the dilemma: "The only way we can survive here on Sapelo now is to have some form of economics brought back to the island to bring descendants back outside of the mass exodus we've already experienced."[164] Another man explained that they need jobs to attract descendants and keep young people on the island: "We can keep the younger generation over here and satisfied with jobs." He envisioned a way to link job creation to Gullah traditions: "You got clamming, you got the oysters, you got fishing and all this other stuff we could also be doing because that's also part of our heritage." He then said to the commissioners, "If y'all were willing to . . . loan us a little money . . . we can get a lot of this stuff done."[165] A different young man told the commissioners that there was plenty of land on the island that could be cultivated in ways that would not hurt the environment while creating viable economic opportunities for residents. He explained that even though he was able to carve out a livelihood on Sapelo, other descendants could not: "We got kinfolk in Germany, California, everywhere. Wasn't no jobs on the island." He remembered, "When I was young, I think we had 120 people on the island. Now we're down to 47 or 50, something like that, it's steadily going down. . . . I would like to stay. It's hard, I'm trying to do it."[166]

In the End

Surely it was hard for Commissioner Hall, and all of the other GGCHC commissioners who attended the meetings, to hear appeals for help that the corridor could not provide. Each of the forty-nine National Heritage Areas in the United States are governed by the same laws and codes—none of which allowed for direct interventions in the types of issues that worried the blacks who lived in the Gullah/Geechee corridor. The corridor was created to recognize, sustain, and celebrate Gullah/Geechee culture and history, to assist with the interpretation and preservation of their culture and history, and to identify and aid in the preservation of historical material and sites associated with the culture.[167] A beautiful mission to be sure, but not one that could solve the problems that plagued black coastal communities in the Low Country.

Some of the residents who went to input meetings may have misinterpreted the power that GGCHC commissioners had to address the issues that they presented, but they used those public forums to speak their truth, to tell their stories, and to name their hardships. When they defined their culture and experience from the "inside out," they told a story about the Gullah that had never been told. Their Gullah story included tragedies, triumphs, strivings, and traditions that were rooted and tangled in the nation's continuously unfolding race and class drama. These accounts clash with primitivist fantasies about groups of backward blacks and Africans stuck in an earlier time that first made the Gullah famous, and their stories chronicled events and experiences that moved the Gullah from mythical isolation into larger contemporary struggles.

The tension between cultural and historic preservation and land and economic preservation that community members called attention to made an impression on the commissioners. Even though the GGCHC was restricted by the NHA constraints, in the final management plan published in 2012, the commissioners acknowledged that land loss and economic development issues were looming concerns that arose in public scoping meetings.[168] Four pages in the published document were dedicated to analyzing and contextualizing the perils of heirs' property.[169] The commissioners also indicated that "educating" was "the key method that the Commission" would use to "assist in sustaining land within the Corridor," and stated that they would "support Gullah

Geechee heritage-related businesses and promote preservation of the land and natural resources needed to sustain the culture, with the goal of enhancing the quality of life for current and future generations."[170] As interpreters of black culture in the corridor, the commission included Gullah people's "Connection with the Land" to the other interpretative themes, which included "Origins and Early Development," "The Quest for Freedom, Equality, Education, and Recognition," "Global Connections," "Cultural and Spiritual Expression," and the "Gullah Geechee Language."[171] These themes would be used to structure the interpretation of Gullah history and culture for audiences that included corridor residents, students, members of the Gullah diaspora who return home for visits, and tourists.[172]

Sapelo Islanders had already attempted many of the approaches outlined in the GGCHC management plan, and their efforts did not dramatically change the prospects for their community's renewed vitality. In fact, the SRS team had documented many of these undertakings. Several of Sapelo's remaining residents who refused to abandon the island created a small-scale tourist industry with bed and breakfasts and rental homes to attract tourists.[173] SICARS initiated a campaign to educate residents and descendants about land and tax issues and had also hosted an annual Cultural Day festival to educate residents, descendants, and tourists alike about the island's culture and history.[174] The organization also partnered with the Savannah College for Art and Design to restore Sapelo's First African Baptist Church and made moves to restore the Farmers' Alliance Hall.[175] In the end, economic forces that had, for generations, pushed their children to the mainland, and scattered them across the nation, dwarfed their efforts and undercut their campaign to reinvigorate their community and secure their land inheritance. For Sapelo Islanders, the GGCHC's educational and promotional initiatives held very little promise of changing the fate of a black community on the verge of being gone, but not forgotten.

EPILOGUE From African Survivals
to the Fight for Survival

During the GGCHC meeting held on Sapelo in June 2009, when describing all of the roadblocks that the Islanders faced while trying to control, protect, and revitalize their community, Cornelia Bailey said, "I'm not here to paint a pretty picture. The picture is not pretty. It is ugly when it comes to us surviving in Hog Hammock. So we are surviving because we are survivors. We had the harshest thing called slavery and we still survived it."[1] For so long, when the word "survival" was paired with Sapelo Island in published works, the coupling invoked traces of African traditions and practices that appeared to live on in the island's black community. But as the new millennium unfolded, when the term "survival" was linked to Sapelo, it referred to the Islanders' battle to stop Hog Hammock from becoming what the island's other black communities had become—long-gone settlements that only *survived* in passages about the island's history in articles and books.

The national and international news media was plugged in to Hog Hammock's campaign for survival.[2] A year before the GGCHC came to Sapelo for the input meeting, *New York Times* reporter Shaila Dewan visited Hog Hammock and found that the price of land in the community had skyrocketed. "Moneyed buyers" such as "Anchorage Holdings and Hammock Haven LLC" had "bought land from heirs who never lived on the island," and Islanders and descendants willing to sell land stood to make a small fortune from family properties that could be sold for $200,000 for half an acre.[3] Dewan's article was clear about the limits of the GGCHC to help the Islanders: "But for a living if aging culture, museums and historical markers can go only so far," and pointed out that state entities like the SIHA, might not be able to meet its mandate to ensure that Hog Hammock remains "occupied by the direct descendants of slaves of Thomas Spalding."[4] Dewan explained that even though SIHA had gained control of "180 acres in Hog Hammock . . . it's not clear whether the authority can legally give preference to descendants over other individuals," and he suggested that questions about their commitment to do so had surfaced.[5] All who read the article could have easily concluded that the final chapter of the Islanders' generations long land fight was coming to an end.

By 2012, media coverage of Hog Hammock's struggle to survive focused on the astronomical tax increase that followed a property value reassessment on the island. Even though Georgia became the second state in the nation to pass the Uniform Partition of Heirs Property Act in 2012 — a law that provided additional court procedures to protect landowners who are cotenants in heirs' property — the future of black landholdings on Sapelo was not bright. New tax rates in Hog Hammock that resulted in tax bills for residents that were in some cases 400 percent to 600 percent higher were covered by numerous media outlets including the *New York Times*, Cable News Network (CNN), and National Public Radio (NPR).[6] With no schools, paramedics, fire departments, police departments, road maintenance, garbage removal services, streetlights, or county-issued ferry transportation on Sapelo, Islanders were especially outraged that they were being asked to pay more than they could afford into a tax system that did not appear to benefit them. As a result, many Islanders made moves to take their grievances to court.

In reporting the dramatic increase in property taxes on the island, the author of another *New York Times* article made clear that because of their past experiences, the Islanders believed that they were once again caught in a scheme to force them off the island. "That kind of history makes it hard for people to believe county officials who say there is no effort afoot to push them from the land."[7] McIntosh County officials were reluctant to comment on the issue, but when they did, they told the *Times* reporter that there was no conspiracy to commit "cultural genocide" and explained that "they are just trying to clean up years of bad management and correct property taxes that were kept artificially low by questionable policies."[8] CNN tried to get county officials to talk about the tax hike on camera, but they declined.[9] However, the tax assessors' board chairman shared his opinion with CNN reporters off camera; he blamed the Islanders for their dilemma, which was featured in the CNN segment: "If they hadn't started selling their property, there wouldn't be a problem."[10] Hog Hammock's property tax crisis was so intertwined with the Islanders' fight for survival, there was no way to talk or write about Sapelo without addressing it. The issue was such a defining feature of their struggle that it even came up in an ESPN segment that featured Kansas City Chief's player Allen Bailey, the island's first descendant to leave Sapelo to pursue a professional sports career.[11]

Lavish houses perched on stilts that had been built in Hog Hammock, structures situated high above the community's original homes in height and economic value, were certainly a factor in the tax increase that made the Islanders' campaign for survival even more tenuous. These modern expensive homes provide a sharp contrast to the ruins of slave cabins at Chocolate, and the small, empty, sagging wooden houses like Emma and Emmitt Johnson's, and the trailer homes and other traditional houses scattered throughout Hog Hammock. In 2009, Reginald Hall, the son of GGCHC commissioner Charles Hall, asked McIntosh County officials to come to Sapelo to investigate fourteen vacation homes that had been built in Hog Hammock because he believed that their architectural designs violated zoning codes in the historic community.[12] He told the county commissioners that "we have this building going on Sapelo Island that's going to run us off the island. . . . They're building a resort-looking structure like what's on Hilton Head."[13] The county attorney responded to Hall's complaint by telling a reporter "he was aware of no violations on Sapelo."[14] More expensive houses were built. And soon, three of the island's first luxury vacation cottages, called Sapelo Island Birdhouses, joined the other structures that dwarfed the community's historic houses and mobile homes, and further transformed Hog Hammock's landscape and economic profile. These luxury cottages, built and managed by outsiders, offer amenities that none of the smaller rentals owned and run by Islanders provide. Lodgers at Sapelo Island Birdhouses can enjoy conveniences that include gourmet kitchens, wireless Internet access, outdoor showers (for beachcombers), and golf cart rentals.[15]

At first glance, it may appear that the Sapelo Island Birdhouses are a sign that profit-seeking coastal developers have finally gained a stronghold in Hog Hammock, but the cottages' property managers say their mission is to help the community. Having managed to avoid television and newspaper reporters who have swarmed the island in recent years, Sapelo Island Birdhouse Cottages' managers finally talked to a journalist who wrote a feature on Sapelo published in *Garden and Gun* magazine during the summer of 2015.[16] Dr. William Thomas and Annita Thomas, a black couple, told the magazine that they intend to help revitalize Hog Hammock.[17] The Thomases had been regular guests at Cornelia Bailey's bed and breakfast since 2000.[18] Having developed a deep affection for the Baileys and the island, they invested a "sizeable sum" into the cottages, "the revenue from which" goes "back into the community."[19] The Thomases' website declares their mission to be to "provide synergy in the community of Hog Hammock . . . by providing job opportunities for the youth to learn marketable skills and participate in business partnerships, that will ultimately encourage them to remain on the island. . . . Partnerships are formed between residents of the island and private investors."[20] In line with their mission, the Thomases have employed Islanders, encouraged and supported entrepreneurial ventures in the community, and Dr. Thomas has even become a SICARS board member.[21] Their written mission also emphasizes that the couple wants to "continually find ways to grow the tourism industry on Sapelo, yet do so with a small foot-print on a beautiful, natural, pristine, undeveloped island."[22] They are working toward achieving their growth goals. A new luxury cottage is available for visitors to rent, but this structure is not a house on stilts. The Thomases renovated Ben Johnson's store—the Islander who told *National Geographic*'s reporter it was time to fight for Sapelo in 1971. They kept its original exterior and turned a portion of the inside into a cottage they have named "The Tea Cake Cottage Suite at B J Confectionary."[23] Their website says that they hope to turn the other part of Johnson's store into a museum.[24] Their mission statement also identifies Dr. Thomas as an insider of sorts: "Doc Bill is from Edisto Island, SC and is a proud Geechee descendant."[25]

The *Garden and Gun* piece also announced Cornelia Bailey's and the Thomases' new plan to resurrect the community's economy by "looking to the island's agricultural past."[26] Pointing out that Dr. Thomas had already worked on cookbooks that had been published about the island's cuisine and had produced digital videos posted on YouTube about the region's culinary treasures, the reporter identifies Thomas as a natural and important partner in the Sapelo Red Peas Project, and a venture cosponsored by Clemson University that will reintroduce a breed of sugarcane grown on Sapelo in the 1800s.[27] Hoping to turn their distinct foodways and rare agricultural products into a viable commodity, supporters of the Red Peas and sugarcane projects believe that they may have found a way to create enough jobs to entice a few descendants back home. Although Bailey is optimistic about these endeavors, she did communicate worries about the work involved in growing and harvesting sugarcane in an interview: "My only concern about the whole project is labor. . . . But I'm trying to bring people back to the island. If this project bears fruit, then we can offer the young people something."[28]

Entrepreneurial opportunities might spark interest in descendants considering moving to the island, but reenacting the type of backbreaking farmwork that drove their ancestors and parents to the mainland and away from the South might be a harder selling point. Will the prospects of becoming partners in agricultural entrepreneurial enterprises and community revitalizers be enticing enough to inspire descendants to leave life on the mainland—and all of the opportunities that mainland life offers—to return to Sapelo to harvest peas and sugarcane? Will descendants embrace the idea of harvesting sugarcane—something their ancestors cultivated as slaves? Many of Sapelo's freedmen and freedwomen grew these crops for their own livelihood after the Civil War, but will young descendants abandon prevailing ideas about "black advancement"—that had, in America, always been measured by diplomas and degrees and professional careers complemented by high incomes—to live on Sapelo?

The lack of jobs on the island is one of many things that discourages young descendants considering a move to Sapelo, but a new deterrent connected to questions about toxins in the island's waterways has recently made the news. Al Jazeera America and various local news outlets reported about the possible impact of the contaminants that LCP Chemicals left behind when it closed its operation in Brunswick, Georgia, in 1998, a city nearly twenty-five miles from Sapelo.[29] In 2010, the Centers for Disease Control (CDC) began its inquiry into the possibility that Sapelo's residents had been "exposed to the same kinds of chemicals as dolphins that live in the same areas" and included nine Islanders in a study conducted in other coastal communities where "dolphins had been examined for their exposure to chemicals in their environments."[30] The fact sheet that the CDC circulated about the study indicates that their research "was not designed to answer questions about" contamination from the LCP Chemical site and claims that the study's main goal was to determine if "dolphins are able to help us predict where people may be exposed."[31] The study focused on polychlorinated biphenyl (PCB) levels in blood samples taken from nine Sapelo residents who regularly consumed locally caught fish.[32] The CDC delicately described their conclusions: "We found that the chemicals in people's bodies are similar to the ones found in the fish that they eat and to the ones in the dolphins"; and "some specific types of PCBs in the participants were higher than the national average, and some were lower. . . . Regional differences are expected around the country, based on which type of PCBs are in the nearby environment."[33] However, Al Jazeera reported that the results from the same "nine of the 47 Geechees on Sapelo Island" that were included in testing conducted by the Agency for Toxic Substances and Disease Registry showed that on average they had levels of a specific PCB produced at the LCP site at rates that were 95 percent higher than the general population's.[34] While questions swirl over how to best eradicate the toxins from the local environment, the Islanders interviewed for the Al Jazeera piece indicate that although they were aware that the fish in local waters may be contaminated, many have made "little to no change in their consumption habits."[35] Now, even the waterways that had for generations given the Islanders, and other people who live throughout the region, sustenance may present yet another problem the community has to face.

For all that recent reports reveal about the Islanders' struggles and aspirations, they also make clear that the nearly one-hundred-year-old stories about their uniqueness will not die anytime soon. In fact, these stories—stories that had been transformed as they passed through the imaginations of so many across time, from 1920s and 1930s researchers to black women writers, and finally to the Islanders themselves—seem to have a more secure place in the national imaginary than the Islanders have in their community. Even as journalists discussed the *changes* that have come to the island's black community, they easily fell into descriptions of an *unchanged* people and culture, stuck in an earlier time. Slavery, the Civil War, the Island's "African feel," and statements about "Creole-speaking" Gullah/Geechee folk are almost always offered as important details that underscore precisely what will be lost if Hog Hammock does not survive. Images of Islanders fishing with cast nets, walking the beach or dock, and sitting on porches underneath trees heavy with Spanish moss that accompany contemporary reports create the impression that the real tragedy is that these quaint scenes will soon pass away forever. The fear is that if the Islanders are ultimately defeated, their cultural world—one whose characteristics, value, and meaning have evolved from the interwar years until today—will only live on in books and films.

And what will live on in books and films is so much more than "factual" or "fictional" accounts of life on Sapelo, and places like it. Embedded in these works are profound histories, chronicles of the American imagination during moments when, over and over again, the nation's scholars, writers, and artists wrestled with race, culture, and *the past*. One only needs to look to the evolution of the many narratives of Bilali Mohammed's life to be reminded of how prominent contemporary ideas and trends have been in shaping perspectives about Sapelo Islanders' folk culture. Depicted as an example of coastal Georgia's "Arabian type" and a respected slave driver by Joel Chandler Harris in the 1890s, cast as exotic evidence of the Islanders' African past in Lydia Parrish's and Mary Granger's works during the interwar years, and imagined as a devout African Muslim defiantly holding on to his religion in black women's fiction in the 1980s and 1990s, Sapelo Island's famed ancestor has been offered as the embodiment of a variety of discourses. In each period, accounts about Mohammed, and the characters he inspired, changed according to the popular ideas about black people's connection to Africa and their past. This too is true for all Sapelo Islanders. And now, the Islanders tell their own story, and they do so brilliantly, pushing all who hear their rendering of their past and present to sincerely commit to the "preservation" of their community. Because the Islanders' celebrity is rooted in their relationship to their African and slave past, each time reports about their land fight recall their history, contemporary stories about Sapelo Islanders inadvertently raise a critical question to the nation: what, if anything, is owed to the descendants of slaves?

If one follows closely how the Islanders describe their predicament, even as they sometimes play to longstanding ideas about their picturesque existence, it becomes clear that their history is not a charming storybook tale. Yes, Sapelo Islanders are connected to their ancestors' ways of thinking about, making, and saying things, and have been close to the very earth that they once walked and farmed, and the places where they lived, laughed, loved, and died. Yes, researchers and writers who studied or imagined this connection marveled at its meaning. But the Islanders carry more than their ancestors' traditions and memories, they carry their ancestors' greatest burden in America—blackness. From the first slaves who came to the barrier island, to the freedmen and freedwomen who resettled the island after the Civil War, to the men and women who called the island home during the Jim Crow years, to those who struck out for the mainland, and the small group who remain on the island, Sapelo Islanders' story has always been inextricably tied to the American race-class drama. Their circumstances may vary from other black communities and families across the United States, but their strivings are the same. Like their counterparts all over the country, the Islanders want justice, equality, opportunity, and they nurture the desire to carve out a safe home space where their families can thrive and survive. Perhaps the greater tragedy in Sapelo Islanders' ultimate displacement would be that black America would have to add one more blow to their long history of losses.

The Islanders and many of Sapelo's descendants plan to keep fighting for their home. They keep fighting even though more land is sold and new houses continue to appear in Hog Hammock. They are not giving up. But there is a somber spirit that hangs over every family reunion, church anniversary, and holiday gathering held on the island—a heaviness that is perfectly articulated in the lyrics of a song collected by Lydia Parrish and once sung by blacks on Sapelo and throughout the region that spoke of the inevitability of death: "I don't know, I don't know. . . . May be the las' time, I don't know. . . . May be the las' time we eat together. . . . May be the las' time we shout together. . . . May be the las' time we pray together. . . . May be the las' time, I don't know."[36]

ACKNOWLEDGMENTS

This book is the end result of many years of research and writing, neither of which would have been possible without the guidance and support that I received from so many people. I am so grateful for Mia Bay's mentorship, and for all of the wisdom, all of the lessons, and all of the laughs that she freely shared with me. I also owe Beryl Satter a debt of gratitude. From the earliest days in the life of this project, Beryl has been a tremendous support and resource, and has always pushed me to dig deeper. To Ann Fabian, thank you for teaching me how to "do" cultural history. All three of you have selflessly donated your time and energy to help me see this through, and for that, and for so much more, I am grateful.

From my graduate school years through the completion of this book, so many wonderful historians and scholars have encouraged and inspired me. I am thankful for Vincent Brown's and Davarian L. Baldwin's guidance—this study grew so much as a result of their insights. Thank you James Goodman and Jan Lewis for motivating me to take the project beyond the master's program. I have learned so much from Deborah Gray White, and I am appreciative for all of the advice that she has shared. Thank you Wanda Hendricks and Cheryl D. Hicks for being both great mentors and true confidantes. I am indebted to my circle of sister scholars who have read chapters and talked me through tough times: Shannen Dee Williams, Krystal Frazier, Zinga A. Fraser, Talitha LeFlouria, Adrienne Petty, Kaia Niambi Shivers, Deidre Cooper Owens, and Keisha-Khan Perry. I consider it a great fortune to have shared my graduate school experience with Melissa Horne, Mekala Audain, and Stephanie E. Jones-Rogers—thank you for all of the good times. These women and so many of my scholar friends have cheered me on. Thank you Davarian L. Baldwin, Minkah Makalani, Andrew Kahrl, Kenneth Janken, and Clare Corbould for your encouragement and counsel. My colleagues at the University of South Carolina were also motivational: Pat Sullivan, Don H. Doyle, Marjorie Spruill, Dianne Johnson, Robert Ellis, Debra Rae Cohen, Bobby Donaldson, Lauren Rebecca Sklaroff, Matt D. Childs, Tracey Weldon-Stewart, Qiana Whitted, and Kimberly Simmons.

This book benefited tremendously from institutional and research support. Thank you Robert Brinkmeyer, director of University of South Carolina's Institute for Southern Studies, and University of South Carolina's College of Arts and Sciences for generously supporting my research. Rutgers University's history departments in Newark and New Brunswick nurtured me intellectually. I had many "research angels" who helped me track down and secure valuable material and shared important insights. William McFeely was gracious and generous when he first took the time to talk to me about Sapelo when I was a graduate student. The University of Georgia Marine Institute Library shared many of the photographs featured in the book; Janet C. Olson at Northwestern University Archives was so kind and helpful to me; and the late Thomas B. Klein of Georgia Southern University and Michael K. Davis at James Madison University helped me put my hands on much needed material—thank you all. Congressman James E. Clyburn, Harvey Granger, and Anne Heard graciously sat for interviews. Thanks to my editor Brandon Proia for working so hard on this project; and to the University of North Carolina Press, thank you for believing that this history is an important story that needs to be told.

So many of my friends—my chosen family—cheered me on. Thank you Steve Fradkin, Po Hong Yu, Chanel Cook-Chukumba, Maryam Myika Day, Jeanine Lee, Pascal Marcelin, and Jonathan Alston for helping me through with kind, and sometimes stern, words and lots of laughter. To Baba David Coleman and Richard Byrd—my soul, my heart, and my ori, thank you.

My family has given so much, for so long, which enabled me to travel this road. My mother Betty Cooper and my father George Cooper, took care of my little ones while I studied, traveled, researched, and wrote. My sister Tanisha Cooper Anderson always showed up for me like only a sister could. My precious nephew Eric Anderson Jr. continually forced me to clarify my mission with adorable questions like, "Auntie, *what* exactly are you doing again?" I would be remiss if I did not acknowledge all of the Sapelo Islanders who sat for interviews and entertained my questions (for some, those interviews began when I was a little girl): the late Ruth Hillery Johnson, the late Fred Johnson, the late Joe A. Johnson, the late Catherine Hillery, Cornelia Bailey, and Paul Walker. Thank you for trusting me with your memories. So many of my Sapelo kinfolk helped to keep me inspired: my late uncle Charles "Chuck" Johnson, my late uncle Melvin Johnson, my late uncle Emmitt Johnson III, my cousin Danielle Williams, and so many others—a group that is too numerous to list. But most of all, I must pay homage to my grandfather Emmitt Johnson Jr. and grandmother Ruth Hillery Johnson for always indulging my curiosities, for driving me around the island, and talking to me about the "old days."

My beloved sons have grown up with and shared their mother with this book. Thank you Menelik and Sundiata for being patient and sweet when I needed it the most. You two are amazing, and for so many reasons, I uncovered this history for you. And to my life partner and soul companion, Daniel, it may seem like a cliché, but there are no words to describe all the ways that you have carried me through this process, and "thank you" seems like an insufficient expression of gratitude for all that you have lovingly given.

NOTES

ABBREVIATIONS

GGCHCDC

Gullah Geechee Cultural Heritage Corridor Digital Collection of Public Meeting Transcripts, www.gullahgeecheecorridor.org

GHS/FWP

Georgia Historical Society, Savannah, Georgia, Federal Writers' Project Savannah Unit Papers

GHS/MGP

Georgia Historical Society, Savannah, Georgia, Mary L. Granger Papers

NARA/FWP

National Archives and Records Administration, College Park, MD, Record Group 69, Records of the Works Project Administration, Records of the Federal Writers' Project, P1-57, Entry 28, Box 2

NUA/LDTP

Melville J. Herskovits Library of African Studies, Northwestern University, Evanston, IL, Lorenzo D. Turner Papers

NUA/MHP

Melville J. Herskovits Library of African Studies, Northwestern University, Evanston, IL, Melville Herskovits Papers

SCHS

South Carolina Historical Society, Charleston, SC

SOHPC

Southern Oral History Program Collection (#4007), Southern Historical Collection, Louis Round Wilson Special Collections Library, University of North Carolina–Chapel Hill

PROLOGUE

1. Many of Sapelo's contemporary visitors have chronicled their experiences on the island. These accounts, published in a variety of media, offer readers impressions of the island and hazy details of the island's history. The feeling of being transported back in time and romantic descriptions of the Islanders' folk culture are common themes in these accounts—whether or not travelers knew much or little about the island before their visit. This can be detected in travel articles about Sapelo such as the short write-up, "Sapelo Island," *Atlanta Magazine*, September 2007, or, in the same magazine, Luke Dittrich's longer feature story "Sweet Nothing: Three Days Adrift on One of Georgia's Most Pristine Barrier Islands." Blogs and posts featuring memories of Sapelo visits are abundant. Examples include "Drive 4 hours and 100 years back in time: Day Trip to Sapelo Island, Georgia," http://www.spoonbred.com/day-trip-to-sapelo-island-georgia/ (accessed May 10, 2016);

and Caroline McCoy, "A Change Is Gonna Come," http://roadsandkingdoms.com/2015
/a-change-is-gonna-come (accessed May 10, 2016). Some accounts highlight the island's
uniqueness in light of its uncertain future, such as "Discovering Sapelo Island, Georgia and the Gullah-Geechees of Hog Hammock," *Going Places Far and Near*, March 7, 2015,
http://goingplacesfarandnear.com/discovering-sapelo-island-georgia-and-the-gullah
-geechees-of-hog-hammock/ (accessed May 10, 2016). Other accounts, written by blacks,
document their desire to spend time in a place where they connect with the black past,
such as Ashon Crawley's post "Peace in Sapelo: On Black Islam and Black Christianity,"
The Hampton Institute: A Working Class Think Tank, February 26, 2010, http://www.hampton
institution.org/peace-in-sapelo.html#.VzIFLgdCAZU (accessed May 10, 2016); and novelist Tina McElroy Ansa's reflection on a writers' retreat on Sapelo, "A Dream of an Island,"
Black Issues Book Review (July–August 2005).

2. Gray, Davis, and Williams, *Lonely Planet*, 224.

3. Keber ("Refuge and Ruin") explores the history of the French Sapelo Company; Sullivan, a Georgia researcher, also writes about the French Sapelo Company, Montalet, Swarbeck, and Spalding in *Early Days on the Georgia Tidewater*; McFeely (*Sapelo's People*) covers similar ground.

4. McFeely (*Sapelo's People*, 37) writes about the crops that Spalding raised on Sapelo;
Sullivan (*Early Days on the Georgia Tidewater*, 102, 109) covers similar ground.

5. Keber, "Refuge and Ruin," 185.

6. Ibid.

7. Sullivan (*Early Days on the Georgia Tidewater*, 84) discusses Thomas Spalding's acquisi-
tion of the French Sapelo Company's holdings.

8. Accounts of Sapelo's Bilali Mohammed appear in a host of works. An article that
mentioned Bilali Mohammed of Sapelo was published in the *African Repository*, a journal
associated with the American Colonization Society, titled "The Gospels: Written in the
Negro Patois of English, With Arabic Characters" (September 1860, 268). His name appears in the works spelled a variety of ways. Charles Spalding Wylly—a descendent of
Thomas Spalding—briefly described Mohammed in *The Seed That Was Sown*. Allan Austin
writes about Bilali Mohammed's African origins in his study *African Muslims in Antebellum
America*. B. G Martin attempts to contextualize Mohammed's diary in "Sapelo Island's Arabic Document," and Michael Gomez discusses Bilali Mohammed and explores the experiences of enslaved Muslims in the region in "Muslims in Early America" and *Exchanging Our
Country Marks*.

9. Austin (*African Muslims in Antebellum America*), McFeely (*Sapelo's People*), and Martin
("Sapelo Island's Arabic Document") present theories about Mohammed's relationship
with his master Thomas Spalding. McFeely and Austin argue that his cotton cultivation
skills afforded him the opportunity to negotiate the terms of his bondage.

10. Gomez, "Muslims in Early America," 696.

11. See Wylly (*The Seed That Was Sown*) and Lovell (*The Golden Isles*, 99) for accounts that depict Spalding as a benevolent slave master. Buddy Sullivan (*Early Days on the Georgia Tidewater*,
120–21) argues that Spalding facilitated the creation of slave villages and gave his slaves
"a great deal of leeway and freedom." Austin (*African Muslims*, 85–98) points to Spalding's
"slave villages" and the fact that Spalding did not force Bilali Mohammed to abandon Islam
as a marker of benevolence.

12. Turner described an account of Behavior's past in his field notes on Sapelo; see Turner Field Notes, Georgia, Series 023, Box 29, Folders 3–4, NUA/LDTP. McFeely writes about the legend of Sapelo's temporary Maroon settlement and the origins of the cemetery's name in *Sapelo's People*, 54. Similarly, Bailey writes about the standoff and the cemetery's name in her memoir, *God, Dr. Buzzard, and the Bolito Man*, 137.

13. McFeely, *Sapelo's People*, 55.

14. McFeely writes about Spalding's children's slave inheritance (ibid., 56).

15. Ibid., 62.

16. Ibid., 64.

17. Ibid., 65.

18. McFeely uncovered records of Wilson's and Lemon's military service during the Civil War (ibid., 67–80).

19. "Bravery of Colored Soldiers—They Are Highly Complimented," *The Liberator*, December 12, 1862.

20. McFeely (*Sapelo's People*, 129–30) explores Sapelo's resettlement during the Civil War and Reconstruction years, and Sullivan (*Early Days on the Georgia Tidewater*, 405–6) includes Ella Barrow Spalding's recollections of events on Sapelo Island during these years.

21. McFeely, *Sapelo's People*, 130–31.

22. Ibid., 22–27, 102–9, 116, 123–24.

23. McCarthy, *Georgia's Lighthouses*, 63.

24. For more on Tunis Campbell see Duncan's *Freedom's Shore*. Dorsey, "'The Great Cry of Our People Is Land!,'" 228.

25. McFeely, *Sapelo's People*, 129–36; Sullivan, *Early Days on the Georgia Tidewater*, 406.

26. McFeely, *Sapelo's People*, 136–41.

27. Ibid., 139–41.

28. Harris, *Deep Souths*, 21–24.

29. McFeely, *Sapelo's People*, 141–42.

30. Sullivan, *Early Days on the Georgia Tidewater*, 600; McFeely, *Sapelo's People*, 146.

31. See "Island Fad Hits South," *New York Times*, February 7, 1937, which chronicled the purchase of "exotic" southern islands by wealthy whites. The Carnegies owned three-fourths of Cumberland Island, and the rest was owned by the Candlers of Atlanta. Jekyll Island was owned by J. Morgan, St. Catherines was owned by C. M. Keys, and Ossabaw Island was owned by a Dr. H. N. Torrey of Detroit.

32. Sullivan, *Early Days on the Georgia Tidewater*, 600–606.

33. Allen Green and Annie Mae Walker Green in Crook et al., *Sapelo Voices*, 102–3.

34. Sullivan, *Early Days on the Georgia Tidewater*, 600–606.

35. Author interview with Paul Walker. Walker describes the Islanders' perception of the role that white "island managers" played on Sapelo when he was growing up on the island.

36. Sullivan (*Early Days on the Georgia Tidewater*, 600–655) writes extensively about Howard Coffin on Sapelo.

37. Shaila Dewan, "A Georgia Community with an African Feel Fights a Wave of Change," *New York Times*, May 4, 2008.

38. Ibid.

39. For example, Charles C. Jones published *Negro Myths from the Georgia Coast* in 1888.

Ruby Moore wrote an article for the *Journal of American Folklore* titled "Superstitions from Georgia" in 1894. John Bennett wrote an article published in the *South Atlantic Quarterly*, "Gullah a Negro Patois," in 1908. Loraine Darby also published an essay in the *Journal of American Folklore* titled "Ring Games From Georgia" in 1917.

40. South Carolina Gullah studies during the interwar years sponsored by the Social Science Research Council include Guy Johnson, *Folk Culture on St. Helena Island, South Carolina*; Kiser, *Sea Island to City*; Guinon Griffis Johnson, *A Social History of the Sea Islands*; and J. T. Woofter's *Black Yeomanry*. All were in part inspired by plans to build a causeway and bridge connecting the once "isolated" island and the mainland. According to Guy B. Johnson ("The Gullah Dialect Revisited," *Journal of Black Studies* 10, no. 4 [1980]) connecting the island to the mainland represented a threat to the island's cultural purity, which made documentation a more urgent matter. Other works, such as Mason Crum's *Gullah*, can also be added to this list. Although the larger intellectual and cultural forces examined in this book surely influenced these works, and some of the scholars and studies listed above will be briefly discussed in the chapters that follow, this work focuses on coastal Georgia blacks, and Sapelo Islanders are the centerpiece.

41. Whisnant, *All That Is Native and Fine*, 7–15.

42. Ibid., 254.

43. Dilworth, *Imagining Indians*, 1–7.

44. Ibid., 1–20.

45. Deloria, *Playing Indian*, 1–10.

46. Matory, "The Illusion of Isolation." Matory also writes about the myth of Gullah/Geechee isolation and all that it obscures in "Islands Are Not Isolated" and briefly introduces the idea in "The Gullah and the Black Atlantic."

CHAPTER 1

1. The University of South Carolina's Moving Image Research Archive holds Fox Movietone's outtakes that feature Sapelo Islanders singing titled "President Hunts from Ox Cart in Dixie Wilds — outtakes." Fox Movietone News Story 1–644, filmed on December 29, 1928.

2. Sullivan (*Early Days on the Georgia Tidewater*, 600–677) documents Coffin's activities and enterprises on Sapelo.

3. "Coolidges at Ease on Sapelo Island," *New York Times*, December 27, 1928, 1; "Coolidge to Spend Holiday on Island," *New York Times*, December 19, 1928, 16.

4. "Five Birds Bagged by President's Gun," *Washington Post*, December 28, 1928, 2; "Coolidge with Gun Bags Wild Turkey," *New York Times*, December 28, 1928, 2.

5. "Sapelo Folk Stage Rodeo for Coolidge," *Daily Boston Globe*, December 30, 1928, A8.

6. "Sapelo Folk Stage Rodeo for Coolidge," *Daily Boston Globe*, December 30, 1928; "Quail Fall Victims to the President's Aim," *Washington Post*, December 29, 1929, 2; "Coolidge Misses on His First Deer Hunt; Watches Unique Rodeo, Rides in Oxcart," *New York Times*, December 30, 1928, 1; "Coolidge at Ease on Sapelo Island," *New York Times*, December 27, 1928.

7. Parrish (*Slave Songs*, xxi) wrote about Howard Coffin's "delight in slave songs."

8. "Sapelo Folk Stage Rodeo for Coolidge," *Daily Boston Globe*, December 30, 1928; "Quail Fall Victims to the President's Aim," *Washington Post*, December 29, 1929; "Coolidge Misses

on His First Deer Hunt; Watches Unique Rodeo, Rides in Oxcart," *New York Times*, December 30, 1928; "Coolidge at Ease on Sapelo Island," *New York Times*, December 27, 1928.

9. Parrish, *Slave Songs*, 208.

10. Ibid.

11. Melissa L. Cooper, "Caught in the Gaze: Sapelo Islanders and the Presidential Visit of 1928," University of South Carolina Moving Image Research Collections Blog, November 7, 2014, http://library.sc.edu/blogs/mirc/caught-in-the-gaze.

12. For more on the roots and legacies of plantation nostalgia see Santiago-Valles, "'Still Longing for de Old Plantation,'" and Anderson, "Down Memory Lane."

13. Williams (*A Devil and a Good Woman*, 52) writes about Peterkin's career as a writer and various aspects of her life and notes that Peterkin often referred to Maum Patsy as the woman who raised her.

14. Ibid.

15. Ibid., 2.

16. Bearden, "Julia Peterkin Discusses Her Carolina Plantation," *Chicago Defender*, June 10, 1933, 15.

17. Lewis, "The Rhetoric of Mobility," 594.

18. Williams, *A Devil and a Good Woman*, 26–27.

19. Ibid., 27–34.

20. Ibid.

21. Durham compiled many of Julia Peterkin's interviews in a collection of her short stories that he edited; the quote is taken from one of the interviews featured in the book (*Collected Short Stories of Julia Peterkin*, 21).

22. Williams (*A Devil and a Good Woman*, 16–17) writes about the time that Peterkin spent in these Low Country locales.

23. Peterkin, *Scarlet Sister Mary*, 11.

24. Ibid., 197.

25. Peterkin, *Green Thursday*, 21–22.

26. This passage in *Scarlet Sister Mary* (210) about new laws imposed on midwives is a good example of Blue Brook Gullahs' views on "whites": "White people try to be too smart. If they keep messing in God's business and trying to change things from the way He meant them to be, the first thing they knew, He would get cross and make Judgment Day wipe the whole world clean of them. . . . They ought to be careful with their laws and projects."

27. Williams (*A Devil and a Good Woman*, 102–3) writes that Peterkin collected clippings from a column published in the South Carolina newspaper *Columbia State* called the "Folklore Corner" and included much of the material from the column pertaining to blacks in her fictional works.

28. Peterkin, *Green Thursday*, 91. Maum Hannah advises Rose to employ her illegitimate ward to heal her sick infant.

29. Durham, *Collected Short Stories*, 21–22. The quote is taken from one of the interviews featured in the book. Peterkin explained, "If I present these people, I want more than anything to do it well, to do them as they really are."

30. Martin ("Sapelo Island's Arabic Document") links the similarities between the main character in Joel Chandler Harris's story *The Story of Aaron (So Named) the Son of Ben Ali* (Boston,

1896)—a Muslim slave who had a leather-bound book that contained writings that looked like "pothooks"—to Rev. Francis R. Goulding, a Georgia writer and storyteller who somehow acquired Bilali Mohammed's diary after Mohammed's death.

31. Harris, "Sea Island Hurricanes," 267–84.

32. Ibid., 274.

33. Ibid.

34. Ibid.

35. Creel ("A Peculiar People," 15–25) provides the most thorough and concise synthesis of the documented origins of the "Gullah" label.

36. *South Carolina Gazette*, May 31, 1783, 2.

37. Bowen, *Central Africa*, 40.

38. Gonzales, *The Black Border*, 9.

39. Creel, "A Peculiar People," 17–20.

40. Georgia Writers' Project, *Drums and Shadows*, 65–66, 99. Lydia Parrish (*Slave Songs*, 48) recorded a song sung by an informant named "Gullah Ben," who she described as having come directly from Africa. The "Gullah" prefix was assigned before the name of an African-born enslaved African who lived in the region.

41. Cornelia Walker Bailey, Betty Cooper, Paul Walker, Joe Johnson, and Catherine Hillery—all Sapelo Islanders who were interviewed for this book—did not call themselves "Gullah," and said that whites used the term to describe them. And some noted that "Geechee" was used as an insult—akin to being called "backwoods" and ignorant. Bailey wrote in her memoir: "There's not a thing wrong with 'Gullah' if that's what you identify with, but a lot of us, including me, have always thought of ourselves as Geechee and we want to be known by our traditional name. Matter of fact, we're Saltwater Geechee" (*God, Dr. Buzzard, and the Bolito Man*, 5).

42. Higginson, *Army Life in a Black Regiment*. Higginson's memoir that recounted the time that he spent as Union soldier stationed in South Carolina during the Civil War included what he interpreted as the Gullah dialect to characterize the speech of the blacks he encountered in the region.

43. Harris, "Sea Island Hurricanes," 274.

44. Ibid., 275.

45. Ibid.

46. Ibid.

47. Ibid., 274.

48. Bennett, "Gullah." Turner (*Africanisms in the Gullah Dialect*, 8) takes on Gonzales's view of the Gullah dialect in his study. In "The Sea Island Hurricanes," 274, Harris, one of the earliest collectors of Gullah lore and dialect, expressed the belief that Sea Islanders' dialect was largely African: "Daddy Jack astonished me with his Gullah talk, half African and less than half English." But the collectors who came after him posited different theories. Gonzales (*The Black Border*) argued that "Gullah" was a form of "baby talk" used by slave owners to speak to their non-English-speaking slaves in the introduction to the collection and told Gullah tales by using the dialect, and George Philip Krapp, a Columbia University professor, similarly concluded that the Gullah dialect was a form of broken English (Turner, *Africanisms in the Gullah Dialect*). However, Turner examined the dialect to prove that it emerged from African languages.

49. Bederman (*Manliness and Civilization*, 1–45) explores the way that race structured and influenced civilization discourse.

50. Ibid., 25–45.

51. Ibid.

52. Singal, *The War Within*, 26–27.

53. Bederman, *Manliness and Civilization*, 20–45. Although Brantlinger ("Victorians and Africans") focuses on British ideas about "Africans," the study does shed light on how "Africa" and "Africans" were characterized in the race fantasies of whites in the West.

54. Bederman, *Manliness and Civilization*, 31.

55. Ibid., 35.

56. Bancroft, *Book of the Fair*, 836.

57. Bederman (*Manliness and Civilization*, 219) points out that Burroughs's novel sold 750,000 copies by 1934.

58. Daniels, *Freedom's Birthplace*, 399–400.

59. Herskovits (*Myth of the Negro Past*, 22–32) cites J. Dollard and J. E. Lind's article "Phylogenic Elements in the Psychoses of the Negro," published in the *Psychoanalytical Review* (303).

60. Huggins, *Harlem Renaissance*, 52.

61. Peterkin, "One Southern View-point."

62. Singal, "Towards a Definition of American Modernism," 1–23.

63. Singal, *The War Within*, 1–10; Singal, "Towards a Definition of American Modernism," 8.

64. Satter, *Each Mind a Kingdom*, 218–23; Dumenil, *The Modern Temper*, 56–58.

65. Huggins (*Harlem Renaissance*, 53–84) discusses the push for racial equality in the wake of the Great War. Bay (*White Image in the Black Mind*, 187–288) covers similar ground.

66. Singal, "Towards a Definition," 17.

67. Baker (*Anthropology*, 5–8) discusses Boas's theories in his study.

68. Singal, *The War Within*, 6–8.

69. Ibid.

70. Peterkin, "One Southern View-point."

71. Peterkin, *Roll, Jordan, Roll*, 12–23.

72. For further analysis on the "uses of the primitive," see Dilworth, *Imagining Indians*, 4–7. Dilworth contextualizes the search for the "primitive" from the 1880s to the 1920s, using Native Americans and fantasies about the "South West" to track this phenomenon.

73. Lemke, *Primitivist Modernism*, 4–29. "By exploring this terra incognita," Lemke writes, "the primitivist discovers the vitality and sensuality of which he feels deprived. The primitivist is drawn to the black other: either figuratively to the mythical other, or literally to the 'other of color.'"

74. Frederickson (*Black Image*, 97–130) describes "romantic racism."

75. Douglas, *Terrible Honesty*, 4–5.

76. Mumford, *Interzones*, 133–56; Heap, *Slumming*, 189–231; Chapman, *Prove It on Me*, 78–114.

77. Baldwin, "Black Belts and Ivory Towers," 421.

78. Lemke (*Primitivist Modernism*, 7) cites W. E. B. Du Bois's recollection of the commencement speech that Franz Boas delivered to Atlanta University's graduating class in

which Boas instructed graduates to "not be ashamed of your African past," and recounted examples of great black kingdoms south of the Sahara.

79. Corbould, *Becoming African Americans*, 129–39.

80. Hutchinson, *Harlem Renaissance in Black and White*, 14–28.

81. Ibid., 29–31, 180–82.

82. These sentiments are communicated in many of the essays in Locke, *The New Negro*.

83. Lewis, *When Harlem Was In Vogue*, 46–49.

84. Hutchinson (*Harlem Renaissance in Black and White*, 30, 137–89) also links black artists and writers to primitivist notions of Africanness, as well as discusses the link between Africa and the New Negro.

85. Corbould, *Becoming African Americans*, 130–60; Huggins, *Harlem Renaissance*, 188–89.

86. Lewis, *When Harlem Was in Vogue*, 219.

87. Renda, *Taking Haiti*, 196–211.

88. Mumford (*Interzones*, 121–32) used these terms when analyzing O'Neill's tendencies with regard to constructing racial difference in a discussion of O'Neil's play "All God's Chillun Got Wings."

89. Lewis, *When Harlem Was in Vogue*, 188.

90. Douglas, *Terrible Honesty*, 98.

91. Lewis, *When Harlem Was in Vogue*, 97.

92. Gregory (*Southern Diaspora*, 40–41) explores the ways that southern migrants were "noticed."

93. Spear, *Black Chicago*, 168.

94. Baldwin, "Black Belts and Ivory Towers," 400–401.

95. Kiser, *Sea Island to City*, 55.

96. Favor (*Authentic Blackness*, 15–16) describes black southerners' unique role in the assessment of black authenticity.

97. Baker (*Anthropology*, 33–35) describes Locke's position on black folklore in relationship to Africa.

98. Nicholls, *Conjuring the Folk*, 13–14, 18; Lewis (*When Harlem Was in Vogue*, 190–91) discusses Hughes's view of "common folk" as the key to art.

99. Williams, *A Devil and a Good Woman*, 29.

100. Peterkin, *Black April*, 18. Peterkin wrote: "Maum Hannah, his own first cousin, had a string of charm beads their old grandmother had brought all the way from Africa when she came on a slave ship."

101. Dorothy Heyward ("Porgy's Native Tongue: A Dissertation in Gullah, the Negro Language of the Play," *New York Times*, December 4, 1927), coauthor of *Porgy*, identified Julia Peterkin as a Gullah dialect expert.

102. Lewis, "The Rhetoric of Mobility," 606.

103. "Again a Serious Study of Negroes in Fiction," *New York Times*, September 28, 1924, BR8.

104. Henry Bellamann, "'Green Thursday,' Julia Peterkin Is an Extraordinary Achievement," *Columbia Record*, November 1924, Peterkin Papers, SCHS, 28-614-8.

105. H. L. Mencken to Julia Peterkin, September 20, 1924, Peterkin Papers, SCHS.

106. A. L. Jackson, "The Onlooker," *Chicago Defender*, October 4, 1924, 12.

107. Lewis, "The Rhetoric of Mobility," 606.

108. Walter White to Julia Peterkin, December 3, 1924, Peterkin Papers, SCHS.

109. Ibid.

110. "Book Chat," Mary White Covington, chairman, board of directors of the National Association of Colored People, October 17, 1924, Peterkin Papers, SCHS.

111. Ibid.

112. Ibid.

113. "Julia Peterkin Will Not Write About White Folks," *Chicago Defender*, June 1, 1929, A1. The article covers her Harlem visit.

114. Williams, *A Devil and a Good Woman*, 170.

115. John R. Chamberlin, "Julia Peterkin Writes Again of the Gullah Negroes," *New York Times*, October 21, 1928, 63.

116. "This Week," *Chicago Defender*, May 18, 1929, A1.

117. Durham, *Collected Short Stories of Julia Peterkin*, 22.

118. "Julia Peterkin Will Not Write About White Folks," *Chicago Defender*, June 1, 1929, A1.

119. Ibid.

120. "The Week: Interesting on the Job Pulitzer Prizes," *Chicago Defender*, May 18, 1929, A1.

121. "Pays for Hundred Julia Peterkin S.C. Negroes," *Atlanta Daily World*, February 12, 1934, 1.

122. Walter White sent Peterkin a confidential copy of the ten-page investigation file into V. H. "Pink" Whaley's execution on October 25, 1928, Peterkin Papers, SCHS.

123. Louise Franklin Bache, Director of Publicity for the Mobilization for Human Needs, to Julia Peterkin, October 8, 1934, Peterkin Papers, SCHS.

124. Williams, *A Devil and a Good Woman*, 39, 65, 67, 68.

125. Ibid., 46.

126. Ibid.

127. "Ethel Barrymore to Play Role in 'Scarlet Sister Mary' Show," *Chicago Defender*, June 22, 1929, 7. Williams (*A Devil and a Good Woman*, 175–201) discusses Peterkin's feelings about the authenticity of the production at length.

128. Williams, *A Devil and a Good Woman*, 208.

129. Ibid., 216.

130. Ibid., 139–42.

131. Durham, *Collected Short Stories*, 22.

132. "The Week," *Chicago Defender*, June 8, 1929, A1.

133. Ibid.

134. Ibid.

135. Williams, *A Devil and a Good Woman*, 130–31.

136. Ibid.

137. An article published in the *Atlanta Daily World* pointed out that Brown broke with the NAACP's assessment of Peterkin's work. "Sterling Brown Raps Julia Peterkin's Latest Book, 'Roll, Jordan, Roll,'" *Atlanta Daily World*, February 19, 1934, 2.

138. Reed Smith ("Reviews") wrote about the proliferation of Gullah material in a footnote to his review of Ambrose Gonzales's folklore collections. He noted that aside from Gonzales, new publications, such as anthropologist Elsie Clews Parsons's *Folk-Tales of the Sea Islands, South Carolina* (1923), Jane Screven Heyward's *Brown Jackets* (1923), J. Palmer Lockwood's *Darkey Sermons from Charleston County* (1925), DuBose Heyward's *Porgy* (1925), Marcel-

lus S. Whale's *The Old Types Pass* (1925), and *Saint Helena Island Spirituals* (1925), collected by Penn Normal Industrial and Agricultural School—a historically black institution founded after the Civil War—were evidence of a marked interest in Gullah folk.

139. Society for the Preservation of Spirituals Papers, SCHS, 28/713.

140. Brown, "Arcadia of the South," 59–60.

141. Ibid., 59.

142. Ibid.

143. Ibid.

144. Ibid.

145. Ibid., 60.

146. Ibid.

CHAPTER 2

1. See Shad Hall's interview (Georgia Writers' Project, *Drums and Shadows*, 167).

2. My interview with Sapelo Islander Betty Cooper involved discussions about Shad Hall and his role as an herbalist and trusted elder. Bailey (*God, Dr. Buzzard, and the Bolito Man*) also describes Hall as a respected elder in her memoir, noting that his name was Shadrach and referring to him as "Uncle Shed" (9, 10, 79, 134, 136, 232, 283, 287, 288, 318). He was identified as "Shad Hall" in *Drums and Shadows* and *Slave Songs*. The Islanders all called him "Uncle Shad" or "Shad," and Hall told Turner that his first name was Shadrack.

3. Contemporary scholars have reexamined studies of Sapelo Islanders in works such as *Drums and Shadows* and have determined that several interviews pointed to the retention of a complex West African cosmology. See Young, *Rituals of Resistance*; Powell, "Summoning the Ancestors"; and Thompson, *The Flash of Spirit*. However, researchers of the twenties and thirties assumed loose links between the spiritual practices they observed and Africa, and their understanding of Africa was largely limited to popular material and skewed information about African societies.

4. Georgia Writers' Project, *Drums and Shadows*, 167–68.

5. Renda (*Taking Haiti*) offers the most in-depth assessment of how "voodoo" emerged in American cultural life during the period relative to the Haitian occupation—reading the trend as a cultural response.

6. Renda (*Taking Haiti*, 5, 6, 126–27, 175–78) unearths the way that race shaped black-white encounters in U.S.-occupied Haiti and charts America's cultural response to Haiti's occupation. Renda also examines the role that voodoo stories played in the U.S. cultural response to the occupation.

7. "Haiti, Land of Voodoos and Many Revolutions," *Washington Post*, August 8, 1915, ES5.

8. Louise James, "Haiti the Land of Tragedy," *Chicago Daily Tribune*, September 12, 1915, B9.

9. "Voodooism Is Faith of Haiti, Admiral Says: Kill Humans, Drink Blood, Knapp Reports," *Chicago Daily Tribune*, December 15, 1920, 5.

10. W. B. McCormick, "Voodooism in Haiti," *New York Times*, February 12, 1922, 92; Richard Loederer, "A Voodoo Castle in Haiti," *New York Times*, May 27, 1923, SM4; "U.S.-Built Hard Roads Lift Haiti Scale of Living," *Chicago Daily Tribune*, March 15, 1928, 12; "Superstition Rules Tropics: Tell Tales of Voodoo in West Indies," *Chicago Defender*, August 11, 1928, A1; William Lawson, " U.S. Nurses Haiti, Filthy and Sick Back to Health," *Chicago Daily Tribune*, December 24, 1929, 8; "Haiti Voodoo Rites Doomed to Extinction: Modern

Civilization Ends Cult Worship," *Chicago Daily Tribune*, April 27, 1930, 16; L. G. Labastille, "Haiti's Native Art: Songs of the Peasant and Voodoo Service," *New York Times*, May 17, 1931, 115; "Yankee Artist Is Praised for Work in Haiti," *Chicago Defender*, January 9, 1932, 3; James Miller, "Voodooism Still Reigns in Haiti," *Washington Post*, November 25, 1934, B3; "Wouldn't You Like to Be in Haiti?" *Chicago Defender*, January 17, 1920, 1; "How Uncle Sam Has Salvaged Haiti," *Washington Post*, December 15, 1929, SM3.

11. "White Negro Allowed to Land," *New York Times*, June 23, 1933, 9.

12. T. R. Potson, "Voodoo Played No Part in Changing Man to White, Haitians Contend," *New York Amsterdam News*, June 28, 1933, 9.

13. Ibid.

14. "Death for Three Voodooists: Two Cuban Men and a Woman Killed Aged White Man for His Blood," *Washington Post*, May 14, 1916, ES18; "Cuban Soldiers Kill 5 Voodoo Worshippers," *New York Times*, June 30, 1919, 12; "Cubans Kill Voodoos: Avenge Sacrifice of Children in Cannibalistic Rites," *Washington Post*, August 10, 1919, ES13; "White Child Voodoo Victim: Body Found in Cuba With Heart Torn Out by Witch Doctors," *Washington Post*, November 17, 1922, 1; "Voodoo Plot to Slay Baby Foiled in Cuba," *New York Times*, September 10, 1929, 16; "Voodoo Plot to 'Sacrifice' Baby Nipped in Cuba," *Chicago Daily Tribune*, September 10, 1929, 21; "3 Seized in Voodoo Lot," *New York Times*, March 2, 1930, 29; "Held as Witch in Killing: Aged Woman Arrested in Cuba as 'Voodoo' Doctor," *New York Times*, March 30, 1930, N9; "Unbidden Attendant Dies in Voodoo Meeting," *Washington Post*, June 7, 1930, 2; "Cuban Boy, 8, Killed as Voodoo Sacrifice," *New York Times*, January 4, 1931, 21; "American Kings in the Caribbean," *Washington Post*, May 10, 1931, MF1; "Cubans Ban Beating of Bongo Drums," *New York Times*, February 17, 1929, 59.

15. "Death for Three Voodooists," *New York Times*, May 14, 1916, ES18; "American Girl Saved From Voodoo Killing," *New York Times*, April 17, 1927, E21; "American Child Saved From Voodoo Sacrifice," *Washington Post*, April 17, 1927, M3.

16. Voodoo reports from Trinidad, Panama and Brazil and other locales also circulated around Chicago, New York, and Washington, DC: "Commits Murder to Escape Voodoo Spell," *Chicago Defender*, March 3, 1928, p. 13; "Letters to Voodooist Cause Brazil Scandal," *Washington Post*, June 22, 1930, A4; "Voodoo Magician Arrested in Trinidad," *New York Times*, May 24, 1931, 11; "Girl Is Slain in Jungle at a Voodoo Ceremony," *New York Times*, August 8, 1933, 12.

17. "Commits Murder to Escape Voodoo Spell," *Chicago Defender*, March 3, 1928, p. 13.

18. "Voodooism in Haiti: Ritualistic Dance and Pig With Ruffled Collar Part of One Ceremony," *New York Times*, February 12, 1922, 92.

19. Many studies executed by scholars from diverse disciplines have taken up the task of either examining black spiritual traditions' African origins, or exploring the origin, meaning, and function of roots, hoodoo/voodoo, and conjure in African American society. For example, Yvonne Patricia Chireau's study *Black Magic: Religion and the African American Conjuring Tradition* (Berkeley: University of California Press, 2003) provides an in-depth examination of the complex intersection of "magic," religion, and "conjuring" traditions among African Americans from slavery through freedom, clarifying the ways that these concepts and practices intermingled and manifested in African American communities "inside" and "outside" formal religious institutions. Other studies, like Timothy Ruppel's, Jessica Neuwirth's, Mark Leone's, and Gladys-Marie Fry's "Hidden in View: African Spiritual Spaces

in North American Landscapes" (*Antiquity*, June 2003) use material culture and historical archaeology to "trace" and locate African spiritual traditions among America's enslaved black communities. Ultimately, these works, and others like them (such as Young's, Thompson's, and Powell's), confirm that black "conjure" traditions were tied to complex African cosmology and spiritual theories.

20. There are too many American voodoo-related murder and violent crime reports to discuss individually in this chapter. And there are likely more reports than what I have collected from very specific newspapers in specific locations. The following is a list of some of the reports that appeared in newspapers that will not be directly addressed in this chapter: "Boy's Torturer Jailed: May Be Voodoo Fanatic," *Chicago Daily Tribune*, October 7, 1921, 9; "Death for Girl's Assailant: Martinsburg Jury Convicts Payton Negro 'Voodoo' Doctor," *Washington Post*, March 15, 1922, 19; "Woman Slayer Gets 10 Years' Imprisonment," *Chicago Defender*, October 31, 1925, 12; "Fulton Given 20 Years," *New York Amsterdam News*, June 2, 1926, 8; "Girl Believed Third Victim of Voodoo Killers," *Chicago Tribune*, December 2, 1928, 8 (race of victim of killer unknown); "Fasting Man Seized in Witchcraft Raid: Cleveland Police Connect Voodoo Cult With Murder Case," *Washington Post*, January 15, 1929, 3; "Fanatic Suspected as Seers' Slayer," *Washington Post*, March 20, 1929, 10; "Patient Kills Voodoo Doctor," *Chicago Defender*, May 18, 1929, 1; "Voodoo Doctor Shot in Battle," *New York Amsterdam News*, April 23, 1930, 3; "Woman Buried Alive 8 Cult Members Held," *Washington Post*, April 3, 1933, 1 (features Filipino voodooists); "Voodoo Slayer Given 33 Years," *Washington Post*, January 4, 1934, 22; "Witch Craft Offered as Murder Defense," *New York Amsterdam News*, April 28, 1934, 15; "Conjure Doctor Slain in Mississippi When He Disturbs Graves," *Chicago Daily Tribune*, October 12, 1935, 8; "Found Guilty of Murder: 'Old Doc Voodoo' of Harlem Convicted of Killing Two," *New York Times*, June 22, 1935, 3; "Killer of 'Voodoo' Man Over Love Charm Jailed," *Washington Post*, February 13, 1935, 3; "'Voodoo' Slaying Stuns East Harlem," *New York Amsterdam News*, February 27, 1929, 1; "Court Hears 'Voodoo' Slaying Plea Tomorrow," *New York Amsterdam News*, March 20, 1929, 2; "Study Sanity of a Man Who Slew in Fear of 'Voodoo,'" *New York Amsterdam News*, April 3, 1929, 1; "Slayer Who Feared 'Voodoo' Sent to Asylum After Study of Lunacy," *New York Amsterdam News*, April 24, 1929; "Phial of Oil, 'Snake Dust' and Cards Figure in Death," *Washington Post*, July 7, 1923, 5.

21. Hale (*Making Whiteness*, 198–239) examines the emergence of "spectator lynching" during the period among other white supremacy strategies and subsequent social and cultural consequences.

22. Baritz, *The Culture of the Twenties*, 85.

23. Hale (*Making Whiteness*, 213–29) describes lynching and mutilation.

24. Bederman, *Manliness and Civilization*, 219–20.

25. "Skull Found May Clear Up Gunness Case," *Chicago Daily Tribune*, May 6, 1916, 1.

26. "Human Bones Found in Voodoo Man's Cave," *New York Times*, April 10, 1925, 21.

27. "Voodoo Doctor Held for Slaying of Negro," *New York Times*, December 22, 1928, 10; "Voodoo Rites Seen in Man's Beheading," *Washington Post*, December 22, 1928, 9; "Hold Voodoo Doctor for Beheading Man," *Chicago Defender*, December 29, 1928, 1.

28. "Lay Death of Babies to Voodoo Sacrifices," *Washington Post*, April 22, 1923, 6; "Seek Voodoos in Killing of Many Infants," *Chicago Daily Tribune*, April 22, 1923, 3.

29. "Lay Death of Babies to Voodoo Sacrifices," *Washington Post*, April 22, 1923, 6.

30. Ibid.

31. Ibid.

32. "Seek Voodoos in Killing of Many Infants," *Chicago Daily Tribune*, April 22, 1923, 3.

33. "Voodoo Tale Shown to Be Absurd," *New York Amsterdam News*, May 9, 1923, 1.

34. "3 Women Found Slain: Night Club Dancer's Throat Slashed; Mother Killed: Baby Left to Starve Dies," *Chicago Defender*, February 21, 1931, 1.

35. Mumford (*Interzones*, pts. 2 and 3) explores sexual "slumming"; Heap (*Slumming*) covers similar ground.

36. "Voodoo Slayer in Court Without Funds," *Chicago Defender*, November 21, 1931, 12; "Voodooism Sifted in Fire Death Case," *New York Times*, July 14, 1929, 16; "Finds Charred Body, Blames Voodooism for Man's Death," *Chicago Defender*, July 20, 1929, 4.

37. "Police Hold Friend of Murder Nurse," *Washington Post*, October 9, 1923, 3; "Occultists Held for Murder," *Amsterdam News*, October 10, 1923, 1; "Voodooist Slew Pittsburgh Nurse," *New York Times*, October 9, 1923, 10; "Nurse's Slayer Executed," *Washington Post*, April 1, 1924, 4.

38. "Voodooist Slew Pittsburgh Nurse," *New York Times*, October 9, 1923, 10.

39. "Nurse's Slayer Executed," *Washington Post*, April 1, 1924, 4.

40. "Misguided Love Caused Death of Nurse, Alleged New Angle Unfolded as Girl's Condition Is Brought to Light," *Pittsburgh Courier*, October 13, 1923, 1.

41. Ibid.

42. "Nurses Slayer Executed," *Washington Post*, April 1, 1924, 4.

43. "Probe Weird Rites of Detroit Voodoo Cult," *Chicago Defender*, December 3, 1932, 1; "Declare Voodoo King Insane," *Chicago Defender*, December 17, 1932, 1. Also see Dewey Jones, "Voodoo Rites of the Jungle in Odd Contrasts With Background of City: Powerful Religious Cults Which Had Beginnings in Africa Still Make Human Sacrifices," *Chicago Defender*, December 10, 1932, 9.

44. Edgar Grey, "Harlem—The Mecca of Fakers," *New York Amsterdam News*, March 30, 1927, 16.

45. John Diaz, "High Negro Mortality," *New York Amsterdam News*, August 31, 1927, 19.

46. Spear (*Black Chicago*, 168) argues that the *Chicago Defender* was one of the first black institutions to criticize black southern migrants' behavior in Chicago.

47. The *New York Amsterdam News* ran advertisements for Professor Salindukee, Professor Domingo, Professor Akpandac, and Professor N. Phoenix. Examples of the display ads commonly found in black papers during the period include "Prof. Salindukee—Display Ad. 13," *New York Amsterdam News*, March 28, 1923, 3; "Prof. Mormordo—Display Ad. 57," *Chicago Defender*, May 10, 1924, A4; "Prof. Akpandac—Display Ad. 3," *New York Amsterdam News*, May 9, 1923, 2; "Prof. Edet Effiong—Display Ad. 73," *Chicago Defender*, February 21, 1925, A4; and "Prof. Domingo—Display Ad 73," *Chicago Defender*, February 21, 1925, A4.

48. Chireau (*Black Magic*, 141–43) discusses the explosion of voodoo advertisements in black newspapers, and Anderson (*Conjure*, 117–20) points out that the majority of voodoo supply businesses were white owned. Long (*Spiritual Merchants*) covers similar ground and traces the rise of large-scale voodoo selling in the United States and finds that the majority of voodoo manufacturers were not black. Here are a few of the advertisements used to sell popular voodoo products: "Display Ad 12," *Chicago Defender*, September 22, 1928, 4; "Display Ad 30," *Pittsburgh Courier*, November 10, 1934, A3; "Display Ad 30," *Pittsburgh Courier*, August 16, 1924, 5; "Lucky Hand-Display Ad 27," *Chicago Defender*, May 18, 1929, A4.

49. "Voodoo Doctor Jailed With 4 'High Priests,'" *New York Times*, August 22, 1927, 5; "Voodoo Doctor Chains Patients Say Police," *Washington Post*, August 22, 1927, 2; "Voodoo Doctor and Four Priest Taken in South," *Chicago Daily Tribune*, August 22, 1927, 11; "Voodoo Doctor Jailed After Patient Dies," *New York Amsterdam News*, August 22, 1927, 1; " 'Doctor Freed in Child's Death," *New York Amsterdam News*, September 12, 1928, 1; African Voodoo Man Dealt 'Pen' Term on Bogus Doctor Charge," *New York Amsterdam News*, September 26, 1928, 1.

50. "Post Office Stops Voodoo Practice," *New York Times*, November 21, 1924, 4; "Seize Price Lists of Voodoo Doctor," *New York Times*, August 14, 1925, 3; "Voodoo Doctor Indicted," *New York Times*, July 1, 1927, 8; "Voodoo Charms Sold by Mail, U.S. Charges," *Washington Post*, July 1, 1927, 8; "Voodoo Doctor Given Additional Six Months," *Washington Post*, January 24, 1929, 20; "U.S. Interrupts Work of Voodoo Mail Order Doctor," *Chicago Defender*, January 10, 1925, A1.

51. "Post Office Stops Voodoo Practice," *New York Times*, November 21, 1924, 4.

52. "Two Voodoos Meet Their One 'Hoodoo'- Jail," *Chicago Defender*, November 29, 1924, 2; "Fortune Teller and Voodoo in Toils Law," *Chicago Defender*, January 24, 1925, 2; "Gets Award for $179 Paid to Remove Evil Spirit," *New York Amsterdam News*, February 4, 1925, 1; "Alleged Voodoo Doctor, Clairvoyant, Palmist, Preacher, Undertaker, Nabbed," *New York Amsterdam News*, April 15, 1925, 1; "Federal Agents Raid Voodoo Doctor's Office," *Chicago Defender*, July 9, 1927, 1; "Doctor Sentenced for Selling Voodoo Charms," *Chicago Defender*, July 16, 1927, A8; "Corks Gilded by Voodoo Man to Represent Gold," *Chicago Defender*, September 24, 1927, 3; "Voodoo Trick Charged: Held Woman for Police," *Chicago Defender*, October 1, 1927, A9; "Nab Voodoo Doctor for Misuse of Mail," *New York Amsterdam News*, July 6, 1927, 6; "Police Arrest Voodoo Doctor," *New York Amsterdam News*, August 10, 1927, 4; "National News Briefs: Jail Voodoo Doctor When Potions Fail," *Chicago Defender*, April 21, 1928, A1; "African Voodoo Man Dealt 'Pen' Term on Bogus Charge," *New York Amsterdam News*, September 26, 1928, 1; "Voodoo Doctor Gets Fine Loitering," *Chicago Defender*, December 19, 1931, 3.

53. "Federal Agents Raid Voodoo Doctor's Office," *Chicago Defender*, July 9, 1927, 1.

54. Seabrook, *The Magic Island*.

55. Ibid., 1–42.

56. Mumford (*Interzones*, 134) describes the popularity of middle-class travel and travel writing; Renda (*Taking Haiti*, 237–55) explores travel writing and, more specifically, exoticism.

57. Seabrook's book was listed among the top-selling books (just under one hundred thousand copies sold) in "Bestsellers of Year Reported by Publishers," *Chicago Daily Tribune*, December 21, 1929, 14.

58. Perry Gitbens, "The New Books," *Life*, January 18, 1929, 33.

59. "Travel Books," *The Living Age*, March 1929, 72.

60. Aubrey Bowser, "Book Review: Long Live King Voodoo!," *New York Amsterdam News*, March 20, 1929, 16.

61. "Haitians Angered by Voodoo Tales," *Chicago Defender*, June 29, 1929, A1.

62. "Projection Jottings; A Picture with Haiti as the Background Has Been Finished—Other Items" *New York Times*, July 17, 1932, X3.

63. "Movie Gossip from Hollywood," *Chicago Tribune*, August 11, 1931, 15.

64. Ibid. "Island Scene of Thrilling Voodoo Tale," *Washington Post*, July 31, 1932, A1.

65. "New Films Reviewed," *Daily Boston Globe*, August 6, 1932, 6.

66. "My Observations," *New York Amsterdam News*, September 21, 1932, 8; "'Black Moon' Gives Many Good Roles," *Atlanta Daily Word*, May 6, 1934, 7; "Coast Codgings," *Chicago Defender*, April 28, 1934, 8; "Supported by Big Negro Cast," *Atlanta Daily World*, September 21, 1934, 2; "Coast Codgings," *Chicago Defender*, May 12, 1934, 9.

67. "Bledsoe to Appear in Opera 'Deep River' as Voodoo King," *New York Amsterdam News*, July 28, 1926, 9.

68. "'Zombie' Play of Thrills and Voodoo Rites," *Chicago Daily Tribune*, March 14, 1932, 19.

69. See Holley, "Black Concert Music," for more on Freeman and his musical roots in Chicago. For Freeman's opera, see "'Voodoo' at 52nd Street," *New York Amsterdam News*, August 29, 1928, 7; "'Voodoo' a Naïve Mélange," *New York Times*, September 11, 1928, 20; "Display Ad 21," *New York Amsterdam News*, September 5, 1928, 6; "New York Hears First Negro Opera Company Sing First Opera by Colored Composer," *Chicago Daily Tribune*, September 6, 1928, G4; "Negro Invades Grand Opera Field," *New York Amsterdam News*, August 22, 1928, 6.

70. "Lawrence Freeman's Opera," *New York Amsterdam News*, September 19, 1928, 16; "'Voodoo' a Naïve Mélange," *New York Times*, September 11, 1928, 20.

71. "Knowing No Jazz, Homer and Nero Knew Not Chaos," *Chicago Daily Tribune*, April 11, 1921, 17; "Calls America Still Savage Musically," *New York Times*, October 11, 1922, 15.

72. "'Zombie' Play of Thrills and Voodoo Rites," *Chicago Daily Tribune*, March 14, 1932, 19.

73. Burns Mantle, "Negro Opus of Deep South Stirs New Yorkers," *Chicago Daily Tribune*, January 10, 1932, C1.

74. J. Brooks Atkins, "Way Down South," *New York Times*, January 1, 1932, 30.

75. "Drums of Voodoos Overheard on Radio," *Washington Post*, October 28, 1928, RS2.

76. Ibid.

77. "Cuba Bans Beating of African Bongo Drums: Used as Jungle Wireless and in Voodoo Rites," *New York Times*, February 17, 1929, 59.

78. *Harlem's Black Magic*, in *The March of Time* newsreel series, volume 3, episode 8, March 19, 1937, HBO Digital Archives.

79. "Latest 'March of Time' on Keith-Memorial Bill," *Daily Boston Globe*, March 17, 1937, 29.

80. *Harlem's Black Magic*, in *The March of Time* newsreel series, volume 3, episode 8, March 19, 1937, HBO Digital Archives.

81. Ibid.

82. For more on the rise and evolution of American spiritualism, see Chapin (*Exploring Other Worlds*) and Weisberg (*Talking to the Dead*). McCabe, *Spiritualism*, 57–58, includes estimates of membership and practitioners.

83. *Harlem's Black Magic*, in *The March of Time* newsreel series, volume 3, episode 8, March 19, 1937, HBO Digital Archives.

84. Ibid.

85. Ibid.

86. Ibid.

87. Ibid.

88. Ibid.

89. Ibid.

90. "Picture Draws Angry Protest," *Los Angeles Sentinel*, March 25, 1937; "Harlem 'Black

Magic' Film Arouses Storm," *New York Amsterdam News*, March 27, 1937, 1; "Score Film on 'Harlem Black Magic': Cites Voodoo Implications as False," *Chicago Defender*, March 27, 1937, 4. "'Voodoo' Film Brings Protest," *Pittsburgh Courier*, March 27, 1937, 13.

91. "The 'March of Time' Slander," *Pittsburgh Courier*, March 27, 1937, 10.

92. "Pennsylvania Voodoo," *New York Amsterdam News*, December 19, 1928, 20.

93. "Voodoo Terror Tales Refuted by Herskovits," *Chicago Daily Tribune*, March 18, 1935, 9.

94. "Drums Are Called the Only Mystery of Voodooist Cult," *Washington Post*, April 7, 1935, R14.

95. Herskovits, review of *Folk Beliefs of the Southern Negro*, 311.

96. Ibid.

97. Hurston, "Hoodoo in America."

98. Baldwin, "Black Belts and Ivory Towers," 425.

99. Baker (*From Savage to Negro*, 21–22) provides a full account of the genesis of anthropology with regard to blacks in America and describes the interplay between anthropology and sociology and their connection to "race."

100. Baker, *Anthropology and the Racial Politics of Culture*, 10.

101. Ibid., 9.

102. Du Bois (*The Souls of Black Folk*, 191–93) identifies African origins of black culture: "The Music of Negro religion is that plaintive rhythmic melody, with its touching minor cadences, which, despite caricature and defilement, still remains the most original and beautiful expression of human life and longing yet born on American soil. Sprung from the African forests, where its counterpart can still be heard, it was adapted, changed, and intensified by the tragic soul-life of the slave, until, under the stress of law and whip, it became the one true expression of a people's sorrow, despair, and hope.... The Negro church of to-day is the social centre of Negro life in the United States, and the most characteristic expression of African character."

103. Ibid., 13.

104. Scott (*Contempt and Pity*, chap. 2) discusses sociological theories relative to race and pathology.

105. Baldwin, "Black Belts and Ivory Towers," 425.

106. Watts, "On Reconsidering Park, Johnson, Dubious, Frazier and Reid."

107. Baker, *From Savage to Negro*, 6.

108. See Baker (*Anthropology and the Racial Politics of Culture*, 12) for a discussion of Boas's race theories relative to Native American subjects; and Hutchinson (*Harlem Renaissance*, 66–77). See Bay (*White Image in the Black Mind*, 187–207) for more on Boas's influence on Du Bois and his activities within, and influence on, the black community. Corbould (*Becoming African Americans*, 63, 194) also describes the relationship between Du Bois and Boas. Hutchinson (*Harlem Renaissance*, 62–63) also writes that New Negroes closely followed Boas's work.

109. Gershenhorn (*Melville J. Herskovits and the Racial Politics of Knowledge*, 54) explains: "Nevertheless, Boas occasionally placed blacks as inferior to whites. For example, in *Anthropology and Modern Life* (1928), Boas said that there were "no pure races" but maintained that "serially the Negro brain is less extremely human than that of the White," because a higher percentage of European people had a higher brain weight than the Negro population.

110. Boas wrote in the preface to Zora Neale Hurston's *Mules and Men* that blacks were likely better scholars of black culture: "She has been able to penetrate through that affected demeanor by which the Negro excludes the White observer effectively from participating in his true inner life."

111. Boas, *The Mind of Primitive Man*, 270.

112. Ibid., 272.

113. See Franz Boas's preface to Zora Neale Hurston's *Mules and Men*.

114. Raushenbush, *Robert E. Park*, 3.

115. Ibid., 29.

116. For more on Park's work with the CRA, see Matthews, "Robert Park, Congo Reform and Tuskegee," and Raushenbush, *Robert E. Park*, 29–42.

117. Raushenbush, *Robert E. Park*, 38.

118. Matthews, "Robert Park, Congo Reform and Tuskegee," 50; Park, "Racial Assimilation in Secondary Groups."

119. See Baldwin, "Black Belts and Ivory Towers," for a discussion of Park and sociology at the University of Chicago.

120. Watts, "On Reconsidering Park, Johnson, Dubious, Frazier and Reid," 280; Baldwin ("Black Belts and Ivory Towers") addresses the role that black Americans played in the construction of sociological theories.

121. Hutchinson, *Harlem Renaissance*, 58; Baldwin, "Black Belts and Ivory Towers," 409.

122. Park, "The Conflict and Fusion of Cultures," 116.

123. Ibid., 112.

124. Ibid., 116.

125. Ibid., 116.

126. Ibid., 121.

127. Ibid., 121–22.

128. Platt, *E. Franklin Frazier Reconsidered*, 12–13.

129. Gershenhorn, *Melville J. Herskovits and the Racial Politics of Knowledge*, 11–13.

130. See Platt (*E. Franklin Frazier Reconsidered*, 12–15) for more on Frazier's academic career. See Gershenhorn (*Melville J. Herskovits and the Racial Politics of Knowledge*, 11–14) for more on Herskovits's academic career.

131. Lewis, *When Harlem Was in Vogue*, 116; Gershenhorn, *Melville J. Herskovits and the Racial Politics of Knowledge*, 32.

132. Gershenhorn (*Melville J. Herskovits and the Racial Politics of Knowledge*, 32) discusses Herskovits's relationship with Charles S. Johnson, Alain Locke, and Du Bois; Baldwin ("Black Belts and Ivory Towers," 418–19) describes Du Bois's influence on Frazier.

133. Gershenhorn, *Melville J. Herskovits and the Racial Politics of Knowledge*, 138.

134. Ibid.

135. Hutchinson (*Harlem Renaissance*, 76) and Corbould (*Becoming African Americans*, 160–61) assert that Herskovits's anthropological theories about racial distinction evolved over time.

136. Baldwin, "Black Belts and Ivory Towers," 400–424.

137. Ibid.

138. Herskovits's and Frazier's debate of the African survivals question is most evident in the footnotes of their respective works. Their back and forth was most direct in

Herskovits's *The American Negro*, "The Negro in the New World," and *The Myth of a Negro Past*, and Frazier's "The Changing Status of the Negro Family," his review of *The American Negro*, and *The Negro Family in the United States*.

139. Frazier, *The Negro Family in the United States*, 3–16.

140. Ibid., 16.

141. Ibid.

142. Ibid., 5–8.

143. Ibid., 3–19.

144. Ibid., 15.

145. Ibid.

146. Herskovits (*Myth of the Negro Past*) describes these survivals in chapters 6, 7, and 8.

147. Ibid., 149.

148. Herskovits, "What Has Africa Given America?," *New Republic*, September 4, 1935, 92–94.

149. Herskovits, "The Negro in the New World."

150. Herskovits, *Myth of the Negro Past*, 236. For more on Herskovits's primitivist tendencies, see Price and Price (*The Root of Roots*).

151. Granger, supervisor of the Savannah unit and lead author of *Drums and Shadows*, and Parrish, author of *Slave Songs*, both thank Herskovits for his assistance and cite his research in their works. Herskovits exchanged many letters with Granger and Parrish—answering their questions and giving advice—during the years that they conducted research in coastal Georgia. For letters exchanged between Granger and Herskovits, see Series 35/6, Box 8, Folder 10, NUA/MHP; for letters exchanged between Parrish and Herskovits, see Series 35/6, Box 18, Folder 2, NUA/MHP. Frazier was asked to review Granger's study.

152. See Hemenway (*Zora Neale Hurston*) and Boyd (*Wrapped in Rainbows*). Hurston frequently cited different birth years—her exact birth year is unknown.

153. Hemenway, *Zora Neale Hurston*, 10–17; Boyd, *Wrapped in Rainbows*, 79–87.

154. Hemenway, *Zora Neale Hurston*, 18; Boyd, *Wrapped in Rainbows*, 80.

155. Hemenway, *Zora Neale Hurston*, 20.

156. Ibid.

157. Ibid., 20–21.

158. Ibid., 88–89. See Gershenhorn (*Melville J. Herskovits and the Racial Politics of Knowledge*, 32–33) for more on Hurston's relationship with Herskovits.

159. Hemenway, *Zora Neale Hurston*, 88.

160. Hurston, *Dust Tracks on a Road*, 127–28.

161. Hemenway, *Zora Neale Hurston*, 91.

162. Ibid., 92.

163. Hurston, "Hoodoo in America."

164. Ibid., 317.

165. Ibid., 317–417.

166. Ibid., 318.

167. Hurston to Boas, October 23, 1934, and letter to Ruth Benedict, 1934, in Caplan, *Zora Neale Hurston*, 319, 329.

168. Hurston, *Mules and Men*, 185.

169. Hurston to Franz Boas, August 20, 1934, in Caplan, *Zora Neale Hurston*, 308.

170. Hemenway, *Zora Neale Hurston*, 227. *Tell My Horse: Voodoo and Life in Haiti and Jamaica* (1937) was the published study that resulted from the research Hurston conducted with Guggenheim funds.

171. Hurston to Langston Hughes, September 20, 1928, in Caplan, *Zora Neale Hurston*, 126.

172. Hurston to Annie Nathan Meyer, March 7, 1927, in Caplan, *Zora Neale Hurston*, 91–92.

173. Renda, *Taking Haiti*, 293.

174. Hemenway, *Zora Neale Hurston*, 218–27.

175. McNeil, Review of *Mules and Men*, 223–25.

CHAPTER 3

1. Although Emmitt's name appears as "Emmett" in several sources featuring the Johnsons, his descendants indicate that his name was misspelled in those publications.

2. Author interview with Fred Johnson; author interview with Joe Johnson.

3. Author interview with Joe Johnson.

4. Fewer newspaper reports about President Hoover's Christmas dinner at Howard Coffin's Sapelo mansion were published than were reports about Coolidge's. "Hoover's Guest on Sapelo for Their Yuletide Dinner," *Daily Boston Globe*, December 26, 1932, 7, was one of the few.

5. The photograph was taken by Folz Studio in 1928 and was published in W. Robert Moore's *National Geographic Magazine* article, "The Golden Isles of Guale." Fred Johnson talked about the day he drove the president and Coffin (author interview with Fred Johnson).

6. McIntosh County Court of Ordinary Marriages, Volumes 1–2, 1869–1926, Georgia State Archives. Author interview with Fred Johnson; author interview with Joe A. Johnson.

7. Crook et al., *Sapelo Voices*, 253. Fred Johnson discussed his family's history on the island with researchers who collected and published interviews with elderly Sapelo Islanders born between 1903 and 1918 beginning in 1991.

8. Author interview with Fred Johnson; author interview with Joe A. Johnson.

9. In Crook et al. (*Sapelo Voices*), Madeline Hudley Carter talked about low wages (57) and Hicks Walker and Samuel Hillery mentioned Islanders who worked on the mainland and on other islands (273, 140).

10. Author interview with Joe A. Johnson.

11. Ibid.

12. Fred Johnson in Crook et al., *Sapelo Voices*, 265.

13. Author interview with Joe A. Johnson.

14. Author interview with Ruth Johnson.

15. Herman Hillery in Crook et al., *Sapelo Voices*, 229.

16. Allen and Annie Mae Green in Crook et al., *Sapelo Voices*, 117–18.

17. Allen Green in Crook et al., *Sapelo Voices*, 106.

18. Author interview with Ruth Johnson.

19. Sullivan, *Early Days on the Georgia Tidewater*, 653–54.

20. Sullivan describes the impact of the depression on Coffin's businesses and the strategies that he employed to salvage his investments (ibid., 655–65).

21. Mumford (*Interzones*, 134) notes exotic travel fad among middle-class whites.

22. Waldon Fawcett, "Island Fad Hits South," *New York Times*, February 7, 1937, 178. Fawcett lists millionaires who owned Georgia Islands. The Carnegie family owned a large portion of Cumberland Island, Georgia. The Candler family (of Coca-Cola) owned what remained of Cumberland Island. J. P. Morgan owned most of Jekyll Island, Georgia. Ossabaw Island was owned by Dr. H. N. Torrey of Detroit—the husband of an heiress to a glass fortune.

23. Thomas and Braden (*High Adventure*, 8–9) discuss the 1888 formation of the National Geographic Society, based in Washington, DC, organized by a group of local white "scientific intellectuals" desiring to create a society "for the increase and diffusion of geographical knowledge." Lutz and Collins (*Reading National Geographic*, xii) explore the history and cultural impact of *National Geographic Magazine*. While the founders of the society and subsequent magazine imagined "geographical knowledge" to be obtainable, objective facts, ideas about racial distinction dictated how "geographic difference" would be described and captured in the magazine's text and photographs.

24. These and other details of Moore's early life can be found in his unpublished memoir, "The First Million Miles: Story of a National Geographic Staff Man," housed at *National Geographic Magazine*'s archive at the National Geographic Society in Washington, DC; "Traveled Million Miles for Magazine: Geographic's W. R. Moore Dies," *Washington Post*, March 23, 1968, B6.

25. W. Robert Moore, "The First Million Miles: Story of a National Geographic Staff Man," 2, *National Geographic Magazine* archives, National Geographic Society, Washington, DC; "Traveled Million Miles for Magazine: Geographic's W. R. Moore Dies," *Washington Post*, March 23, 1968, B6.

26. The *Washington Post* announced many of Moore's speaking engagements; see, for example, "Ancient Shrines of Orient Snapped in Natural Colors," March 24, 1932, 8; "Geographical Expert to Address Educators," July 1, 1934, 10; "Barbaric Splendor of Ethiopia Recalled by D.C. Journalist," July 21, 1935, 10; "W. R. Moore Will Deliver Travel Lecture Tonight," February 21, 1936, 3; "W. R. Moore to Describe Modern French Life," January 29, 1937, 19.

27. W. Robert Moore, "The First Million Miles: Story of a National Geographic Staff Man," 1–2, *National Geographic Magazine* archives, National Geographic Society, Washington, DC.

28. Bederman, *Manliness and Civilization*, 21–22.

29. Lutz and Collins (*Reading National Geographic*, 2, 6) estimate *National Geographic*'s readership.

30. W. Robert Moore, "The First Million Miles: Story of a National Geographic Staff Man," 279, *National Geographic Magazine* archives, National Geographic Society, Washington, DC.

31. *National Geographic Magazine* archivists explain that staff writers generally covered domestic stories while on vacation.

32. W. Robert Moore, "The Golden Isles of Guale."

33. Ibid.

34. See Gillis (*Islands of Mind*) for more analysis on islands and the imagination.

35. W. Robert Moore, "The Golden Isles of Guale."

36. Ibid., 245, 256.

37. Ibid., 262.

38. Ibid.

39. Ibid.

40. W. Robert Moore, "Golden Isles of Guale," draft, 26, *National Geographic Magazine* archives, National Geographic Society, Washington, DC.

41. "Barbaric Splendor of Ethiopia Recalled by D.C. Journalist," *Washington Post*, July 21, 1935, 10.

42. Ibid.

43. Peterkin, *Roll, Jordan, Roll*, includes over 230 pages of text and a photographic study conducted by Doris Ulman featuring "Gullah" blacks.

44. Green (Crook et al., *Sapelo Voices*, 119) said that Coffin was a good man.

45. Fred Johnson in Crook et al., *Sapelo Voices*, 269–70.

46. Ibid.

47. W. Robert Moore, "The Golden Isles of Guale," 251.

48. Ibid.

49. Ibid., 253.

50. Ibid.

51. Ibid.

52. Ibid., 249.

53. Ibid.

54. Wilson in (Crook et al., *Sapelo Voices*, 184–85).

55. Author interview with Joe Johnson.

56. W. Robert Moore, "The Golden Isles of Guale," 253.

57. Ibid.

58. Author interview with Joe Johnson. According to Mae Ruth Green's genealogy of Sapelo Island's black families, Morrison Johnson died of food poisoning sometime in 1933, and Eldora Johnson died in 1931, the same year she was born. Green, a genealogist and former president of the Georgia Genealogical Society, recorded Sapelo Islanders familial ties in a study designed to trace the genealogy of forty-four Hog Hammock families—commissioned by the Georgia Department of Natural Resources in 1980. For more on Mae Ruth Green and the unpublished genealogy, see "Mae Ruth Green, 85, Landmark Genealogist of Geechee Community," *Atlanta Journal-Constitution*, February 8, 2007.

59. Author interview with Joe Johnson.

60. Stott (*Documentary Expression and Thirties America*) explores the role of documentary expressions in books and journalism of the 1930s.

61. W. Robert Moore, "The Golden Isles of Guale," 253.

62. Ibid.

63. Ibid., 240.

64. Ibid., 251; author interview with Fred Johnson.

65. W. Robert Moore, "The Golden Isles of Guale," 258.

66. Ibid., 244.

67. Author interview with Cornelia Walker Bailey.

68. Cornelia Walker Bailey (author interview) and Paul Walker (author interview) described a contentious relationship between "Cap'n Frank" and Sapelo Islanders, in par-

ticular, tensions between Cap'n Frank and the Islanders who refused to work for Coffin or Reynolds. However, it is unlikely that his name was "Frank" because that island manager didn't work on the island until R. J. Reynolds purchased Coffin's holdings.

69. Author interview with Paul Walker. Walker discussed the distinction between the Islanders whites trusted and those whom they did not trust.

70. Author interview with Joe Johnson.

71. Ibid.; author interview with Fred Johnson. Neither Joe Johnson nor Fred Johnson had seen the book. They indicated that it was likely their parents knew nothing about it.

72. Parrish, Slave Songs, 9–41.

73. Ibid., xxi.

74. Rosenbaum, a folk music researcher, performer, and professor at the University of Georgia, interviewed Ronister Johnson in 1976 and asked him about Lydia Parrish's activities on Sapelo Island. Ronister Johnson's recollection was included in Rosenbaum's essay in ibid., xiii. Again, his brother Joe Johnson explained that Ronister likely knew little about the publication.

75. Parrish commented on the racial composition of the community where she grew up in a letter to Herskovits, January 29, 1936, Series 35/6, Box 18, Folder 2, NUA/MHP.

76. Parrish, Slave Songs, xxv.

77. Ibid.

78. Ibid.

79. Ibid., xxvi.

80. Ibid., 9.

81. Author interview with Anne Heard, Lydia Parrish's granddaughter. Heard explained that Lydia Parrish visited Georgia's coast alone, and other times, she traveled to St. Simons with her children. Lydia eventually moved to the island.

82. Parrish, Slave Songs, 9.

83. Ibid.

84. Ibid., 9–10.

85. Author interview with Anne Heard.

86. Ramey (Slave Songs and the Birth of African American Poetry, 2) explains that a significant interest in "slave songs" was expressed between the 1850s and 1880s. Fredrika Bremer, The Homes of the New World: Impressions of America (1853); Francis Anne Kemble, Journal of a Residence on a Georgia Plantation 1838–1839 (1863); William Francis Allen, Charles Pickard Ware's, and Lucy McKim Garrison's Negro Slave Songs of the United States (1867); Thomas Fenner, Frederic G. Rathbun, and Miss Bessie Cleveland, Cabin and Plantation Songs as Sung by Hampton Students (1874); J. B. T. Marsh, The Story of the Jubilee Singers (1875); Theodore F. Seward, As Sung by the Jubilee Singers of Fisk University (1872); and Rev. Marshall W. Taylor, Plantation Melodies (1882) were all slave song collections produced during these years.

87. James Weldon Johnson and J. Rosamond Johnson published The Books of American Negro Spirituals in 1925.

88. Parrish, Slave Songs, 11.

89. Parrish composed a letter to Herskovits on January 15, 1936 (Series 35/6, Box 18, Folder 2, NUA/MHP) after reading an article he published in the New Republic titled "What Has Africa Given America?" and his book Rebel Destiny, explaining that she believed he was

best qualified to teach her how to read film recordings of blacks performing the ring shout and buzzard lupe.

90. Parrish, in letters that she wrote to Herskovits between 1936 and 1942, several times commented on "self-seeking" commercial collectors of black culture, and he agreed. In particular, this topic came up in correspondence from Parrish to Herskovits on January 15, 1936, January 29, 1936, February 5, 1936, and May 6, 1936, Series 35/6, Box 18, Folder 2, NUA/MHP.

91. Series 35/6, Box 18, Folder 2, NUA/MHP.

92. Ibid.

93. Parrish confessed that she had a vague awareness of the black African cultural connection and hoped Herskovits would help her learn more in a letter to Herskovits on March 19, 1936; she discussed her academic training in a letter to Herskovits on December 14, 1936, both in Series 35/6, Box 18, Folder 2, NUA/MHP.

94. Parrish to Herskovits, January 29, 1936, Series 35/6, Box 18, Folder 2, NUA/MHP.

95. Parrish to Herskovits, May 18, 1936, Series 35/6, Box 18, Folder 2, NUA/MHP.

96. Parrish to Herskovits, March 28, 1937, Series 35/6, Box 18, Folder 2, NUA/MHP.

97. Ibid.

98. Herskovits to Parrish, April 3, 1937, Series 35/6, Box 18, Folder 2, NUA/MHP.

99. Ibid.

100. Parrish to Herskovits, April 28, 1937, Series 35/6, Box 18, Folder 2, NUA/MHP.

101. Ibid.

102. Ibid.

103. Parrish, Slave Songs, xxix.

104. Ibid.

105. Ibid.

106. Ibid., 9.

107. Ibid., 3.

108. Ibid.

109. Ibid., 12–13.

110. Ibid., 54.

111. Since the publication of Slave Songs, scholars and writers have referenced Parrish's descriptions of ring shouts and shout songs and have posited many theories about the practice and its origins in their explorations of black American traditions. Parrish's research is cited in other studies that examine coastal Georgia black folk during the period (such as Turner's Africanisms in the Gullah Dialect), and shows up in a wide range of contemporary scholarship representing various disciplines, such as Stuckey, Slave Culture; Rosenbaum, Shout Because You're Free; Gomez, Exchanging Our Country Marks; Twining, "I'm Going to Sing and 'Shout'"; Hazzard-Donald, "Hoodoo Religion and American Dance Traditions"; Cartwright, Reading Africa into American Literature; and many more.

112. Parrish to Herskovits, February 4, 1936, Series 35/6, Box 18, Folder 2, NUA/MHP.

113. Parrish, Slave Songs, 12.

114. Ibid.

115. Ibid.

116. Ibid., 10.

117. Ibid.

118. Ibid., 20.

119. Ibid., 22.

120. Ibid., 23.

121. Ibid., 10.

122. Ibid., 11.

123. Ibid.

124. Kodish (*Good Friends and Bad Enemies*, 119–51) chronicles Gordon's collecting mission in Darien, Georgia (1925–28).

125. Kodish, *Good Friends and Bad Enemies*, 124–25.

126. Parrish to Herskovits, April 28, 1937, Series 35/6, Box 18, Folder 2, NUA/MHP.

127. Author interview with Catherine Hillery.

128. "'Ring Around the Rosy' Probe Will Be Held as Climax to GA Lynching," *Pittsburgh Courier*, October 18, 1930, A1; "Potentialities of Inter-Racial Lynchings," *Atlanta Daily World*, October 11, 1934, 6.

129. Parrish to Herskovits, July 30, 1937, Series 35/6, Box 18, Folder 2, NUA/MHP.

130. Parrish to Herskovits, October 23, 1939, Series 35/6, Box 18, Folder 2, NUA/MHP.

131. Parrish, *Slave Songs*, 29–31.

132. Parrish to Herskovits, April 28, 1937, Series 35/6, Box 18, Folder 2, NUA/MHP.

133. Parrish to Herskovits, November 24, 1936, Series 35/6, Box 18, Folder 2, NUA/MHP.

134. Herskovits to Parrish, December 1, 1936, Series 35/6, Box 18, Folder 2, NUA/MHP.

135. Greenberg, "The Decipherment."

136. Ibid.

137. Author interview with Catherine Hillery. Hillery talked about the Islanders' reliance on herbal remedies and cited poverty among the other factors that encouraged the blacks who lived there to learn about the abundance of medicines to be found "in the woods."

138. Parrish, *Slave Songs*, 111.

139. Ibid.

140. Ibid.

141. Bailey, *God, Dr. Buzzard, and the Bolito Man*, 178–83.

142. Ibid., 182.

143. Ibid.

144. Ibid., 234.

145. Ibid.

146. Ibid.

147. Ibid.

148. Woodson, "Review: Slave Songs."

149. Ibid., 466.

150. Ibid.

151. Ibid.

152. Ibid.

153. Parrish to Herskovits, February 24, 1936, Series 35/6, Box 18, Folder 2, NUA/MHP.

154. Wade-Lewis (*Lorenzo Dow Turner*, 82) writes about Turner's relationship to Lydia Parrish; and Parrish mentioned helping him in letters.

155. Parrish to Herskovits, January 17, 1940, Series 35/6, Box 18, Folder 2, NUA/MHP.

156. Parrish to Turner, March 27 and April 14, 1938, Series 023, Box 3, Folder 4, NUA/LDTP. Parrish also referred to Turner's findings and research several times in *Slave Songs*.

157. Parrish to Herskovits, January 17, 1940, Series 35/6, Box 18, Folder 2, NUA/MHP.

158. Letter from Parrish to Turner, March 27, 1938, Series 023, Box 3, Folder 4 NUA/LDTP.

159. Wade-Lewis (*Lorenzo Dow Turner*, 12) writes about Turner's parents.

160. Ibid., 13–26.

161. Ibid., 35.

162. Ibid., 36.

163. Ibid.

164. Turner, *Africanisms in the Gullah Dialect*, 5–14.

165. Ibid., 6.

166. Ibid., 8.

167. Wade-Lewis, *Lorenzo Dow Turner*, 66.

168. Ibid., 81–98.

169. Ibid., 81.

170. Turner, *Africanisms in the Gullah Dialect*, 291.

171. Ibid.

172. Wade-Lewis, *Lorenzo Dow Turner*, 81.

173. Turner, *Africanisms in the Gullah Dialect*, lx.

174. Ibid.

175. Ibid.

176. Turner sent a summary of his findings and a research statement to Herskovits—the list described can be found on page 9 of that summary. Turner to Herskovits, February 17, 1940, Series 023, Box 3, Folder 4, NUA/LDTP.

177. Turner, *Africanisms in the Gullah Dialect*, 12.

178. Ibid.

179. Ibid., 11–12.

180. Author interview with Cornelia Bailey.

181. Wade-Lewis, *Lorenzo Dow Turner*, 82.

182. Taken from Lorenzo Dow Turner's Sapelo Recordings, courtesy of Professor Thomas B. Klein, PhD, Georgia Southern University.

183. Turner Field Notes, Georgia, Series 023, Box 29, Folders 3–4, NUA/LDTP.

184. Ibid.

185. Ibid.

186. Ibid.

187. Lorenzo Dow Turner's Sapelo Recordings, courtesy of Professor Thomas B. Klein, PhD, Georgia Southern University.

188. Ibid., Katie Brown recording (July/August 1933).

189. Ibid., Reverend John Dunham recording (July/August 1933).

190. Ibid., Shad Hall recording (July/August 1933).

191. Wade-Lewis, *Lorenzo Dow Turner*, 90.

192. Ibid., 98–105.

193. Turner, *Africanisms in the Gullah Dialect*, 292.

194. Ibid., lx.

195. Ibid., 2–42.

196. Ibid., 42.

197. Turner, *Africanisms in the Gullah Dialect*, 255–57.

198. Ibid., 191, 199. These terms are still used by older Sapelo Islanders.

CHAPTER 4

1. Georgia Writers' Project, *Drums and Shadows*, 159. In a letter to Sterling Brown, Mary Granger notes that she had visited Sapelo for the first time in November 1937, NARA/FWP.

2. Georgia Writers' Project, *Drums and Shadows*, 158–72. The Savannah unit toured the island in an oxcart driven by "a Negro boy named Julius."

3. Sullivan, *Early Days on the Georgia Tidewater*, 677; Bailey, *God, Dr. Buzzard, and the Bolito Man*, 92–103.

4. Brown's memories of Bilali Mohammed's prayer rituals can be found in Parrish, *Slave Songs*, 27, and Georgia Writers' Project, *Drums and Shadows*, 161.

5. Georgia Writers' Project, *Drums and Shadows*, 162.

6. Ibid.; Parrish, *Slave Songs*, 27.

7. The *Drums and Shadows* study section that features Sapelo mentions what Katie Brown was offered in exchange for the interview (159). Muriel and Malcolm Bell, the photographers who took the photos included in the book, remembered that their longtime friend, Mary L. Granger, the supervisor of the Savannah unit, frequently conducted interviews and offered potential informants gifts to encourage their participation (ibid., xxx). Although the Georgia Writers' Project is credited as the author of *Drums and Shadows*, research, interviews, and other tasks associated with drafting the book also involved Granger's staff. Granger was always careful to use terms such as "us" and "we" when writing to national Federal Writers' Project officials about the manuscript, but the work is unquestionably her brainchild. The Bells recall that Granger "told us of her proposed study of African cultural survivals she believed to be extant along the Georgia coast" (ibid., xxix). Henry G. Alsberg, Guy B. Johnson, W. F. Ogburn, W. T. Couch, Melville Herskovits, and others identified Granger as the person responsible for the study's direction and content in correspondences. Granger took responsibility for the manuscript that extended beyond her duties as Federal Writers' Project state unit bureaucrat: she twice visited the University of North Carolina to consult with researchers on the manuscript; and she actively recruited scholars to aid her research. Her personal interest in the African survivals question was enduring. When interviewed for an article in 1963, Granger talked about her sustained interest in African survivals with a reporter: "She became so caught up in studying the Negro origins that she planned to go to West Africa with a professor from Northwestern University to do field work when World War II began" ("Hobbies Keep Her Busy," *Savannah News*, May 19, 1963, 2E).

8. Benyon, "The Voodoo Cult."

9. Georgia Writers' Project, *Drums and Shadows*, xliv.

10. Charles Joyner mentions the tensions and debates that surrounded Mary Granger's study in his 1986 introduction to the Brown Thrasher Edition of *Drums and Shadows*, but his brief discussion of the issues that surrounded the publication does not include an exten-

sive review of the archival materials that reveal, in detail, the depth of this debate and the forces that propelled the work's publication. In the introduction, Joyner poses questions about Granger, her advisors, and her adversaries that chapter 4 in this book tries to answer.

11. Mary L. Granger's Barnard College Occupation Bureau card, Barnard College Archives.

12. Ibid.

13. See Heap (*Slumming*), Mumford (*Interzones*), and Douglas (*Mongrel Manhattan*) for more on "slumming" and racial boundary crossing in New York City during the 1920s.

14. Mary L. Granger's Barnard College Occupation Bureau card, Barnard College Archives; "Hobbies Keep Her Busy: She Has No Time for Boredom," *Savannah News*, May 19, 1963, section 2E.

15. Author interview with Harvey Granger Jr.

16. Ibid.

17. Mary Granger's novels were reviewed in "The New Books," *Saturday Review*, February 12, 1927, and June 22, 1929.

18. Author interview with Harvey Granger Jr.

19. GHS/MGP, Collection Number 321.

20. R. B. Eleazer to Granger, December 28, 1932, GHS/MGP.

21. *America's Tenth Man: A Brief Survey of the Negro's Part in American History* (3), GHS/MGP.

22. "Hobbies Keep Her Busy: She Has No Time for Boredom," *Savannah News*, May 19, 1963, section 2E.

23. *America's Tenth Man: A Brief Survey of the Negro's Part in American History* (4), GHS/MHP.

24. *America's Tenth Man: A Brief Survey of the Negro's Part in American History* (5), GHS/MHP.

25. Ibid.

26. Ibid.

27. Ibid., 6.

28. GHS/MGP.

29. *America's Tenth Man: A Brief Survey of the Negro's Part in American History* (13), GHS/MGP.

30. "Georgia Writers' Project: Works Progress Administration 1940 Brochure," Georgia Historical Society, Collection Number 1308, Folder 30.

31. Ibid. lists the projects the Savannah unit worked on.

32. See Mangione (*The Dream and the Deal*, 8) and Penkower (*The Federal Writers' Project*, 19–29) for a discussion of Eleanor Roosevelt's and Henry G. Alsberg's efforts to institute relief for writers. Penkower (*The Federal Writers' Project*, 1–7) also describes the Writers' Union 1935 strike, and Mangione (*The Dream and the Deal*, 36–39) writes about their strike.

33. Mangione, *The Dream and the Deal*, 373.

34. Hirsch, *Portrait of America*, 2–13.

35. Ibid.

36. Ibid., 2.

37. See Stott (*Documentary Expressions*, 1–73) for more on the "common man" vernacular.

38. Hutchinson, *The Harlem Renaissance in Black and White*, 437.

39. Stott, *Documentary Expressions*, 1–73.

40. Mangione (*The Dream and the Deal*, 125–256) writes about FWP's black artists and writers.

41. Hirsch, *Portrait of America*, 111.

42. See Mangione (*The Dream and the Deal*), Hirsch (*Portrait of America*), and Skalroff (*Black Culture*) for more on the numbers of writers employed by the FWP.

43. Bold (*WPA Guides*, 3–6) explains the "double authority" of FWP projects.

44. Sklaroff, *Black Culture*, 81–121; Hirsch, *Portrait of America*, 125–26.

45. "Folklore and Customs," Writers' Guide, Federal Writers' Project, File Box A7, Library of Congress, Washington, DC, 1.

46. Ibid., 2.

47. Ibid.

48. Ibid.

49. Ibid., 1–5.

50. Savannah unit, "Studies of Negro Survival Types in Coastal Georgia," NARA/FWP. The manuscript cited Peterkin's *Roll, Jordan, Roll* on 13, 36, 42, 43, 46, 47, 50, 52, 59, and 67.

51. Savannah unit, "Studies of Negro Survival Types in Coastal Georgia," NARA/FWP.

52. Du Bois's book *The Gift of Black Folk* (1924) appeared in two notes about black people's musical gifts and inheritances in Savannah unit, "Studies of Negro Survival Types in Coastal Georgia," NARA/FWP.

53. Georgia Writers' Project, *Drums and Shadows*, xxix.

54. Savannah unit, "Studies of Negro Survival Types in Coastal Georgia," NARA/FWP, 1.

55. Ibid.

56. Ibid., 10.

57. Ibid., 11.

58. Ibid., 10–11.

59. Ibid., 12.

60. Ibid., 13.

61. Ibid., 5–8.

62. Ibid., 14.

63. Ibid.

64. Ibid., 15.

65. Ibid., 16.

66. Ibid.

67. Ibid., 24.

68. Ibid.

69. Ibid., 25.

70. Ibid.

71. Ibid., 27.

72. Ibid., 27–28. In reviews of Weatherford's book, Carter G. Woodson and Robert E. Park denounced his poor attempt at a scholarly study of the origins of black cultural life in their published reviews: for Woodson's review, see *Journal of Negro History* 9, no. 4 (October 1924): 574–77; for Park's review, see *American Journal of Sociology* 31, no. 2 (September 1925): 259–60.

73. Savannah Unit, "Studies of Negro Survival Types in Coastal Georgia," NARA/FWP, 29–30.

74. Ibid., 45–68.

75. Ibid., 45.

76. Ibid., 46.

77. Ibid., 44.

78. Ibid., 2n4.

79. Ibid., 73.

80. Ibid., 74–75.

81. "Georgia Writers' Project: Works Progress Administration 1940 Brochure," GHS/FWP.

82. Gabbin, *Sterling Brown*, 67–70.

83. Ibid.

84. Brown, "Arcadia of the South."

85. Gabbin (*Sterling Brown*, 70) describes Brown's staff, and Sklaroff (*Black Culture*, 81–21) discusses the challenges inherent to Brown's role in the FWP.

86. Sklaroff, *Black Culture*, 97; Hirsch, *Portrait of America*, 157.

87. Carolyn Dillard, Georgia State FWP director, to Mary Granger, July 15, 1937, NARA/FWP.

88. Samuel Tupper Jr. to Sterling Brown, August 14, 1937; Sterling Brown to Samuel Tupper Jr., August 18, 1937, NARA/FWP.

89. Brown to Tupper, August 18, 1937, NARA/FWP.

90. Tupper to Brown, August 24, 1937, NARA/FWP.

91. Brown to Tupper, August 18, 1937, NARA/FWP.

92. Ibid.

93. Mary Granger to Samuel Tupper Jr., July 19, 1937, NARA/FWP.

94. Granger to Brown, October 18, 1937, NARA/FWP.

95. Guy B. Johnson to Mary Granger, October 13, 1937, NARA/FWP; Granger to Melville Herskovits, October 4, 1937, Series 35/6, Box 8, Folder 10, NUA/MHP. The Institute for Research in Social Science had, in conjunction with the Social Science Research Council, published several studies about coastal South Carolinians during the 1930s, including Guy B. Johnson's St. Helena study.

96. Granger to Brown, October 18, 1937, NARA/FWP.

97. Johnson to Granger, October 13, 1937, NARA/FWP; Johnson, *Folk Culture on St. Helena Island, South Carolina*.

98. Johnson, *Folk Culture on St. Helena Island, South Carolina*.

99. Ibid.

100. Ibid.

101. Ibid.

102. W. T. Couch to Mary Granger, October 25, 1937, NARA/FWP.

103. Granger to Herskovits, October 4, 1937, Series 35/6, Box 8, Folder 10, NUA/MHP.

104. Ibid.

105. Lydia Parrish began writing to Melville Herskovits in January 1936; see Series 35/6, Box 18, Folder 2, NUA/MHP.

106. Parrish to Herskovits, September 8, 1939; January 17, 1940; July 31, 1940, Series 35/6, Box 18, Folder 2, NUA/MHP.

107. Herskovits to Granger, November 22, 1937, Series 35/6, Box 8, Folder 10, NUA/MHP.

108. Ibid.

109. Granger to Brown, October 18, 27, 1937, NARA/FWP.

110. Granger to Brown, October 27, 1937, NARA/FWP.

111. Sklaroff (*Black Culture*, 99) briefly discusses Sterling Brown's reduced role in the FWP during the fellowship. Granger inquired about the impact that his absence would have on her project in letters she wrote to Brown on October 18 and 27, 1937, NARA/FWP.

112. Brown to Granger, October 30, 1937, NARA/FWP.

113. Granger to Brown, November 10, 1937, NARA/FWP.

114. Brown to Granger, November 18, 1937, NARA/FWP.

115. Ibid.

116. Ibid.

117. Gabbin (*Sterling Brown*, 87–117) writes about the influence of "folk tradition" on Brown's work.

118. Brown wrote: "I am able, as you know, to give only so much time to the project, and the rest of my staff is quite overburdened" (Brown to Tupper, January 4, 1938, NARA/FWP).

119. Frazier ("A Folk Culture in the Making," 197) wrote: "Although investigation is now in progress to determine just what the Negro has brought from Africa, it may be asserted without fear of contradiction that when the Negro was brought to America there was a well nigh complete break with his African past." Frazier expressed this anti-African survivals position in most of the works that he published during the 1920s and 1930s.

120. Frazier to Brown, February 1, 1938, NARA/FWP.

121. Ibid.

122. Ibid.

123. Ibid.

124. Ibid.

125. Ibid.

126. W. O. Brown to Sterling Brown, NARA/FWP.

127. Ibid.

128. Ibid.

129. Ibid.

130. Ibid.

131. Ibid.

132. Ibid.

133. Author interview with Paul Walker; author interview with Catherine Hillery.

134. W. O. Brown to Sterling Brown, NARA/FWP.

135. Ibid.

136. Henry G. Alsberg to Sterling Brown, February 16, 1938, NARA/FWP.

137. Ibid.

138. Ibid.

139. Ibid.

140. Ibid.

141. Sterling Brown to Granger, February 24, 1938, NARA/FWP.

142. Ibid.

143. Granger to Sterling Brown, February 28, 1938, NARA/FWP.

144. Ibid.

145. Ibid.

146. Ibid.

147. Ibid.

148. Guy B. Johnson continued to review and suggest strategies to improve Granger's manuscript. Johnson to Granger, March 24, 1938, NARA/FWP.

149. William F. Ogburn to Granger, March 3, 1938, NARA/FWP.

150. Granger to Sterling Brown, March 25, 1938, NARA/FWP.

151. Ibid.

152. Ibid.

153. Ibid.

154. Ibid.

155. Ibid.

156. Ibid.

157. Ibid.

158. Johnson to Granger, April 15, 1938, NARA/FWP.

159. Granger to Sterling Brown, July 28, 1938, NARA/FWP.

160. Ibid.

161. Granger to Herskovits, July 27, 1938, Series 35/6, Box 8, Folder 10, NUA/MHP.

162. Herskovits to Granger, September 12, 1938, Series 35/6, Box 8, Folder 10, NUA/MHP.

163. Ibid.

164. Ibid.

165. Ibid.

166. Ibid.

167. Ibid.

168. Granger to Herskovits, September 15, 1938, Series 35/6, Box 8, Folder 10, NUA/MHP.

169. Herskovits to Granger, October 10, 1938, Series 35/6, Box 8, Folder 10, NUA/MHP.

170. Letters exchanged between Granger and Herskovits, Series 35/6, Box 8, Folder 10, NUA/MHP.

171. Herskovits to Couch, Series 35/6, Box 8, Folder 10, April 25, 1939, NUA/MHP.

172. Herskovits to Granger, September 27, 1939, Series 35/6, Box 8, Folder 10, NUA/MHP.

173. Benjamin Botkin to Sterling Brown, January 1939, NARA/FWP.

174. Ibid.

175. Ibid.

176. Ibid.

177. Sterling Brown, "General Criticism," August 16, 1939, NARA/FWP.

178. Ibid.

179. Ibid.

180. John C. Rogers to Benjamin A. Botkin, December 21, 1939, NARA/FWP.

181. "Editorial Report on State Copy," January 9, 1940, NARA/FWP.

182. Georgia Writers' Project, Drums and Shadows, xxx. Photographers Muriel and Malcolm Bell described the strategies that Granger used to gain the cooperation of coastal Georgia blacks in their 1986 foreword to the study.

183. The University of North Carolina Press told Granger that they could not publish

the book for two or three years after it was complete; the University of Georgia presented a more favorable timeline. Tupper to Henry G. Alsberg, July 17, 1939, NARA/FWP.

184. Georgia Writers' Project, *Drums and Shadows*, xlii.

185. Ibid., xxix–xxx ("Photographer's Note"): "We had seen the Julia Peterkin-Doris Ullman collaboration . . . and resolved that our photographs of the Negroes would be as sharply focused as had been our Savannah houses."

186. Ibid., 2.

187. Ibid., 195–249.

188. Ibid.

189. Ibid., xliv.

190. Ibid., 3.

191. Ibid., 30.

192. Ibid., 27.

193. Ibid., 159.

194. The following *New York Times* articles reported the details of the car accident and the murder trial: "Reynolds on Trial for Manslaughter," July 23, 1929; "Three Doctors Aid in Reynolds' Defense," July 31, 1929; and "Reynolds Guilty; Gets Five Months," August 1, 1929. An obituary announcing Reynolds's death published in the *Chicago Tribune* also mentioned that the tycoon spent five months in prison on a manslaughter charge, "R. J. Reynolds, Heir to Camel Millions Dies," December 16, 1964.

195. Sullivan (*Early Days on the Georgia Tidewater*, 677) notes, "In the later 1930s and early 1940s, R. J. Reynolds acquired tracts of land settled by blacks around the island by a series of property exchanges and purchases." Reynolds's land swaps continued through the 1950s, a strategy that was described as "peculiar" in "Peculiar Land Swaps Leave Little of Ancestors' SE Georgia Island," *Atlanta Daily World*, December 6, 2001.

196. Bailey (*God, Dr. Buzzard, and the Bolito Man*, 114) discusses the work Islanders did for Reynolds.

197. Author interview with Joe Johnson.

198. Author interview with Ruth Johnson.

199. Allen Green in Crook et al., *Sapelo Voices*, 93.

200. Bailey, *God, Dr. Buzzard, and the Bolito Man*, 261.

201. Ibid., 97–99.

202. Ibid.

203. Georgia Writers' Project, *Drums and Shadows*, 165.

204. Ibid., 159.

205. Ibid., 160.

206. Ibid., 167.

207. Ibid.

208. Ibid., 168.

209. Ibid., 158–65.

210. Ibid., 163.

211. Ibid.

212. Ibid.

213. Ibid.

214. Ibid., 164.

215. Herskovits to Granger, February 15, 1939, Series 35/6, Box 8, Folder 10, NUA/MHP.

216. Ibid., 161.

217. Ibid.

218. Ibid., 166.

219. Ibid., 165.

220. Ibid., 168.

221. Ibid., 171.

222. Author interview with Betty Johnson Cooper; author interview with Paul Walker.

223. Herskovits to Granger, February 15, 1939, Series 35/6, Box 8, Folder 10, NUA/MHP.

224. Herskovits, review of *Gullah*.

225. C. McD. Puckette, "Sea Island Negroes," *New York Times*, April 6, 1941, BR17.

226. Ibid.

227. Ibid.

228. Herzog, "Review: Drums and Shadows."

229. Bascom, "Acculturation Among the Gullah Negroes."

230. Ibid., 43.

231. Ibid.

232. Author interview with Paul Walker.

233. Author interview with Betty Johnson Cooper.

234. Author interview with Joe Johnson.

235. Author interview with Cornelia Walker Bailey.

CHAPTER 5

1. Cerruti, "Sea Islands."

2. W. Robert Moore, "The Golden Isles of Guale."

3. Cerruti, "Sea Islands," 381.

4. Ibid.

5. Ibid., 384.

6. Mae Ruth Green, a genealogist and former president of the Georgia Genealogical Society, recorded Sapelo Islanders' military service in her unpublished Sapelo Island Genealogy—a study designed to trace the genealogy of forty-four Hog Hammock families—commissioned by the Georgia Department of Natural Resources in 1980 (A23-A42). For more on Mae Ruth Green and the unpublished genealogy, see Green's obituary, "Mae Ruth Green, 85, Landmark Genealogist of Geechee Community," *Atlanta Journal-Constitution*, February 8, 2007.

7. U.S. Census, Population Schedules, McIntosh County; Crook et al., *Sapelo Voices*, 28; Sullivan, "Sapelo Island Settlement and Land Ownership."

8. Betty Johnson Cooper described her commute to Todd Grant High School in author interview.

9. As noted in "Peculiar Land Swaps Leave Little of Ancestors' SE Georgia Island," *Atlanta Daily World*, December 6, 2001, Reynolds's "land swaps" persisted and increased through the 1950s.

10. Bailey, *God, Dr. Buzzard, and the Bolito Man*, 255.

11. Reynolds and Shachtman, *The Gilded Leaf*, 235.

12. Greene, *Praying for Sheetrock*.

13. Ibid., 21, 87.

14. Ibid., 37.

15. Ibid., 82, 240.

16. Sullivan (*Early Days on the Georgia Tidewater*) and Reynolds and Shachtman (*The Gilded Leaf*) discuss the marine life research that Reynolds supported and encouraged on Sapelo at length. Sullivan (*Early Days on the Georgia Tidewater*, 685) also writes about the sale of the island's north end.

17. Author interview with Betty Johnson Cooper.

18. Greene, *Praying for Sheetrock*, 117–38.

19. Bailey, *God, Dr. Buzzard, and the Bolito Man*, 274–75.

20. Ibid.

21. Reynolds and Shachtman (*The Gilded Leaf*) discuss Reynolds's disinheriting of his sons (1–9) and the promises that R. J. Reynolds allegedly made to his favorite black workers (265). Buddy Sullivan writes about the sale of the island's north end in *Early Days on the Georgia Tidewater*, 685.

22. See Bailey (*God, Dr. Buzzard, and the Bolito Man*, 113–16) for more on the tactics that Reynolds used to force blacks to sell their land and Sullivan (*Early Days on the Georgia Tidewater*, 677) for a discussion of Reynolds's consolidation of black landholdings on Sapelo Island.

23. See Bailey (*God, Dr. Buzzard, and the Bolito Man*, 271–72) for a discussion about legal challenges to the sale and suspicions that Reynolds did not have clear title to the land; Sullivan (*Early Days on the Georgia Tidewater*, 685) does not mention these accusations but does note the sale.

24. Bailey, *God, Dr. Buzzard, and the Bolito Man*, 275.

25. Ibid.

26. Ibid.

27. Terence Smith, "President Vacationing on Island in Georgia, to 'Read, Sleep, Fish,'" *New York Times*, April 13, 1979, A10.

28. Bailey, *God, Dr. Buzzard, and the Bolito Man*, 276–78.

29. See Erenberg and Hirsch, *The War in American Culture*, for more on the cultural impact of World War II.

30. Granger to Herskovits, January 3, 1941, Series 35/6, Box 8, Folder 10, NUA/MHP.

31. Glicksberg, "The Negro Cult of the Primitive."

32. Glicksberg, "Negro Americans and the African Dream."

33. Ibid., 323–25.

34. Horton (*Race and the Making of American Liberalism*) explores the rise of racial liberalism. Horton examines the complex relationship between race, racism, and liberalism in American history. She posits that 1940s postwar racial liberalism is embodied in Myrdal (*An American Dilemma*, 121), which argued that racial discrimination stood in opposition to the nation's most cherished ideals and contends that this new racial liberalism obscured the complex dynamics that constitute racial and economic inequality in America.

35. Southern, *Gunnar Myrdal and Black-White Relations*, 3–49.

36. Myrdal, *An American Dilemma*, lix–lxx.

37. Southern, *Gunnar Myrdal and Black-White Relations*, 16–17.

38. Ibid.

39. Myrdal, *An American Dilemma*, 753.

40. Horton (*Race and the Making of American Liberalism*, 141–43) examines the complex negotiation of the black cultural reconfiguration during the civil rights years.

41. Ibid., 144.

42. Works like Joseph's *Waiting 'Til the Midnight Hour* chronicle the history of the movement and identify key leaders and prominent ideologies embraced by its adherents.

43. See Deburg, *A New Day in Babylon*, and Ongiri, *Spectacular Blackness*, for more on this topic. Ford (*Liberated Threads*) also examines Black Power's aesthetic expressions during this moment.

44. Glazer and Moynihan, *Beyond the Melting Pot*, 78–79: "One can reject white standards of beauty, one can devote oneself to the study of African history and culture, one may support policies of African states. There will be more and more of this, and this is all to the good. But Africa and nationalism and exclusivism will have as little to do with changing the conditions of American Negro life as Israel and Zionism have to do with the conditions of American Jewish life."

45. Murch, *Living for the City*, 85–87. Murch explores the study groups organized by students at various colleges in the California university system.

46. Ibid.

47. See Rojas, *From Black Power to Black Studies*, and Biondi, *The Black Revolution on Campus*, for more on the Black Studies movement.

48. Biondi, *The Black Revolution on Campus*, 23–24; Murch, *Living for the City*, 85–87.

49. Biondi (*The Black Revolution on Campus*, 241–67) explores debates that emerged among black educators about black studies. See also Dagbovie (*What Is African American History?*) for an in-depth discussion of the evolution of Black Studies.

50. See Hale (*A Nation of Outsiders*, 84–131) for more on race, white youth, and the folk revival of the 1960s and 1970s.

51. Blassingame, *The Slave Community*, 3–105. Many other historians engaged in analysis of enslaved blacks' cultural lives in the 1970s; George Rawick, Peter Wood, Eugene Genovese, Leslie Howard Owens, Albert J. Raboteau, Charles Joyner, and Paul Escott are a few.

52. Levine, *Black Culture and Black Consciousness*, xxvii.

53. Ibid., 51–52, 57, 64.

54. A special edition of the *Journal of Black Studies* is dedicated to Sea Island culture. In this volume, numerous writings about the uniqueness of Sea Islanders appear. *Journal of Black Studies* 10, no. 4 (June 1980).

55. Ibid.

56. Ibid, 380.

57. Janie Gilliard Moore, "Africanisms among Blacks of the Sea Islands," 468.

58. Ibid.

59. Blockson, "Sea Change in the Sea Islands."

60. Dubey (*Black Women Novelists*, 1–9) examines, among other things, how black women writers explore their "dual subjectivity."

61. Wall, *Worrying the Line*, 5–9.

62. Blassingame, *The Slave Community*, 3–49.

63. Levine, *Black Culture and Black Consciousness*, 4.

64. Powell ("Summoning the Ancestors") reconstructs the possible connection between flying Africans and an 1803 uprising.

65. Georgia Writers' Project, *Drums and Shadows*, 169.

66. Ibid., 79.

67. Toni Morrison interview by Thomas LeClair in "A Conversation with Toni Morrison: 'The Language Must Not Sweat,'" *New Republic*, March 21, 1981, 26–27.

68. Ibid., 28.

69. Ibid.

70. Georgia Writers' Project, *Drums and Shadows*, 161.

71. Ibid., 163.

72. Ibid., 162.

73. Morrison, *Song of Solomon*, 303.

74. Ibid.

75. W. Robert Moore, "The Golden Isles of Guale," 253.

76. Paule Marshall interview by Melody Graulich and Lisa Sisco in "Meditations on Language and the Self," 292–93.

77. Ibid.

78. Ibid., 293.

79. Georgia Writers' Project, *Drums and Shadows*, 185.

80. Marshall, *Praisesong for the Widow*, 30–35.

81. Georgia Writers' Project, *Drums and Shadows*, 158–72; photo of Hall, xviia.

82. Marshall, *Praisesong for the Widow*, 38–39.

83. Ibid., 67, 107.

84. Ibid., 126, 165.

85. Ibid., 225.

86. Georgia Writers' Project, *Drums and Shadows*, 56, 143.

87. Carabi, "An Interview with Gloria Naylor," 36.

88. Ibid.

89. Ibid.

90. Ashford, "Gloria Naylor on Black Spirituality: An Interview," 81.

91. Ibid., 77.

92. Ibid.

93. Eugenia Collier, "Once Again, the White Liberal to the Rescue," *New York Times*, April 21, 1974, 137; Kevin Kelly, "'Conrack' Is Sad, Sticky Sweetness," *Boston Globe*, April 25, 1974, 69; Greg Mims, "'Conrack'–T'suh Wit Luv?," *New Pittsburgh Courier*, May 4, 1974, 18.

94. Eugenia Collier, "Once Again, the White Liberal to the Rescue," *New York Times*, April 21, 1974, 137.

95. Dash, *Daughters of the Dust: The Making of an African American Woman's Film*, 1–5.

96. Ibid., 5.

97. Ibid., 4–5.

98. Ibid., 6.

99. Ibid., 10, 31.

100. "Interview of Julie Dash by Valerie Smith," 32.

101. Dash, *Daughters of the Dust: The Making of an African American Woman's Film*, 36–37.

102. Ibid., 77.

103. Ibid., 85.

104. Ibid., 81.

105. Ibid., 85.

106. Ibid., 81.

107. Ibid., 80.

108. Georgia Writers' Project, *Drums and Shadows*, 114.

109. Ibid., 160.

110. Ibid., 125, 129, 140, 171, 187, 194, and 48.

111. Dash, *Daughters of the Dust: The Making of an African American Woman's Film*, 86.

112. Georgia Writers' Project, *Drums and Shadows*, 117.

113. Marshall, *Praisesong for the Widow*, 37–38; Dash, *Daughters of the Dust: The Making of an African American Woman's Film*, 141. Dash noted on the script that the Ibo Landing story came from *Praisesong for the Widow*.

114. Dash, *Daughters of the Dust: The Making of an African American Woman's Film*, 99.

115. Georgia Writers' Project, *Drums and Shadows*, 42–43.

116. Ibid., 109.

117. Dash, *Daughters of the Dust: The Making of an African American Woman's Film*, 158.

118. Ibid., 159–60.

119. hooks, "Talking Art with Carrie Mae Weems," 75.

120. Thompson (*Flash of the Spirit*) uses Granger's study—among other sources—to establish the presence of Kongo cosmology in America. Sterling Stuckey's study, *Slave Culture*, includes references to Granger's study and Parrish's book *Slave Songs*. Margaret Washington Creel cites *Drums and Shadows* in her book "*A Peculiar People*," which connects the Gullah's African past to their Christian religious practices and ideologies of resistance during slavery. Julia Floyd Smith references *Drums and Shadows* in her study *Slavery and Rice in Low Country Georgia* as evidence of an African-styled folk culture on Georgia's coast. William McFeely cites Granger's interviews in *Sapelo's People*, a book on his reflections on his encounter with the Islanders and their history. Allan Austin uses *Drums and Shadows* Sapelo Islanders' interviews to reconstruct Bilali Mohammed's life in *African Muslims in Antebellum America*. Michael Gomez similarly draws from the study to explore the island's Muslim past in *Exchanging Our Country Marks*; anthropologist William Pollitzer does the same in his study *The Gullah People and Their African Heritage*; Granger's reports also make an appearance in Philip Morgan's edited collection, *African American Life in the Georgia Lowcountry* (2010).

121. Georgia Writers' Project (*Drums and Shadows*) and Parrish (*Slave Songs*) have become frequently cited sources.

122. For a description of Opala's research capturing the attention of Sierra Leone officials, see the documentary film *The Language You Cry In*, directed by Angel Serrano and Alvaro Toepke (San Francisco, CA: California Newsreel, 1998). The visits to the Low Country and Sierra Leone were announced in "Africans See Their Culture in the U.S. South," *New York Times*, October 25, 1987, 5. Matory (*Black Atlantic Religion*) analyzes these visits.

123. *The Language You Cry In*.

124. Robin Toners, "Bible Is Being Translated into a Southern Coastal Tongue Born of Slavery," *New York Times*, March 1, 1987, A24.

125. Bailey, *God, Dr. Buzzard, and the Bolito Man*, 301.

CHAPTER 6

1. "Gullah/Geechee Cultural Heritage Corridor Public Input Meeting," June 29, 2009, 10:30 A.M., at Sapelo Island Cultural and Revitalization Society on Sapelo Island, Georgia. Transcript recorded by Kathleen Dore, Certified Court Reporter, B-2041; Meeting Discussion 003, lines 1–24 (speaker: Charles Hall), GGCHCDC.

2. Ibid., speaker: Cornelia Bailey, Meeting Discussion 0011, lines 12–17.

3. See Bailey, "Still Gullah," and Bailey, *God, Dr. Buzzard, and the Bolito Man*. The documentaries Bailey appears in are *Will to Survive* (2006) and *This Far by Faith* (2003).

4. "Gullah/Geechee Cultural Heritage Corridor Public Input Meeting," June 29, 2009, 10:30 A.M., at Sapelo Island Cultural and Revitalization Society on Sapelo Island, Georgia. Transcript recorded by Kathleen Dore, Certified Court Reporter, B-2041; Meeting Discussion 0012, lines 8–11 (speaker: Cornelia Bailey), GGCHCDC.

5. Ibid., lines 11–14.

6. "Islanders Worry as Young People Leave," *Miami Herald*, July 21, 1983, 12C.

7. Jingle Davis, "The Haven of Hog Hammock," *Atlanta Journal-Constitution*, June 25, 1995, C/1.

8. Ibid.

9. The legislation that created the Sapelo Island Heritage Authority is cited in "Islanders Worry As Young People Leave," *Miami Herald*, July 21, 1983, 12C.

10. Jingle Davis, "The Haven of Hog Hammock," *Atlanta-Journal Constitution*, June 25, 1995, C/1.

11. John Cheves Morris, "Agency's Intervention Causes Rift," *Augusta Chronicle*, July 4, 1995, C07.

12. Jingle Davis, "The Haven of Hog Hammock," *Atlanta Journal-Constitution*, June 25, 1995, C/1.

13. Ibid.

14. Ibid.

15. Ibid.

16. Jingle Davis, "State Sets Hearings on Sapelo Land Rules—Plan Drawn to Protect Gullah Community," *Atlanta Journal-Constitution*, August 24, 1995.

17. Jingle Davis, "The Haven of Hog Hammock," *Atlanta Journal-Constitution*, June 25, 1995, C/1.

18. John Cheves Morris, "Agency's Intervention Causes Rift," *Augusta Chronicle*, July 4, 1995, C07.

19. Jingle Davis, "The Haven of Hog Hammock," *Atlanta Journal-Constitution*, June 25, 1995, C/1, and "State Sets Hearings on Sapelo Land Rules—Plan Drawn to Protect Gullah Community," *Atlanta Journal-Constitution*, August 24, 1995.

20. Roger Soiset, Letter to the Editor, "Culture Evolves," *Atlanta Journal-Constitution*, July 2, 1995, B/6.

21. Ibid.

22. Ibid.

23. Jingle Davis, "The Haven of Hog Hammock," *Atlanta Journal-Constitution*, June 25, 1995, C/1. The *Augusta Chronicle* article states that Hog Hammock residents "resent the DNR for restricting blacks as well as whites, and for making its decisions without input from the islanders themselves." John Cheves Morris, "Agency's Intervention Causes Rift," *Augusta Chronicle*, July 4, 1995, C07.

24. John Cheves Morris, "Agency's Intervention Causes Rift," *Augusta Chronicle*, July 4, 1995, C07.

25. Ibid.

26. Ibid.

27. Ibid.

28. Ibid.

29. Ibid.

30. Ibid.

31. Author interview with Paul Walker.

32. Ibid.

33. Ibid.

34. Ibid.

35. Ibid.

36. Mitchell ("From Reconstruction to Deconstruction," 507) cites the acreage that black southerners acquired in the decades that followed the Civil War.

37. Foner (*Reconstruction*, 109) discusses blacks' desire to own land in the post–Civil War South; Hahn (*A Nation Under Our Feet*, 173, 239–41) discusses the importance of land ownership to newly freedmen and freedwomen in the South — and includes discussion of the way this aspiration was expressed in political activities in McIntosh County, Georgia, which includes Sapelo Island. See McFeely (*Sapelo's People*, 141) for a discussion of William Hillery, John Grovenor, and Bilally Bell's land company.

38. Author interview with Paul Walker.

39. Several researchers have suggested that Low Country blacks did not leave wills, perhaps, because it was an African survival of sorts — an expression of a preference for communal property. See Cross, *Gullah Culture in America*, 78; Dyer and Bailey, "A Place to Call Home," 318. However, I argue that other forces played a more significant role in the trend.

40. Author interview with Paul Walker.

41. The following studies examine, among other things, the difficulties that blacks in the South have faced when trying to hold on to land and the perils of heirs' property: Kahrl, *The Land Was Ours*; Marable, "The Politics of Black Land Tenure"; Mitchell, "Reforming Property Law to Address Devastating Land Loss" and "From Reconstruction to Deconstruction; and Dyer and Bailey, "A Place to Call Home."

42. Kahrl, *The Land Was Ours*.

43. Conley (*Being Black, Living in the Red*) offers a critical review of racialized wealth gaps in America.

44. Satter (*Family Properties*) and Connolly (*A World More Concrete*) are two more-recent studies that examine the convergence of race, class, and real estate in American history.

45. "Metro Georgia in Brief: Sapelo Vote Delayed," *Atlanta Journal-Constitution*, September 28, 1995, C/6.

46. Ibid.

47. Ibid.

48. "Rules Aim at Protecting Sapelo Island's Beauty," *Atlanta-Journal Constitution*, January 25, 1996, B1.

49. In July 1996, applications were filed with the National Register of Historic Places to include Sapelo's Hog Hammock, First African Baptist Church, and Behavior Cemetery on its registry. See the National Register of Historic Places digital database for applications submitted by Kenneth H. Thomas Jr. of the Historic Preservation Division, Georgia Department of Natural Resources.

50. Bailey, "Still Gullah," 134.

51. Ibid.

52. Ibid.

53. Bailey, *God, Dr. Buzzard, and the Bolito Man*, is a good example of the balance that she strikes in storytelling.

54. Ibid.

55. Ibid.

56. Dana Clark, "Geechee Champion to Be Awarded $115,000—Ford Foundation Honors Carolyn Dowse of Sapelo Island Cultural And Revitalization Society for Her Preservation Work," *Savannah Morning News*, October 12, 2004, 1B.

57. Ibid.

58. Ibid.

59. Ibid.

60. Lee Shearer, "Hog Hammock Community Struggles for Survival," *Athens Banner-Herald*, June 1, 2002, section: UGA Life.

61. Heather Duncan, "Tied to the Land: African-Influenced Culture Fighting to Stay Alive on the Coast," *Macon Telegraph*, September 22, 2003, 4.

62. Queen Quet discussed her motivations for addressing the United Nations in an oral history interview conducted by Rachel Martin, "Queen Quet, Carlie Towne, Lesa Wineglass-Smalls, Halim Gullahbemi," Interview Number U-0399, SOHPC, 2.

63. Ibid.

64. Ibid.

65. For more on Queen Quet's use of the Internet to organize, see oral history interview conducted by Rachel Martin, "Queen Quet, Carlie Towne, Lesa Wineglass-Smalls, Halim Gullahbemi," Interview Number U-0399, SOHPC, 14. "Queen Quet Steps away from the Keyboard to Become Gullah/Geechee Head of State," *Charleston City Paper*, September 5, 2012, reported on an interview with Queen Quet and indicated that she attended Fordham University and Columbia University to study math and computer science.

66. The Gullah/Geechee Sea Island Coalition's work with Native American nations is mentioned in "Save the Gullah, Tell the World Coalition Preserves Native S.C. Culture," *Florida-Times Union*, December 19, 1999, B-1. Scholars have explored connections between black Seminoles and Gullah folk; see, for example, Amos, "Black Seminoles."

67. Oral history interview conducted by Rachel Martin, "Queen Quet, Carlie Towne, Lesa Wineglass-Smalls, Halim Gullahbemi," Interview Number U-0399, SOHPC, 3–5.

68. Ibid., 13.

69. Ibid.

70. Oral history interview conducted by Rachel Martin, "Michael Allen," Interview Number U-0394, SOHPC, 19.

71. Ibid.

72. Ibid., 19–20.

73. Ibid.

74. Ibid., 7.

75. See Merringolo (*Museums, Monuments, and National Parks*) for more on the history of the National Park Service.

76. Author interview with Congressman James E. Clyburn.

77. Ibid.

78. Ibid.

79. Ibid.

80. Ibid.

81. Oral history interview conducted by Rachel Martin, "Michael Allen," Interview Number U-0394, SOHPC, 7.

82. The "National Park Service Study Act of 1999" included "Low Country Gullah Culture, multi-state" among the list of study areas (H.R. 3423, Interior Appropriations).

83. Oral history interview conducted by Rachel Martin, "Michael Allen," Interview Number U-0394, SOHPC, 7.

84. National Park Service, *Low Country Gullah*, 246. The document features a complete list of the study team, which identifies Porcher as the "Principal Researcher."

85. Ibid., 6.

86. Oral history interview conducted by Rachel Martin, "Queen Quet, Carlie Towne, Lesa Wineglass-Smalls, Halim Gullahbemi," Interview Number U-0399, SOHPC, 32.

87. Ibid., 33–34.

88. Ibid., 34.

89. Audra Burch, "A Culture at Risk: The Low-Profile Gullah Community, Descended from African Slaves, Is Fighting for the Preservation of Its Ways," *Miami Herald*, November 30, 2003, 1A; Dan Huntley, "Reversing the Tide against the Gullah—National Park Service Completing Study That Could Save the Culture," *Charlotte Observer*, March 3, 2002, 1A.

90. Dan Huntley, "Reversing the Tide Against the Gullah—National Park Service Completing Study That Could Save the Culture," *Charlotte Observer*, March 3, 2002, 1A.

91. Ibid.

92. Robert Behre, "Preserving Gullah Culture Is Aim of Federal Agency," *Charleston Post and Courier*, December 26, 2005, B1.

93. Ibid.

94. Audra Burch, "A Culture at Risk: The Low-Profile Gullah Community, Descended from African Slaves, Is Fighting for the Preservation of Its Ways," *Miami Herald*, November 30, 2003, 1A.

95. National Park Service, *Low Country Gullah*, 1–6.

96. Ibid., 3.

97. The section of the published report that discusses how the report was composed does not list or identify the Gullah/Geechee experts who reviewed the document. However, two scholars, professors William Pollitzer and Richard A. Long, offered research and

a statement of significance that supported the study. See National Park Service, *Low Country Gullah*, 9.

98. Ibid., 13.

99. Ibid., 1. Anthropologist Matory ("The Illusion of Isolation") directly challenges what he describes as the "myth of isolation" with regard to the Gullah.

100. National Park Service, *Low Country Gullah*, 10.

101. In the special section that he prepared for the NPS special resource study (National Park Service, *Low Country Gullah*, D1) and in the introduction to his *The Gullah People* (17) Pollitzer admitted that he knew little about black life on the coast.

102. See Wailoo and Nelson (*Genetics and the Unsettled Past*) for larger discussions of the tension between genetic research, history, and racial identity and categories in contemporary science. Pollitzer did not see himself making a "traditional" argument about biology and race; he envisioned "genes" as a more reliable measure of sameness and difference than morphology (National Park Service, *Low Country Gullah*, D2).

103. Pollitzer, *The Gullah People*, 13–21.

104. National Park Service, *Low Country Gullah*, 11. The report also noted that they included two additional bibliographies in the appendix that itemized other works written about the Gullah and black history and culture in the Low Country.

105. The section of the study titled "Demographic History," which contains fewer than five pages, is the only section of the document in which the authors argue that the Gullah had been "genetically isolated" (National Park Service, *Low Country Gullah*, 51–55).

106. Ibid., 13–51.

107. Ibid.

108. Ibid., 75–81.

109. Ibid., 43–49.

110. Ibid., 55–81.

111. Ibid., 49.

112. Ibid.

113. Ibid., 100.

114. Professor Long's letter can be found in ibid., 101–3.

115. Ibid., 2.

116. Ibid.

117. Ibid., 107–35.

118. Each alternative is presented with cost estimates; see ibid., 134–35.

119. Ibid., 136.

120. Ibid.

121. Ibid.

122. "Heritage Areas 101: Place-Based Community-Driven Conservation & Economic Development," National Park Service, U.S. Department of the Interior, April 2012, 1, http://ca-contracostacounty.civicplus.com/DocumentCenter/Home/View/6364 (accessed September 8, 2016).

123. National Park Service, *Low Country Gullah*, 93–100.

124. Ibid., 6; Queen Quet also discussed the fact that some community members were reluctant to be recorded and were uncomfortable with Porcher (oral history interview

conducted by Rachel Martin, "Queen Quet, Carlie Towne, Lesa Wineglass-Smalls, Halim Gullahbemi," Interview Number U-0399, SOHPC, 32–33.

125. National Park Service, *Low Country Gullah*, 93–99.

126. Davis, "Unless God Take My Life."

127. National Park Service, *Low Country Gullah*, 9.

128. Clyburn, *Blessed Experiences*, 262.

129. Ibid., 262–63.

130. Gullah Geechee Cultural Heritage Corridor Commission, *Gullah Geechee Cultural Heritage Corridor*, 13.

131. National Park Service News Release, "Commissioners Named for Gullah-Geechee Cultural Heritage Corridor," October 22, 2007, http://anthropology.usf.edu/faculty /personal/publications/Press%20Release%20Gullah-Geechee.pdf (accessed September 8, 2016).

132. Ibid.

133. Ibid.

134. Ibid.

135. Gullah/Geechee Cultural Heritage Corridor Commission, "Cultural Management Plan Newsletter #1," February 2009, National Park Service website, https://parkplanning .nps.gov/document.cfm?parkID=423&projectID=24119&documentID=25847 (access date September 8, 2016).

136. "Gullah/Geechee Cultural Heritage Corridor Public Input Meeting," May 5, 2009, Atlantic Beach, SC. Transcript recorded by Melissa M. Decker, Certified Court Reporter (commenter, Commissioner Veronica Gerald), pp. 11–12, GGCHCDC.

137. Court reporters transcribed the comments made at the public meetings held between February and August 2009, and these transcripts can be accessed on the GGCHC's digital archive of public meetings on their website. The National Park Service public scoping comment analysis report produced from the transcriptions—"Gullah/Geechee Cultural Heritage Corridor Public Scoping Analysis Report," October 15, 2009—can also be retrieved from the GGCHC digital collection.

138. GGCHC Public Input February 2009–August 2009 transcripts, GGCHCDC. The "Gullah/Geechee Cultural Heritage Corridor Public Scoping Analysis Report," October 15, 2009, GGCHCDC, also indicated that the vast majority of comments made at public input meetings and communicated on comment cards, emails, and letters reflect these themes.

139. "Gullah/Geechee Cultural Heritage Corridor Public Input Meeting," July 7, 2009, Johns Island, SC. Transcript recorded by Mary Ann Ridenour, Certified Court Reporter (commenter, Mr. Jenkins), comment 00259–00263, GGCHCDC.

140. "Gullah/Geechee Cultural Heritage Corridor Public Input Meeting," April 7, 2009, Georgetown, SC. Transcript recorded by Melissa M. Decker, Certified Court Reporter (commenter, Ms. Carr), p. 35, GGCHCDC.

141. GGCHC Public Input February 2009–August 2009 transcripts, GGCHCDC.

142. "Gullah/Geechee Cultural Heritage Corridor Public Input Meeting," June 2, 2009, Savannah, GA. Transcript recorded by Kathleen Dore, Certified Court Reporter (commenter, Ms. Dixon), p. 46, GGCHCDC.

143. "Gullah/Geechee Cultural Heritage Corridor Public Input Meeting," June 9, 2009,

Savannah, GA. Transcript recorded by Kathleen Dore, Certified Court Reporter (commenter, Ms. Kadalie), comment 0017, GGCHCDC.

144. Gullah/Geechee Cultural Heritage Corridor Public Input Meeting," June 5, 2009, Mount Pleasant, SC. Transcript recorded by Mary Ann Ridenour, Certified Court Reporter (commenter, Mr. Wilder), comment 00020–00022; (commenter, Mr. Freeman), comment 00025, GGCHCDC.

145. Gullah/Geechee Cultural Heritage Corridor Public Input Meeting," June 5, 2009, Mount Pleasant, SC. Transcript recorded by Mary Ann Ridenour, Certified Court Reporter, (commenter, Ms. Carter), comment 00037–00043.

146. Ibid.

147. Ibid.

148. "Gullah/Geechee Cultural Heritage Corridor Public Input Meeting," April 28, 2009, Conway, SC. Transcript recorded by Melissa M. Decker, Certified Court Reporter (commenters, Ms. Rodgers and Mr. Gilliard), pp. 19, 57, GGCHCDC.

149. "Gullah/Geechee Cultural Heritage Corridor Public Input Meeting," April 27, 2009, McClellanville, SC. Transcript recorded by Melissa M. Decker, Certified Court Reporter (commenter, Ms. McCormick), p. 52, GGCHCDC.

150. "Gullah/Geechee Cultural Heritage Corridor Public Input Meeting," June 9, 2009, Savannah, GA. Transcript recorded by Kathleen Dore, Certified Court Reporter (commenter, Mr. Grant), comment 0035–0038, GGCHCDC.

151. "Gullah/Geechee Cultural Heritage Corridor Public Input Meeting," June 9, 2009, Savannah, GA. Transcript recorded by Kathleen Dore, Certified Court Reporter (commenter, Ms. Gumb), comment 0057, GGCHCDC.

152. "Gullah/Geechee Cultural Heritage Corridor Public Input Meeting," June 9, 2009, Savannah, GA. Transcript recorded by Kathleen Dore, Certified Court Reporter (commenter, Ms. Brown), comment 0017–0018.

153. "Gullah/Geechee Cultural Heritage Corridor Public Input Meeting," June 26, 2009, Darien, GA. Transcript recorded by Kathleen Dore, Certified Court Reporter (commenter, Ms. Collins), pp. 14–15.

154. Ibid., 16–18.

155. "Gullah/Geechee Cultural Heritage Corridor Public Input Meeting," June 5, 2009, Mount Pleasant, SC. Transcript recorded by Mary Ann Ridenour, Certified Court Reporter (commenter, Ms. Goesthceus), comment 00049–00051, GGCHCDC.

156. "Gullah/Geechee Cultural Heritage Corridor Public Input Meeting," June 16, 2009, St. Helena, SC. Transcript recorded by Mary Ann Ridenour, Certified Court Reporter (commenter, Mr. Barnwell), comment 00090, GGCHCDC.

157. "Gullah/Geechee Cultural Heritage Corridor Public Input Meeting," June 26, 2009, Darien, GA. Transcript recorded by Kathleen Dore, Certified Court Reporter (commenter, Mr. Grant), pp. 44–45, GGCHCDC.

158. National Park Service, *Low Country Gullah*, 86–87.

159. "Gullah/Geechee Cultural Heritage Corridor Public Input Meeting," June 29, 2009, Sapelo Island, GA. Transcript recorded by Kathleen Dore, Certified Court Reporter (commenter, Commissioner Cyriaque), comment 0007, GGCHCDC.

160. Gullah/Geechee Cultural Heritage Corridor Public Input Meeting," June 29, 2009,

Sapelo Island, GA. Transcript recorded by Kathleen Dore, Certified Court Reporter (various comments), GGCHCDC.

161. Gullah/Geechee Cultural Heritage Corridor Public Input Meeting," June 29, 2009, Sapelo Island, GA. Transcript recorded by Kathleen Dore, Certified Court Reporter (commenter, Mr. Benjamin Hall), comment 0009, GGCHCDC.

162. Gullah/Geechee Cultural Heritage Corridor Public Input Meeting," June 29, 2009, Sapelo Island, GA. Transcript recorded by Kathleen Dore, Certified Court Reporter (commenter, Mr. Reginald Hall), comment 0017. Mr. Hall also commented at the meeting in Georgetown, SC, on May 14, 2009. Transcript recorded by Melissa M. Decker, Certified Court Reporter, pp. 43–47, GGCHCDC.

163. Gullah/Geechee Cultural Heritage Corridor Public Input Meeting," June 29, 2009, Sapelo Island, GA. Transcript recorded by Kathleen Dore, Certified Court Reporter (commenter, Mr. Dixon), comment 0029, GGCHCDC.

164. Gullah/Geechee Cultural Heritage Corridor Public Input Meeting," June 29, 2009, Sapelo Island, GA. Transcript recorded by Kathleen Dore, Certified Court Reporter (commenter, Mr. Hall), comment 0017–0023, GGCHCDC.

165. Gullah/Geechee Cultural Heritage Corridor Public Input Meeting," June 29, 2009, Sapelo Island, GA. Transcript recorded by Kathleen Dore, Certified Court Reporter (commenter, Mr. Walker), comment 0032–0033, GGCHCDC.

166. Gullah/Geechee Cultural Heritage Corridor Public Input Meeting," June 29, 2009, Sapelo Island, GA. Transcript recorded by Kathleen Dore, Certified Court Reporter (commenter, Mr. Grovenor), comment 0033–0034, GGCHCDC.

167. Gullah Geechee Heritage Corridor Commission, *Gullah Geechee Cultural Heritage Corridor*, 1.

168. Ibid., 17.

169. Ibid., 98–101.

170. Ibid., 116.

171. Ibid., 170–82.

172. Ibid., 183–84.

173. National Park Service, *Low Country Gullah*, 87.

174. Ibid., 94–95.

175. Ibid.

EPILOGUE

1. Gullah/Geechee Cultural Heritage Corridor Public Input Meeting," June 29, 2009, Sapelo Island, GA. Transcript recorded by Kathleen Dore, Certified Court Reporter (commenter, Mrs. Cornelia Bailey), comment 0037, GGCHCDC.

2. Numerous articles and news reports chronicling Sapelo Islanders' land fight have been featured in local, national, and international news outlets—too many to discuss here.

3. Shaila Dewan, "A Georgia Community with an African Feel Fights a Wave of Change," *New York Times*, May 4, 2008.

4. Ibid.

5. Ibid. The SIHA had leased 1.13 acres to Emmitt and Emma Johnson's grandson in 1997 for an annual payment of $320—an arrangement that could be passed on to his de-

scendants—with the caveat that he could not sell or sublet land (Lawrence Viele, "Descendants Given Lease on Hog Hammock," *Florida Times-Union*, January 23, 1997, B-1), but Dewan told the story of another Sapelo descendant who tried to secure a lease, the SIHA "said it would limit her to a 25-year lease at market rates," while "a non-descendant who had bought an interest in some land in the state's wildlife management area was allowed to swap it for a 60-year lease in Hog Hammock."

6. Kim Severson, "Taxes Threaten Culture in Georgia," *New York Times*, September 25, 2012; NPR *Tell Me More* segment titled "Property Taxes Causing Slaves' Descendants to Lose Homes," October 9, 2013; CNN segment titled "Property Tax Avalanche Threatens Homeowners on Historic Coastal Island," October 28, 2013.

7. Kim Severson, "Taxes Threaten Culture in Georgia," *New York Times*, September 25, 2012.

8. Ibid.

9. CNN segment titled "Property Tax Avalanche Threatens Homeowners on Historic Coastal Island," October 28, 2013.

10. Ibid. The quote appears in the video segment at 2:39.

11. ESPN segment titled "OTL: Sapelo Island," February 24, 2013.

12. Mike Morrison, "Sapelo Man Decries Buildings: He Says the Vacation Homes Don't Mesh with the Historic Homes on the Island," *Florida Times-Union*, December 9, 2009, B-1.

13. Ibid.

14. Ibid.

15. "Sapelo Island Birdhouses Luxury Island Vacation Rental Cottages," Sapelo Island Birdhouses, http://sapeloislandbirdhouses.com/sapelo-island-birdhouse-cottages.html (accessed October 14, 2015).

16. Dixon, "The Heart of Sapelo."

17. Ibid., 125.

18. Ibid.

19. Ibid.

20. "Sapelo Island Birdhouses Luxury Island Vacation Rental Cottages: Our Mission . . . is our passion," Sapelo Island Birdhouses, http://sapeloislandbirdhouses.com/our -mission.html (accessed October 14, 2015).

21. Dixon, "The Heart of Sapelo."

22. Sapelo Island Birdhouses Luxury Island Vacation Rental Cottages: Our Mission . . . is our passion," Sapelo Island Birdhouses, http://sapeloislandbirdhouses.com/our -mission.html (accessed October 14, 2015).

23. "Sapelo Island Birdhouses Luxury Island Vacation Rental Cottages: The Teacake Cottage Suite at BJ Confectionary," Sapelo Island Birdhouses, http://sapeloislandbird houses.com/the-tea-cake-cottage-suite.html (accessed October 14, 2015).

24. Ibid.

25. Sapelo Island Birdhouses Luxury Island Vacation Rental Cottages: Our Mission . . . is our passion," Sapelo Island Birdhouses, http://sapeloislandbirdhouses.com/our -mission.html (accessed October 14, 2015); Dixon, "The Heart of Sapelo," 125.

26. Dixon, "The Heart of Sapelo."

27. Ibid. *Targeted News Service* announced the sugarcane project in an article titled "Clemson Joins Effort to Reintroduce Sugarcane to Sapelo Island," May 25, 2015.

28. "Clemson Joins Effort to Reintroduce Sugarcane to Sapelo Island," *Targeted News Service*, May 25, 2015.

29. "Human Tests Suggest Contamination from Superfund Site Stretches at Least 25 Miles," December 1, 2014, http://www.thebrunswicknews.com/news/local_news/human-tests-suggest-contamination-from-superfund-site-stretches-at-least/article_71224c1c-dea9-52d2-bed6-fcd7b4b23841.html (accessed October 17, 2015); Al Jazeera America, "Locals, Activists Slam EPA Proposal to Clean Georgia Superfund Site," January 12, 2015, http://america.aljazeera.com/articles/2015/1/12/georgia-pollutionlcpsuperfund.html (accessed October 17, 2015), chronicle growing concerns about contamination in the region.

30. Centers for Disease Control Fact Sheet, "Comparing Environmental Chemical Levels in Dolphins, Fish and People: A Sample of Sapelo Island Residents," http://www.cdc.gov/nceh/hsb/cwh/Sapelo_study_factsheet.pdf.

31. Ibid.

32. Ibid.

33. Ibid.

34. Al Jazeera America, "Locals, Activists Slam EPA Proposal to Clean Georgia Superfund Site," January 12, 2015, http://america.aljazeera.com/articles/2015/1/12/georgia-pollutionlcpsuperfund.html (accessed October 17, 2015).

35. Ibid.

36. Parrish, *Slave Songs*, 166–67.

BIBLIOGRAPHY

ARCHIVAL COLLECTIONS

Barnard College Archives, New York, New York
    Mary L. Granger Records
Georgia Historical Society, Savannah, Georgia
    Federal Writers' Project Savannah Unit Papers
    Mary L. Granger Papers
Gullah Geechee Cultural Heritage Corridor Digital Collection of Public Meeting
    Transcripts, www.gullahgeecheecorridor.org
HBO Digital Archives
    The March of Time newsreel series
Library of Congress, Washington, DC
    Federal Writers' Project Collection
Melville J. Herskovits Library of African Studies, Northwestern University, Evanston,
    Illinois
    Melville Herskovits Papers
    Lorenzo D. Turner Papers
National Archives and Records Administration, College Park, Maryland
    Federal Writers' Project Collection
National Geographic Society, Washington, DC
South Carolina Historical Society, Charleston, South Carolina
    Julia Peterkin Papers
    Society for the Preservation of Spirituals Papers
University of North Carolina–Chapel Hill, Louis Round Wilson Special Collections
    Library, Southern Oral History Program Collection, The Southern Historical
    Collection
    Interview Number U-0394
    Interview Number U-0399
University of South Carolina Moving Image Research Archive, Columbia, South Carolina
    Fox Movietone Collection

NEWSPAPERS

Athens Banner-Herald
Atlanta Daily World
Atlanta Journal-Constitution
Augusta Chronicle
Charleston Post-Courier
Charlotte Observer
Chicago Daily Tribune
Chicago Defender
Daily Boston Globe
The Liberator
Los Angeles Sentinel
Macon Telegraph
Miami Herald
New York Amsterdam News
New York Times
Pittsburgh Courier
Savannah Morning News
Savannah News
South Carolina Gazette
Washington Post

INTERVIEWS BY THE AUTHOR
Cornelia Walker Bailey, July 3, 2009
Betty Johnson Cooper, April 9, 2010
Congressman James E. Clyburn, July 1, 2014
Harvey Granger, June 30, 2009
Anne Heard, July 23, 2009
Catherine Hillery, July 3, 2009
Fred Johnson, August 9, 2005
Joe Johnson, July 1, 2009
Ruth Johnson, August 8, 2002
Paul Walker, June 4, 2009

BOOKS, ARTICLES, THESES, AND DISSERTATIONS
Amos, Alcione M. "Black Seminoles: The Gullah Connections." *Black Scholar* 41, no. 1 (2011): 32–47.
Anderson, David. "Down Memory Lane: Nostalgia for the Old South in Post–Civil War Plantation Reminiscences." *Journal of Southern History* 71, no. 1 (2005): 105–36.
Anderson, Jeffrey E. *Conjure in African American Society.* Baton Rouge: Louisiana State University Press, 2005.
Ashford, Tomeiko R. "Gloria Naylor on Black Spirituality: An Interview." MELUS 30, no. 4 (2005): 73–87.
Austin, Allan. *African Muslims in Antebellum America: Transatlantic Stories and Spiritual Struggles.* New York: Routledge, 1997.
Bailey, Cornelia Walker. *God, Dr. Buzzard, and the Bolito Man: A Saltwater Geechee Talks about Life on Sapelo Island, Georgia.* New York: Anchor Books, 2000.
———. "Still Gullah." *Essence,* February 1998, 134.
Baker, Lee. *Anthropology and the Racial Politics of Culture.* Durham, NC: Duke University Press, 2010.
———. *From Savage to Negro: Anthropology and the Construction of Race, 1896–1954.* Berkeley: University of California Press, 1998.
Baldwin, Davarian. "Black Belts and Ivory Towers: The Place of Race in U.S. Social Thought, 1892–1948." *Critical Sociology* 30, no. 2 (2004): 397–451.
Bancroft, Hubert Howe. *The Book of the Fair: An Historical and Descriptive Presentation of the World's Science, Art and Industry, as Viewed through the Columbian Exposition at Chicago in 1893.* Vol. 3. Chicago: Bancroft Company, Publishers, 1893.
Baritz, Loren. *The Culture of the Twenties.* New York: Bobbs-Merril, 1970.
Bascom, William R. "Acculturation Among the Gullah Negroes." *American Anthropologist* 43, no. 1 (1941): 43–50.
Bay, Mia. *White Image in the Black Mind: African-American Ideas about White People, 1830–1925.* New York: Oxford University Press, 2000.
Bederman, Gail. *Manliness and Civilization: A Cultural History of Gender and Race in the United States, 1880–1917.* Chicago: University of Chicago Press, 1995.
Bennett, John. "Gullah: A Negro Patois." *South Atlantic Quarterly* 7, no. 4 (1908): 332–47.
Benyon, Ederman Doane. "The Voodoo Cult among Negro Migrants in Detroit." *American Journal of Sociology* 43, no. 6 (1938): 894–907.

Biondi, Martha. *The Black Revolution on Campus*. Berkeley: University of California Press, 2012.

Blassingame, John W. *The Slave Community: Plantation Life in the Antebellum South*. New York: Oxford University Press, 1972.

Blockson, Charles L. "Sea Change in the Sea Islands: 'Nowhere to Lay Down Weary Head.'" *National Geographic* 172, no. 6 (December 1987): 734–63.

Boas, Franz. *The Mind of Primitive Man*. New York: Macmillan, 1921.

Bold, Chrsitine. *WPA Guides: Mapping America*. Jackson: University of Mississippi Press, 1999.

Bowen, T. J. *Central Africa and Adventures and Missionary Labors in Several Countries in the Interior of Africa: From 1849 to 1856*. Charleston Southern Baptist Publication Society, 1857.

Boyd, Valerie. *Wrapped in Rainbows: The Life of Zora Neale Hurston*. New York: Scribner, 2003.

Brantlinger, Patrick. "Victorians and Africans: The Genealogy of the Myth of the Dark Continent." *Critical Inquiry* 12, no. 1 (Autumn 1985): 166–203.

Brown, Sterling. "Arcadia of the South." *Opportunity: Journal of Negro Life* 12 (1934): 59–60.

Carabi, Angels. "An Interview with Gloria Naylor." *Belles Lettres: A Review of Books by Women* 7, no. 3 (Spring 1992): 36–42.

Cartwright, Keith. *Reading Africa into American Literature: Epics, Fables, and Gothic Tales*. Lexington: University Press of Kentucky, 2002.

Cerruti, James. "Sea Islands: Adventuring along the South's Surprising Coast." *National Geographic Magazine*, March 1971, 367–92.

Chapman, Erin D. *Prove It on Me: New Negroes, Sex, and Popular Culture in the 1920s*. New York: Oxford University Press, 2012.

Chireau, Yvonne Patricia. *Black Magic: Religion and the African American Conjuring Tradition*. Berkeley: University of California Press, 2003.

Clyburn, James. *Blessed Experiences: Genuinely Southern, Proudly Black*. Columbia: University of South Carolina Press, 2014.

Conley, Dalton. *Being Black Living in the Red: Race, Wealth, and Social Policy in America*. Berkeley: University of California Press, 1999.

Connolly, Nathan. *A World More Concrete: Real Estate and the Remaking of Jim Crow South Florida*. Chicago: University of Chicago Press, 2014.

Corbould, Clare. *Becoming African Americans: Black Public Life in Harlem*. Cambridge: Harvard University Press, 2009.

Creel, Margaret Washington. *"A Peculiar People": Slave Religion and Community among the Gullahs*. New York: New York University Press, 1988.

Crook, Ray, Cornelia Bailey, Norma Harris, and Karen Smith. *Sapelo Voices: Historical Anthropology and the Oral Traditions of Gullah Geechee Communities on Sapelo Island, Georgia*. Carrolton: State University of West Georgia, 2003.

Crum, Mason. *Gullah: Negro Life in the Carolina Sea Islands*. Durham, NC: Duke University Press, 1940.

Dagbovie, Pero. *What Is African American History?* Cambridge: Polity Press, 2015.

Daniels, John. *In Freedom's Birthplace: A Study of the Boston Negroes*. Boston: Houghton Mifflin, 1914.

Darby, Loraine. "Ring Games from Georgia." *Journal of American Folklore* 30 (1917): 218–21.

Dash, Julie. *Daughters of the Dust*. Screenplay. 1991.

——. *Daughters of the Dust: The Making of an African American Woman's Film*. New York: The New Press, 1992.

Davis, Michael K. "Unless God Take My Life, I'm Going to Be at Those Meetings: A Rhetorical Analysis of the 2000 National Park Service Low Country Gullah Special Resource Study." PhD dissertation, University of Georgia, 2005.

Deburg, William L. Van. *A New Day in Babylon: The Black Power Movement and American Culture, 1965–1975*. Chicago: University of Chicago Press, 1992.

Deloria, Philip. *Playing Indian*. New Haven: Yale University Press, 1998.

Dilworth, Leah. *Imagining Indians in the Southwest: Persistent Visions of a Primitive Past*. Washington, DC: Smithsonian Institution Press, 1996.

Dixon, Charles. "The Heart of Sapelo." *Garden and Gun*, June/July 2015, 120–25.

Dorsey, Allison. "'The Great Cry of Our People Is Land!' Black Settlement and Community Development on Ossawbaw Island, Georgia, 1865–1900." In *African American Life in the Georgia Lowcountry: The Atlantic World and the Gullah Geechee*, edited by Philip Morgan, 224–52. Athens: University of Georgia Press, 2010.

Douglas, Ann. *Terrible Honesty: Mongrel Manhattan in the 1920s*. New York: Farrar, Straus and Giroux, 1995.

Dubey, Madhu. *Black Women Novelists and the Nationalist Aesthetic*. Bloomington: Indiana University Press, 1994.

Du Bois, W. E. B. *The Souls of Black Folk*. Chicago: A. C. McClurg, 1903.

Dumenil, Lynn. *The Modern Temper: American Culture and Society in the 1920s*. New York: Hill and Wang, 1995.

Duncan, Russell. *Freedom's Shore: Tunis Campbell and the Georgia Freedmen*. Athens: University of Georgia Press, 1986.

Durham, Frank. *Collected Short Stories of Julia Peterkin*. Columbia: University of South Carolina Press, 1970.

Dyer, Janice, and Conner Bailey. "A Place to Call Home: Cultural Understandings of Heir Property among Rural African Americans." *Rural Sociology* 73, no. 3 (2008): 317–38.

Erenberg, Lewis A., and Susan Hirsch. *The War in American Culture: Society and Consciousness during World War II*. Chicago: University of Chicago Press, 1996.

Favor, J. Martin. *The Folk in the New Negro Renaissance*. Durham, NC: Duke University Press, 1999.

Foner, Eric. *Reconstruction: America's Unfinished Revolution, 1863–1877*. New York: Harper & Row, 1988.

Ford, Tanisha. *Liberated Threads: Black Women, Style, and the Global Politics of Soul*. Chapel Hill: University of North Carolina Press, 2015.

Frazier, E. Franklin. "The Changing Status of the Negro Family." *Social Forces* 9 (1931): 386–93.

——. "A Folk Culture in the Making." *Southern Workman* 51, no. 6 (1928): 195–99.

——. *The Negro Family in the United States*. Chicago: University of Chicago Press, 1939.

——. Review of *The American Negro: A Study in Racial Crossing*, by Melville J. Herskovits. *American Journal of Sociology* 33, no. 6 (1928): 1010–12.

Fredrickson, George M. *The Black Image in the White Mind: The Debate on Afro-American Character and Destiny, 1817–1914*. New York: Harper & Row, 1971.

Gabbin, Joannes V. *Sterling Brown: Building the Black Aesthetic Tradition*. Charlottesville: University of Virginia Press, 1994.

Georgia Writers' Project, Savannah Unit. *Drums and Shadows: Survival Studies Among the Georgia Coastal Negroes*. Athens: University of Georgia Press, 1940.

Gershenhorn, Jerry. *Melville J. Herskovits and the Racial Politics of Knowledge*. Lincoln: University of Nebraska Press, 2004.

Gillis, John. *Islands of Mind: How Human Imagination Created the Atlantic World*. New York: Palgrave-Macmillian, 2004.

Gitbens, Peter. "The New Books." *Life*, January 18, 1929, 33.

Glazer, Nathan, and Daniel P. Moynihan. *Beyond the Melting Pot: The Negroes, Puerto Ricans, Jews, Italians, and Irish of New York City*. Cambridge: MIT Press, 1963.

Glicksberg, Charles I. "Negro Americans and the African Dream." *Phylon* 8, no. 4 (1947): 323–30.

———. "The Negro Cult of the Primitive." *Antioch Review* 4, no. 1 (1944): 44–55.

Gomez, Michael. *Exchanging Our Country Mark: Transformation of African Identities in the Colonial and Antebellum South*. Chapel Hill: University of North Carolina Press, 1998.

———. "Muslims in Early America." *Journal of Southern History* 60, no. 4 (November 1994): 671–710.

Gonzales, Ambrose. *The Black Border: Gullah Stories of the Carolina Coast*. Columbia, SC: The State Company, 1922.

Graulich, Melody, and Lisa Sisco. "Meditations on Language and the Self: A Conversation with Paule Marshall." *NWSA Journal* 4, no. 3 (1992): 282–302.

Gray, Jeremy, Jeff Davis, and China Williams. *Lonely Planet: Georgia and the Carolinas*. Melbourne: Lonely Planet Publications, 2002.

Greenberg, Joseph. "The Decipherment of the 'Ben-Ali Diary,' a Preliminary Statement." *Journal of Negro History* 25, no. 3 (July 1940): 372–75.

Greene, Melissa Fay. *Praying for Sheetrock: A Work of Nonfiction*. Reading, MA: Addison-Wesley, 1991.

Gregory, James. *The Southern Diaspora: How the Great Migrations of Black and White Southerners Transformed America*. Chapel Hill: University of North Carolina Press, 2005.

Gullah Geechee Cultural Heritage Corridor Commission. *Gullah Geechee Heritage Corridor Management Plan*. National Park Service, Denver Service Center, 2012.

Hahn, Steven. *A Nation under Our Feet: Black Political Struggles in the Rural South from Slavery to the Great Migration*. Cambridge: Harvard University Press, 2003.

Hale, Grace Elizabeth. *Making Whiteness: The Culture of Segregation in the South, 1890–1940*. New York: Pantheon Books, 1998.

———. *A Nation of Outsiders: How the White Middle Class Fell in Love with Rebellion in Postwar America*. New York: Oxford University Press, 2011.

Harris, J. William. *Deep Souths: Delta Piedmont and Sea Island Society in the Age of Segregation*. Baltimore: Johns Hopkins University Press, 2003.

Harris, Joel Chandler. "The Sea Island Hurricanes II The Relief." *Scribner's Magazine*, March 1894, 267–85.

———. *Uncle Remus: Legends of the Old Plantation*. London: R. Clay, Sons, and Taylor, 1881.

Hazzard-Donald, Katrina. "Hoodoo Religion and American Dance Traditions: Rethinking the Ring Shout." *Journal of Pan African Studies* 4, no. 6 (September 2011): 194.

Heap, Chad. *Slumming: Sexual and Racial Encounters in American Nightlife, 1885–1940*. Chicago: University of Chicago Press, 2009.

Hemenway, Robert. *Zora Neale Hurston: A Literary Biography*. Champaign: University of Illinois Press, 1977.

Herskovits, Melville. *The American Negro: A Study in Racial Crossing*. New York: Alfred A. Knopf, 1928.

———. *Myth of the Negro Past*. Boston: Beacon Press, 1941.

———. "The Negro in the New World: The Statement of a Problem." *American Anthropologist* 32, no. 1 (1930): 145–55.

———. Review of *Folk Beliefs of the Southern Negro*, by Newbell Niles Puckette. *Journal of American Folklore* 40, no. 157 (1927): 310–12.

———. Review of *Gullah: Negro Life in the Carolina Sea Islands*, by Mason Crum. *American Sociological Review* 6, no. 3 (1941): 423–24.

———. "What Has Africa Given America?" *New Republic*, September 4, 1935, 92–94.

Herzog, George. "Review: *Drums and Shadows*." *Social Forces* 20, no. 1 (1941): 120–21.

Higginson, Thomas Wentworth. *Army Life in a Black Regiment*. Boston: Fields and Osgood, 1870.

Hirsch, Jerrold. *Portrait of America: A Cultural History of the Federal Writers' Project*. Chapel Hill: University of North Carolina Press, 2003.

Holly, Ellistine Perkins. "Black Concert Music in Chicago, 1890s to the 1930s." *Black Music Research Journal* 10, no. 1 (1990): 141–49.

hooks, bell. *Art on My Mind: Visual Politics*. New York: The New Press, 1995.

Horton, Carol. *Race and the Making of American Liberalism*. New York: Oxford University Press, 2005.

Huggins, Nathan. *The Harlem Renaissance*. New York: Oxford University Press, 1971.

Hurston, Zora Neale. *Dust Tracks on the Road: An Autobiography*. Philadelphia: J. B. Lippincott, 1942.

———. "Hoodoo in America." *Journal of American Folklore* 44, no. 174 (1931): 317–417.

———. *Mules and Men*. New York: Harper & Row, 1935. Reprint, New York: Perennial Library, 1990.

Hutchinson, George. *The Harlem Renaissance in Black and White*. Boston: Harvard University Press, 1995.

"Interview of Julie Dash by Valerie Smith." In *Artist and Influence*, by James Hatch and Leo Hamalian. New York: Hatch Billops Collection, 1990.

Johnson, Guinon Griffis. *A Social History of the Sea Islands: With Special Reference to St. Helena Island, South Carolina*. Chapel Hill: University of North Carolina Press, 1930.

Johnson, Guy B. *Folk Culture on St. Helena Island, South Carolina*. Chapel Hill: University of North Carolina Press, 1930.

Jones, Charles C. *Negro Myths from the Georgia Coast, Told in the Vernacular*. Boston: Houghton Mifflin, 1888.

Joseph, Peniel. *Waiting 'Til the Midnight Hour: A Narrative History of Black Power in America*. New York: Henry Holt, 2006.

Kahrl, Andrew. *The Land Was Ours: African American Beaches from Jim Crow to the Sunbelt South*. Cambridge: Harvard University Press, 2012.

Kaplan, Carla. *Zora Neale Hurston: A Life in Letters*. New York: Anchor Books, 2002.

Keber, Martha L. "Refuge and Ruin: The French Sapelo Company." *Georgia Historical Quarterly* 86 (Summer 2002): 173–200.

Kiser, Clyde Vernon. *Sea Island to City: A Study of St. Helena Islanders in Harlem and Other Urban Centers*. New York: Columbia University Press, 1932.

Kodish, Debora. *Good Friends and Bad Enemies: Robert Winslow Gordon and the Study of American Folksong*. Urbana: University of Illinois Press, 1986.

The Language You Cry In. Directed by Angel Serrano and Alvaro Toepke. Produced by Inko Producciones. California Newsreel, 1998.

LeClair, Thomas. "'The Language Must Not Sweat:' A Conversation with Toni Morrison." *New Republic*, March 21, 1981, 25–29.

Lee, Catherine, Alondra Nelson, and Keith Wailoo. *Genetics and the Unsettled Past: The Collision of DNA, Race, and History*. New Brunswick: Rutgers University Press, 2012.

Lemke, Sieglinde. *Primitivist Modernism: Black Culture and the Origins of Transatlantic Modernism*. New York: Oxford University Press, 1998.

Levine, Lawrence. *Black Culture and Black Consciousness: Afro-American Folk Thought From Slavery to Freedom*. 30th Anniversary Edition. New York: Oxford University Press, 2007.

Lewis, David Levering. *When Harlem Was in Vogue*. New York: Oxford University Press, 1979.

Lewis, Nghana Tamu. "The Rhetoric of Mobility, the Politics of Consciousness: Julia Mood Peterkin and the Case of a White Black Writer." *African American Review* 38, no. 4 (2004): 589.

The Living Age. "Travel Books." *The Living Age*, March 1929, 72.

Locke, Alain. *The New Negro: An Interpretation*. New York: Albert and Charles Boni, 1925.

Long, Carolyn Morrow. *Spiritual Merchants: Religion, Magic, and Commerce*. Knoxville: University of Tennessee Press, 2001.

Lovell, Caroline Couper. *The Golden Isles of Georgia*. Boston: Little, Brown, 1932.

Lutz, Catherine, and Jane Lou Collins. *Reading National Geographic*. Chicago: University of Chicago Press, 1993.

Mangione, Jerre. *The Dream and the Deal: The Federal Writers' Project, 1935–1943*. Boston: Little, Brown, 1972.

Marable, Manning. "The Politics of Black Land Tenure: 1877–1915." *Agricultural History* 53, no. 1 (January 1979): 142–52.

Marshall, Paule. *Praisesong for the Widow*. New York: Plume, 1983.

Martin, B. G. "Sapelo Island's Arabic Document: The 'Bilali Diary' in Context." *Georgia Historical Society* 78, no. 3 (1994): 589–601.

Matory, J. Lorand. *Black Atlantic Religion: Tradition, Transnationalism, and Matriarchy in the Afro-Brazilian Candomblé*. Princeton: Princeton University Press, 2005.

———. "The Gullah and the Black Atlantic." *Footsteps: African American History and Heritage Magazine* 3, no. 2 (2001): 6–9.

———. "The Illusion of Isolation: The Gullah/Geechees and the Political Economy of African Culture in the Americas." *Comparative Studies in Society and History* 50, no. 4 (2008): 949–80.

———. "Islands Are Not Isolated: Reconsidering the Roots of Gullah Distinctiveness." In *Transcendent Traditions: Baskets of Two Continents*, edited by Dale Rosengarten, Theodore Rosengarten, and Enid Schildkrout, 232–43. Long Island City, NY: Museum for African Art, 2008.

Matthews, Fred H. "Robert Park, Congo Reform and Tuskegee: The Molding of a Race Relations Expert, 1905–1913." *Canadian Journal of History* 8, no. 1 (1979): 37–65.

McCabe, Joseph. *Spiritualism: A Popular History from 1847*. New York: Dodd, Mead, 1920.

McCarthy, Kevin M. *Georgia's Lighthouses and Historic Coastal Sites*. Sarasota, FL: Pineapple Press, 1998.

McFeely, William. *Sapelo's People: A Long Walk into Freedom*. New York: W. W. Norton, 1994.

McNeil, B. C. Review of *Mules and Men*, by Zora Neal Hurston. *Journal of Negro History* 21, no. 2 (1936): 223–25.

Merringolo, Denise D. *Museums, Monuments, and National Parks: Toward a Genealogy of Public History*. Amherst: University of Massachusettes Press, 2012.

Mitchell, Thomas. "From Reconstruction to Deconstruction: Undermining Black Landownership, Political Independence, and Community through Partition Sales of Tenancies in Common." *Northwestern University Law Review* 95, no. 2 (2001): 505–80.

———. "Reforming Property Law to Address Devastating Land Loss." *Alabama Law Review* 66, no. 1 (January 2014): 1–61.

Moore, Janie Gilliard. "Africanisms among Blacks of the Sea Islands." *Journal of Black Studies* 10, no. 4 (1980): 467–49.

Moore, Ruby Andrews. "Superstitions of Georgia, No. 2." *Journal of American Folklore* 9, no. 34 (1896): 226–28.

Moore, W. Robert. "The Golden Isles of Guale." *National Geographic Magazine*, February 1934, 235–64.

Morgan, Philip, ed. *African American Life in the Georgia Lowcountry: The Atlantic World and the Gullah Geechee*. Athens: University of Georgia Press, 2010.

Morrison, Toni. *Song of Solomon*. First Plume Printing. New York: Plume, 1987.

Muhammad, Khalil Gibran. *The Condemnation of Blackness: Race, Crime, and the Making of Modern America*. Cambridge: Harvard University Press, 2010.

Mumford, Kevin. *Interzones: Black/White Sex Districts in Chicago and New York in the Early Twentieth Century*. New York: Columbia University Press, 1997.

Murch, Donna Jean. *Living for the City: Migration, Education, and the Rise of the Black Panther Party in Oakland, California*. Chapel Hill: University of North Carolina Press, 2010.

Myrdal, Gunnar. *An American Dilemma: The Negro Problem and Modern Democracy*. New York: Harper & Row, 1944.

National Geographic. *High Adventure: The Story of the National Geographic Society*. Washington, DC: National Geographic Society, 2008.

National Park Service. *Low Country Gullah Culture: Special Resource Study and Final Impact Statement*. Atlanta, GA: National Park Service Southeast Regional Office, 2005.

Naylor, Gloria. *Mama Day*. Vintage Contemporaries Edition. New York: Vintage Contemporaries, 1993.

Nicholls, David. *Conjuring the Folk: Forms of Modernity in African America*. Ann Arbor: University of Michigan Press, 2000.

Ongiri, Amy Abugo. *Spectacular Blackness: The Cultural Politics of the Black Power Movement and the Search for a Black Aesthetic*. Charlottesville: University of Virginia Press, 2010.

Park, Robert E. "The Conflict and Fusion of Cultures with Special Reference to the Negro." *Journal of Negro History* 4, no. 2 (1919): 111–33.

———. "The Negro from Africa to America. W. D. Weatherford." *American Journal of Sociology* 31, no. 2 (1925): 259–60.

———. "Racial Assimilation in Secondary Groups with Particular Reference to the Negro." *American Journal of Sociology* 19, no. 5 (1914): 606–23.

Parrish, Lydia. *Slave Songs of the Georgia Sea Islands*. Brown Thrasher Edition. Athens: University of Georgia Press, 1992.

Penkower, Monty Noam. *The Federal Writers' Project: A Study in Government Patronage of the Arts.* Champaign: University of Illinois Press, 1977.

Peterkin, Julia. *Black April: A Novel*. Indianapolis: Bobbs-Merrill, 1927.

———. *Green Thursday: Stories*. Alfred A. Knopf, 1924.

———. "One Southern View-Point." *North American Review* 244, no. 2 (1937): 389–98.

———. *Roll, Jordan, Roll*. New York: Robert O. Ballou, 1933.

———. *Scarlet Sister Mary*. New York: Bobbs-Merrill, 1928.

Platt, Anthony. *E. Franklin Frazier Reconsidered*. New Brunswick: Rutgers University Press, 1991.

Pollitzer, William S. *The Gullah People and Their African Heritage*. Athens: University of Georgia Press, 1999.

Powell, Timothy. "Summoning the Ancestors: The Flying Africans' Story and Its Enduring Legacy." In *African American Life in the Georgia Lowcountry: The Atlantic World and the Gullah Geechee*, edited by Philip Morgan, 253–80. Athens: University of Georgia Press, 2010.

Price, Richard, and Sally Price. *The Root of Roots: Or, How Afro-American Anthropology Got Its Start*. Chicago: Prickly Paradigm Press, 2003.

Ramey, Lauri. *Slave Songs and the Birth of African American Poetry*. New York: Palgrave Macmillan, 2008.

Raushenbush, Winifred. *Robert E. Park: A Biography of a Sociologist*. Durham, NC: Duke University Press, 1979.

Renda, Mary. *Taking Haiti: Military Occupation and the Culture of U.S. Imperialism, 1915–1940*. Chapel Hill: University of North Carolina Press, 2001.

Reynolds, Patrick, and Tom Shachtman. *The Gilded Leaf: Triumph, Tragedy, and Tobacco: Three Generations of the R. J. Reynolds Family and Fortune*. Boston: Little, Brown, 1989.

Rojas, Fabio. *From Black Power to Black Studies: How a Radical Social Movement Became an Academic Discipline*. Baltimore: Johns Hopkins University Press, 2007.

Rosenbaum, Art. *Shout Because You're Free: African American Ring Shout Tradition in Coastal Georgia*. Athens: University of Georgia Press, 1998.

Ruppel, Timothy, Jessica Neuwirth, Mark P. Leone, and Gladys-Marie Fry. "Hidden in View: African Spiritual Spaces in North American Landscapes." *Antiquity* 77, no. 296 (2003): 321–35.

Santiago-Valles, Kelvin. "'Still Longing for de Old Plantation': The Visual Parodies and Racial National Imaginary of Overseas Expansionism, 1898–1903." *American Studies International* 37, no. 3 (1999): 18–43.

Satter, Beryl. *Each Mind a Kingdom: American Women, Sexual Purity, and the New Thought Movement, 1875–1920*. Berkeley: University of California Press, 2001.

———. *Family Properties: How the Struggle Over Race and Real Estate Transformed Chicago and Urban America*. New York: Metropolitan Books, 2010.

Scott, Daryl Michael. *Contempt and Pity: Social Policy and the Image of the Damaged Black Psyche, 1880–1996*. Chapel Hill: University of North Carolina Press, 1997.

Seabrook, William. *The Magic Island*. New York: The Literary Guild of America, 1929.

Singal, Daniel Joseph. "Towards a Definition of American Modernism." In *Modernist Culture in America*, edited by Daniel Joseph Singal, 1–23. Belmont: Wadsworth Publishing Company, 1991.

———. *The War Within: From Victorian Thought to Modernist Thought in the South, 1919–1945*. Chapel Hill: University of North Carolina Press, 1982.

Sklaroff, Laura Rebecca. *Black Culture and the New Deal: The Quest for Civil Rights in the Roosevelt Era*. Chapel Hill: University of North Carolina Press, 2009.

Smith, Julia Floyd. *Slavery and Rice Culture in Low Country in Culture Georgia, 1750–1860*. Knoxville: University of Tennessee Press, 1985.

Smith, Reed. "Reviews." *American Speech* 1, no. 10 (1926): 559–62.

Southern, David W. *Gunnar Myrdal and Black-White Relations: The Use and Abuse of an American Dilemma, 1944–1969*. Baton Rouge: Louisiana State University Press, 1987.

Spear, Allen. *Black Chicago: The Making of the Negro Ghetto, 1890–1920*. Chicago: University of Chicago Press, 1967.

Stott, William. *Documentary Expression and Thirties America*. Chicago: University of Chicago Press, 1973.

Stuckey, Sterling. *Slave Culture: Nationalist Theory and the Foundations of Black America*. New York: Oxford University Press, 1987.

Sullivan, Buddy. *Early Days on the Georgia Tidewater: The Story of McIntosh County and Sapelo*. McIntosh County Board of Commissioners, 1990.

———. "Sapelo Island Settlement and Land Ownership: An Historical Overview, 1865–1970." *Occasional Papers of the Sapelo Island National Estuarine Research Reserve* 3 (2014): 1–24.

Thompson, Robert Farris. *Flash of the Spirit: African and Afro-American Art and Philosophy*. New York: Vintage Books, 1984.

Turner, Lorenzo. *Africanisms in the Gullah Dialect*. Southern Classics Series Edition. Columbia: University of South Carolina Press, 2002.

Twining, Mary A. "'I'm Going to Sing and 'Shout' While I Have the Chance: Music, Movement and Dance on the Sea Islands." *Black Music Research Journal* 15, no. 1 (Spring 1995): 1–15.

Twining, Mary A., and Keith E. Baird. "The Significance of Sea Island Culture." *Journal of Black Studies* 10, no. 4 (June 1980): 379–86.

Wade-Lewis, Margaret. *Lorenzo Dow Turner: Father of Gullah Studies*. Columbia: University of South Carolina Press, 2007.

Walker, Alice. "In Search of Zora Neale Hurston." *Ms.*, March 1975, 74–90.

Wall, Cheryl. *Worrying the Line: Black Women Writers, Lineage, and Literary Tradition*. Chapel Hill: University of North Carolina Press, 2005.

Watts, Jerry G. "On Reconsidering Park, Johnson, DuBois, Frazier and Reid: Reply to Benjamin Bower's 'The Contribution of Blacks to Sociological Knowledge.'" *Phylon* 44, no. 4 (1983): 273–91.

Whisnant, David E. *All That Is Native and Fine: The Politics of Culture in an American Region*. Chapel Hill: University of North Carolina Press, 1983.

Williams, Jeremy, Jeff Davis, and China Williams. *Lonely Planet: Georgia and the Carolinas.* Melbourne: Lonely Planet Publications, 2002.

Williams, Susan Millar. *A Devil and a Good Woman Too: The Lives of Julia Peterkin.* Athens: University of Georgia Press, 2008.

Woodson, Carter G. Review of *Slave Songs of the Georgia Islands,* by Lydia Parrish and Olin Downes. *Journal of Negro History* 27, no. 4 (October 1942): 465–67.

Woofter, T. J., Jr. *Black Yeomanry: Life on St. Helena Island.* New York: Henry Holt, 1930.

Wylly, Charles Spalding. *The Seed That Was Sown in the Colony of Georgia: The Harvest and the Aftermath, 1740–1870.* New York: Neale Publishing Company, 1910.

Young, Jason R. *Rituals of Resistance: African Atlantic Religion in Kongo and the Lowcountry South in the Era of Slavery.* Baton Rouge: Louisiana State University Press, 2007.

INDEX

Page numbers in italics refer to illustrations.

Bailey, Allen, 208
Bailey, Cornelia Walker, 149, 209, 239–40n68, 256n3; *God, Dr. Buzzard, and the Bolito Man*, 85, 98–99, 221n12, 224n41, 228n2; Moore and, 85; Reynolds and Reynolds Foundation and, 143, 154–55; Sapelo preservation and, 179, 181, 184, 204, 207, 210; "Still Gullah," 188–89; Turner and, 106
Bailey, Maurice, 180, 189, 190
Baird, Keith E., 161
Baker, Josephine, 29
Baldwin, Davarian, 30
Bancroft, Hubert Howe, 26–27
Banks, Bernice, 184
Baptisms, 21, 123, 141
Barrett, Lonice, 182–85, 187
Barrymore, Ethel, 36
Barthell, Elise, 46–47
Bascom, William R., 149
Beaufort, SC, 178
Behavior Cemetery, 3, 80, 187–88, 258n49
Bell, Belali, 5
Bell, Muriel and Malcolm, Jr., 140, 244n7, 249n182, 250n185
Bellamann, Henry, 20, 34
Bellamy, Madge, 50
Belle Marsh, 7, 85, 143, 154
Bennett, John, 23, 25, 104, 125, 222n39, 224n48
Beyond the Melting Pot (Moynihan and Glazer), 159, 253n44
Bible, 179
Bilal (character), 173–74, 176
Black April (Peterkin), 20, 149, 226n100
Black art, vogueness of, 30–32
Blackbeard Island, 3, 6
The Black Border (Gonzales), 25, 224n48
Black Culture and Black Consciousness (Levine), 160–61
Black Feminism, 9, 162, 163, 176
Black inferiority, 24, 27, 48, 56, 57, 61, 104, 234n109. *See also* White supremacy
Black Moon, 50
Black northerners, 32–33, 47, 48

Black Panthers, 159
Black pathology, 48, 56, 61
Black Power movement, 156, 158–59, 163
Black press: Peterkin's work and, 35–36; voodoo craze and, 43, 46–48, 49–50, 53–54. *See also specific newspapers*
Black spaces, 19, 29–30
Black spiritual practices. *See* Conjure; Roots, root doctors, and rootworking; Voodoo
Black Studies movement, 9, 159–63, 170–71, 194
Blassingame, John W., 160, 164
Bledsoe, Julius, 51
Blockson, Charles S., 162
Blue Brook Plantation (fictional place), 20–22, 33–35, 37–38
Board of Natural Resources, 187
Boas, Franz: about, 30, 57–58, 110; African survivals debate and, 55–58, 59–60; Hurston and, 62, 63–64, 65, 235n110; views on race and culture, 28, 225–26n78, 234n109
The Book of the Fair (Bancroft), 26–27
The Books of American Negro Spirituals (Johnson and Johnson), 240n87
Boston blacks, 27
Botkin, Benjamin A., 9, 114, 119, 138
Bottle tree, 175
Boulton, Laura, 89
Bowen, T. J., 23
Brazil and voodoo, 43, 229n16
Bright Skin (Peterkin), 20, 22
Brooklyn Museum, 30
Brown, Evan, 141
Brown, Katie, 110–11, 143–46, 144; Granger and, 112–13, 146, 147, 166–67, 174, 244n7; Parrish and, 95–98; Turner and, 107–8
Brown, Sterling, 9, 14, 114, 119, 157; as Federal Writers' Project editor, 126–27, 129–31, 133–35, 138–39, 248n111, 248n118; Peterkin and, 37, 38, 227n137; use of black southern dialects, 33
Brown, William Oscar, 9, 131, 132–34, 135–36, 157

Brunswick, GA, 211
Bunche, Ralph, 126
Burials, 75, 80, 89–90, 95–96, 99, 112, 124. *See also* Funerals
Burroughs, Edgar Rice, 27, 45, 225n57
Buzzard-prey song/dances, 98–99

Cable News Network (CNN), 208
Campbell, Emory, 179, 199
Campbell, Tunis, 4, 5
Candler family, 221n31, 238n22
Cap'n Frank, 85, 143, 239–40n68
Caribbean and voodoo, 43
Carnegie family, 221n31
Carnegie Foundation, 157
Carpenter, William, 48
Carter, Jimmy, 155
Causeways connecting isolated islands, 95, 222n40
Cemeteries, 3, 79–80, 174, 175, 201, 258n49
Centers for Disease Control (CDC), 211
Cerruti, James, 151–52
Charleston, SC, 196, 201
Chicago Daily Tribune, 42, 45–46
Chicago Defender: black southern migrants and, 231n46; on Peterkin, 34, 35–36, 37; voodoo craze and, 43, 45, 46, 48, 49–50, 124–25
Chicago Tribune, 41, 54–55, 250n194
Chorus for Calvin Coolidge visit, 17, 18–19
Christianity, black, 74–75, 108, 170; CIC on, 117–18; Granger and, 123; Moore on, 80; Park on, 59; in SRS report, 196; voodoo and, 53
Churches, black, 118, 234n102; First African Baptist, 4, 75, 187, 206, 258n49; spirituality and, 52–53; St. Luke Baptist, 75, 154
CIC (Commission on Interracial Cooperation), 116–18
Civilization disillusionment, post–World War I, 26, 27
Civilized culture, Victorian thinking on, 26

Civil rights movement, 152–53, 154, 156, 158
Civil War, 4, 108, 196, 221n18
Clemson University, 210
Cloister Hotel and Resort, 6, 75, 92
Clyburn, James E., 192–93, 199
CNN (Cable News Network), 208
Coastal capitalism, 187
Coffin, Howard: Cloister hotel and, 75, 92; Coolidge visit and, 17–18, 70, 71, 83; Islanders and, 70–72, 79, 95, 99, 100, 171, 239n44; Moore and, 75, 76–77, 83, 85; Parrish and, 86, 87, 92, 101; Reynolds's purchase of Sapelo from, 142; take over of Sapelo by, 6–7, 75
Cohen, Louise Miller, 199
Collecting: Granger and, 133, 137–38; Hurston and, 63–66; overview, 10–11, 12, 75; Parrish and, 86, 87–89, 92–94, 241n90; Turner and, 105–6, 107, 109–10
Colorblind liberalism, 157–58, 252n34
Colored Farmers' Alliance and Cooperative Union, 80
Columbia Record, 34, 37
Columbia State, 223n27
Combing the Caribbees (Foster), 49
Commission on Interracial Cooperation (CIC), 116–18
"The Conflict and Fusion of Cultures with Special Reference to the Negro" (Park), 58
Congo Reform Association (CRA), 58
Congo type, 23
Conjure, 41. *See also* Voodoo
Conrack (film), 172
Conroy, Pat, 172
Coolidge, Calvin, 17–19, 70, 71, 83, 237n4
Coolidge, Grace, 18
Cooper, Betty Johnson, 149, 224n41, 228n2
Cortor, Eldzier, 136
Couch, W. T., 119, 128, 244n7
Counting systems, 110
Creel, Margaret Washington, 23–24, 173, 255n120
Crisfield voodoo mystery, 45–46

Harlem Renaissance, 30–32, 119
Harlem's Black Magic (film), 52–54
Harris, J. William, 13
Harris, Joel Chandler, 22–23, 24–25, 96, 117, 223–24n30, 224n48
Harris Neck, 105, 110, 178
Heard, Anne, 240n81
Heirs' property, 186–87, 188, 203, 205–6, 207–8, 257n41
Herbal medicine: Granger on, 124–25, 132, 138–39; Hall and, 41, 96–97; Hurston and, 64–65; Naylor and, 170
Heritage conservation, 198. *See also* Preservation
"Heritage" (Cullen), 31
Herskovits, Melville: about, 8; African survivals and, 60–62, 64, 117, 131, 159, 235n135, 235–36nn138; Crum and, 148; Glicksberg on, 156; Granger and, 114, 128–29, 136–38, 140, 146, 155–56, 236n151, 244n7; *Myth of the Negro Past*, 62, 157, 164; Naylor and, 170; Parrish and, 88–90, 92–94, 95–96, 240–41n89, 241n93; on religious ceremonies, 123; Turner and, 243n176; voodoo and, 54–56
Herzog, George, 148
Higginson, Thomas Wentworth, 224n42
Hillery, Catherine, 224n41, 242n137
Hillery, Gibb, 143
Hillery, William, 5
Hirsch, Jerrold, 119
Historic landmarks, 187–88, 258n49
Hog Hammock: about, 1; land swaps and, 142–43, 152; preservation attempts for, 182–85, 187–88, 203–4, 257n23, 258n49; Reynolds Foundation and, 154–55; survival question of, 190, 207–13, 263n2
Hog Hammock Community Foundation, 154–55, 181
Hollywood filmmakers and voodoo craze, 50
Holt, Jack, 50
Home in black women's writings, 177
Hoodoo, 41, 64–65. *See also* Voodoo

"Hoodoo in America" (Hurston), 64–65
Hoover, Herbert, 70, 237n4
Hughes, Langston, 31, 33, 34, 36, 136
Human sacrifice, 42, 43, 45–46, 50, 55, 65
Hurst, Fannie, 63
Hurston, Zora Neale, 33, 119, 136, 236n152; about, 62–63; Herskovits and, 55; "Hoodoo in America," 63–66, 235n110, 237n170; Parrish and, 93–94; resurrection of works of, 160, 170

Ibo Landing, 151, 167–69, 175, 176
Ibos, 109, 175, 176–77
Identity, Gullah: background, 6, 12–13, 14, 25; black women writers and, 9, 155, 162–64, 170; *Drums and Shadows* and, 115; Julia Peterkin and, 25; revival of, 178–79; of Sapelo Islanders, 149–50, 155; SRS study and, 194, 196–97
"The Illusion of Isolation" (Matory), 222n46, 260n99
Imagining Indians in the Southwest (Dilworth), 11–12
Input meetings of Gullah Geechee Cultural Heritage Corridor (GGCHC), public, 199–205, 207
"In Search of Zora Neale Hurston" (Walker), 160
Institute for Research in Social Science, 128, 247n95
Island fad, 75, 238n22
Isolation of Gullah territory, 2, 12, 59, 222n40, 260n99, 260n105

Jabati, Bendu, 178
Jallon, Futa, 3
James, Curtis, 94
Jazz, 30, 51
Jekyll Island, 221n31, 238n22
Jim Crow, 5–6, 110, 117, 152–53, 158, 200–201
Johns Island, 200, 201, 202
Johnson, Andrew, 5
Johnson, Anna Lee, 50
Johnson, Ben, 151–52, 210

Matory, J. Lorand, 12, 222n46, 260n99

Maum Hannah (character), 21–22, 34, 223n28, 226n100

Maum Patsy, 20, 223n13

Maxwell, Susan, 169

McClain, Billy, 50

McFeely, William, 13, 220n9, 255n120

McGregor, Alan, 182–83

McIntosh County, GA, 153–54, 183, 208–9

McIntosh County Commission, 183

McQueen, Peter, 175–76

Mencken, H. L., 34–35

Meyer, Annie Nathan, 63

Migration of blacks from the South, 19, 32–33, 107, 172, 185

Military service of Sapelo Islanders, 152, 251n6

Milkman Dead (character), 165, 166, 167, 176

Minis, Wevonneda, 7

Missionary reports, white, 131, 135–36, 137

Mitchell, Thomas, 186

Mobile home ban, 183, 184

Mobilization for Human Needs, 36

Modernity: Granger and FWP and, 115, 118; in Gullah region, 77, 95, 104–5, 110; New Negro movement and, 30–31, 94; in Peterkin literature, 21; shift to, 19, 26, 27–29

Mohammed, Bilali: African Muslims in Antebellum America and, 255n120; background and overview, 3, 174, 212, 220nn8–9, 220n11; black women writers and, 173, 176–77; diary of, 96, 129, 146–47, 224n30; fictionalizations of, 22, 173–74; Granger and, 113, 146–47, 166; in SRS, 203

Momoh, Joseph Saidu, 178

Moore, Janie Gilliard, 161–62

Moore, W. Robert: about, 8, 69–70, 75, 76; Africanness of Gullah and, 102, 110, 150; Ethiopia and, 78; "The Golden Isles of Guale" (see "The Golden Isles of Guale"); Islanders' names and, 167

Moorish Scientists, 47

Morgan, J. P., 238n22

Morgan, Philip, 14, 255n120

Morrison, Toni, 162–67, 176–77

Motley, Willard, 119

Mount Pleasant, SC, 192, 201, 203

Movies: Conrack, 172; Daughters of the Dust (Dash), 9, 164, 171–76, 255n113; fictionalizing Sapelo interviews, 17–18, 39, 222n1; voodoo craze and, 50–51, 52–54

Moynihan, Daniel P., 159, 253n44

Ms. Magazine, 160

Mules and Men (Hurston), 65–66, 235n110

Murder reports and voodoo, 44–47, 230n20

Muse, Clarence, 50

Music: of black religion, 158, 234n102; Coolidge visit and, 18; jazz, 30, 51; racial trait of exuberance for, 18, 77–78, 81, 83, 91, 110, 117, 122; theater and, 50–51. See also Slave songs; Songs

Muslims, 3, 9, 47, 113, 117, 146–47, 166–67, 173. See also Mohammed, Bilali

Muslim Slaves in Antebellum America (Austin), 14

Myrdal, Gunnar, 157–58, 252n34

Myth of the Negro Past (Herskovits), 62, 157, 164

NAACP, 35, 36, 53, 60, 227n137

Naming, 109–10, 166–67

Nana Peazant (character), 171, 174, 175, 176

National Geographic Magazine, 8; about, 76, 82, 238n23, 238n31; Blockson and, 162; "The Golden Isles of Guale" (see "The Golden Isles of Guale"); Moore and, 76–77, 238n31; Sapelo Island article of 1971, 151–52

National Geographic Society, 76

National Heritage Area (NHA), 180, 197–98, 205. See also Gullah Geechee Cultural Heritage Corridor

Nationalism, black, 158–59, 253n44

National Park Service (NPS), 9, 183–84; criticism of, 202; GGCHC and, 191–93, 199; SRS on Low Country Gullah cul-

ture and, 193–99, 259n84, 259–60n97, 260n101, 260nn104–5, 260–61n124
National Public Radio (NPR), 208
National Register of Historic Places, 187, 258n49
National Trust for Historic Preservation, 197
A Nation Under Our Feet (Hahn), 13
Native American groups, 191
Naylor, Gloria, 9, 162–64, 169–71, 173, 176–77
NBC Radio, 52
"Negro Americans and the African Dream" (Glicksberg), 156
The Negro from Africa to America (Weather-ford), 124, 246n72
"The Negro Speaks of Rivers" (Hughes), 31
Neill, Roy William, 50
The New Negro (Locke), 60, 226n82
New Negro movement: African survivals debate and, 56, 57, 60, 61, 234n108; background and overview, 19, 30–32, 33, 44, 159; failure of, 156–57; Parrish and, 94; Peterkin and, 34, 36, 37; voodoo craze and, 47, 66
Newspapers and the voodoo craze, 40–41, 42–47, 230n20. *See also specific newspapers*
Newsreels, 52
New York Amsterdam News, 43, 46, 47, 49, 51, 54, 124–25, 231n47
New York Times: on *Drums and Shadows*, 148; on Peterkin, 34, 35; Sapelo land story, 7, 207–8, 263–64n5; voodoo craze and, 43, 45, 46–47, 50, 51
Nickelodeon Network, 178
"Nigger Heaven," 80
Nigger Heaven (Van Vechten), 32
Night funerals, 89–90, 96, 112
Nobel Prize in literature, 165
NPS (National Park Service). *See* National Park Service
De Nyew Testament, 179

Odum, Howard, 57, 128, 134, 157
Ogburn, W. F., 134–35, 244n7

O'Neill, Eugene, 31–32, 226n88
Opala, Joseph, 178
Operas, 51, 93
Ophelia (character), 169–70
Opportunity: A Journal of Negro Life (John-son), 63
Ossabaw Island, 77, 238n22
Ovington, Mary White, 35

Panama, 43, 229n16
Paredes, J. Anthony, 194
Park, Robert E.: about, 30, 58, 131; Afri-can survivals debate and, 55–56, 58–61; Myrdal and, 157; review of *The Negro from Africa to America*, 246n72
Parrish, Lydia, 88, 224n40; about, 8, 86–87, 240n75; beliefs on slave song survival, 92–93, 94; Brown and Hall and, 95–98; fear of other collectors, 93–94; Herskovits and, 88–90, 93–94, 96, 129, 236n51, 240n75, 240–41nn89–90, 241n93; Johnson family and, 86, 98–100, 240n71; Levine on, 160–61; Mohammed and, 173; racial assump-tions of, 13, 89–92, 94–95, 99–102, 104, 110; slave song collecting and, 87–89, 100; *Slave Songs of the Georgia Sea Islands* (see *Slave Songs of the Georgia Sea Islands*); Turner and, 101–2, 107, 242n154, 243n156
Parrish, Maxfield, 86, 87
Partition sales, 186
Pathology, black, 48, 56, 61
"Pay Me My Money Down," 18–19, 99
Pearce, Samuel Kojoe, 48
Peazant family (characters), 171, 174, 175, 176
A Peculiar People (Creel), 24, 173, 255n120
Penn, Ada, 50
Penn Center, 172, 192
Penn Normal Industrial and Agricultural School, 228n138
Penny-a-head campaign, 36
Personal names, Gullah, 109–10
Peterkin, Julia Mood: about, 19–20, 23, 27,

223n27, 223n29, 226n101; *Black April*, 20, 149, 226n100; *Bright Skin*, 20, 22; criticism of, 37–38; on evolution of southern literature, 27–28; *Green Thursday*, 20, 21, 34–35, 62, 223n29; Gullah identity and, 25–26; Herskovits and, 62; literary praise and respect for, 33–36; primitivism and, 28–29; racial politics of, 36–37; *Roll, Jordan, Roll*, 17, 20, 38, 121, 140, 239n43, 246n50; *Scarlet Sister Mary*, 19, 20, 21, 35, 36, 37, 62, 223n26

Peterkin, William George, 20

Phylon, 156

Picasso, Pablo, 29

Pittsburgh Courier, 47, 54, 125

Playing Indian (Deloria), 12

Politics of culture, 10–11

Pollitzer, William, 195, 197, 255n120, 259–60n97, 260nn101-2

Polychlorinated biphenyl (PCB), 211

Popular culture, 49–54

Population of Sapelo Island, 2, 152, 185, 205

Porcher, Cynthia, 193–94, 259n84, 260–61n124

Porgy and Bess, 114

Post office and voodoo practices, 48

Praise houses, 77, 80, 196

Praisesong for the Widow (Marshall), 151, 167–69, 175, 255n113

Praying for Sheetrock (Greene), 153

Preservation: Gullah Geechee Cultural Heritage Corridor, 199–206, 261nn137-38; Gullah/Geechee Sea Island Coalition, 190–91; land and economic versus historic and cultural, 180–81, 204–6; National Park Service and SRS, 191–99; of Sapelo Island, 181–86, 188–89, 206; SICARS, 1, 179, 185, 188, 189–90, 206, 209

Press, black. *See* Black press

Primitive Negro Art exhibit, 30

Primitivism, 33, 104, 105, 120, 157; in anthropology and sociology studies, 56, 58, 59, 62, 63, 64; background and

overview, 7, 11–12; Granger and, 121–22, 123–24, 126, 132, 142, 164; Moore and, 78, 80, 81, 83, 86; obsession with and vogueness of, 26–32, 225n73; Parrish and, 89, 93, 95, 102; Peterkin and, 28–29, 36–37; in popular culture, 49, 50, 51, 52, 53–54; spiritual, 15, 59, 80, 121; voodoo and, 66, 69, 121

Prince Hough, 48

Products, voodoo, 48, 231n48

Progressive Club, 200

Puckett, Newbell Niles, 55, 64, 136

Pulitzer Prize of Julia Peterkin, 19, 35–36

Queen Quet, 190–92, 193, 199, 260–61n124

Raccoon Bluff, 5, 6, 75, 143, 154, 185

Race fantasies, 19, 31; Herskovits and, 62; Peterkin and, 22–23; voodoo and, 41, 48, 50; white Sapelo researchers and, 69–70, 79, 81, 99–100, 113–14

Race relations, 116, 152, 157

Racial boundaries, crossing, 30, 31, 44, 46, 94, 115

Racial discrimination, 158

Racial equality, 28, 30–31, 36, 157

Racial liberalism, 157–58, 252n34

Racial segregation, 19, 29–30

Racial stereotypes, 54, 69, 132

Racial superiority, 13, 26, 28, 29, 36, 42, 57, 119

Racism: African survivals debate and, 56, 58, 60; civil rights movement and, 158

Radio City Music Hall, 52

Ramos, Arthur, 61

Red Peas Project, 210

Religiosity of blacks, 117–18

Reparations, 187, 203

Retention of African culture. *See* African survivals

Revival, Gullah. *See* Gullah revival

Reynolds, R. J., 112–13, 142–43, 152–53, 154, 240n68, 250nn194-95, 251n9

Reynolds Foundation, 152, 154–55

Rice, fanning, 73

Made in the USA
Coppell, TX
15 February 2023